ART in TURMOIL

Contemporary Chinese Studies

This series, a joint initiative of UBC Press and the UBC Institute of Asian Research, Centre for Chinese Research, seeks to make available the best scholarly work on contemporary China. Volumes cover a wide range of subjects related to China, Taiwan, and the overseas Chinese world.

Glen Peterson, *The Power of Words: Literacy and Revolution in South China, 1949-95*

Wing Chung Ng, *The Chinese in Vancouver: The Pursuit of Power and Identity, 1945-80*

Yijiang Ding, *Chinese Democracy after Tiananmen*

Diana Lary and Stephen MacKinnon, eds., *Scars of War: The Impact of Warfare on Modern China*

Eliza W.Y. Lee, ed., *Gender and Change in Hong Kong: Globalization, Postcolonialism, and Chinese Patriarchy*

Christopher A. Reed, *Gutenberg in Shanghai: Chinese Print Capitalism, 1876-1937*

James A. Flath, *The Cult of Happiness: Nianhua, Art, and History in Rural North China*

Erika E.S. Evasdottir, *Obedient Autonomy: Chinese Intellectuals and the Achievement of Orderly Life*

Hsiao-ting Lin, *Tibet and Nationalist China's Frontier: Intrigues and Ethnopolitics, 1928-49*

Xiaoping Cong, *Teachers' Schools in the Making of the Modern Chinese Nation-State, 1897-1937*

Diana Lary, ed., *The Chinese State at the Borders*

Norman Smith, *Resisting Manchukuo: Chinese Women Writers and the Japanese Occupation*

Hasan H. Karrar, *The New Silk Road Diplomacy: China's Central Asian Foreign Policy since the Cold War*

ART in TURMOIL

The Chinese Cultural Revolution 1966-76

Edited by Richard King

With Ralph Croizier, Shengtian Zheng, and Scott Watson

UBCPress · Vancouver · Toronto

20 19 18 17 16 15 14 13 12 11 10 5 4 3 2 1

Printed in Canada on acid-free paper

Library and Archives Canada Cataloguing in Publication

Art in turmoil: the Chinese Cultural Revolution, 1966-76 / edited by Richard King.

(Contemporary Chinese studies, 1206-9523)
Includes bibliographical references and index.
ISBN 978-0-7748-1542-0 (bound); ISBN 978-0-7748-1543-7 (pbk.);
ISBN 978-0-7748-1544-4 (e-book)

1. Arts, Chinese – 20th century. 2. China – History – Cultural Revolution, 1966-1976. I. King, Richard II. Series: Contemporary Chinese studies

NX583.A1A78 2009 700.951'09046 C2009-906602-5

Canada

UBC Press gratefully acknowledges the financial support for our publishing program of the Government of Canada (through the Canada Book Fund), the Canada Council for the Arts, and the British Columbia Arts Council.

This book has been published with the help of a grant from the Canadian Federation for the Humanities and Social Sciences, through the Aid to Scholarly Publications Programme, using funds provided by the Social Sciences and Humanities Research Council of Canada.

Additional funding from the
MM Millard Meiss Publication Fund of the College Art Association,
the Chiang Ching-kuo Foundation,
and the University of Victoria is greatly appreciated.

UBC Press
The University of British Columbia
2029 West Mall
Vancouver, BC V6T 1Z2
www.ubcpress.ca

Contents

Illustrations / vii

Preface / xi

Introduction: Vibrant Images of a Turbulent Decade / 3
Richard King and Jan Walls

Part 1: Artists and the State

1 The Art of the Cultural Revolution / 27
Julia F. Andrews

2 Summoning Confucius: Inside Shi Lu's Imagination / 58
Shelley Drake Hawks

Part 2: Artists Remember: Two Memoirs

3 Brushes Are Weapons: An Art School and Its Artists / 93
Shengtian Zheng

4 When We Were Young: Up to the Mountains, Down to the Villages / 107
Gu Xiong

Part 3: Meanings Then and Now

5 The *Rent Collection Courtyard,* Past and Present / 121
Britta Erickson

6 Hu Xian Peasant Painting: From Revolutionary Icon to Market Commodity / 136
Ralph Croizier

Part 4: Beyond the Visual Arts

7 Model Theatrical Works and the Remodelling of the Cultural Revolution / 167
Paul Clark

8 Feminism in the Revolutionary Model Ballets *The White-Haired Girl* and *The Red Detachment of Women* / 188
Bai Di

9 Fantasies of Battle: Making the Militant Hero Prominent / 203
Richard King

Notes / 216

Bibliography / 245

Acknowledgments / 256

Contributors / 257

Index / 259

Illustrations

0.1 Wang Zhaoda, *Invincible Mao Zedong Thought Illuminates the Revolutionary Arts Stage* (painting released as poster, 1969) / after page 8

0.2 *Let's Go and Watch the Model Theatrical Works* (poster, 1976) / 12

0.3 *Consolidate Our Forces: Enter Deeply into Condemnation of Deng Xiaoping's Counter-Revolutionary Revisionist Line* (poster, 1976) / 13

0.4 Wang Keping, *Idol* (wood carving, 1979) / 18

0.5 Shen Jiawei, *1966 Beijing Jeep* (painting, 2002) / before page 9

1.1 *Revolution Is No Crime, Rebellion Is Justified* (poster, 1966) / after page 34

1.2 *Chairman Mao's Heart Beats as One with the Hearts of the Revolutionary Masses* (poster, 1967) / before page 35

1.3 *We Must Implement the Proletarian Cultural Revolution to the Finish* (detail of painting released as poster, 1972) / before page 35

1.4 Hou Yimin, *Liu Shaoqi and the Anyuan Coal Miners* (painting, 1961) / 37

1.5 Weng Rulan, *A Parade of Clowns* (poster, 1967) / 40

1.6 Liu Chunhua, *Chairman Mao Goes to Anyuan* (painting, 1967) / after page 44

1.7 Dong Xiwen, *Founding of the Nation* (painting, 1952-53) / before page 45

1.8 Lin Yong, *Great Job! Investigating the Peasant Movement in Hunan* (painting, 1970) / after page 46

1.9 He Kongde, *Gutian Meeting* (painting, 1972) / 49

1.10 Tang Xiaohe and Cheng Li, *Follow Chairman Mao Closely, Grow Up Tempered by Wind and Waves* (painting, 1972) / 51

1.11 Tang Muli, *Acupuncture Anaesthesia* (painting, 1972) / 52

1.12 Shen Jiawei, *Standing Guard for Our Great Motherland* (painting, 1974) / before page 47
1.13 Liu Wenxi, *New Spring in Yan'an* (poster, 1972) / after page 54
1.14 Li Shan, *The Rouge Series, no. 8* (painting, 1990) / before page 55
2.1 Shi Lu, *Fighting in Northern Shaanxi* (painting, 1959) / 63
2.2 Shi Lu, *Indian Sage-King* (1955 sketch revised in 1970 in colour) / after page 74
2.3 Shi Lu, *Eastern Venus de Milo,* alternatively titled *Goddess of Beauty* (1970 ink drawing poured with red ink, inscription added c. 1972) / before page 75
2.4 Shi Lu, *Winter Plum Illustration* (painting, 1972) / 80
2.5 *Indian Fort/Tower to Recognize the Heart of Lu Ban* (1955 sketch revised 1970 in colour) / 82
2.6 Shi Lu, *Confucius* (drawing, 1974-75) / 85
2.7 Shi Lu, *Qin Shihuang* (drawing, 1974-75) / 89
3.1 *Man's World Is Mutable, Seas Become Mulberry Fields: Chairman Mao Inspects the Situation of the Great Proletarian Cultural Revolution in Northern, South-Central, and Eastern China* (painting, 1967) / after page 94
3.2 Shengtian Zheng at work on a mural portrait of Mao early in the Cultural Revolution (photograph) / 94
3.3 Wang Liuqiu, *Labour-Reform Farm Inmate* (painting, n.d.) / before page 95
3.4 *Great Yak* (jade sculpture) / 105
4.1 Gu Xiong on the eve of his journey to the countryside (photograph) / 109
4.2 Gu Xiong and friends in the countryside (photograph) / 110
4.3 Gu Xiong, *Qingping Village Scene in the Daba Mountains* (drawing, 1972) / 111
4.4 Gu Xiong, *Our Kitchen* (drawing, 1973) / 111
4.5 Gu Xiong, *Grinding Grain* (drawing, 1973) / 113
4.6 Gu Xiong, *The Moon Is Up* (drawing, 1974) / 114
4.7 Gu Xiong, *The Entertainment Troupe Shows a Movie to the Educated Youth* (drawing, 1974) / 115
4.8 Gu Xiong, *Shattering Illusions* (drawing, 1974) / after page 116
4.9 Gu Xiong, *From Brother Laowan* (drawing, 1973) / before page 117

5.1 *Rent Collection Courtyard* (mixed media installation, 1965) / 122
5.2 *Rent Collection Courtyard* (detail of mixed media installation, 1965) / 122
5.3 Cai Guo-Qiang, *Venice's Rent Collection Courtyard* (mixed media installation, 1999) / 123
5.4 *Rent Collection Courtyard* (detail of mixed media installation, 1965) / 125
5.5 *Rent Collection Courtyard* (detail of mixed media installation, 1974-78) / 127
5.6 Cai Guo-Qiang, *Venice's Rent Collection Courtyard* (detail of mixed media installation, 1999) / 132
6.1 Liu Zhide, *Old Party Secretary* (painting, 1973) / after page 148
6.2 Liu Zhigui, *Attending Party Class* (painting, 1972-73) / before page 149
6.3 Bai Tianxue, *Raising Goats* (painting, c. 1973) / 150
6.4 Li Fenglan, *Spring Hoeing* (painting, n.d.) / after page 150
6.5 Dong Zhengyi, *Communal Fish Pond* (painting, 1972) / before page 151
6.6 Fan Zhihua, *Digging a Well* (painting, n.d.) / 151
6.7 Cao Jinying, *Fish Pond* (painting, c. 1982) / 154
6.8 Liu Zhide, *Night Melody* (painting, 1983) / 155
6.9 Liu Fengtao (photograph) / 157
6.10 Liu Fengtao, *Artistic Family* (painting, n.d.) / 158
7.1 Assembled characters from the model theatrical works (drawing, 1967) / 168
7.2 Fang Haizhen, Communist Party branch secretary and heroine of *On the Docks* (opera) / 183
8.1 Xi'er from *The White-Haired Girl* (ballet) / 196
8.2 The slave-girl Wu Qinghua from *The Red Detachment of Women* (ballet) / after page 198
8.3 Wu Qinghua from *The Red Detachment of Women* (ballet) / before page 199
9.1 Qingdao Workers' Fine Arts Creation Collective, with Jiang Baoxing in charge of the brush, *Steady as a Rock* (painting, 1976) / 204
9.2 Yang Zirong, hero of *Taking Tiger Mountain by Strategy* (opera) /210

Preface

In 2002, an exhibition titled Art of the Great Proletarian Cultural Revolution, 1966-1976, appeared at the Morris and Helen Belkin Art Gallery in Vancouver.[1] Visitors to the exhibition were bombarded with the iconic images of that extraordinary decade – vivid red banners, slogans, and denunciations in bold cursive calligraphy on huge sheets of paper in the tradition of the Cultural Revolution big-character poster *(dazibao),* posters of peasant and proletarian heroes in attitudes of triumph and defiance, televisions playing continuous performances of revolutionary opera and ballet, and the fibreglass statue of a young Red Guard that had been created by Vancouver sculptor Arthur Cheng Shuren for the exhibition, in the style of the heroic sculptures of the mid-1960s.

Presiding over the exhibition, inevitably, was the ubiquitous image of Communist Party chairman Mao Zedong, in posters, paintings, portrait busts, and other memorabilia of the times, his face "red, smooth, and luminescent" *(hong, guang, liang)* in the manner prescribed for the artists of the period. Mao appeared in scenes embellished or imagined from his years as a youthful revolutionary, and in a robust middle age as a benign leader, occasionally with his colleagues but more often in isolation or surrounded by throngs of enthusiastic young people or loyal crowds carefully selected to present a wholesome blend of ages, nationalities, and the revolutionary categories of worker, peasant, and soldier, male and female. To be at the exhibition was to be transported back to the Cultural Revolution, three decades after the event, and to a country that is now barely recognizable from those days.

In recent years, there has been a resurgence of interest in the Cultural Revolution not only as a massive political and social upheaval resulting from philosophical differences and personal antagonisms, but also as a time of both brutal iconoclasm and radical experimentation in the arts, the effects of which resonate long after the Cultural Revolution was condemned in

China and the outside world. The chapters in this volume cover the visual, literary, and performing arts of this tumultuous decade, both as they were created and appreciated in the 1960s and 1970s, and as they have been interpreted, appropriated, and reinvented in the years since then. They are written by both scholars and artists, the latter having begun their careers as creators of heroic images of the Cultural Revolution and having since attained international renown as artists, art historians, and curators. All strive to understand and explain what lay behind the creation of those celebrated iconic images during the Cultural Revolution and what meaning they continue to offer in the twenty-first century, in China and beyond.

ART in TURMOIL

Introduction
Vibrant Images of a Turbulent Decade

Richard King and Jan Walls

Piecing together the history of the Cultural Revolution decade remains a difficult undertaking. Many histories and memoirs of the period have been written in the four decades since the Cultural Revolution began, and it has provided material for films, novels, and works of art by those who lived through it. The political campaigns, the mass rallies, and the major documents are all matters of public record. However, much remains unclear about events away from the political centre, and the motivation of the leading participants for their actions is often a matter for contentious debate. The post–Cultural Revolution national leadership has discouraged research and teaching on the period at the nation's universities and has focused public attention on the economic successes of the present rather than revisiting a past in which the ruling Communist Party was responsible for chaos and injustice. Thus, the history of the Cultural Revolution has largely been told by those writing outside China: expatriates such as the husband-and-wife team of Yan Jiaqi and Gao Gao, authors of *Turbulent Decade: A History of the Cultural Revolution,* or Western scholars such as Roderick MacFarquhar and Michael Schoenhals, who wrote *Mao's Last Revolution,* and Paul Clark, author of *The Chinese Cultural Revolution: A History.*[1] Scholars of China's arts have tended to focus on the more cosmopolitan, sophisticated, and commercial art, literature, and film of the post-Mao years in preference to the more strident images of the Cultural Revolution.[2] Cultural Revolution art has proved strangely persistent, however, demanding attention with its return as nostalgia or kitsch in an age when the market, rather than the Communist Party, is the arbiter of popular taste.

The visual images of the Cultural Revolution do not provide a reliable documentary record of the period; they cannot be used as evidence of historical events or of popular sentiment. The arts of the Cultural Revolution were (in the official formulation of their day) a combination of revolutionary realism and revolutionary romanticism, not a picture of the world as it then was, but a vision of a utopian society to which the Communist Party (or at least that element of the party that controlled cultural policy and the media) aspired. Histories and memoirs of the period tell a very different story, presenting the Cultural Revolution as a time of vicious internecine warfare within the ruling party, merciless persecution of officials, teachers, writers, and artists, betrayals of family members, friends, and colleagues, desperation among the youth sent to the countryside, wanton destruction of China's heritage, and barrenness and stultification in the nation's cultural life. We see a hint of the savagery of the mid-1960s in the cartoons by Red Guards that lampoon the senior officials who were among the first victims of the movement. We cite only the most famous (or notorious) of examples: Weng Rulan's 1967 *A Parade of Clowns,* discussed by Julia F. Andrews in Chapter 1, is a masterful political cartoon, showing the excellent training the young artist had received. It portrays the members of the Chinese establishment who were condemned in the early months of the Cultural Revolution in the order of their downfall, each skilfully caricatured and further identified by an individual quirk. Even as we admire the considerable skill with which the artist represented the objects of her scorn, we have to remember that few of them escaped imprisonment and torture, that many were killed or driven to suicide, and that all endured humiliation and ostracism, a poor reward indeed for their loyal service to the communist cause.

The art of the period cannot be understood without a grasp of the historical and cultural background from which it arose and of the personalities, chief among them Mao Zedong and his wife, Jiang Qing, who shaped the age and the artistic images it left behind.

The Great Leader and the Standard-Bearer

Nowhere is the disjuncture between the historical record as it now stands and the polemic and familiar images of the Cultural Revolution more acute than in their contrasting presentations of Chairman Mao, the man who was, beyond any doubt, the instigator of the movement. The healthy, genial figure who appears on the posters surrounded by his people, and who was praised in the communist anthem "The East Is Red" as "planning happiness for the people," is now portrayed as a vindictive, reclusive hypochondriac plotting against his enemies and friends alike, and pursuing grandiose and wasteful schemes without regard for the sufferings these imposed on the people (see, for example, the memoir by his doctor Li Zhisui and the recent biography by Jung Chang and Jon Halliday).[3]

In the mid-1960s, as he was setting in motion what was to be his final great campaign, Mao was in his early seventies. He had been leader of the

Communist Party for thirty years and ruler of China for half of that time, since the founding of the People's Republic in 1949. Under him, the Communist Party had won victory in the Civil War against the Nationalists that had followed the Second World War and had embarked on the transition of China to become the world's most populous socialist state, bringing all aspects of the life of the nation under central control. Mao's prestige among his colleagues in the Chinese leadership had declined during the early 1960s following the Great Leap Forward campaign of the late 1950s, which had failed in its bid to propel China into the ranks of the world's most industrially advanced and militarily powerful nations and had led to the death by starvation of millions, mostly peasants in the poorer provinces, through unrealistic production targets, excessive grain levies, and massive construction projects that squandered material resources and exhausted the population. Mao's most trenchant critic in the leadership, Marshal Peng Dehuai, had been dismissed from his post for his blunt assessment of the Great Leap in 1959 when other leaders sided with Mao against him, but Mao was still obliged to give up some of his authority. Claiming to be stepping back from the front line and allowing others to direct the state, Mao formed a close alliance with Lin Biao, who succeeded Peng Dehuai as commander of the armed forces, to plan his revenge on those who were now managing the country and taking control of its huge bureaucracy. Lin Biao worked to build the cult of Mao's personality in the army, in part by his promotion of the "Little Red Book" of quotations from Mao's speeches and writings. Sensing a frustration with officialdom, particularly among the young, Mao was prepared to capitalize on it to overturn the entire system, if that was what it took to effect his return to power. He was, he told the visiting French novelist and cultural affairs minister André Malraux in 1965, alone with the people.

Mao was to launch his counterattack, the Cultural Revolution, in the field of the arts, specifically in opera. In most cultures, it would seem strange for a massive political upheaval to begin with an argument over allegorical readings of a new drama about a historical figure, but in China, and even more so in Mao's China, politics and art were irrevocably intertwined. In the early 1940s, with the Red Army confined to "revolutionary base areas" around Yan'an in the poor and mountainous Shaanxi Province, Mao had convened a forum at which he imposed his own view of the arts on the leftist intellectuals who had joined the communist cause.[4] For Mao, following the practice of Stalin in the Soviet Union and using Lenin's memorable metaphor, the arts were "cogs and screws" in the revolutionary machine; art was to be produced by "cultural workers" under the supervision of the

Communist Party, rather than being the independent expression of writers and artists. In the years that followed the Yan'an Forum, Mao had intervened periodically in the arts, turning academic and aesthetic discussions into political movements aimed at contesting views of history or culture that differed from his own, but never with the ferocity that he was to demonstrate in the mid-1960s.

Shortly after the 1959 dismissal of Peng Dehuai for criticizing the Great Leap, Wu Han, a historian who was also the deputy mayor of Beijing, had begun to write his first work for the stage, which focused on a sixteenth-century "upright official" named Hai Rui. In 1961, this appeared as the Beijing opera *Hai Rui Dismissed from Office,* in which Hai Rui stands up for villagers tyrannized by a powerful family and is dismissed by the emperor for his temerity. The historical analogy was clear enough: Peng Dehuai had also taken the side of a devastated peasantry after the Great Leap Forward and had then been dismissed from his office by the supreme ruler. Wu's opera represented an indirect assault that Mao was not prepared to tolerate. The attack on *Hai Rui Dismissed from Office,* in November of 1965, came not from Mao directly, but from one of his allies, the Shanghai journalist and critic Yao Wenyuan. He denounced the opera as portraying the peasantry as a downtrodden class dependent on the favour of the ruling elite for its salvation, rather than being, as he claimed it was, a revolutionary class capable of overthrowing its oppressors by itself.[5]

Yao's criticism of Wu Han and his opera was the first of many increasingly vicious attacks that led to the denunciation of members of the intellectual elite and the official establishment. It also launched an offensive against the Chinese theatrical tradition, which, Mao complained, was dominated by emperors and generals, scholars and beauties, and against almost all of the cultural heritage then available to the Chinese people. This encompassed the classical and traditional, imported foreign culture, and even works created during the years following the communist assumption of power, when the arts had been managed, in Mao's name, by people he no longer trusted. The destruction of the old was to be accompanied by the creation of an unprecedented new proletarian culture true to a radical interpretation of Mao's vision of the arts at the Yan'an Forum a quarter of a century before. This revolution in the arts also began in the world of opera, and Mao's agent was his wife, Jiang Qing, who was to assume the role of his "standard-bearer" in the arts.

Jiang Qing, Mao's fourth wife, had been a stage and screen actress in Shanghai during the 1930s before joining the communist forces in Yan'an, where she met and married Mao. Neither welcomed nor respected by the nation's political and cultural elites, she was thus disposed to share her husband's increasing animosity toward the establishment. Her opportunity for advancement came in 1964, with her attendance at a festival of Beijing operas on modern themes, at which she gave a speech that called for an operatic theatre that was tightly controlled and politically engaged, portraying communist heroes overcoming their enemies. She maintained an active interest in opera and ballet, making increasingly extreme pronouncements on the arts as her influence grew; in speeches given during the mid-1960s, she furiously denounced both Chinese tradition, which she presented as feudal, and Western traditions, which she regarded as decadent. A European scholar of Chinese literature then resident in China offered the opinion that "no Chinese authority has ever spoken so disparagingly of Western culture yet with so little knowledge of it."[6]

Jiang Qing's major contribution to the arts of the Cultural Revolution was a group of performances, principally opera and ballet, the first eight of which appeared in 1967, known collectively as the revolutionary model theatrical works *(geming yangbanxi).* They are discussed in Chapters 7 and 8 by Paul Clark and Bai Di, who evaluate their influence and content. Jiang Qing did not claim authorship of the works, most of which had been in existence for several years before her involvement with opera at the 1964 festival, but she took credit for their transformation into models of a new revolutionary art, a task to which she relentlessly devoted herself for a decade. She clearly identified herself with the heroes of the model works and was portrayed in association with them in propaganda posters (Figure 0.1). The hyperbole often repeated by proponents of the model theatrical works was that "every word and every phrase, every tone and every beat, is soaked through with the heart's blood of Comrade Jiang Qing."[7] These works, with their focus on revolutionary heroism and struggle, were intended to serve not only as models for subsequent works in the same genres, but also for all other arts: some works in other forms subsequently attained "model" *(yangban)* status, including Liu Chunhua's oil painting *Chairman Mao Goes to Anyuan* and the assemblage of sculptures known as the *Rent Collection Courtyard,* which are discussed below by Julia F. Andrews (Chapter 1), Shengtian Zheng (Chapter 3), and Britta Erickson (Chapter 5). The models were also intended to play a role in the transformation of human behaviour, through a process whereby the heroic actions in the performances mirrored the finest qualities of the audience and were in turn imitated by them, to the point where, in the parlance of the day, those on the stage and those in front of the stage would all be heroes. Some of the central heroic figures of the newly created model theatrical works were female, precursors of strong and militant heroines in films, novels, and the visual arts, and prompting suspicion that Jiang Qing's advocacy of leading roles for women onstage was a move to prepare public opinion for her own accession to supreme power when her husband died. If this had been her intention, she had seriously overestimated the suasive power of the arts: her political influence survived her husband's death less than a month, and she was to spend the last fifteen years of her life in prison for her part in the persecutions of intellectuals and party officials during the Cultural Revolution.

The Establishment and the Red Guards

The attack on the Chinese establishment instigated by Mao in the mid-1960s was carried out on his behalf by the young members of the first generation raised under socialism. They were told by Mao that "rebellion is justified" *(zaofan you li)* and, in a quotation immortalized in the Little Red Book, promised the world, in words Mao had spoken almost a decade earlier: "The world is yours as well as ours, but in the final analysis, it is yours. You young people, full of vigour, are in the bloom of life, like the sun at eight or nine in the morning. Our hope is placed in you ... The world belongs to you. China's future belongs to you."[8] Children who had been raised to venerate Mao above all others were turned by him against their families, their teachers, and almost all other figures of authority. In the spring of 1966, the first Red Guard organizations were formed; they were sanctioned by Mao when he accepted a Red Guard armband and, in what were to be almost his only public appearances of the Cultural Revolution, reviewed the Red Guards at huge rallies in Tian'anmen Square that summer, during which he stood on the same balcony from which he had announced the foundation of the People's Republic.

From the summer of 1966, as Mao and his associates wrested power from their rivals, the country sank into chaos. A *People's Daily* editorial with the title "Sweep Away All Ox-Demons and Snake-Spirits" effectively sanctioned acts of horrific brutality against all those who had suddenly changed from authority figures to targets of the Cultural Revolution.[9] Most of the atrocities of the first two years of the Cultural Revolution (1966-68) were committed by Red Guards. These included the beating, often to death, not only of teachers, but also officials, artists, and authors. Red Guards were responsible for the ransacking of houses owned by families under suspicion and the destruction of books, paintings, and antiques in private collections, as well as public buildings and the treasures they contained. One celebrated early victim of Red Guard violence was the novelist and playwright Lao She,

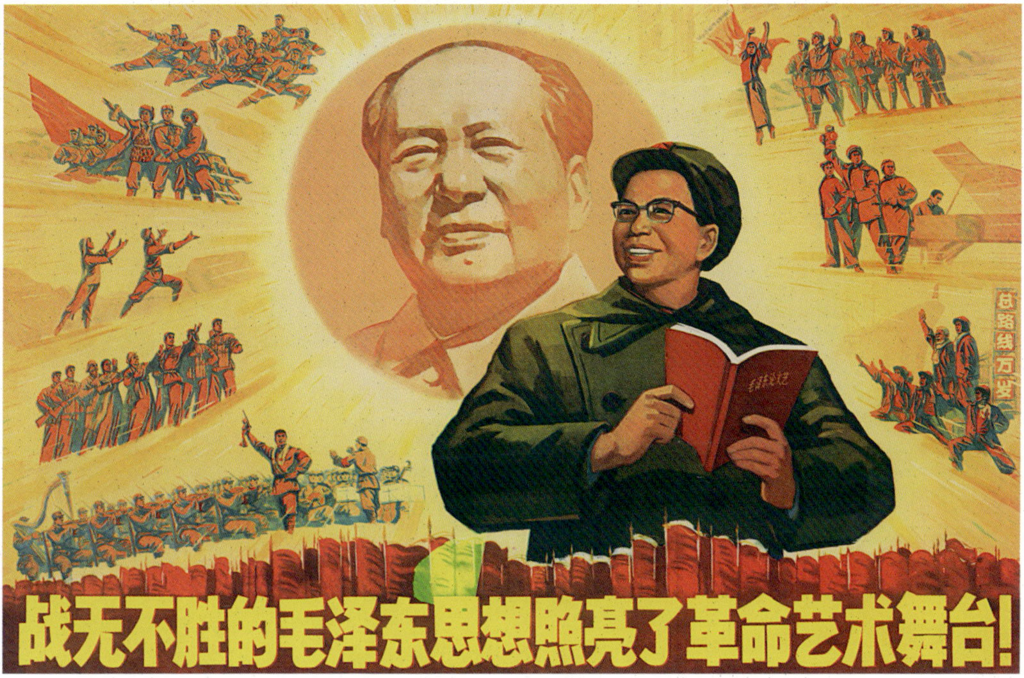

Figure 0.1 *Wang Zhaoda, Invincible Mao Zedong Thought Illuminates the Revolutionary Arts Stage* (January 1969). Poster. Jiang Qing, holding a volume of Mao's writings on the arts and with his image behind her, is circled by scenes from stage performances and recitals of the Model Theatrical Works. *Zhejiang Worker-Peasant-Soldier University of Fine Arts* (n.p.: Zhejiang People's Fine Arts Pulishers, 1969).

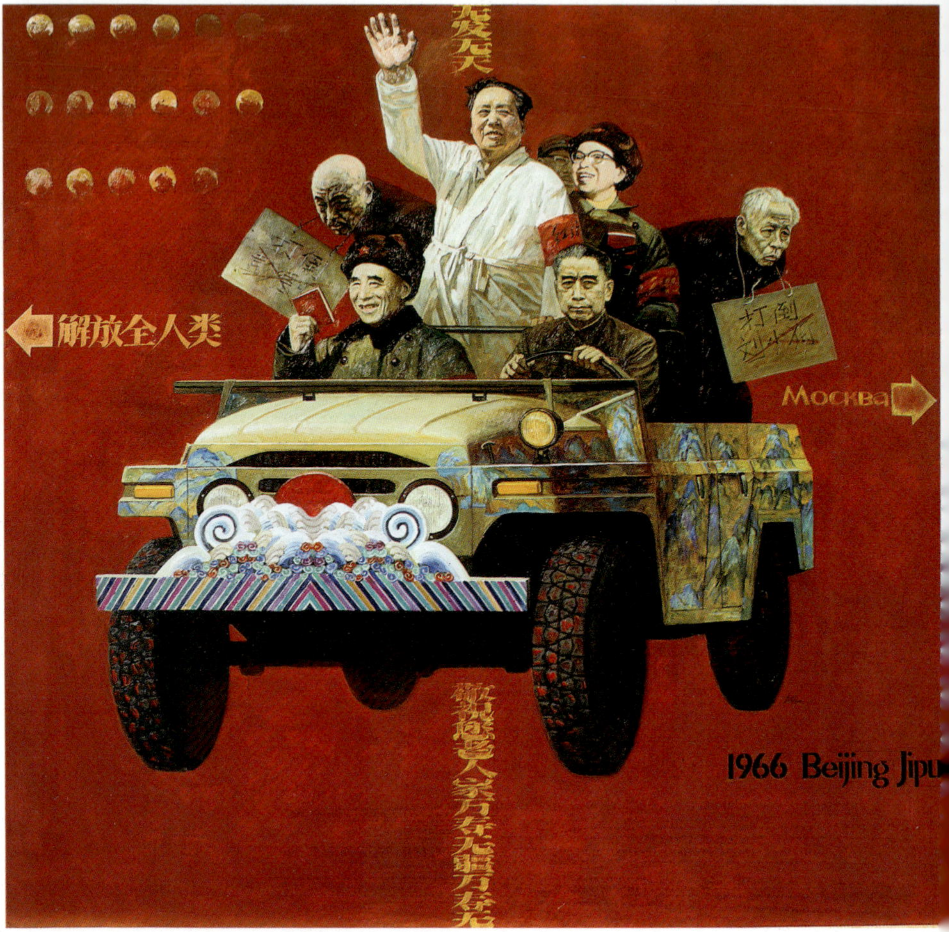

Figure 0.5 Shen Jiawei, *1966 Beijing Jeep* (2002). The painting is a collage of images of the most famous winners and losers of the early Cultural Revolution, at the time of Mao's reviews of massed Red Guards in August 1966. Premier Zhou Enlai is driving, with Mao's (then) chosen successor Lin Biao beside him; Mao stands, dressed as he appears in pictures of his celebrated dip in the Yangtze River, with Jiang Qing at his side. Behind them are two of the major victims of the Cultural Revolution, former army marshal Peng Dehuai (left, behind Lin Biao) and President Liu Shaoqi (right), both with placards round their necks condemning them by name. Reproduced by permission of the artist.

who had been honoured with the Soviet-style title of "people's artist" following his return to China from the West in 1949; his closeness to members of the cultural establishment may have made him particularly vulnerable to attack. In August 1966, Lao She's house was raided by young Red Guards, he and his wife were bound, and he was beaten with Beijing opera props the Red Guards found in his home. The following day, the author drowned himself. In Chapter 3, Shengtian Zheng gives some examples of senior artists and art professors who were victimized by the Red Guards; the painter Shi Lu, the subject of Chapter 2, by Shelley Drake Hawks, was one of many artists abused and humiliated for their supposed enmity to the ideals of the Cultural Revolution. In his case, his earlier painting of Mao failed to meet the heroic standards of the mid-1960s.

Schools and universities were closed in the early months of the Cultural Revolution, though many continued to be occupied by students who had formed themselves into Red Guard factions. At the Central Academy of Fine Arts, Red Guards mounted an exhibition of works they considered "black" (counter-revolutionary) and wanted to expose to public humiliation, in August 1966; later the same month, with the assistance of Red Guards from another university, Beijing Normal, they burned teaching materials and paintings at the academy and smashed the plaster reproductions of Western sculptures that had been used as models, forcing their teachers to witness the destruction. Many of those teachers, and other artists and intellectuals, were confined in cells and rooms that were known as ox-sheds *(niu peng),* a name derived from the ox-demons they were accused of being.

Although subsequent accounts of Red Guard activities emphasize the violence and chaos of the mid-1960s, for many of the youth of the day, the experience was exhilarating: they had heard Mao himself express his confidence in them, they had the chance to attend the mass rallies in Tian'anmen Square, and they were able to travel the country, riding trains without paying and meeting up with young people from other parts of China in "revolutionary liaisons." Many former Red Guards look back from middle age to their Cultural Revolution youth with nostalgia, as the best days of their lives.

The Red Guards, who included many of the most talented members of their generation, were also responsible for the creation of the earliest Cultural Revolution art, much of it in the form of caricatures and propaganda posters.[10] Some of these works were preserved in journals put out by Red Guard organizations at universities and colleges. The year 1967 saw a number of exhibitions of Red Guard art, first in Beijing and then in other major cities and as touring shows. The first of these opened to the public at the Beijing Planetarium on 5 February 1967 and was titled Caricatures: Smashing the

Reactionary Line Advocated by Liu Shaoqi and Deng Xiaoping. This exhibition was organized by student groups from twenty Beijing educational institutions, with help from factories, governmental and cultural organizations, and the military. Most of the displayed works had been shown before as big-character posters, a fact referred to in the exhibition's subtitle – A Grand Review of the Works of Art of the Great Proletarian Cultural Revolution.

The first shows were of works from Beijing alone, but the Red Guards were soon sufficiently organized to mount an exhibition of works from around the country. On 1 October, the eighteenth anniversary of the founding of the People's Republic, Long Live the Victory of Chairman Mao's Revolutionary Line opened at the National Art Gallery in Beijing. The scale of this show was unprecedented, displaying more than sixteen hundred works, including traditional Chinese paintings, oil paintings, prints, picture posters, clay sculptures, and arts and crafts. The press praised the exhibition for its revolutionary character, its fighting spirit, and its mass participation. Many of the paintings exhibited were portraits of Mao, including a huge oil painting titled *The East Is Red,* which showed Mao, Lin Biao, Premier Zhou Enlai, Jiang Qing, and other leaders at Tian'anmen reviewing the Red Guards. A series of woodcuts by a Red Guard group from Beijing showed Mao at various key historical moments.

The Red Guard movement was to last only two years. It became increasingly violent and factionalized, with opposing groups, each claiming to represent Chairman Mao, fighting pitched battles on university campuses (including what was referred to as the "hundred days' war" at Beijing's prestigious Qinghua University) and the streets of some of China's major cities. By late 1968, with his rivals overthrown and the nation close to anarchy, Mao brought the Red Guard era to an end, instructing graduates of city schools to volunteer to leave their homes and go to the state farms of China's northern and western borders or to the villages of rural China to be "re-educated" by the peasantry. Between 1968 and 1979, more than 17 million of China's urban youth went "up to the mountains and down to the villages." Their departure from the cities brought the most violent period of the Cultural Revolution to an end. It also deprived millions of a chance for higher education and gave some young artists and writers a unique insight into the poverty of rural China. Many of the finest artists of the post-Mao age had spent some of their formative years as rusticated urban youths. These include the multimedia artist Gu Xiong, now based in Vancouver, whose reflections on his "rustication" experience appear in Chapter 4 of this volume.

The Brave New World and the Final Struggle

Although some historians have suggested that the year 1969 marks the end of the Cultural Revolution, the editors of this volume have followed the dating conventionally used in China, which regards it as a ten-year period, beginning in the spring of 1966 when Mao issued the "May Sixteenth Directive" and effectively turned a power struggle within the party into a national movement, to the death of Mao in September 1976 and the arrest of Jiang Qing and her three closest associates (the Gang of Four) the following month. Certainly, the rhetoric of the Cultural Revolution continued in the Chinese media throughout the ten-year period.

The end of the Red Guard movement and the departure of the first wave of students, comprising the high school graduating classes of the mid-1960s, for the countryside, was a prelude to a return of something approaching normality in the educational system. Schools that had been closed since the first months of the Cultural Revolution reopened, as did the universities, with an intake of "worker-peasant-soldier" students selected for their political reliability, as well as their academic potential. Journals that had ceased publication in 1966 resumed circulation, and publications other than the works of Mao or party documents began to appear: there was new fiction published from the early 1970s, one of the earliest works to appear being the first volume of Hao Ran's monumental *The Golden Road,* by far the most popular Chinese novel of the 1970s. The film industry, which, during the years since 1966 had generated little but documentaries celebrating Mao and the Cultural Revolution, resumed more varied production. The first features to appear were filmed versions of the model theatrical works, which became required viewing for the years that followed and were unremittingly promoted in the media and on posters (Figure 0.2). These were followed by dramatic movies that rewrote the history of the Chinese revolution to bring all credit to Mao and the heroes who idolized him, as well as by tales of political activism and class struggle taking place in what was presented as a new world of opportunity for the proletariat and peasantry.

Much of the visual art of the 1970s was similarly engaged in portraying a new and better world, the beginnings of a Maoist utopia: posters and paintings celebrated acts of heroism in the cause of the revolution, innovations in science and technology, the advance of women in jobs previously dominated by men, and the enthusiastic participation of the general populace in political activity. The artists who created these new images were themselves lauded as a cultural innovation – peasants, proletarians, and educated youths creating work in areas that had previously been the province of

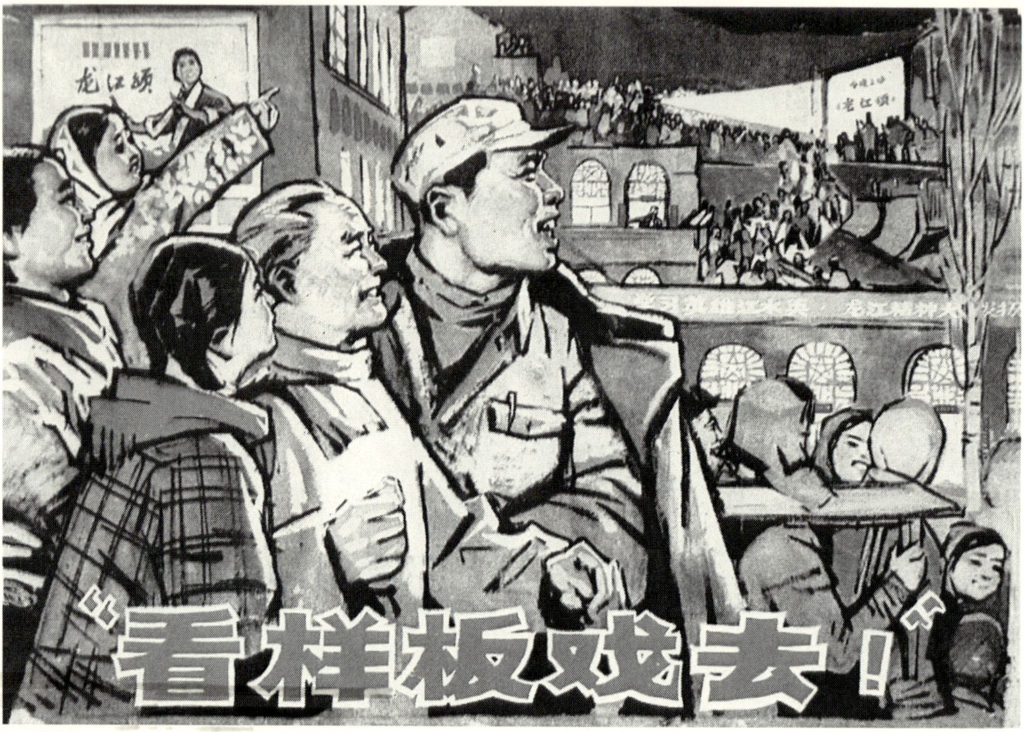

Figure 0.2 ***Let's Go and Watch the Model Theatrical Works*** **(March 1976). Poster.** *Yangquan Municipal People's Cultural Palace* (Beijing: People's Fine Arts Publishers, 1976).

professional artists. Peasant painters, most notably those from Hu County in Shaanxi Province, achieved national and international prominence with images of a new rural utopia. As Ralph Croizier demonstrates in Chapter 6, on the changes in the forms and messages of Hu County artists, the paintings ranged from the artfully primitive to a sophisticated realism, which demonstrated that the peasant artists had been taught by academy instructors. Although the visual arts of the 1970s featured new political content and imagery, the styles were an eclectic blend of the Chinese elite and folk traditions and techniques learned from the West, including the socialist realism of the Soviet painting instructors of the 1950s, as can be seen in the posters released during the campaign to condemn Deng Xiaoping during the final months of the Cultural Revolution (Figure 0.3). Many of the figures portrayed are depicted in militant or even military postures, an indication of the

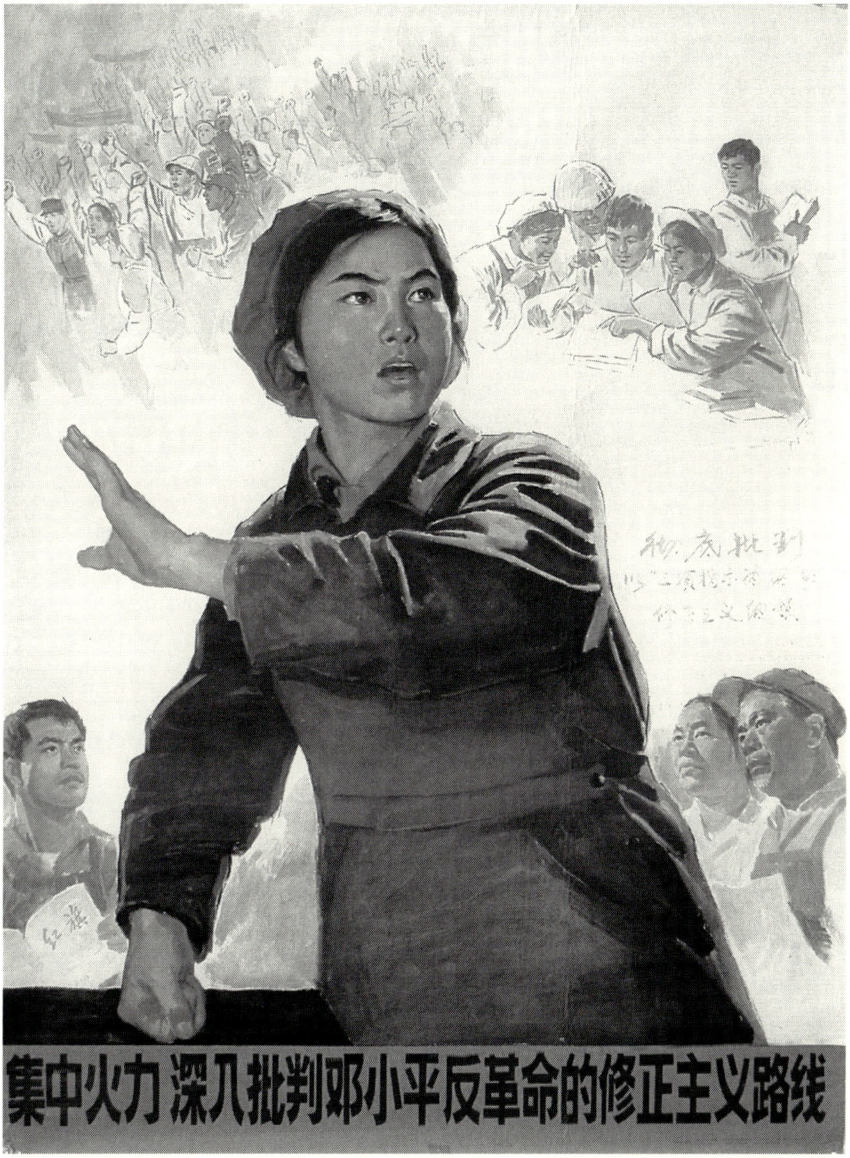

Figure 0.3 ***Consolidate Our Forces: Enter Deeply into Condemnation of Deng Xiaoping's Counter-Revolutionary Revisionist Line*** **(April 1976). Poster.** *Propaganda Art Group of the Shanghai Fine Arts Publishers* (Shanghai: Shanghai Fine Arts Publishers, 1976).

Cultural Revolution leadership's fixation with struggle. Battle-readiness, even at a time when the nation was not at war, is a recurrent theme in the visual, performing, and literary arts of the Cultural Revolution, as is demonstrated in Richard King's Chapter 9 discussion of fantasies of battle.

Political life in China during the 1970s was characterized by a series of increasingly strident campaigns, which reflected an intense struggle to replace the generation of leaders now close to death, chief among them Mao and State Premier Zhou Enlai. First, Marshal Lin Biao, who had been known as Mao's close comrade-in-arms in the early years of the Cultural Revolution and had risen to second place in the party hierarchy, just below Mao, staged an abortive coup in 1971 and was killed with his family when their plane crashed during an attempted flight to the Soviet Union. A year elapsed before the events surrounding Lin's death were made public; for many of those who had believed in the Cultural Revolution, including former Red Guards now in the countryside, Lin Biao's fall and subsequent denunciation marked the beginning of their disillusionment. A political campaign to denounce Lin – called Criticizing Lin Biao and Confucius – linked him with Chinese tradition and attacked Zhou Enlai and his protégé Deng Xiaoping. Deng had been removed from office during the mid-1960s but was reinstated by Mao in 1973, to the chagrin of Jiang Qing and her allies.

The Past and the Present: Allegorical Attacks on Moderate Leaders

The practice of retelling historical events as allegorical criticism of contemporary political issues had been adopted by Wu Han in his 1961 opera *Hai Rui Dismissed from Office,* the first work to be criticized as the Cultural Revolution began. As early as the 1950s, Mao had advocated the study of history from the perspective of "making the past serve the present" *(gu wei jin yong).* This practice has had a long history in China, where historical documents have been seen as "mirrors" to be used by contemporary government; philosophers and rhetoricians dating back to Confucius found that the most persuasive arguments were those that could be backed by quoting a universally admired passage or citing a parallel from the distant past. But when Chairman Mao used his famous phrase, he meant that history should be seen and used as a tool to advance the interest of the working class today. One intriguing example of its application began, surprisingly, with a statement by Mao criticizing his former comrade-in-arms Lin Biao, almost two years after his failed coup attempt in the fall of 1971.

In July 1973, Chairman Mao observed to two of his confidants that, like the Nationalists whom he had defeated in the Civil War, Lin Biao revered Confucianism and opposed Legalism. Mao believed that Legalism, the system of government practised by the unifying Qin dynasty in the third century BC, represented a positive, progressive force in Chinese history, whereas Confucianism was regressive, always glorifying and seeking to reinstate the ways of the ancient past. Mao compared Lin Biao to the Confucianists because he believed that Lin Biao and his supporters sought to negate the Cultural Revolution and restore the earlier, and less radical, system. The ultra-leftist faction (led by Jiang Qing and her allies Yao Wenyuan, Zhang Chunqiao, and Wang Hongwen, a group later castigated as the Gang of Four) used this pronouncement by the supreme leader to launch the Criticizing Lin Biao and Confucius movement, which was a thinly veiled attack against the moderates in the party, whose leading spokesman was Premier Zhou Enlai. Indeed, this movement was sometimes even referred to as a campaign to criticize Lin Biao, Confucius, and the Duke of Zhou *(pi-Lin pi-Kong pi-Zhou Gong)*, and references were often made to "the modern-day Confucianist" and "the Communist Party Confucianist."[11]

The same anti-moderate criticism was promoted through another movement called the Confucianist-Legalist Struggle *(Ru-Fa douzheng)*. Classical Chinese stories with anti-Confucian and anti-traditionalist themes were performed in all genres of popular storytelling and ballads, published as cartoon series and poster art, and discussed in polemical essays as conveying lessons from the past that showed the need for vigilance and aggressive action against the conservative and moderate forces of the present. The stories were used to support the ultra-leftist assertion that conservative and moderate leaders in the Communist Party were analogous to the reactionary Confucianist forces in ancient times. Typically, the retelling of these old stories would end with an explicit comment by the narrator, to the effect that "we must constantly stay alert and be on guard against contemporary Confucianists in our midst today!" Everyone understood that the target of criticism was Premier Zhou Enlai and the moderates who backed him.

Kitsch and Nostalgia: The Afterlife of Cultural Revolution Art

Although the Chinese media were controlled by the group around Mao, which included Jiang Qing and Yao Wenyuan, whose essay censuring Wu Han's opera had been the first salvo in the counterattack that began the Cultural Revolution, there were indications by the mid-1970s that public sentiment had not been won over to the cause. This constituted a setback for Jiang Qing, whose role as Mao's cultural standard-bearer was a major part of her claim to succeed him as leader of the Communist Party; she had told her

American biographer Roxanne Witke that "drama shapes consciousness" and that "the superstructure [the media and the arts] could lead the base [politics and the economy]."[12] Events were to prove that she had seriously overestimated the success of her cultural initiatives and the media campaigns that had supported them. Evidence of popular disenchantment with the Cultural Revolution came at Qingming, the festival for commemorating the dead, in early April 1975: demonstrators took wreaths to Tian'anmen Square in Beijing in memory of Zhou Enlai, who had died in January of that year, and wrote poems condemning Jiang Qing and others close to Mao. The demonstrations were suppressed and condemned in the official press, Deng Xiaoping was ousted a second time, and a final campaign was unleashed to "beat back the right deviationist wind" and attack "capitalist-roaders" who would abandon the policies of the Cultural Revolution; but these increasingly desperate attempts were ineffective in securing the position of Jiang Qing and her allies beyond Mao's death. Within weeks, the Gang of Four was accused of trying to take credit for any achievements that rightly belonged to Mao and of instigating all the atrocities that had occurred during what became known as the "ten-year disaster" of the Cultural Revolution, including half a million deaths and the imprisonment, torture, and maltreatment of countless innocent victims.

Almost immediately, in an ironic application of Chairman Mao's principle of "making the past serve the present," opera stages, storytellers, ballad singers, and serial cartoon publications throughout China were presenting the episode "Sun Wukong san-da Baigujing" (Sun Wukong beats the White Bone Demoness) from the medieval epic *Journey to the West (Xiyouji),* which was instantly perceived by all Chinese as an allegory on the current situation. In the story, a revered Tang monk (Chairman Mao) searches for the highest truth and is deceived three times by the disguises of the evil White Bone Demoness (Jiang Qing), who would destroy him. His clever disciple Sun Wukong (Deng Xiaoping) sees through each of her ruses and vanquishes her, only to be sternly punished by his master for harming her, until finally revealing her true demonic nature and proving his ability to do the right thing. Before long, the Cultural Revolution was denounced as a revolt against culture, with the model theatrical works and the other art of the period dismissed as aesthetically barren and motivated by the political ambitions of Jiang Qing and her allies. As established artists returned from imprisonment and exile, they joined in the chorus of scorn and derision. The art of the Cultural Revolution, it seemed, was to be consigned to the dustbin of history.

China's rapid transition since the end of the Cultural Revolution from socialist austerity to capitalist consumerism has not meant the end of the visual imagery of the Mao era. On the contrary, the iconic images of the Cultural Revolution have demonstrated a resilience that could not have been foreseen in the years immediately following the death of Mao and the arrest of the Gang of Four. The fiction and other writing of the period is largely forgotten, as new and adventurous authors such as Mo Yan, Yu Hua, and Nobel laureate Gao Xingjian have brought Chinese literature onto a global stage; the films of the so-called fifth- and sixth-generation directors, who learned their craft after the Cultural Revolution, have also won awards and commanded audiences worldwide, eclipsing the work of the directors who preceded them. But, in commercial popular culture, itself a product of the economic and social policies of the post-Mao years, images and icons from the Cultural Revolution have enjoyed a curious resurrection. Similarly, in formal (or at least expensive) high art, Cultural Revolution images, given a new and often ironic twist, have become profitable commodities. Mao's fear that lingering cultural influences from the old society would poison the socialism he was trying to build was a factor in his launching of a "cultural" revolution. Do the songs, plays, and pictures recycled from the "ten-year disaster" now threaten the new post-socialist China? The posthumous history of Cultural Revolution art provides something of an answer.

In the immediate aftermath of Mao's death and the fall of the Gang of Four, political rhetoric and political posters continued in much the same vein, except that the stalwart soldiers, workers, and peasants were now condemning the disgraced radicals instead of alleged revisionists such as Deng Xiaoping. In formal art, traditional Chinese painting enjoyed a prominent revival, with famous painters who only a few years before had been the target of Jiang Qing's black painting exhibitions now praised and commissioned to execute the murals for Mao's mausoleum. The ubiquitous portraits and statues of Mao did not disappear immediately as his successors tried to absolve the great architect of the Cultural Revolution from responsibility for its disastrous results. Still, in unofficial, briefly tolerated protest art at the end of the seventies, some satiric portraits did appear, notably the small wooden statue *Idol* by Wang Keping, shown at the 1979 exhibition of the group of unofficial and unauthorized artists who took the name "Stars" (Xingxing pai) (Figure 0.4). Otherwise, attacks on Mao, now covertly referred to as the fifth member of the Gang of Four in private conversations, were taboo.

By the 1980s, the official policy of "[economic] reform and opening [to the West]" had made it possible for a few artists to join the growing flow of Chinese students out of the country. Some of them found that the styles and images of Cultural Revolution art could, when given an ironic or satirical

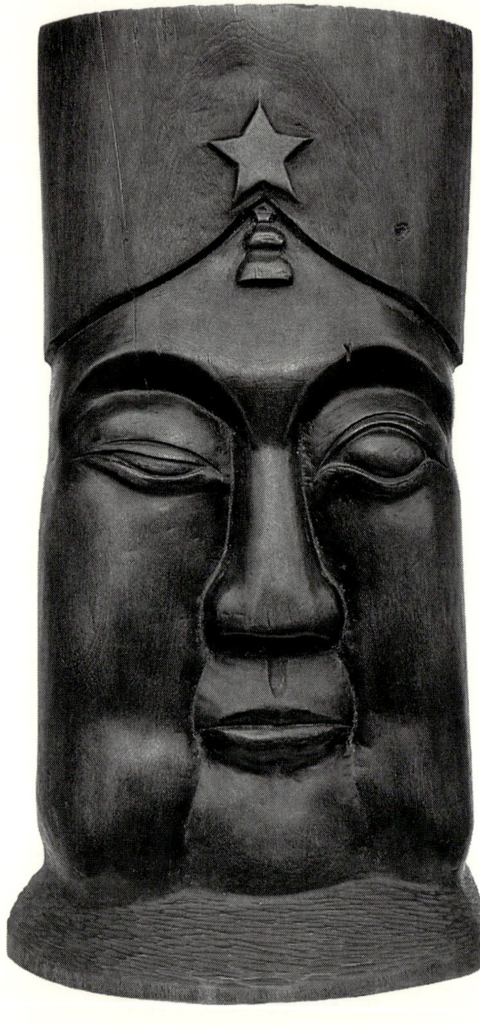

Figure 0.4 Wang Keping, *Idol* (1979). Birchwood, height 57 centimetres. Reproduced by permission of Wang Keping.

postmodern twist, find a ready market in the West. Two innovative pioneers of this development were Zhang Hongtu in New York and Shen Jiawei in Australia. Both were young but accomplished artists who experienced all the rigours of the Cultural Revolution. Zhang was perhaps the earliest to rework Mao's image for the benefit of foreign capitalist collectors. For him and others of his generation, this was a liberating but wrenching experience marking the final separation from the goals and ideals of their youth. His monumental oil painting *Last Supper* (1984), executed in a socialist-realist style, played on the Leonardo da Vinci version by replacing Jesus and all his disciples with images of Mao. The painting aroused some controversy in the United States, where a conservative congressman attacked it for blasphemy in associating Mao with Christ. Subsequently, Zhang, and a few other émigré artists, produced a series of Pop Art representations of Mao, in some ways following upon Andy Warhol's famous Mao prints of the 1960s but with much greater feeling and inventiveness. Shen Jiawei, on the other hand, successfully pioneered the overtly humorous political pop art that would emerge in China itself only after the Tian'anmen crisis of 1989. Appropriating, or cannibalizing, famous images from the Cultural Revolution in the same glossy popularized style of that time was fair game in a postmodernist Western art world where originality was no longer indispensable for serious art and Cold War news coverage enabled Westerners to recognize many of the subjects. Even if a Western audience could not identify all the figures in Shen's *Beijing Jeep,* a pastiche including celebrated images of Mao and Lin Biao reviewing the Red Guards in Tian'anmen Square, they at least knew it was from a China that no longer represented a revolutionary threat to the West (Figure 0.5). They could indulge in a little radical chic, while safely enjoying the joke. In China, however, the unravelling of radical socialism was not necessarily so amusing for those involved in its cultural devolution.

After 1979, the unofficial work of the Stars artists and other subversives was driven underground along with the activists of the short-lived democracy movement. Both movements were almost entirely composed of young people, whose formative experience had been the early years of the Cultural Revolution; the later disillusionment had imbued them with unprecedented independence of thought and hunger for freedom of expression. Mao had his "revolutionary successors," but they may not have been quite what he had had in mind.

In 1985, not coincidently the year when student protests for greater democracy broke out, the New Wave art movement surfaced, led by students and graduates of China's elite art academies. Unlike earlier dissidents, the young artist rebels of the 1980s concentrated almost exclusively on stylistic innovation and avoided the overtly political. This presented the reformist regime of Deng Xiaoping with a dilemma: how was it to maintain a socialist agenda for the arts while opening to the West and consumer culture? Generally, the cultural authorities, often themselves rehabilitated victims of Cultural Revolution political persecution, maintained a fairly tolerant attitude toward stylistic innovation, so long as it did not directly challenge the communist state. Some young artists, notably a group at the

Zhejiang Academy of Fine Arts in Hangzhou (now the National Academy of Fine Arts), drew on symbols from the Cultural Revolution not only for paintings, but also for experimental performance and installation art.

Then, out of the same questioning of the communist system that produced the New Wave art, came the political crisis that culminated in the Tian'anmen massacre of June 1989. This might have been expected to mark a return to a socialist, if not exactly Cultural Revolution, style for art and society, but it did not. The experimentation with modern Western styles and the drive toward a consumer society integrated with world economy resumed and picked up speed. But, in the midst of rapid social and economic change, the old symbols of the Cultural Revolution resurfaced in commercialized popular culture and some of the fine arts. The Mao fever (Mao *re*) of the early 1990s was part of this. As the hundredth anniversary of his birth approached in December 1993, Cultural Revolution images of the chairman were suddenly everywhere again: Red Guard badges, portrait busts of Mao, posters, and copies of the Little Red Book, by no means all of them authentic, were sold at inflated prices to Chinese and foreign buyers alike. Oil portraits of the chairman tended to be sold to foreigners, thus creating a profitable, no longer state-controlled market in political pop imagery. In a sense this development was an extension of what émigré artists had already achieved during the eighties, but in China it funded a new generation of financially independent artists who no longer depended on government patronage.

On the whole, the recycled cultural products of the Mao fever era were short-lived kitsch providing an income for China's new entrepreneurs. The Mao badges, clocks, and wristwatches, and reprinted Cultural Revolution posters remain staples of the tourist trade, but little more. The revival of Cultural Revolution–era songs, music, and stage performances seems to have had more staying power. First came the best-selling tapes and CDs of the early 1990s, with titles that were variations on the name *Red Sun,* rehashing revolutionary anthems in a Hong Kong–Cantopop style to a synthesized disco beat. More surprisingly, the model theatrical works of the mid-1960s – the ballets *The White-Haired Girl* and *The Red Detachment of Women,* and the operas *The Red Lantern, Taking Tiger Mountain by Strategy,* and *Shajiabang* – were revived in the 1990s and after 2000 to popular acclaim. At a 1996 revival of *The Red Detachment of Women* in Beijing, a full house gave ovations to the overture, to the first ensemble scene of the female recruits dancing a rifle-drill routine, and at several points thereafter; there are reports of similar receptions for other revivals, some of which featured dancers from the original productions returning four decades after their first triumphs. Anachronistic as their political message is, the model theatrical works appeal to nostalgia in an older audience and seem quaint, even charming, to those who were born long after the operas and ballets lost their model status and political currency.

This afterlife of the cultural products of the Cultural Revolution continues into the twenty-first century. Filmmakers and visual artists still draw on its images and songs for stories set in that period or juxtapose them with contemporary images to make sometimes ambivalent contrasts between the present and that relatively recent past. In that sense, just as the cultural images of traditional China continued to haunt Mao and his standard-bearer Jiang Qing as they attempted to build a new revolutionary culture, these ghosts of the Cultural Revolution persist in post-socialist China. The study of the art of the Cultural Revolution, both for what it meant then and what it continues to mean, remains an important undertaking.

Nine New Takes on the Cultural Revolution

The chapters in this book shed light on the arts of the Cultural Revolution, their creators, and their changing meaning from the time of their production to the early years of the twenty-first century.

The first two chapters look back on the turmoil of the Cultural Revolution decade and its effect on those who experienced it. In Chapter 1, an overview of the art of the decade, Julia F. Andrews reminds us of the waste, the suffering, and the destruction that the Cultural Revolution brought to the Chinese people and demonstrates the various effects it had on the generations that lived through it. Her chapter provides a periodization of the Cultural Revolution and the art that it produced, from the frenzied iconoclasm of the early cartoons to the optimistic work of the young artists entrusted with the creation of a new socialist visual culture. The Cultural Revolution museum called for by the eminent writer Ba Jin may be built one day, but until then, the work of artists during and after the event can offer a virtual museum, the record of an assault on tradition and an age of (often contrived) revolutionary fervour. Chapter 2, by Shelley Drake Hawks, offers an extraordinary case study of one prominent artist who suffered at the hands of the Red Guards and the cultural authorities for his alleged ideological crimes. This was the painter Shi Lu; his tribulations, and the unique form of his resistance, are the focus of Hawks' study. Shi Lu, who was incarcerated, condemned, and mistreated while suffering from serious mental illness, situated himself in his tormented imagination within a long-standing tradition of righteous literati protest, expressing himself in poetry modelled after that of the third century BC statesman and poet Qu Yuan, and revisiting (or defacing) his earlier work to express his anguish.

Chapters 3 and 4, memoirs written by artists Shengtian Zheng and Gu Xiong, recall very different experiences of their youth in the Cultural Revolution. Both men are now international artists based in Vancouver: Shengtian Zheng is an art historian and curator, editor of a journal on Chinese art, and honorary professor at his alma mater, the Zhejiang Academy of Fine Arts in Hangzhou; Gu Xiong is a painter, illustrator, installation artist, and art professor at the University of British Columbia. As the Cultural Revolution began, Shengtian Zheng was a young instructor at the Zhejiang Academy, whereas Gu Xiong was a high school student in Chongqing, the largest city in Sichuan Province. Shengtian Zheng's chapter recalls the persecution suffered by the faculty at the academy, including senior established artists and younger ones like himself. In striking contrast to Shengtian Zheng's experience was that of his former student, the Red Guard leader Zhang Yongsheng, whose political radicalism brought him to national prominence in the Cultural Revolution but disgrace and imprisonment thereafter. Gu Xiong was one of the millions of young people sent down to the countryside after 1968; his memoir details not only the hardships he and his peers endured, but also their quest for a cultural life. Gu Xiong recorded his life in the countryside in a series of sketchbooks, which present a truthful and evocative portrait of a young man's physical and emotional life, and of the development of his artistic talent.

Chapters 5 and 6 look at two of the most vaunted artistic achievements of the Cultural Revolution – the sculptures that comprise the *Rent Collection Courtyard,* and the peasant paintings of Hu County – chronicling their elevation to iconic status. In addition, they address the question of what revolutionary art becomes in a post-revolutionary age, where exploitation of the vagaries of the market (and frequently the international market), rather than the whims of the Communist Party leadership, is the key to survival and success. They also treat the issue of who owns works that were collectively constructed or created by amateur artists working under the close direction of experts sent to instruct them, when these works become valuable commodities. As Britta Erickson shows in Chapter 5, the expatriate Chinese artist Cai Guo-Qiang (whose name is given here in the form preferred by him, rather than as the standard *pinyin* romanization Cai Guoqiang) aroused considerable hostility in China when he appropriated the images of the *Rent Collection Courtyard,* staging a partial reconstruction of the ensemble at the 1999 Venice Biennale under his own name. The creators of the original works emerged from their collective anonymity to protest the theft of their intellectual property, though their proposed lawsuit came to nothing. Britta Erickson's account of this furor raises the question not only of ownership, but of meaning: what did the reconstruction of the images for a Western audience signify, more than three decades after the originals were created to teach a lesson in resistance to feudal oppression? In the case of the Hu County painters, Ralph Croizier shows in Chapter 6 how village artists adapted their style to accommodate differing political demands as Communist Party policy became more extreme, producing a strategically naive revolutionary art to meet the mood of the Cultural Revolution and then changed again to offer images of bucolic charm for a domestic and foreign market nostalgic for an unchanging rural China.

Whereas the previous chapters focus on the visual arts, the final three bring in other genres in the performing and literary arts: opera, ballet, and fiction. The most dominant works of art, and certainly the most highly praised in the media of their day, were the model theatrical works, particularly the first eight launched in 1967 by Jiang Qing. These were heralded, on Jiang Qing's behalf, as the first truly proletarian works of art since the composition of the revolutionary anthem the "Internationale" almost a century before, at the time of the Paris Commune.[13] The militant spirit and glorification of revolutionary heroism in the model theatrical works set the tone for the arts throughout the rest of the Cultural Revolution; after they were filmed in the early 1970s, their repeated viewing became more political duty than entertainment or education. The pre-eminence of the model works in the Cultural Revolution led to the criticism, after 1976, that the culture of the period had been limited to 800 million people watching eight shows *(bayi ren kan bage xi)*. Chapters 7 and 8 challenge previous assumptions about the model theatrical works. The former, by Paul Clark, examines the cultural fare presented to Chinese audiences in major cities at two key points in the year – the May anniversary of Mao's Yan'an Talks and the October National Day – and reveals that the models were not the only entertainment available and that their influence waxed and waned during the ten-year period. In Chapter 8, Bai Di discusses the two ballets among the model theatrical works, *The White-Haired Girl* and *The Red Detachment of Women,* which had their origins respectively in an opera performed in the liberated areas during the 1940s and a 1961 feature film. She demonstrates that, by creating a "feminist utopia" in which women are freed of domestic constraints to achieve heroic status, they can be seen as revolutionary in a manner differing from that claimed by their promoters at the time. Chapter 9, by Richard King, looks at one theme, the readiness to do battle, in three manifestations, one each in the visual, performing, and literary arts; the political and aesthetic principles established during the reform of the model theatrical works in the mid-1960s can be seen to exert their influence throughout the arts of the Cultural Revolution, most notably in the portrayal of principal heroic characters.

To appreciate the persistence of militant socialist Cultural Revolution iconography in an age of rampant capitalism, it is necessary to follow the changes in meaning that these images carried, from their origins, in most cases during the years preceding the Cultural Revolution, to their place in contemporary Chinese, and global, culture. We must also assess their significance for the survivors of those days, as well as for that majority of China's (and the world's) population born since the end of China's turbulent decade.

PART 1

Artists and the State

1
The Art of the Cultural Revolution

Julia F. Andrews

The art of the Cultural Revolution documents both the extraordinary enthusiasm of Chinese artists for the movement launched by Mao Zedong in 1966 and the twists and turns of the party politics they tried to support. Yet, as the visual culture of this era, the bright, confident, and compelling images call to mind the shattered ideals and great human tragedies of the ten-year disaster. Cultural Revolution art speaks of the dreams of an idealistic generation but at the same time carries the burden of the lies it was told by its leaders. Those who lived through the period may have fond childhood memories associated with some of the images, but equally terrible visions are brought back by the sight of others.

The Great Proletarian Cultural Revolution was one of the most profound of the many horrors to which China's people were subjected during the twentieth century. A hideous abuse of totalitarian power, perhaps second only to that of the Nazi period in Germany, its traumas were all the greater because of the naive willingness and complicity of China's people in the abuses visited upon their fellow citizens. In Germany, the party in whose name horrendous crimes were committed was defeated, its surviving leaders were brought to swift justice, and the causes of such murderous behaviour were publicized, analyzed, condemned, and taught as warnings in the schools. In China, however, political leaders did not confront the Cultural Revolution, choosing instead to use euphemistic labels such as the "ten lost years" and addressing it in the most abstract terms. Art historians Zhang Shaoxia and Li Xiaoshan begin their discussion of Cultural Revolution art with a quotation from a 1981 Communist Party document: "History has proved that the Cultural Revolution was erroneously launched by the leadership, was used by a counter-revolutionary group, and was an internal disturbance that brought severe suffering to the nation and to the people of all its nationalities."[1]

The burst of public lamentation concerning the tragedies of the Cultural Revolution, which assisted Deng Xiaoping in his 1979 rise to power, was quickly shut down once he had gained control of key parts of the government. After a show trial during the fall of 1980, in which Mao's wife and three others were convicted and sentenced, many Cultural Revolution policies were revoked, and the nation, unable to look back, began rebuilding. Some, but not all, of the most vicious officials and former Red Guards were arrested and quietly sent away. The call by prominent writer and Cultural Revolution victim Ba Jin for a Cultural Revolution museum was ignored. The causes, the culprits, and the effects of the Cultural Revolution were all too well understood by those who witnessed it, but this collective experience and memory was left largely unspoken and for the most part has not been passed on to the generations that followed.

Most historians agree that the Cultural Revolution was launched by Mao Zedong with the goal of removing his rivals in the party. Because he came to view his most senior colleague, President Liu Shaoqi, as an opponent yet was unable to rally Communist Party support for his purge, he mobilized millions of students to destroy the party apparatus. His goals were not known to most of his supporters in 1966, and his failure to control the activity he set in motion led to massive human suffering and loss of life.[2]

Three generations suffered in the terrors that began in 1966. Members of the first generation, who had grown up in the Republic of China (1911-49) and had assisted the communist regime to take power, had already reached retirement age by 1966 and had nothing left but their reputations, on the basis of which they contributed their opinions and knowledge to the new society. It was easy to deprive them of their good names by dragging them before crowds that publicly humiliated them and only slightly more difficult to hasten their departure from this world by withholding proper nutrition and needed medical care. The second-generation victims, then in their forties or fifties, had idealistically contributed their adult lives to building New China. They happily sent their teenage children to Beijing in 1966 to see Chairman Mao at Tian'anmen Square, but then, at the peak of their creative and professional careers, they too were seized, humiliated, and denounced. Many were exiled to rural areas for as long as a dozen years. Prohibited or otherwise unable to pursue the specialties for which they had been trained, few had retained the skills or creativity to resume their work when they returned to their homes after the Cultural Revolution. They survived, but that was all, and most have been too scarred to let others know what happened to them. The world will never see the scientific discoveries they might have made, the books they might have written, or the images they might have painted.

Finally, the youngest, the post-war baby boom generation, who grew up entirely in Mao's China, suffered in a different way. Because schools were closed or radically restructured, the formal learning of all children was interrupted and in many cases terminated. Most of China's baby boom generation lost its chance for education and a normal career. Some, as Red Guards, had abandoned all humane scruples to carry out Mao's most vicious and paranoid retribution, actions that in some cases led to the deaths of his imagined or real enemies. Red Guards participated in publicly humiliating and even torturing their elders, as well as in fighting to the death against heretics in other Red Guard factions believed to be less loyal to Chairman Mao. In the end, once Mao's destructive acts were successfully carried out, the Red Guards were discarded and sent out of the cities for "re-education," to live as peasants, workers, or soldiers in China's most remote or impoverished areas. There, they learned to farm, to survive on the most meagre of rations, and to endure the abuse of the local officials, before whose absolute power they were helpless. Only a small percentage of the brightest, most self-motivated, or best-connected were able to re-enter the educational system when the Cultural Revolution concluded in 1976. The vast majority, left behind as farmers or labourers in rusting factories, form the huge cohort of unskilled and now unemployed labourers who have been forced into an impoverished early retirement by the new economic policies. The silence of most members of this generation comes from a mixture of disillusionment, shame, and fear.

It is on the human wreckage left by the Cultural Revolution that China is building its twenty-first century. Silence on the part of those who know what happened has made it possible for China and its new generation to emerge, since about 1993, on the world economic, political, and military stage as a new nation, one that seems to have no modern history and to lack the baggage of the past. It is probably much too late to provide any meaningful recompense to those whose lives were destroyed, though the new economic possibilities opened to the younger generation may restore some measure of hope to damaged families. However, the failure to document what happened, and how it happened, deprives China and the world of a necessary admonition about what can transpire if the crimes of political leaders are ignored, propaganda is unchallenged, and patriotism is misused for cynical ends. It was the trust and idealism of China's citizens that permitted them to be so willingly led into disaster.

The Cultural Revolution also destroyed China's traditional culture in a way that the most iconoclastic reformers of the early twentieth century could not have imagined. Although most old art and archaeological sites survived the campaigns against the "four olds" *(sijiu)*, the people who practised and taught traditional forms of art, and who understood the culture of the past, were thoroughly demoralized, their spirits broken and their passion wiped away. The entire succeeding generation was taught to ridicule tradition rather than respect it. Replacing traditional art with a new socialist imagery had been on Mao's agenda since the 1940s, but, during the Cultural Revolution, China's steady progress in this direction was brought to its culmination. With the close supervision of Mao's wife, Jiang Qing, all old art was replaced by socialist images executed in a uniform style.

The art of the Cultural Revolution may be divided into two periods that correspond with the political history of the movement. The first period lasted from its outbreak in 1966 until the mysterious death of Mao's chosen successor Lin Biao, killed as he and his family tried to flee China by air in September of 1971. This phase produced visual art primarily focused on destroying the old culture and system, and on codifying the cult of Mao, in whose name the destruction was carried out. Much of this art was ephemeral, consisting of cartoons, drawings, gouache drafts, or woodcuts produced for broadsheets or posters. A great deal of it seems to emulate the wartime publications made by art workers at the communist base in Yan'an, a high point in Mao's revolutionary career, and thus revives the iconoclastic art trends of early years of the People's Republic, including the Korean War era. It sought authenticity in wartime revolutionary styles and images. The early Cultural Revolution also produced the iconic images of Mao Zedong that became permanent elements of the nation's visual landscape. The second period of Cultural Revolution art, from 1971 to 1976, saw Mao's actress-wife, Jiang Qing, assert more centralized control over a re-established art bureaucracy, which yielded images now made in the mediums of high art, such as oil on canvas or ink on Chinese paper, as well as a remarkably uniform national style. Although images of Mao's benevolence continued to be produced, vignettes of the heroism and happiness of everyday people became much more common, a way of implementing Mao's dictum that art should serve the workers, peasants, and soldiers. Thus, art moved from models of revolutionary artistic activity and revolutionary artistic styles developed by the Eighth Route Army and veterans of the Lu Xun Academy of Arts and Literature in Yan'an during the late 1930s and 1940s to a more academic socialist manner. In subject matter, the concerns of Cultural Revolution artists seem to repeat at a radically accelerated pace and miniature scale the developments of the preceding decades of Chinese communist history: first, a call to arms; second, praise for the leadership; third, a quasi-historical phase, including praise for martyrs and exemplary communists; and finally, praise for the unity of the people and the regime.

The Chinese of the 1960s and 1970s lived in a world ornamented with inspiring visual and auditory images, from posters to broadcast music to movies and local propaganda dramas, the entire society as though (or actually) in pursuit of a utopian fantasy. At the same time, the practical needs of material existence, such as food and clothing, became ever more difficult to obtain. An entire generation grew up nourished by the same music, that of the model theatrical works of the Cultural Revolution, and the same imagery – Cultural Revolution cartoons, posters, and paintings – and all artists were trained to paint in essentially the same style. This art, like the policies that produced it, may trace its origins and aesthetic principles to the earlier history of the Communist Party, and like them, it is the result of a continuous development pushed onto an extremist byway.

The Cultural Revolution was not simply a ten-year aberration, as the euphemism the "ten lost years" implies. Instead, it built very directly on the procedures and system put in place by the Communist Party during the preceding twenty-five years, a system on which the party based its legitimacy and in which all party leaders were complicit. Political purges, arrests, and thought reform conducted within the party during the 1940s and throughout society during the 1950s provided the groundwork for the massive persecutions that took place between 1966 and 1976. The Anti-rightist Campaign of 1957, in which all work units *(danwei)* were ordered to identify between 5 and 20 percent of their staff as anti-party rightists, might be viewed as a trial run for the purges of the Cultural Revolution. People from all walks of life were condemned, often on fabricated charges, and their families and friends threatened with retribution for any attempt at defence. The party's enormous propaganda machine rolled out such detailed and often-repeated accounts of the alleged crimes that people learned to recite them from memory. Demonizing the victims through propaganda was effective, and the victims, or "rightists," came to be viewed as something "other," less than human and not worthy of sympathy. Notable, in retrospect, is the vigour with which party members pursued attacks on their colleagues and the weakness of any defence of the rightists. The few people who loyally insisted on the innocence of their colleagues or family members were immediately labelled rightists themselves and removed from the scene. Trust in the government and fear for their own safety led colleagues and even family members to assist in patently unfair attacks. Numerous examples may be found of wives or husbands who divorced their "rightist" spouses, changed the names of their children, and completely cut off contact. Acceptance of the government's claims and its right to persecute its citizens laid the groundwork for what would follow during the Cultural Revolution.

It was only after the Cultural Revolution, with the wisdom of hindsight, that these "movements" to rectify political thinking, which dated all the way back to the early 1940s at the Yan'an communist base, were understood as part of a continuum. Privately, many individuals came to realize that their own words of condemnation in the Anti-rightist Campaign constituted not loyalty to the party, but betrayal of the innocent, a perspective gained by suffering a similar fate themselves in 1966 or 1967. Since virtually every party official had been involved in implementing these movements, exposing them would have required admissions of culpability that the party as a whole was not willing to make. From this viewpoint, a thorough analysis of the Cultural Revolution would require a hard look at the history of the Communist Party and the past activities of its subsequent leaders, including Deng Xiaoping, who ruled China from 1979 to 1989 and retained substantial power until his death in 1997.

The First Phase (1966-71)

The first phase of Cultural Revolution art (1966-71), produced spontaneously and quickly, supported the ever-developing political movements as they responded to every new directive or suggestion from Mao and his close supporters, including his wife, Jiang Qing.[3] In February 1966, Jiang Qing held a conference on military arts and literature at which praise for the thought of Chairman Mao was the dominant theme. She singled out the *Rent Collection Courtyard,* a life-sized sculptural installation made at the Sichuan Arts Academy, as a "model" for the art world, the first such canonization in the Cultural Revolution. This installation, and its subsequent history, is the subject of Chapter 5, by Britta Erickson, in this volume. Jiang Qing's critical stance was justified, according to the Red Guards, by the approval of workers, peasants, and soldiers.

Late in the spring of 1966, the party, on Mao's orders, issued a paper referred to as the "May Sixteenth Directive." It criticized Liu Shaoqi and Deng Xiaoping for "having let all of the ox-demons and snake-spirits out of their cages," for "stuffing up our newspapers, broadcasts, periodicals, books, textbooks, performances, works of literature and art, films, plays, operas, art, music, dance, and so forth," and for refusing to accept the leadership of the proletariat.[4] Four high Communist Party officials were dismissed: Army Chief of Staff Luo Ruiqing, Beijing Mayor Peng Zhen, head of the Central Propaganda Department Lu Dingyi, and Director of the Communist Party

Central Committee Office Yang Shangkun.[5] Staffing shifts were made throughout the propaganda apparatus so that major newspapers became more responsive to Mao's wishes. A new Cultural Revolution Small Group was appointed directly under the Standing Committee of the Politburo to direct the movement.

The most frequently seen, yet transitory, art form of the period may have been the big-character posters *(dazibao)* handwritten in bold calligraphy to attack the person or policy to be discredited. Young people who had learned the traditional skills of calligraphy were much sought after, urged to turn their talents against their own birthright. Of course, the messages conveyed by the posters were intended to take pride of place, but the somewhat less revolutionary attraction of style seems to have been appreciated as well, as witnessed by the many stories of posters written by well-known calligraphers disappearing almost as quickly as they were displayed.

On 1 June, Mao approved broadcast of the text of a big-character poster that denounced the president of Beijing University. In the view of the Red Guards, he personally launched the Cultural Revolution by this act.[6] With Mao's support withdrawn from college administrations and party committees, most collapsed. Student activists, garbed in Yan'an-style faded army uniforms, marched from school to school in demonstrations against academic administrators. Wide leather belts with heavy buckles, a standard part of the costume, were used by some students as weapons against those who failed to pay proper respect.

By mid-June, all schools were closed. On 4 June, some middle school students at Qinghua University wrote a big-character poster with the slogan "Rebellion is justified!" (Figure 1.1). The title "Red Guard" was recognized by Mao on 1 August as the name for student activists who supported him.[7] A meeting of Maoist members of the Communist Party's Central Committee in early August set forth guidelines on the goals of the Red Guard movement. The Red Guards were mandated, first, to overthrow those within the party who had taken the capitalist road and, second, to uproot and destroy the "four olds." On 5 August, Mao himself displayed a big-character poster on the door of the room where the Central Committee met, calling upon the Red Guards to "bombard the headquarters" *(paoda silingbu)* of his party opponents who exercised "bourgeois dictatorship."[8] The four olds were defined as old ideas, old culture, old customs, and old habits of the exploiting classes to corrupt the masses.[9] Normal cultural activity in the capital largely ceased as students and teachers organized to support the Red Guard movement.

Over the course of 1967, well-known artists were attacked in the press and in their studios.[10] In general, all who reached adulthood before 1949 had "historical problems" that made them targets. In January 1967, when the communist bureaucracy was overthrown nationwide, the Chinese Artists' Association was "smashed."[11] In this period, many young artists devoted more energy to political activities than to art of any kind. Nevertheless, academic artists, including Red Guard art students, were crucial in establishing the visual images of the Cultural Revolution.[12] For example, two contending Red Guard groups from the Central Academy of Arts and Crafts – the East Is Red and Mount Jinggang – seized control of the giant billboards at the northeast and northwest corners of Tian'anmen Square. Their competition was played out in the design and execution of huge painted images, which became models for billboards throughout the nation.[13] Students threw themselves into painting murals, cartoons, and posters in support of Chairman Mao and the Cultural Revolution.

Ideological struggles and personal hostilities then factionalized the Red Guard movement. The crisis of the matched couplet debate began in July 1966 when a group of middle school students at the Beijing Aeronautical Institute posted a slogan in the form of a matched couplet, which read "If the father's a hero, the son's a brave; if the father's a counter-revolutionary, the son's a bastard."[14] The slogan, which codified Maoist class distinctions as hereditary, spread throughout the capital, provoking controversy and antagonism within the Red Guard movement. Red Guard students in the colleges of music, drama, and art had particularly intense reactions to the slogan, for many of them came from "bad" class backgrounds and risked permanent exclusion from the upper social stratum of revolutionary society. Red Guards from revolutionary families, the new elite, began marching, demonstrating, and chanting in support of the slogan. Pro-slogan students eventually prevailed nationwide, and Red Guards from bad backgrounds were required to denounce their parents or quit the patriotic movement. A Hong Kong newspaper reported in November that students from politically suspect backgrounds were expelled from schools in Guangzhou by the Red Guards unless they condemned their families.[15] For most of the subsequent decade, a person's class background determined access to employment and education.

On eight occasions between August and December 1966, Mao Zedong and the reorganized Communist Party leadership received Red Guards who travelled to Beijing from all over the nation. It has been estimated that the total number of Red Guards assembled at Tian'anmen Square during the course of these receptions was between 10 and 13 million.[16] Mao's meeting with the Red Guard became a favourite subject for young artists. An anonymous oil painting titled *Chairman Mao's Heart Beats as One with the*

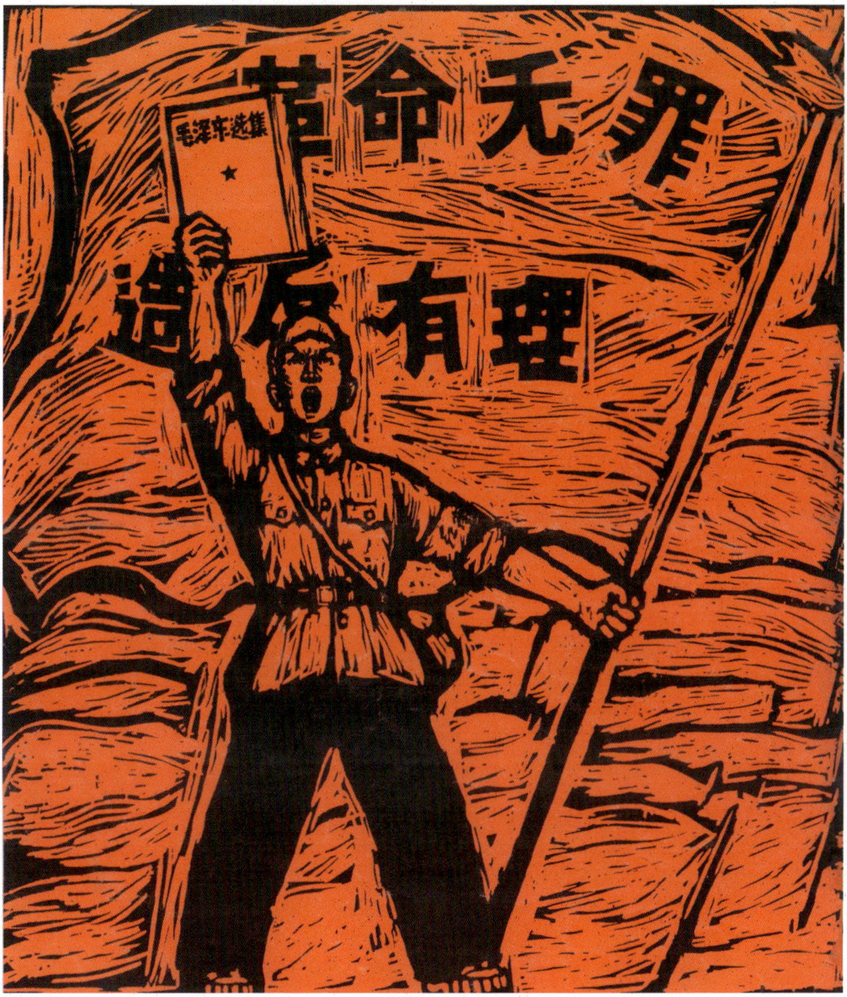

Figure 1.1 ***Revolution Is No Crime, Rebellion Is Justified*** **(1966). Red Guard poster.** *China Pictorial* 4 (1967): back cover.

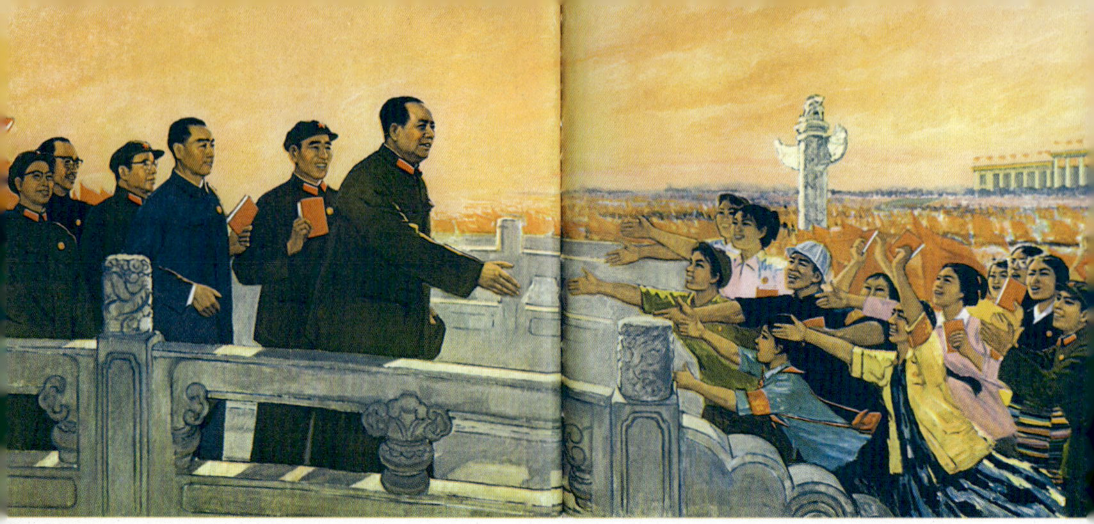

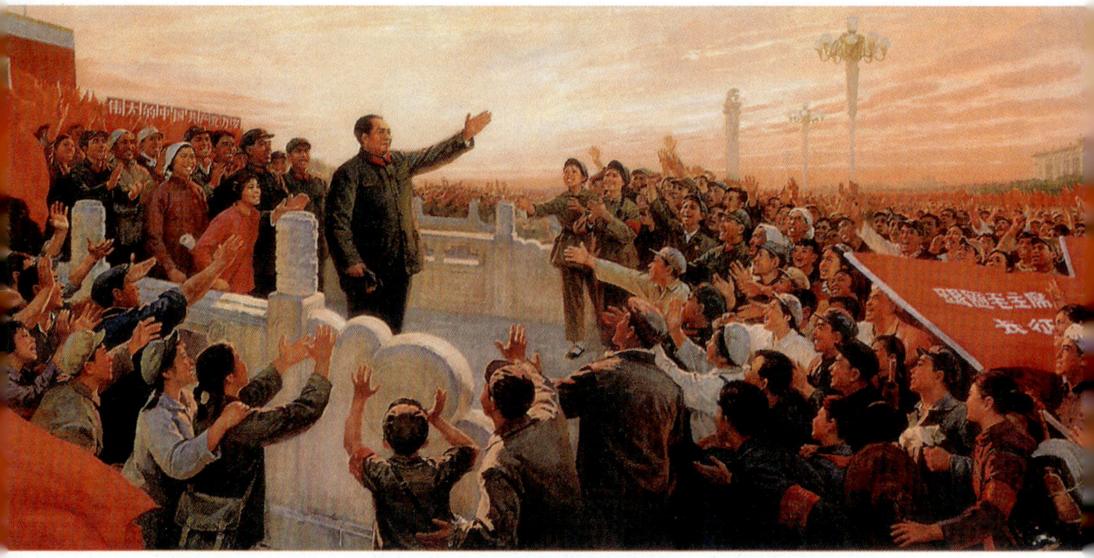

Figure 1.2 *Chairman Mao's Heart Beats as One with the Hearts of the Revolutionary Masses* (1967). Poster. From left are Cultural Revolution leaders Jiang Qing, Kang Sheng, Chen Boda, Zhou Enlai, Lin Biao, and Mao Zedong. *China Reconstructs,* February 1968, 22.

Figure 1.3 *We Must Implement the Proletarian Cultural Revolution to the Finish.* Detail of oil painting published as a poster. Mao Zedong, now unaccompanied by other leaders, greets his followers in this revised and retitled version of Figure 1.2. This version was painted collaboratively for the 1972 national art exhibition by senior artists Hou Yimin, Deng Shu, Jin Shangyi, Zhan Jianjun, Luo Gongliu, Yuan Hao, and Yang Lin'gui. Collection of Wang Mingxian.

Hearts of the Revolutionary Masses (Figure 1.2), published in February of 1968 but painted slightly earlier, commemorated the event. Mao, dressed in a military uniform, strides across a stone bridge in front of the old palace to shake the hands of his young supporters on Tian'anmen Square. The demonstrators are a carefully varied group of student Red Guards, workers, and soldiers of both genders. Behind Mao are key Cultural Revolution leaders: Lin Biao, Zhou Enlai, Chen Boda, Kang Sheng, and Jiang Qing. All but Kang and Zhou are in military uniforms, emphasizing Mao's reliance on the army to maintain order after his purge of the party.

The authorship of this painting is not known, but it is clearly a collective work. The socialist-realist style encouraged by Jiang Qing and other Cultural Revolution leaders required more technical training than most Red Guards had received. Because the paintings tended to be extraordinarily large and painted on short deadlines, the young artists would often plan and execute their compositions collaboratively. If Mao were to be the focus of the picture, as he usually was, it was especially important that his face be delineated as skilfully as possible. In many cases, an experienced painter would be sought to help with this crucial part of the picture. There may have been at least three hands involved in the production of this work, typical of the collaboration encouraged by the "communistic" ideals of the Cultural Revolution. A group of Central Academy of Fine Arts professors, including Hou Yimin and Jin Shangyi, was required to paint a more polished version of this composition for the 1972 national exhibition (see Figure 1.3).

Early in the 1966 frenzy of student activism, revolutionary students and teachers of the Central Academy of Fine Arts conducted a dramatic symbolic event, the smashing of the plaster statues, which occurred on about 25 August. Sketching from plaster casts of famous European and Asian sculptures was an integral part of the Central Academy of Fine Arts curriculum, following that of the European academies on which it was based. The Red Guards decided in 1966 that the plaster reproductions of the four olds should be smashed. The academy's collection of casts, including reproductions of such works as Michelangelo's *David,* the Venus de Milo, and the Apollo Belvedere, were ritually destroyed with axes and shovels and then burned. Red Guards paraded around the fire in a victory celebration. Completion of the ambitious undertaking required a great deal of physical exertion, and the art students were assisted in this task by students from the Physical Education Department of Beijing Normal University.

Some of the most appalling incidents of the early Cultural Revolution period involved violence against people, as well as property. In order to smash the "power-holding faction," an exhibition of newly condemned "black paintings" was held at the Central Academy of Fine Arts by the Red Army group of the academy's middle school, a Red Guard body composed chiefly of the sons and daughters of high-cadre families. Works of art were brought out of the academy gallery for castigation. At least four faculty members, Ye Qianyu, Luo Gongliu, Li Kuchan, and Huang Yongyu, were beaten with belts and belt buckles by Red Guard students and faculty. After being physically humiliated in front of their students, colleagues, and families, most old artists and administrators were incarcerated in makeshift campus prisons called ox-sheds, for "ox-demons and snake-spirits."

During January and February of 1967, the National Assembly of Red Art Rebels met in the National Art Gallery in Beijing to attack the seventeen years of the black line in literature and art and to struggle against capitalist-roaders in the art world. The "rebels" *(zaofanpai)* included students and young artists affiliated with art and film academies, the Chinese Artists' Association, and institutes of Chinese painting, who had travelled to Beijing from all over the nation. The Ministry of Culture auditorium, the National Art Gallery, and the Central Academy of Fine Arts auditorium were converted into "national liaison stations" for Red Guards from arts institutions. The primary targets of their campaign were the national leaders of the artists' association and the academies. According to a former Red Guard leader, his group was granted 3,000 *yuan* by the Ministry of Culture to fund its criticism meetings and to publish a set of propaganda posters. The "rebellion" in the art world was government-funded.

The Red Guards published a number of new tabloids to record and encourage Cultural Revolution activities. Among them was *Art Storm (Meishu fenglei),* first published in June 1967 by Red Guards at the academy but with co-sponsorship from many Beijing art groups.[17] Although its editorial offices were on the Central Academy of Fine Arts campus, and groups associated with that institution played a prominent role in its activities, it was a joint effort of Red Guard groups from most Beijing art institutions. The extravagant names of the sponsoring organizations give a sense of the atmosphere of the time and indeed demonstrate both revolutionary zeal and an impulse to remake a bureaucracy to replace the one they had just overthrown: Great United Congress of Central Academy of Fine Arts Classes and Departments, Beijing Painting Institute Mao Zedong Thought Armed Struggle Group Revolutionary Committee, Red [Guard] Congress Central Academy of Fine Arts Prairie Fire Armed Struggle Team, Red [Guard] Congress Central Academy of Arts and Crafts East Is Red Commune, Museum of Revolutionary History Revolutionary Rebel United Committee, and National Art Gallery Red Rebel Group, to name only a few.[18]

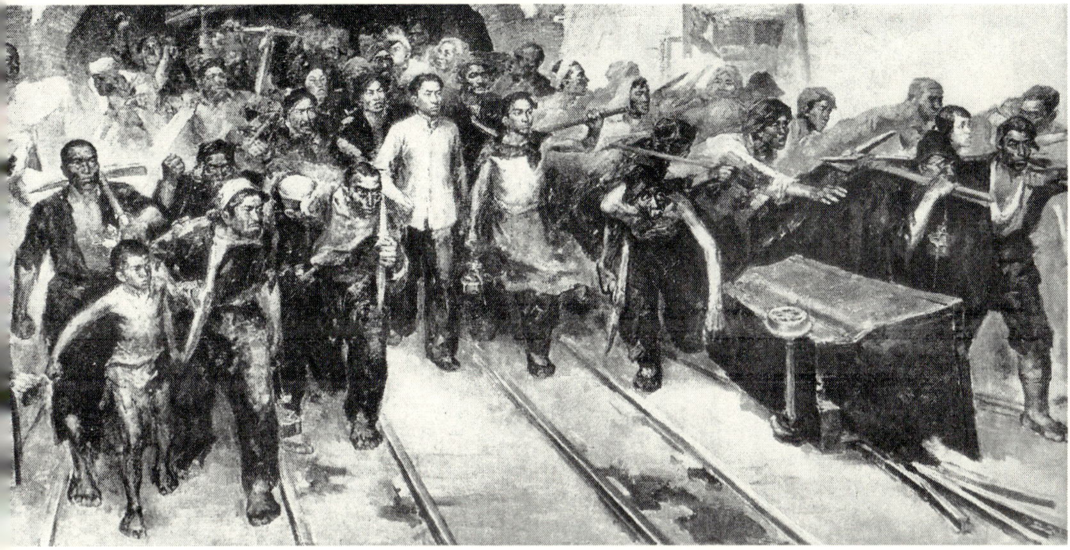

Figure 1.4 Hou Yimin, *Liu Shaoqi and the Anyuan Coal Miners* (1961). In official party histories of the 1950s, Liu Shaoqi, the picture's central figure in a white tunic, is credited with leading a 1922 coal miners' strike in Anyuan, Jiangxi, that initiated the party's successful effort to overturn the capitalist system. This version of the oil painting was destroyed during the Cultural Revolution, but the artist subsequently painted a new one for the Museum of Revolutionary History. *Meishu* 4 (1961): 33.

The first issue of *Art Storm* reported on a 6 June conference titled "Cut Off Liu Shaoqi's Black Hand in the Art World – Thoroughly Eliminate the Poisonous Weeds Glorifying Liu Shaoqi." At that staged circus, art world leaders were brought to the Museum of Revolutionary History to face public attack in front of delegates of the labour congress *(gongdaihui),* military, and art circles. Those criticized were held responsible for production and publication of "dog portraits" of Liu Shaoqi, many of which had been commissioned by the museum.[19] *Art Storm* devoted the remainder of its first issue to castigating portraits of Liu Shaoqi and their creators. In one heinous example, it was found that 172,077 copies of Hou Yimin's oil painting *Liu Shaoqi and the Anyuan Coal Miners* (Figure 1.4) had been published by People's Art Press between 1962 and 1965. Other Red Guard targets were the Hangzhou oil painting professor Wang Dewei, whose picturesque portrait of Liu Shaoqi's forest meeting with workers from the timber industry was exhibited in 1964, and the Central Academy of Fine Arts professor Li Qi, who had painted a portrait of Liu in the traditional medium of ink and colour on paper. The "erroneous" art produced between 1961 and 1965 was blamed on both the artists and their political masters, in this case Deng Xiaoping, Lu Dingyi, and Zhou Yang.[20]

On 23 May 1967, after a year of destruction, the Cultural Revolution Small Group announced the establishment of a Literature and Arts Group (Wenyizu) directed by Jiang Qing. Other members of the group were Zhang Chunqiao, Yao Wenyuan, and Qi Benyu. In May an exhibition of paintings by the Proletarian Cultural Revolution Red Painting Guard was held at the former Rongbaozhai Gallery. It was sponsored by various Red Guard publications, including the journal *Art War Gazette (Meishu zhanbao).*[21] Five days later, eighty rebel units opened an even larger exhibition, called Long Live the Victory of Mao Zedong Thought Revolutionary Painting Exhibition, at the National Art Gallery, in honour of the twenty-fifth anniversary of the Yan'an Talks. Former art leaders were once again humiliated and attacked before an audience of almost a thousand people.[22]

Soon after, *Art Storm* issued an attack on the Beijing Chinese Painting Institute, which had been founded in 1957 to preserve China's endangered traditional art, for being a "royal academy" run by Deng Xiaoping and Liu Shaoqi. The Red Guards asserted that Mao and Zhou Enlai, the latter of whom was actually a strong supporter of the institute, had intended it to produce socialist-realist pictures but that the Central Propaganda Department and Beijing municipal government had led it astray.

Between 10 and 12 June 1967, a "ten-thousand person meeting" was held at the Beijing Workers Stadium under the auspices of the Literature and Arts Group of the Cultural Revolution Small Group. Cultural leaders were presented for "criticism and struggle" by the masses, a euphemism for verbal attack and physical humiliation, and one of the *Rent Collection Courtyard* artists gave a formal speech.[23] In July and August 1967, many meetings were held to "criticize and struggle" arts administrators in the Central Academy of Fine Arts. Another black painting exhibition in late 1968 attacked the classical tradition of ink painting. Many of the leading masters of this genre were on the Central Academy of Fine Arts faculty – Qi Baishi (who had died by this time) and the senior professors Ye Qianyu, Li Keran, and Li Kuchan. Most old artists were under surveillance and were prohibited from painting during these years.

As factional loyalties to competing Red Guard groups were solidified in 1967, their allies from outside the Central Academy sought to participate in criticizing victims.[24] In some instances, a faction would spirit away works of art or even people to be criticized and hide them from opposing groups. At the height of the factional struggles in 1967, opposing Red Guard groups at the Central Academy of Fine Arts occupied the two largest buildings on campus as forts. Older faculty (and a few unlucky students) at the school continued to be physically and mentally abused throughout the first eighteen months of the Cultural Revolution. To take one notorious example – the Central Academy of Fine Arts party committee member and oil painting instructor Hou Yimin, who had been an underground party member before 1949 and had fought hard to swing the school into the communist camp during the Civil War, had initially been sympathetic to Mao's movement but nevertheless became a Red Guard target himself. Not only had he painted the disgraced *Liu Shaoqi and the Anyuan Coal Miners* for the Museum of Revolutionary History, he also had a "landlord" family background and he liked to collect antiques. For these crimes, he was reportedly hung by his arms and beaten; his wife, Deng Shu, suffered a heart attack during her assault. His Japan-educated colleague Wang Shikuo was tortured into confessing to espionage; his wife was dragged by her hair down two flights of stairs. This violence at the centre of the Chinese art establishment reflected the general situation in cultural and educational circles. The desire to forget the "ten lost years" on the part of both victims and victimizers is understandable.

Red Guard Caricature: *A Parade of Clowns*

The Central Academy of Fine Arts in Beijing attracted national attention for its propaganda work at the height of the movement. A *People's Daily (Renmin ribao)* report of 23 February 1967 records that "rebel artists" from the Central Academy of Fine Arts had drawn propaganda pictures based on Mao's quotations and described this as "a new event in the Great Proletarian Cultural Revolution and a great initiative of the fine arts circle."[25] The following day, a foreign reporter described lines of workers at post offices and other public institutions waiting to purchase a "news sheet caricaturing thirty-nine targets of the Cultural Revolution."[26] This poster fits the description of an elaborate cartoon designed by Weng Rulan, an advanced undergraduate in the academy's *guohua* (traditional Chinese painting) department.[27] The version reproduced below bears the title *A Parade of Clowns* and was issued by a transitory Red Guard group, the Preparatory Office for the Struggle against Peng [Zhen], Lu [Dingyi], Luo [Ruiqing], and Yang [Shangkun]'s Counter-Revolutionary Revisionist Group (Figure 1.5).[28] When the poster was made, this organization occupied offices in the municipal government

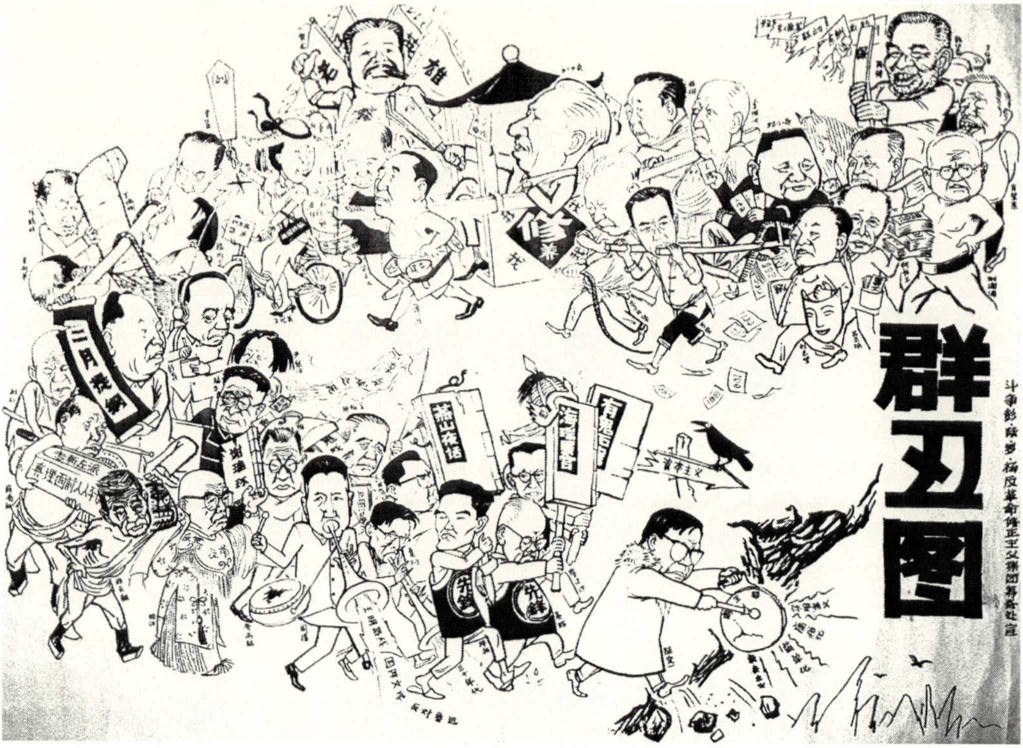

Figure 1.5 Weng Rulan, *A Parade of Clowns* (1967). Poster. Collection of the artist.

complex, a situation no doubt resulting from the January overthrow of the city government. The work is unsigned, but the artist and her classmates confirm her authorship.

According to Weng Rulan, the poster depicts the first thirty-nine high-ranking targets of the Cultural Revolution in the order that they were purged from government. The caricatured figures convey both their personal quirks and their political positions, and are based on the artist's visual imagination and crucial details she learned from her parents' circle of friends. One of the many ironies of the Cultural Revolution is that the young people Mao used for his political ends were products of the system they overthrew. Weng Rulan was a twenty-two-year-old Beijing native who had received an elite education at China's premier art school from the age of twelve. Her undergraduate advisor was Ye Qianyu, chairman of the academy's *guohua* department and a renowned cartoonist and satirist. Weng, like her teacher, became a specialist in the outline style.

By the time the Cultural Revolution began in 1966, Weng had completed ten years of professional art training at the Central Academy of Fine Arts and was thoroughly steeped in the principles and history of communist art. The complex composition and amusing caricatures of *A Parade of Clowns* are very much a product of that careful training. The legacy of her teacher's ink painting and comic style, which includes slightly squared shoulders and knees as well as lively variations in line width, is evident in her cartoon, a stylistic heritage she did not reject even though Ye Qianyu was an early target of the Red Guards. Ye's own penetrating characterization was clearly a model for this extraordinary work by his student.

The composition of *A Parade of Clowns* has other sources within the academy, including a well-published revolutionary New Year's picture by Hong Bo from the Civil War period. In his work, twenty-five north Chinese peasants and communist cadres parade across the picture in serpentine fashion to celebrate heroes of the Civil War. Just as wartime woodcuts reworked the established iconographic forms of folk art to help Mao Zedong in propaganda battles of the 1940s, so Weng Rulan manipulated icons of early communist art to attack the Communist Party's ousted leaders on Mao's behalf. The first of the thirty-nine figures in *A Parade of Clowns* is Lu Dingyi, director of the Communist Party's Central Propaganda Department and minister of culture. Lu beats a broken drum that emits noises such as "dogmatism," "pragmatism," and "simplification." Wu Han, Liao Mosha, and Deng Tuo, who had been attacked for criticizing Mao in their writings, follow. Deposed vice-minister of culture Xia Yan blows a trumpet that sounds "the thirties," alongside Zhou Yang, whose own trumpet urges "The Wang Ming Line," "Literature of National Defence," and "Down with Lu Xun." Each figure is labelled and satirized. The playwright Tian Han wears a Beijing opera robe, the collar of which is embroidered with the word "counter-revolutionary." General Luo Ruiqing, whose leg is in a cast, is carried in a basket. Luo had broken his leg the previous year in an unsuccessful suicide leap from a building.[29]

Wang Guangmei, Liu Shaoqi's wife, rides a bicycle in the high heels, sheath dress, and jewellery for which the Red Guards ridiculed her.[30] A book, *The Sayings of Chairman Liu,* rests on the front of her bicycle and a pile of hats on the rear. The hats are labelled counter-revolutionary, true rightist, false leftist, anti-party type, and so forth. Marshall He Long stands behind her, depicted with exaggerated emphasis on his hairy chest, arms, and moustache. He wears Beijing opera flags on his back that read "If the father's a hero," thus portraying him as a supporter of the "bloodlines" Red Guard group. Following in sedan chairs are Liu Shaoqi, Deng Xiaoping, and their supporters. Deng plays bridge with cards that read "king" and "work teams," the latter a reference to party officials who attempted to pacify the student rebels in the early days of the movement.

The ridicule of purged party leaders had a venerable history by the time Weng made her poster. Her work treats her subject much more mildly than some humourless cartoons conceived during the 1955 anti–Hu Feng movement, which used homophones to vilify the disgraced communist writer as a thoroughly evil tiger *(hu).* Weng Rulan's work mocks rival Red Guard factions as well as the thirty-nine politicians. Trailing behind the last purged leader is a ragged line of small figures carrying the tattered flags of rival rebel groups: West Guard, East Guard, United Action Committee, Red Flag Army, and so forth.[31] These groups were all associated with the slogan "If the father's a hero, the son's a brave; if the father's a counter-revolutionary, the son's a bastard." He Long's flags bear this slogan, an intentional irony, for his son was a leader of the United Action Committee, which promoted the elitist ditty.[32] The Red Guard leader was thus attacked with his own slogan, for once his venerable father had been condemned, he must become the bastard his group had labelled others.[33] Weng herself, as the daughter of two professors, was the product of what the other faction had declared to be a bad class background and thus was one who would be deprived of political and civil rights in the new social structure codified by the Cultural Revolution.

A Parade of Clowns enjoyed wide distribution and marked a short-lived publicity victory for the artist's Red Guard faction. In poster form, it was made available to workers in Beijing, displayed throughout the diplomatic district of the city, and even mailed to foreign purchasers of Chinese books and periodicals. It documented serious business, however: two years later, the primary target of Mao Zedong's wrath, Liu Shaoqi, died in prison of untreated pneumonia.

Much Red Guard art sought to create the directness and urgency of wartime propaganda produced in the 1940s at Yan'an. The revolutionary agenda that generated Cultural Revolution art was accompanied by claims of collectivism in the process of production, and *A Parade of Clowns* is typical of Red Guard propaganda pictures in being unsigned. Many bold woodcuts were also published during this period, most anonymously. Figure 1.1 incorporates the new tenets of socialist realism with the simplicity of the folk-inspired Yan'an style.

Many of the published images from the early years of the Cultural Revolution were painted for one of the many Red Guard–organized exhibitions. Red Guards, inspired by the cult of Mao Zedong and guided by Jiang Qing, set out to construct a new pictorial history for the People's Republic of

China – one that dramatized Mao's revolutionary role and minimized that of most other communist leaders. A publication of the period asserts, "It is Chairman Mao who points the correct direction for the revolutionary literary and art workers. It is Comrade Jiang Qing, courageous standard-bearer of the great Cultural Revolution, who persists along Chairman Mao's revolutionary line in literature and art and leads the proletarian revolutionaries in these fields in creating 'model' revolutionary productions for the stage."[34]

One well-publicized exhibition of the period was Long Live the Victory of Chairman Mao's Revolutionary Line, which opened at the National Art Gallery on 1 October 1967 and subsequently toured the nation. Sixteen hundred works were shown, of which 60 percent were advertised as by workers, peasants, and soldiers.[35] (Presumably, the other 40 percent were by professionals.) *Chairman Mao's Heart Beats as One with the Hearts of the Revolutionary Masses* (Figure 1.2), an oil painting prepared for this exhibition, may have been the result of amateur-professional collaboration.

An event that was even more memorable for the young artists in Beijing was Mao Zedong's Thought Illuminates the Anyuan Workers' Movement, an exhibition that opened in October 1967. It featured the Cultural Revolution icon *Chairman Mao Goes to Anyuan* (Figure 1.6).[36] The exhibition was organized at the Museum of Revolutionary History by the national labour union. Its political purpose was explicit, for it was part of an intensified campaign to discredit Liu Shaoqi. As *Art Storm* had indicated some months earlier, the purge of Mao's chosen successor meant that well-known history paintings such as Hou Yimin's *Liu Shaoqi and the Anyuan Coal Miners* (Figure 1.4) and Dong Xiwen's *Founding of the Nation* (Figure 1.7), with its prominent image of Liu Shaoqi, were inappropriate for display. The exhibition sought to redefine the iconography of China's revolutionary history by replacing Liu with Mao as the primary organizer of the important 1922 coal miners' strike. Liu Chunhua's oil painting *Chairman Mao Goes to Anyuan* was a remarkable exception to the convention of anonymity. The young artist, whose education paralleled that of Weng Rulan, was then a college student at the Central Academy of Arts and Crafts, which he had entered from the elite art middle school of the Lu Xun Academy of Art in Shenyang.

His painting of the young Mao visiting Anyuan in 1921 would not have inspired such interest were it not for the official response it received. Jiang Qing requested that a viewing be held at the governmental compound at Zhongnanhai and in 1967 declared it a "model" for Cultural Revolution art. *People's Daily* reproduced it in colour and distributed it nationwide. Parades and festivals were organized to commemorate the publication, with pretty girls in new blue overalls dancing in front of multiple reproductions of the picture.[37] By the fall of 1968, it was institutionalized as a model painting, copied by aspiring artists nationwide, and reproduced on everything from Mao badges to pocket mirrors. Years later, in the 1980s, the artist estimated that 900 million copies had been printed during the course of the Cultural Revolution, a number greater than the entire Chinese population at that time.

The painting was an important contribution to Mao's cult, for it possessed clear devotional appeal. Indeed, the artist claimed to have taken his inspiration from a Raphael Madonna, although a more immediate source for the composition might have been contemporary Chinese oil painting of Mao executed in the Soviet manner by the well-known Chinese portraitist Jin Shangyi.[38]

Although *Chairman Mao Goes to Anyuan*'s links to earlier academic art are more evident than its innovations, it was affirmed by Cultural Revolution authorities as an icon of the new art. Features of Liu's work that became characteristic of Cultural Revolution painting are Mao's exaggerated eyebrows, his smooth face, and the artificially arranged clouds, which allow nature to echo Mao's divine movements.

As Maurice Meisner has observed, by 1968 the cult of Mao had shifted from the iconoclasm of the Red Guard movement, here exemplified by the work of Weng Rulan, to the production of icons.[39] Liu Chunhua's *Chairman Mao Goes to Anyuan* was the most important pictorial manifestation of this trend, but it was not alone. Lin Yong, in his *Great Job! Investigating the Peasant Movement in Hunan* (1970), is similarly successful in his portrayal of the youthful Mao as a handsome heroic figure, the perfect object of admiration for the young (Figure 1.8). Lin Yong's attainment was all the more remarkable in winning official approval of a painting in the traditional medium of ink and colour on paper, thus setting a standard for a socialist, non-traditional, form of Chinese painting.

If the delicately refined young Mao of the paintings by Liu and Lin might present a certain view of history and serve as a model for China's youth, an oil painting of the mature, ruddy-faced Mao by Shengtian Zheng, then a young art teacher at the Zhejiang Academy of Fine Arts in Hangzhou (now the National Academy of Fine Arts), and his collaborators served to reassure China's people of the glories of their present under Mao's firm and wise control (see Figure 3.1 in Chapter 3). This painting enjoyed less celebrity than Liu Chunhua's, due to the preferences of Jiang Qing and the artist's troubles at the hands of increasingly radical Zhejiang Red Guards; Shengtian Zheng's account of the creative process, and of the contrasting fates of his

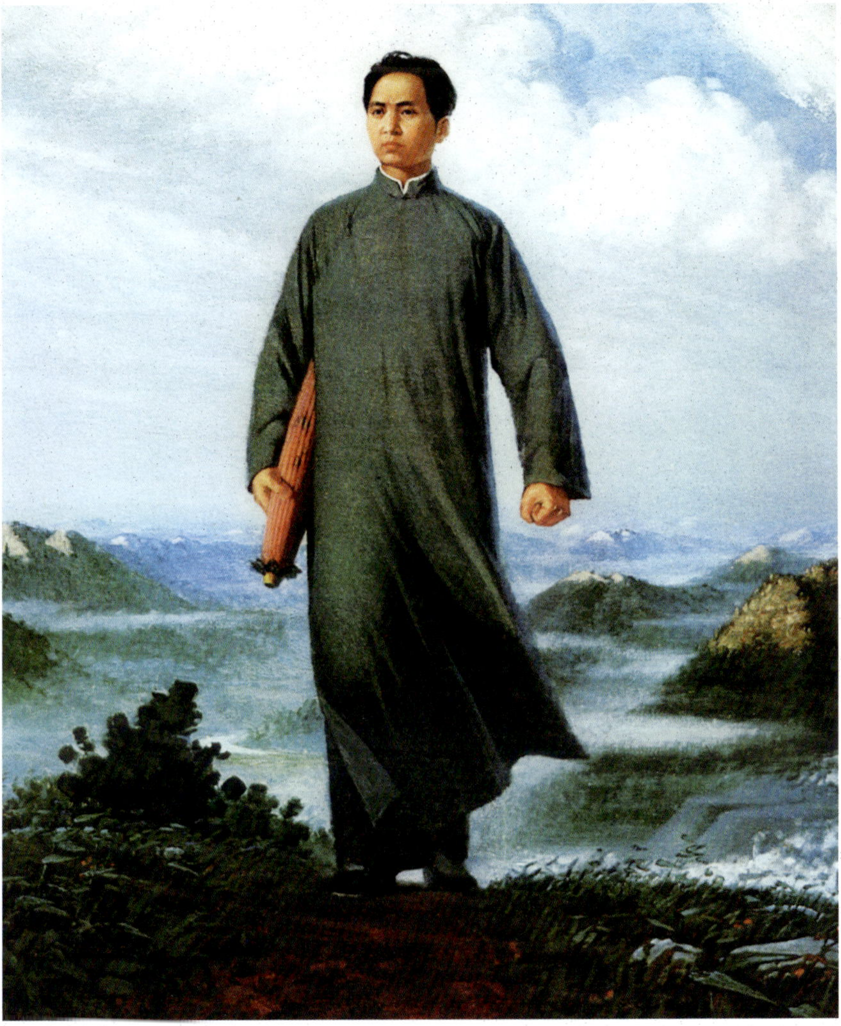

Figure 1.6 Liu Chunhua, *Chairman Mao Goes to Anyuan* (1967). Oil painting reproduced as a poster. This painting responded to the Cultural Revolution's program of destroying the reputations of Mao's rivals as revolutionary founders and was specifically intended to replace Figure 1.4. Mao is here depicted as arriving in Jiangxi in the fall of 1921 to begin organizing the coal miners. The claim is thus asserted that Mao enjoyed precedence over the disgraced Liu Shaoqi in organizing the urban proletariat and that he personally ignited the revolutionary conflagration. Collection of Wang Mingxian.

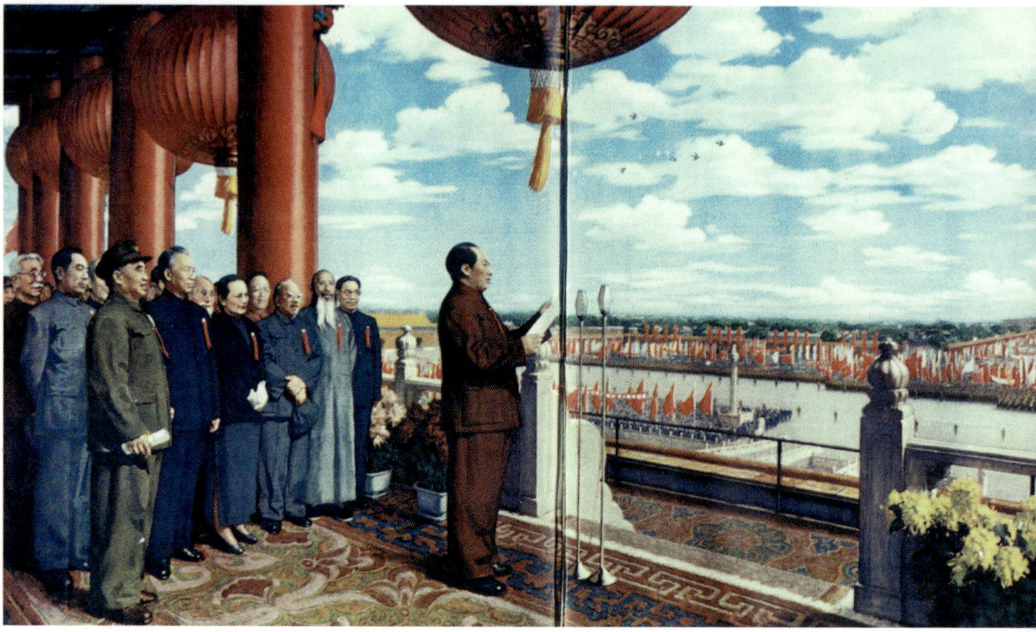

Figure 1.7 Dong Xiwen, *Founding of the Nation* (1952-53). Oil painting reproduced as a poster (painting now damaged). Behind Mao, in the front row, from left, are General Zhu De, Liu Shaoqi, Madame Song Qingling, Li Jishen, Zhang Lan, and Gao Gang, who were the six vice-chairmen of the Central People's Government; among those in row two are Zhou Enlai at left, the elderly and bearded Shen Junru, and Guo Moruo at right; in the back row, at left, is Lin Boqu. *China Pictorial* 10 (1953): 20-21.

painting and Liu Chunhua's *Chairman Mao Goes to Anyuan,* appears in Chapter 3 of this volume.

The rampant chaos of 1967 and 1968, which threatened the nation with civil war, led to a crackdown against student activism. In 1968 and 1969, all urban high school graduates were sent to labour in China's distant hinterlands – the Siberian border in the northeast, the remote mountains of Sichuan, the Mongolian steppes, and the southwestern jungles of Yunnan – in a mass rustication that brought the Red Guard art movement to its close. Simultaneously, most professional artists were removed from the art world and sent to the countryside for labour reform.

There were some regional differences in art administration during the unsettled period before 1971. In Shanghai, as in Beijing, artists who were not in prison were sent, by 1969, to do farm work at May Seventh Cadre-schools, as labour camps in the rural suburbs were called, and they remained there until 1971. Although art periodicals had ceased publication, major Shanghai newspapers continued to function and began to seek revolutionary paintings for reproduction on their pages. In 1969, for example, a young amateur named Xu Chunzhong, who had learned to paint at a Children's Palace, was commissioned to illustrate an important article in *Liberation Daily (Jiefang ribao)* about the heroic death of Jin Shunhua, a Shanghai student who had drowned in Heilongjiang while trying to prevent timber from being swept away by flood waters.[40] The Shanghai-born Jin was thus depicted as a martyr by another Shanghai-born rusticated youth. Technical skill was not sacrificed to political correctness, however, as Xu was assisted in this commission by one of the most talented of the young Shanghai professional artists, Chen Yifei, and the work was published under the pseudonym Yi Zhong. According to their colleagues, top Cultural Revolution administrators decided to promote Jin Shunhua as a national model of selfless sacrifice. The image was repeatedly published, including as a colour poster.

Reconstruction of the National Bureaucracy

The Ministry of Culture, the Central Propaganda Department, and the Chinese Artists' Association, organizations within the party and government that were responsible for art in the centralized socialist structure before 1966, were rendered powerless and ineffective during the early years of the Cultural Revolution. By about 1970, their functions were assumed by a Culture Group under the State Council. Jiang Qing, as director of this group, was the highest authority on cultural matters. Art activities were directed by

Wang Mantian, one of the ten directors of the Culture Group, a shadowy figure who is believed to have studied art at the Lu Xun Academy of Arts and Literature in Yan'an.[41]

Wang Mantian began planning for a 1972 exhibition to commemorate the thirtieth anniversary of Mao's Yan'an Talks, with a meeting at the Zhejiang Academy of Fine Arts. The choice of location for the meeting may have been due to the presence there of Zhang Yongsheng (a Red Guard leader at the Zhejiang Academy who had risen to a leadership position in the rebel factions of Hangzhou).[42] Zhang Yongsheng's Cultural Revolution exploits and his subsequent downfall are described in Chapter 3. Wang Mantian selected a young oil painting instructor, Gao Jingde, to head the exhibition effort.

Gao Jingde visited all provinces and major art institutions in the country, with the goal of assembling an unprecedented national exhibition to promote the thought of Chairman Mao. Although worker-peasant-soldier art remained extremely important, Gao sought high technical standards, which had not been the case during the spontaneous and disorganized artistic activity of the 1966-70 period.

That Gao and his assistants were products of the academy system strongly affected the direction taken by Chinese painting of the 1970s. The 1972, 1973, and 1974 exhibitions were dominated by a narrowly defined academic style. The painting that they promoted was a synthesis of the Soviet-influenced academic painting of the art colleges and the more restrictive requirements Jiang Qing developed for the model theatrical works she promoted at the same time. This style combined socialist realism with some aspects of folk art, especially its bright colour, and certain idiosyncratic Western elements derived from Jiang Qing's personal taste, some of which may have come from her early life as an aspiring movie actress in the commercial mecca of Shanghai. Eclectic as her taste may have been, Jiang Qing's antipathy to traditional Chinese art was almost total.

Before selection of work for the national exhibition began in the spring of 1972, all provincial and municipal Cultural Revolution Committees were asked to organize submissions. Orders were given that many artists, old and young, who had been incarcerated but not convicted were to be liberated for the purpose. A small number of old professional artists who had enjoyed Zhou Enlai's appreciation during the 1950s were asked to paint for the exhibition; among these were Guan Shanyue, partner in a major 1959 commission illustrating Mao's poetry for the Great Hall of the People, and Qian Songyan, active in forging the new Jiangsu style of traditional Chinese painting

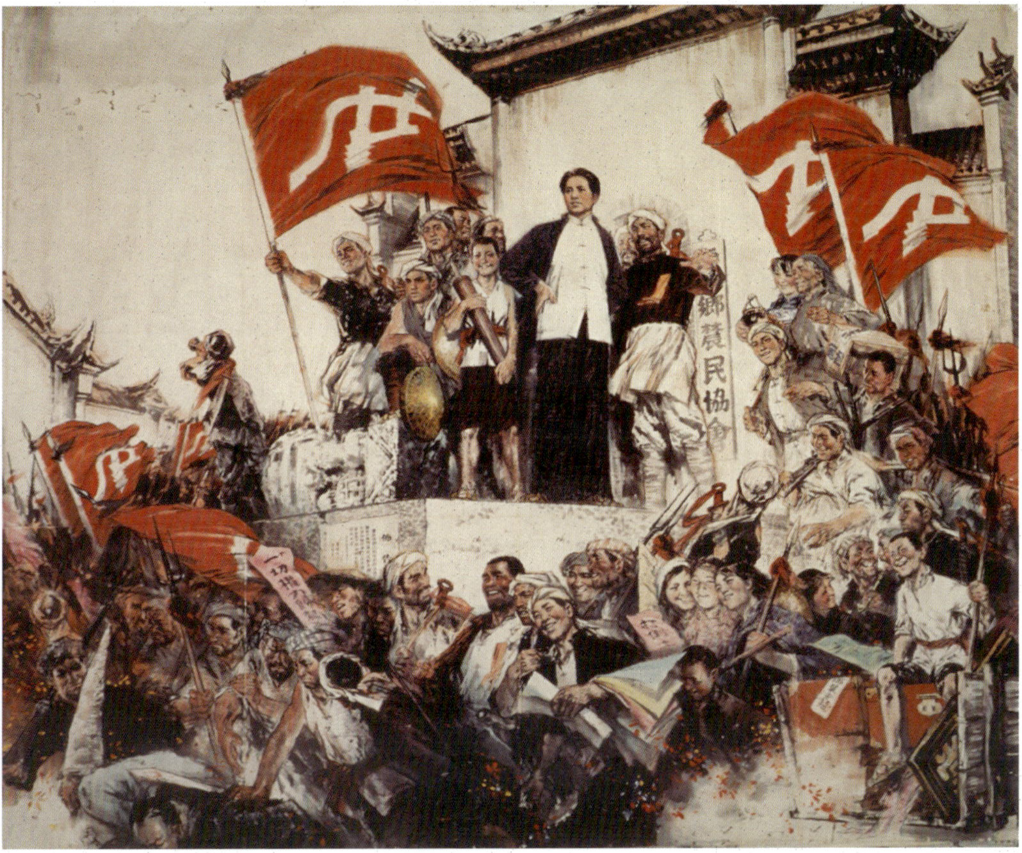

Figure 1.8 Lin Yong, *Great Job! Investigating the Peasant Movement in Hunan* (1970). The artist has imagined the young Hunanese, Mao Zedong, conducting the fieldwork that produced his seminal 1927 essay advocating the overthrow of landlords by peasant associations. Mao's theory for implementation of China's revolution through rural organization, in contrast to that of rivals in the party who focused more on the industrial urban proletariat, became an essential Maoist text. Collection of the artist.

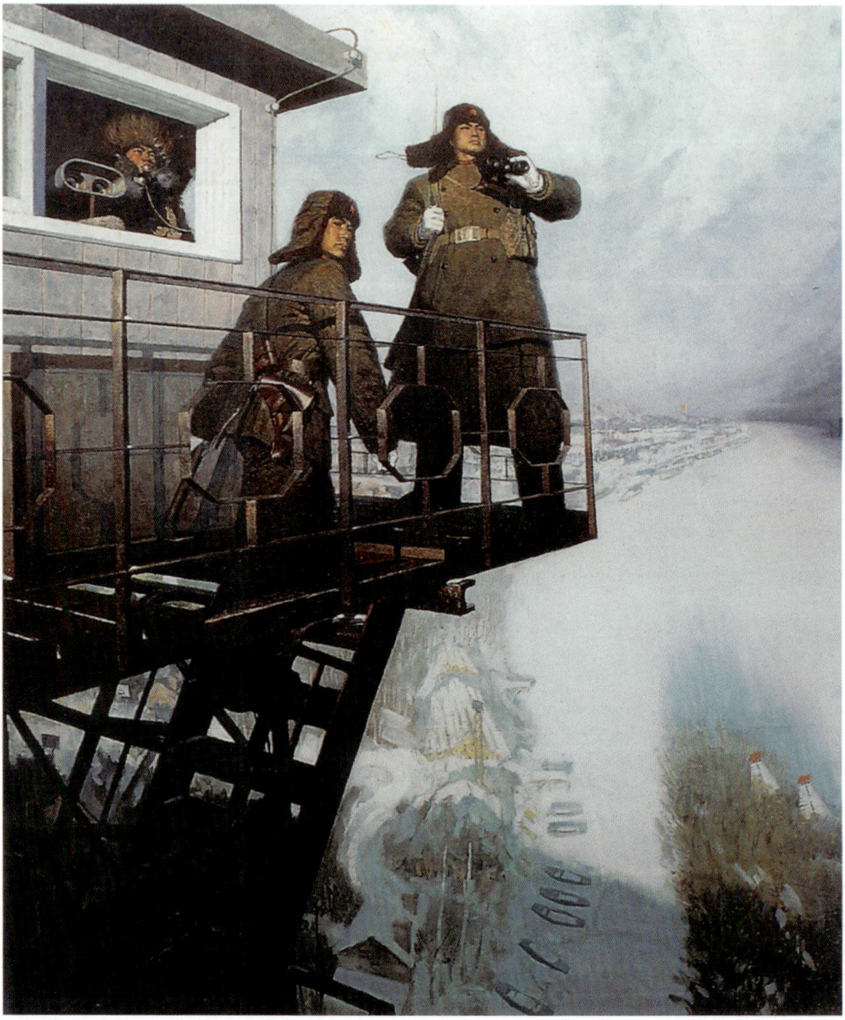

Figure 1.12 **Shen Jiawei, *Standing Guard for Our Great Motherland* (1974).** Collection of the artist.

during the late 1950s. A larger number of middle-aged professionals re-emerged, as did some former Red Guard painters.

A jury of well-known professional artists was formed to make the final selection of the many pictures submitted by provincial authorities. The dual mandate of high technical standards and "serving the people" led to an odd combination of professional and amateur activity. In spite of Gao's efforts to include some professional artists, the Cultural Revolution's emphasis on proletarian art by workers, peasants, and soldiers ensured that most of the successful submissions were by amateurs.

The inherent contradiction between Gao's mandate to seek high standards and the politically correct but technically weak images by workers, peasants, and soldiers was resolved by forming Painting Correction Groups. Works by amateurs might have interesting subject matter but be poorly executed. In response to criticisms by jury members, officials, and other artists, such paintings were "corrected" by prominent young professionals who had accompanied them when each region shipped them to the capital. For the oil painting section, a representative of the artist's own region would simply repaint problematic sections. If the officials still found the work inadequate, artists from other regions might complete the repainting. Some of the most highly skilled realists of the younger generation were selected: these included Jin Shangyi, from Beijing, a young oil painting professor at the Central Academy of Fine Arts trained a decade earlier by the Soviet expert Constantine Maksimov; from Shanghai, Chen Yifei, who had studied at the Shanghai Art College; from Wuhan, Tang Xiaohe, a graduate of the Hubei Art Academy; from Kunming, Sun Jingbo, a graduate of the Central Academy of Fine Arts Middle School; from Guangzhou, Chen Yan'ning, a graduate of the Guangzhou Academy of Arts; from Qinghai, Zhu Naizheng, a talented Central Academy of Fine Arts graduate; and from Shenyang, Guang Tingbo, from the Lu Xun Academy of Art. Several other Beijing artists were given special assignments. Most of the artists were called back from labour camps or prison to participate in the exhibition.

In a departure from the conventions learned from Soviet painters, it was widely accepted among Cultural Revolution-era artists that images of Mao should be red, smooth, and luminescent. Although Soviet socialist realism was still the most evident stylistic source for such compositions, details of colour and texture may be related to the more elegant of preliberation New Year's pictures *(nian hua).* Cool colours were to be avoided; Mao's flesh should be modelled in red and other warm tones. Conspicuous displays of brushwork should be eschewed, and Mao's face should be smooth.

The entire composition should be bright and should be illuminated in such a way as to imply that Mao himself was the primary source of light. If Mao were in the centre of a group of people, all efforts should be made to illuminate surfaces that faced him. In this way, slogans such as "Chairman Mao is the red sun in our hearts" could be made visible.

He Kongde's *Gutian Meeting* (Figure 1.9), which was prominently hung in the oil painting section of the exhibition, does not specifically fulfill all the requirements of the red, smooth, and luminescent formulation, for the artist, unlike many graduates of the Soviet expert Maksimov's class, never abandoned the loose textural handling of the paint common to many Soviet-trained Chinese artists. Nevertheless, he was particularly favoured by the art administrators because he combined two qualities they sought. As a member of the People's Liberation Army, he could be considered a worker-peasant-soldier, but he was, at the same time, a professionally trained history painter.

He Kongde chose a military theme in this work, depicting Mao Zedong as he presented instructions from the party central to soldiers of the Red Fourth Army in Gutian village, Fujian, in December of 1929. This new doctrine was considered to have established the communist military structure, in which the party and its ideology possessed authority over the army. Most importantly, this painting demonstrates the party's acceptance of Mao's military strategy of surrounding and strangling Guomindang-controlled cities with rural communist troops, and thus implicitly credits the communist victory to his wisdom.

In *Gutian Meeting,* He Kongde made few concessions to Cultural Revolution styles: he did not banish cool colours from his palette, modify his rough brushwork, or employ irrational sources of illumination. Nevertheless, the work does not contradict the underlying aesthetic of the Cultural Revolution, for red tonalities dominate and Mao is the most brightly lit figure in the composition; furthermore, the Painting Correction Group repainted Mao's face so that it was more smoothly rendered than the remainder of the image.

Organizing the *guohua* section of the exhibition, held the following year, was more difficult, in part due to Jiang Qing's aversion to traditional art. Local authorities generally believed that *guohua* was part of the four olds to be eradicated by the Cultural Revolution. It was only after Gao received explicit authorization from Wang Mantian to permit *guohua* painting that he was able to persuade local art circles to submit such works. As was the case with oil painting, a Painting Correction Group was assembled to assist with preparations for the exhibition. It, like the oil painting group,

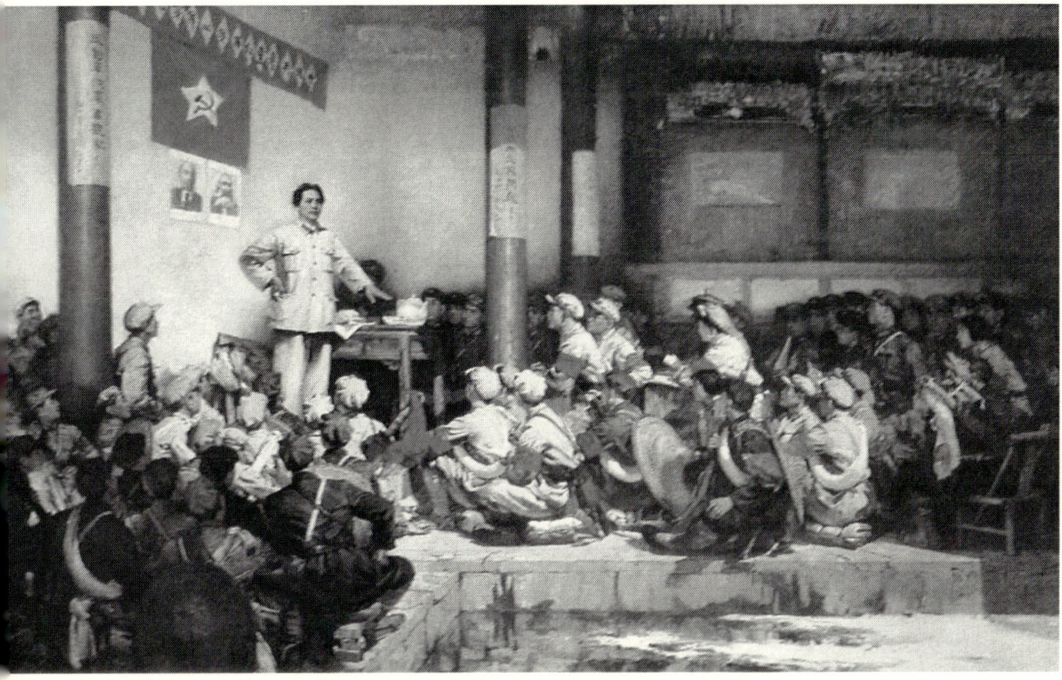

Figure 1.9 He Kongde, *Gutian Meeting* (1972). Oil painting published as a poster. The military artist He Kongde has depicted Mao Zedong speaking to soldiers of the Red Fourth Army in December of 1929. The party central had accepted his proposal for establishing rural armies. *Gaoju Mao zhuxi de weida qizhi shengli qianjin: Meishu zuopin xuan* [Victoriuosly advance, raising high the great banner of Chairman Mao: Selected artworks] (Beijing: Beijing People's Art Press, 1977).

consisted of academically trained *guohua* painters from each of China's major regions: these included, from Hangzhou, Fang Zengxian, a *guohua* figure painting professor at the Zhejiang Academy of Fine Arts; from Xi'an, Liu Wenxi, a graduate of the Zhejiang Academy of Fine Arts *guohua* figure painting program; from Guangzhou, Wu Qizhong, a Guangzhou Academy of Arts graduate; from Shenyang, Xu Yong, a professor at the Lu Xun Academy of Art; and from Beijing, Zhou Sicong, a graduate of the Central Academy of Fine Arts *guohua* figure painting program.

Faulty sections of a work painted in permanent ink on paper could not be overpainted, as they might be in an oil painting. The correctors were thus required to make new paintings based on the amateurs' compositions. The late Zhou Sicong recalled her assignment to fix a painting by a worker in a shoe factory. The worker had attempted to depict the actress of a model opera trying on her new ballet slippers at the factory. The theme was appealing to authorities at all levels: it flattered Jiang Qing and her model theatrical works, and it also documented the contribution the artist's shoe factory was making to the Cultural Revolution. Unfortunately, the subject was difficult for an amateur to paint with any semblance of anatomical accuracy. Zhou completely repainted the work, basing her picture on the worker's composition, and it was exhibited under the worker's name.

The emphasis on rusticated urban youth in the 1972 exhibition left the final group of paintings with comparatively few portraits of Chairman Mao. He Kongde's *Gutian Meeting* was prominently hung in the main room of the gallery. A monumental work by the young Wuhan professionals Tang Xiaohe and Cheng Li depicted Mao on the occasion of his famous 1966 swim in the Yangtze River near Wuhan (Figure 1.10). This work combined several desirable characteristics. On 16 July 1966, the elderly Mao Zedong demonstrated the virtues of physical fitness by floating and swimming for over an hour in the Yangtze River. At this crucial juncture, in the early phase of the Cultural Revolution, this praise of Mao's physical health (whether factually accurate or not) was politically significant. It also fell into the class of revolutionary paintings of local subjects, by taking a theme specific to the artists' own home locale and thus demonstrating the loyalty of the people of Hubei Province to Mao and the Cultural Revolution (Wuhan had experienced large-scale armed strife in 1967). Multiplied by China's thirty provinces and cities, such local testimonials became key visual and propaganda statements.

Gao Jingde specifically commissioned another Mao portrait – *We Must Implement the Proletarian Cultural Revolution to the Finish* – that spoke to both Beijing events and the nation (Figure 1.3).[43] To accomplish the creation of this large oil painting with the optimum quality and speed, he freed a group of Beijing professional artists from nearby labour camps. Thus released, Hou Yimin, Deng Shu, Jin Shangyi, Zhan Jianjun, Luo Gongliu, Yuan Hao, and Yang Lin'gui reworked the Red Guard composition discussed above (Figure 1.2). A major iconographic change is that the Cultural Revolution leadership has been removed from the composition so that Mao crosses the bridge alone. Zhou Enlai reportedly insisted that his own image be removed from the painting, which may have precipitated the revision.

The greatest number of paintings shown in 1972 were executed by amateurs, many of whom were sent-down urban youth facing permanent careers as peasants or factory labourers. When the Cultural Revolution authorities announced the forthcoming exhibition to commemorate the

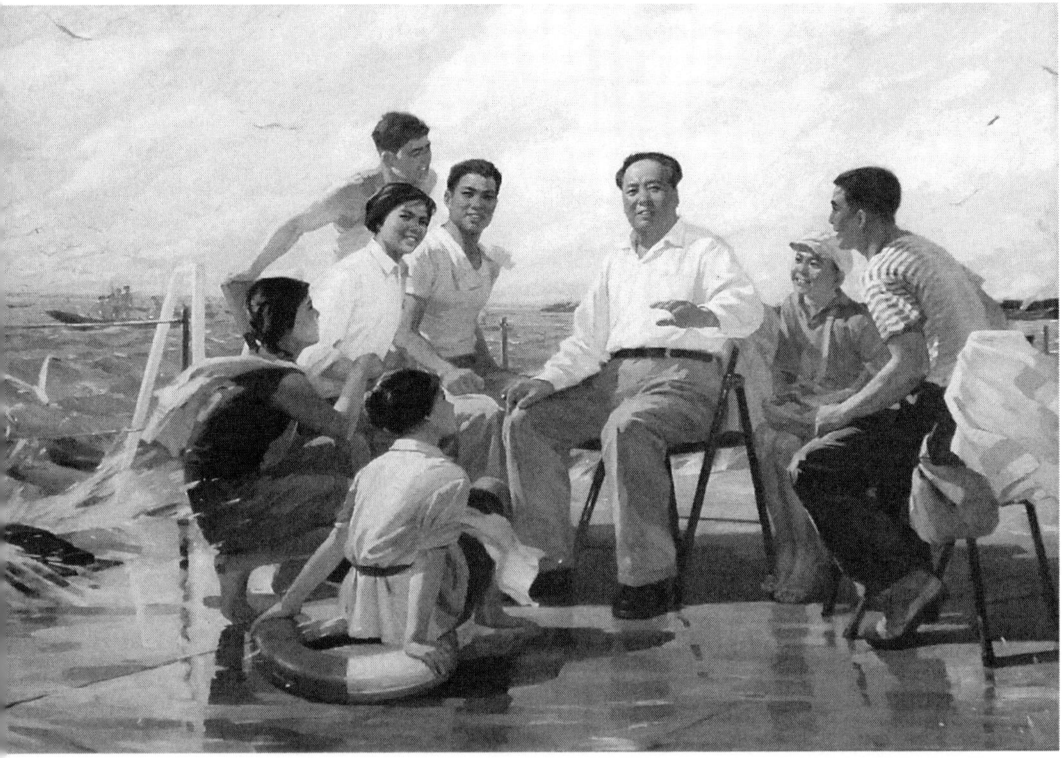

Figure 1.10 **Tang Xiaohe and Cheng Li, *Follow Chairman Mao Closely, Grow Up Tempered by Wind and Waves* (1972). Oil painting published as a poster. On 16 July 1966, the seventy-three-year-old Mao Zedong swam for over an hour in the Yangtze River. Wind and waves here are metaphors for the complicated and dangerous situation in the confrontation of Mao's revolutionary line and Liu Shaoqi's bourgeois revisionist line. Mao urges his young followers to steadfastly follow him, despite all difficulties.** Collection of Wang Mingxian.

thirtieth anniversary of the Yan'an Talks, some amateurs began avidly painting in their spare time. Instructions went out to all units to gather submissions from workers, peasants, and soldiers, particularly those glorifying the patriotic contributions of rusticated urban youth. The results were paintings such as *Milk Maid,* by the Shanghai student turned dairy farmer Tang Muli.

The Shanghai-born Tang Muli, son of a successful film director, began painting as a child; like Weng Rulan and Xu Chunzhong, he was a gifted product of the Children's Palace system. Before the Cultural Revolution, Tang had studied at one of Shanghai's best secondary schools in preparation

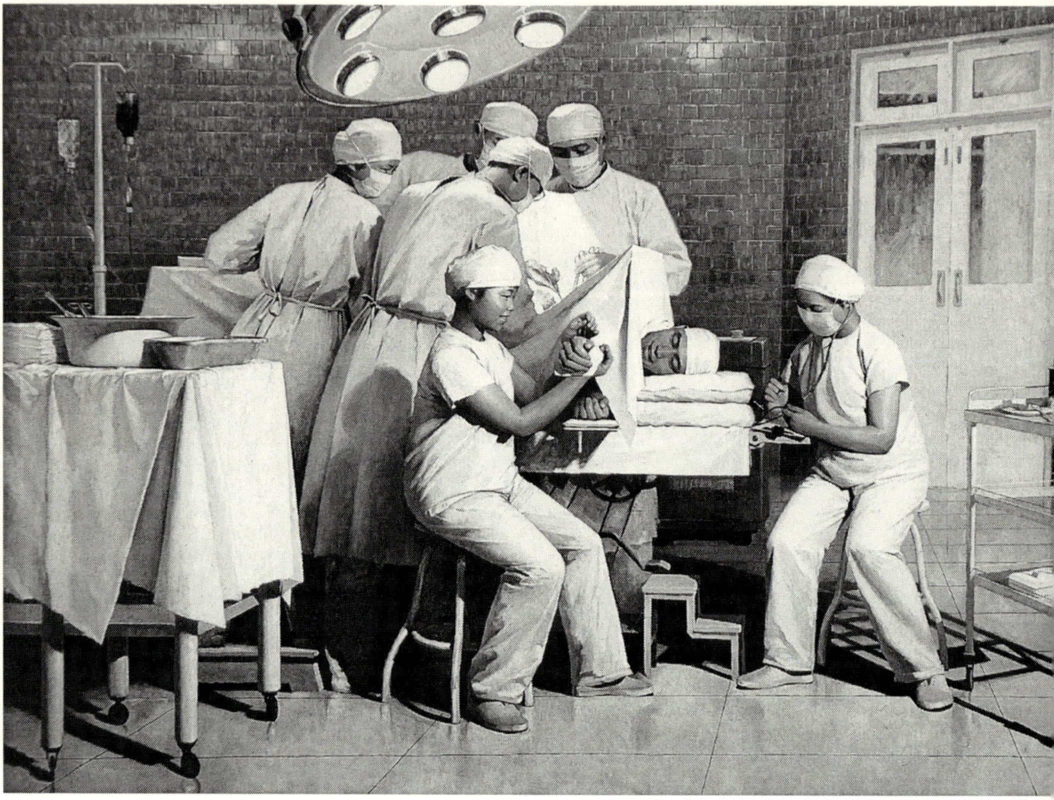

Figure 1.11 Tang Muli, *Acupuncture Anaesthesia* (1972). Oil on canvas. Collection of the artist.

for a career in physics. Sent to work on a dairy farm in the Shanghai suburbs rather than to college, he turned to his hobby of drawing and in 1971 submitted his first oil painting for the upcoming exhibition.[44] In *Milk Maid,* Tang Muli, now considered a peasant, depicted a healthy dairy farmer surrounded by cows. In 1972, he was commissioned by the health service to prepare a picture highlighting acupuncture's use as a surgical anaesthetic, a development seen as the victory of indigenous Chinese science over that of the West. *Acupuncture Anaesthesia* was well received when exhibited in Shanghai that spring. Tang was then freed from farm work to concentrate full-time on a final version to be exhibited in the national exhibition in the fall (Figure 1.11). His *Milk Maid* paints a pretty picture of the situation of his cohort of rusticated urban youth and thus indirectly praises the policy that sent them all to the countryside. Ironically, by virtue of his recognition as a painter, Tang took the first step to escaping his rural destiny.

The next major show was held in October of 1974 at the National Art Gallery, in celebration of the twenty-fifth anniversary of the People's Republic. Jiang Qing, then involved in a power struggle with the cancer-stricken Zhou Enlai, stepped up her personal involvement with the visual arts. She personally inspected the gallery before the opening of the exhibition, which she had not done in 1972, and she reportedly spent most of one night studying the display. The Politburo attended the opening, according unprecedented political importance to the event.

A rusticated urban student from Zhejiang, Shen Jiawei, exhibited a painting depicting the heroic activities in Heilongjiang, his new home near the Siberian border (Figure 1.12). His story would be typical of other such young artists, were it not for the extraordinary short-term success the picture brought him. Shen Jiawei's painting, *Standing Guard for Our Great Motherland,* reportedly won Jiang Qing's enthusiastic approval. Like Tang Muli, Shen was a rusticated urban youth, but because he worked on a military farm in Beidahuang, he was considered a soldier rather than a peasant. Born in 1949 in Jiaxing, Zhejiang, Shen was one of the 400,000 middle school graduates sent in 1968 to a farm in Heilongjiang. He was assigned to the second regiment of the fourth division of the Heilongjiang Production and Construction Corps, which had its headquarters in Jiamusi. His farm, with a population of ten or twenty thousand demobilized soldiers, rightists, and rusticated urban youth, was located in the eastern corner of Heilongjiang, an area of border conflicts with the Soviet Union, near the Muleng River. Among the many young people in Heilongjiang were some who had aspired to enter art academies before the colleges were closed. About thirty of them were graduates of the Central Academy Middle School. With the national leadership's decision to sponsor national art exhibitions, the authorities in Heilongjiang, like those elsewhere, began organizing painters. Hao Boyi, a young oil painter and printmaker, was assigned to find and supervise the young soldier-artists. In 1971, he ordered a select group of young farmers to attend an art creation class in Jiamusi.

Hao Boyi taught printmaking in the local Beidahuang style, and some of his pupils excelled at printmaking. Students who wished to work in other media experimented and taught one another. The program continued for the next five years, with artists dividing their time between artwork in Jiamusi and manual labour on their farms. Heilongjiang prints were shown in most major exhibitions of the 1970s, and many were published anonymously in *Chinese Literature* and other magazines for distribution abroad. Shen Jiawei entered the group in 1973 and produced his vision of heroic border guards during the next year. The leading national art magazine of the late Cultural Revolution period, Zhejiang-based *Art Materials (Meishu ziliao),* published an article in which Shen elaborated upon his creative process.[45] He wrote that the theme of his painting was suggested by a widely heard patriotic song of the period. While participating in a class for amateur artists in 1973, he was given an opportunity to visit the Wusuli River and to climb a watchtower where soldiers monitored the Sino-Soviet border. The spectacular natural scenery reinforced the importance of the soldiers' patriotic duty.

Upon his return to the military camp, his sketch of the scene was approved by local authorities, who also gave him permission to collect further material during a future visit to the site. His composition, he wrote, was guided further by principles of Chairman Mao, such as "Our requirement is the unification of politics and art, the unification of contents and form, the unification of revolutionary political contents and the most perfect artistic form" and "The life reflected in artistic and literary works can be and should be loftier, more intense, more concentrated, more typical, and more ideal than ordinary actual life; thus it will be more universal."[46] Shen claimed additional inspiration from the study of the model theatrical works, which emphasized heroic characters. One soldier was made more prominent by following the suggestions of classmates to place him against an empty sky. His height was emphasized by shortening the railing and by aligning his head and feet with the exaggerated diagonals bordering the tower roof and the walkway floor. This construction was indeed perfectly in keeping with one of Jiang Qing's revolutionary aesthetic principles: the three prominences *(san tuchu).* As discussed in *Art Materials* in 1973, the three prominences required that, when depicting figures, artists should emphasize those associated with positive qualities; for positive figures, they should emphasize the heroic; and for heroic characters, they should emphasize the central or most important one.[47] What Shen did not mention was his extreme dissatisfaction with the alteration made to his painting in Beijing by a Painting Correction Group, whose representative repainted the main character's face in the red, smooth, and luminescent manner. Because Shen Jiawei was singled out for praise by Jiang Qing, his experience resembled that of Liu Chunhua more than that of Tang Muli. Rocketed to national attention on the basis of his first major painting, he was an overnight celebrity – a fame that lasted less than two years, until Mao died and Jiang Qing was arrested. Shen Jiawei was later to find international celebrity following his move to Australia, with paintings such as *Beijing Jeep* (Figure 0.5 in the Introduction).

From 1973, socialist-realist ink painting *(guohua),* was also exhibited. Typical of the *guohua* of this period were works such as Liu Wenxi's *New*

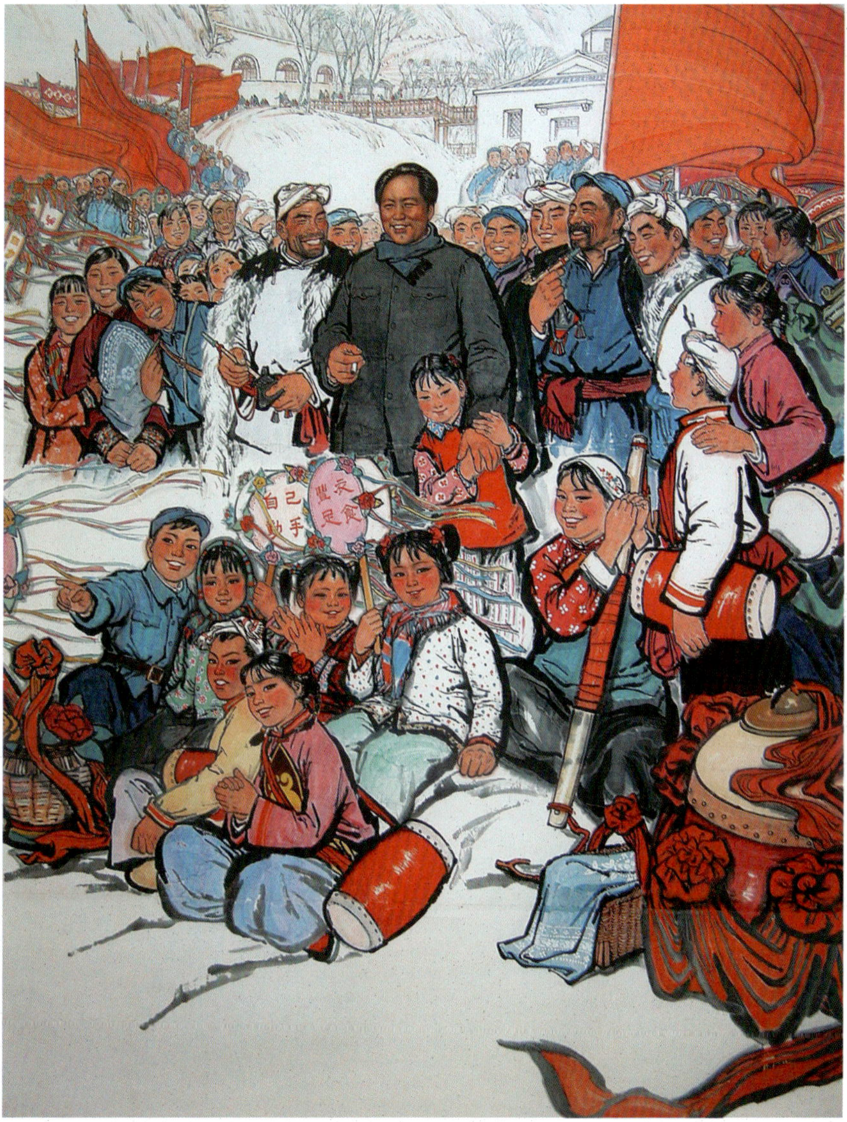

Figure 1.13 Liu Wenxi, *New Spring in Yan'an* (1972). Ink and colour on paper printed as a poster. Mao joins the now prosperous peasants in enjoying a New Year's performance. China International Exhibition Agency, Beijing.

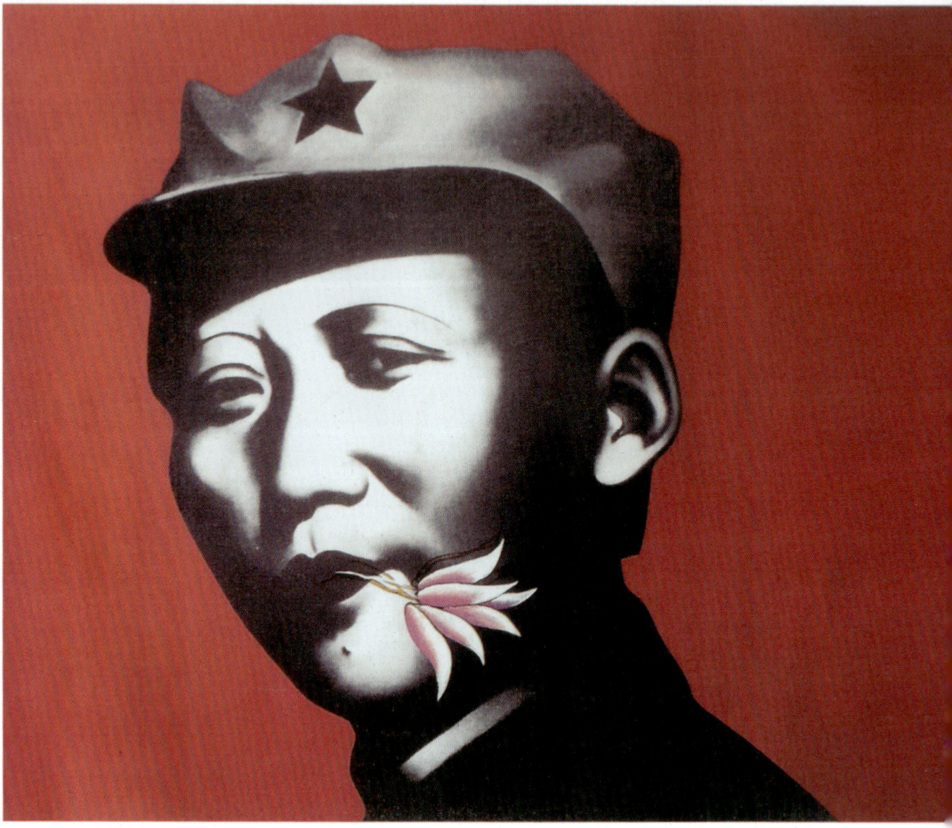

Figure 1.14 Li Shan, *The Rouge Series, no. 8* (1990). Collection of the artist.

Spring in Yan'an, painted in 1972 (Figure 1.13). Liu Wenxi, a Xi'an artist who had been two classes ahead of Gao Jingde in art school, had developed an unmistakable style of figure painting characterized by strong outlines and bold colours. In this commission, the artist emphasizes the close connections between the region of his own residence and the revolutionary heritage of Mao Zedong. The work appears to document a happy reunion between Chairman Mao and the now liberated peasants of the area around Yan'an. Themes of the wartime communist base at Yan'an were considered part of the regional territory of the Xi'an artists, and the work thus combines two desirable subjects: the portrait of Chairman Mao and a scene based on the artist's life experience.

Trained in the ink-and-colour socialist-realist figure painting program that had come to dominate Chinese painting at the former National Academy at Hangzhou, Liu Wenxi went on to develop a personal style more closely related to the crisp New Year's picture aesthetic than to the self-expressive aspirations of Shanghai and Hangzhou ink painters. His *guohua* figures, carefully modelled with rich flesh tones, achieve a pronounced three-dimensionality as well as the theatricality required by Jiang Qing. The garments, less heavily shaded than they might be in an oil painting, are outlined with thick black lines, and all have much the same volumetric quality. Although principles of Western perspective dominate, the background is paler and plainer than it might be in an oil painting. During the heyday of this style, Liu was one of China's most technically competent socialist-realist *guohua* figure painters.

Most of the visual images that were reproduced as posters, calendars, or in pictorial magazines from about 1971 to 1976 were prepared in the context of the new bureaucratic structure, which culminated in the series of local and national exhibitions. The close controls over official art in the late Cultural Revolution yielded an extreme and easily recognizable period style. Examination of the careers of individual artists who were part of this national phenomenon demonstrates that, as remarkable or even strange as this body of work might seem to our eyes today, it is very much part of a continuous history of modern Chinese art. The professional artists who made many of the canonical images of the era were thoroughly trained socialist realists. Many of the so-called amateurs were rusticated urban youth with years of art practice in weekend and after-school art programs at Children's Palaces; some were graduates of elite art middle schools. A number of them have subsequently gone on to careers as professional artists and critics.

This institutional and, to some extent, stylistic continuity is not difficult to understand, as the Cultural Revolution brought to a culmination thirty years (1949-79) of fairly steady artistic and political development. More puzzling is the emergence, three decades after the end of the ten-year disaster, of a large body of contemporary art that appropriates iconic images from the Cultural Revolution for satirical or playful purposes. Some of the earliest examples might be understood as a personal reckoning with shattered beliefs and wasted effort by artists who themselves had produced images in support of Mao and the Cultural Revolution. Li Shan's *Rouge Mao* of 1991 (Figure 1.14), which presents China's leader as an object of androgynous erotic desire, critiques the passion felt by many of the artist's generation and exposes the expression of that passion in the iconic images of the day. Lin Yong's *Great Job!* of 1970 (Figure 1.8), in which the young Mao is depicted with the utmost sincerity as an object of adoration, is only one of many such adolescent fantasies that formed the devotional canon of Maoist iconography.

Outside China, émigré artists who had escaped both their youthful Maoist hero-worship and the remaining political constraints on artistic expression in Deng Xiaoping's China also exorcised demons from their Cultural Revolution past by recycling and subverting its iconography. Zhang Hongtu, working in New York during the 1990s, produced a series of images on the theme of Mao's absence. The cleverest but most devastatingly bitter may be his *Pingpong Mao,* in which a hole in the shape of Mao's head and shoulders has been cut into each side of a ping-pong table.[48] Playing a normal game is impossible: a ball shot up the centre of the table cannot win a point, for it will simply fall through the hole; if it is shot up the side to avoid the absent Mao, it will easily go out of bounds. Another piece, evoking paranoia and nightmares, is constructed from an old apartment door. The peephole lens through which one inspects visitors has been altered to reveal not the apartment corridor, but a looming image of Mao. Such a seemingly playful work, amusing in its unexpectedness, may be interpreted more darkly when one considers the artist's youth at the height of the Cultural Revolution's Mao-worship and Mao-fear. For artists of the Red Guard generation now in their fifties, the utopian images of the Cultural Revolution bring forth the complicated emotions of nostalgia for the passion and simplicity of youth, a remembered pride in paintings well painted, and bitter anger at the betrayal of their idealistic faith. Older people, however, associate the Cultural Revolution pictures much more directly with the torture and humiliation they suffered, and many feel outright revulsion at their sight.

Some artists and filmmakers too young to have participated in the Cultural Revolution are now interested in its imagery. Some portray it with the innocent eyes of their own childhood selves: for them, there was no suffering, only festive displays of colour and music, and many happy days without school. They appropriate Cultural Revolution images with no trace of the bitterness or pain such pictures might evoke in the victims. Others, as though regretful at having missed out on the intense Cultural Revolution experience, now aestheticize an otherwise meaningless violence and cruelty. In performance pieces that centre on sadism or masochism, passion and heroism may be absent, but the quest for a similarly extreme intensity of physical or emotional experience seems to become the purpose of art. These legacies are quite diverse in almost every way but have in common the public presentation of a kind of fictionalized remembrance. That the Cultural Revolution images – happy pictures masking a tragic reality – were often fiction themselves has been forgotten. Those that survive have outlived the truth that has not. One hopes that Ba Jin's Cultural Revolution museum, or its virtual equivalents, will indeed preserve and document not only the art and material remains, but even more importantly, record what they meant.

2

Summoning Confucius: Inside Shi Lu's Imagination

Shelley Drake Hawks

No other Chinese artist pitted himself against the Cultural Revolution as boldly as Shi Lu (Feng Yaheng, 1919-82). A proud and committed revolutionary who joined the Communist Party in the Chinese communists' wartime headquarters of Yan'an, Shi Lu vehemently disagreed with the Cultural Revolution's assault on inherited culture. An artist of high standing until his disgrace in 1964, he had completed several portraits of Mao Zedong prior to the Cultural Revolution. Although he was not personally acquainted with the chairman, he felt a strong spiritual kinship with him and joined the communist movement because he recognized the "inside stuff" of himself in Mao.[1] His son recalls that strangers sometimes mistook Shi Lu for Mao because Shi Lu's face and swooping hair bore a resemblance to those of the Communist Party chairman. Thus, having his reputation defamed as a result of a dispute over *Fighting in Northern Shaanxi,* his prized portrait of Mao, exacted a huge psychological toll on Shi Lu. Wounded at his rejection by the political idol he had placed at the centre of his revolutionary identity, Shi Lu underwent a profound transformation. A close reading of selected examples of his Cultural Revolution artwork provides a window on the erosion and final collapse of his Mao-centred faith.

The removal in 1964 of his famous (or infamous) portrait of Mao to a storeroom, and a party-imposed ban on his recently published catalogue, struck a profound blow to Shi Lu's self-esteem. As early as 1961-62, his exploratory approach to landscape painting had sparked criticism within Beijing art circles. However, official disapproval did not take a grave turn until 1964 when representatives of the Beijing art establishment asked him to revise his publicly commissioned masterpiece *Fighting in Northern Shaanxi,* and he refused.[2] Shi Lu experienced physical and mental trauma as a result of these battles to defend his reputation. To obtain relief from a painful liver condition, he took time off from his administrative duties as chairman of the Xi'an Art Association and began practising *qigong* meditation. He spent hours in a trance without eating or sleeping and devised strange herbal concoctions to treat what he described as a virus. One cold day in 1965, he created a public spectacle when, wearing little clothing, he wallowed in the snow on the grounds of the Xi'an Art Academy.[3] On the recommendation of a family friend who recognized that he required urgent medical attention, Shi Lu's wife, Min Lisheng, urged authorities to hospitalize him for mental illness. He was still under treatment at a psychiatric institution near Xi'an for symptoms related to schizophrenia when the Cultural Revolution broke out in the summer of 1966.

Despite his medically diagnosed mental condition, the Red Guards offered Shi Lu no immunity from political persecution. On the contrary, activists were convinced that the former chairman of the Xi'an Art Association was feigning insanity in order to escape punishment for his political "crimes." They carted off a heavily medicated Shi Lu to a makeshift jail within the art academy and held him captive for three years. Sedated, he passively endured humiliation and constant beatings for the first two of these. Red Guards were particularly brutal to his family, once arranging for one of his sons to be hung from a tree for hours until he denounced his father. Aware of these acts of cruelty, Shi Lu resolved to stop taking sedatives and began to fight back. During a political education meeting in 1969, he pointedly criticized Mao's wife, Jiang Qing. The worker's group in charge of the art academy could not tolerate his frank criticism of a high-ranking revolutionary leader. They sent him to be detained at the Law Department of the Xi'an Art Academy's provincial offices, accusing him of the very serious crime of being a "recent counter-revolutionary," one who opposes current policies. Although the allegation was serious, the provincial authorities in charge of detaining Shi Lu permitted him to make occasional visits home as he awaited a verdict. Twice, he took advantage of these periods of lax surveillance to escape from imprisonment, once eluding his captors for several months. After he was re-arrested in the fall of 1969, he was sentenced to capital punishment and came close to being executed. Although he was finally permitted to return home in December 1969 and spent the 1970s in the care of his family, his political crimes continued to be regarded as very serious throughout the late Cultural Revolution era.

What sets Shi Lu's story apart from that of other Chinese artist victims is not merely the severity of his persecution or the drama of his life story. Simply outlasting the Cultural Revolution was in itself a heroic feat, but Shi Lu achieved something far greater. He was that rare individual who dared to argue with the logic of the Cultural Revolution as the movement unfolded. Of those Chinese artists who, like him, were victims subjected to prolonged persecution and surveillance, only a handful managed to produce private art at all during the late 1960s and early 1970s.[4] Arguably, no other Chinese artist produced such thoughtful and original poems and paintings during this period. Shi Lu demonstrated a unique capacity for forging art into a weapon of spiritual resistance. He stretched the limit of what was possible to say and do under extremely repressive circumstances, aiming his "missiles" (his privately produced poems and paintings) squarely at the false claims and callous indifference of Maoist extremism. In doing so, he exploited the fact of his madness, using it as a form of camouflage that enabled his open defence of China's cultural inheritance against the exterminatory impulses of the Cultural Revolution. Most of his contemporaries were unable to grasp the true significance of his behaviour, but a retrospective audience can approach a fuller appreciation.

What nourished Shi Lu's stubborn independence? Once his Mao-centred faith came into question, what underlying values remained? A surprising aspect of his response to the Cultural Revolution is the degree to which he invoked Confucian legacies as a strategy for protest and psychological compensation. In 1969, during his brief escape from confinement, Shi Lu composed a poem in the persona of the unjustly persecuted poet-official, Qu Yuan. This venerated historical figure was a perennial favorite of Confucian scholars, who summoned Qu Yuan's memory as a way to affirm their loyalty and self-worth in the face of doubts. During the early 1970s, Shi Lu protested the radical Maoists' defamation of Confucius by drawing a portrait of Confucius in his poetry diary and, in a related painting, dedicating a castle to the ancient philosopher's name. In the diary, Shi Lu claimed to have seen a statue of Confucius on the grounds of an ancient Indian castle in Old Delhi during 1955. This recollection (or dream) of an Indian-made statue of Confucius wearing plain cotton clothing inspired the portrait in the diary. Elsewhere in the same diary, Shi Lu wrote a historical fable describing a fictional encounter between Confucius and China's notorious first emperor Qin Shihuang (a historical figure with whom Mao was closely associated). By inventing an apocryphal Confucius who gains audience with Qin Shihuang (the historical Confucius actually lived during a different century), Shi Lu seemed to be playing out his own fantasy of admonishing the communist "emperor." Speaking sometimes as narrator and sometimes as "Confucius" himself, Shi Lu challenged Mao on ethical grounds for the Cultural Revolution's cruel repetition of Qin Shihuang's policy, two millennia earlier, of "burning books and burying scholars alive."[5]

Shi Lu's evocations of Confucius and Qu Yuan situated his contemporary dilemma within a long-standing literature concerned with moral integrity amidst persecution. He summoned and impersonated these heroic figures as a strategy to bolster his own remonstrating courage.[6] The spirit of the ancestors was to him a living force, not a fossilized relic in need of discarding. The Confucius Shi Lu imagined grew out of his specific political and psychological needs during the Cultural Revolution, and his work should not be misinterpreted as advocating a serious restoration of Confucianism (though he was accused of this by censoring authorities in the context of the "black painting" exhibition of 1974). Until his death in 1982, Shi Lu continued to think of himself as defending an idealized, uncorrupted version of communism associated in his mind with the revolutionary community of Yan'an. He affiliated himself with Confucius and the Confucian tradition of righteous remonstrance as a counterweight to the Cultural Revolution's total rejection of the past and its insistence on a totally new present. To summon Confucius affirmed his conviction that true creativity was not possible without nurturing deep roots within one's own cultural inheritance. That he dared to create art honouring Confucius during the publicly declared Criticizing Lin Biao and Confucius movement of 1973-74 attests to his willingness to court danger and underlines the boldness of his resistance art.

Shi Lu was one of the first devout communists of his generation to recognize that a reconstituted Confucianism still had value for modern living, and that it need not be seen as incompatible with communism. Having been on the receiving end of the Red Guard assault, he came to understand that revolutionary ethics focused on eliminating social evils through struggle could not entirely supplant the millennia-old Confucian ethical system premised on humaneness and moderation. The Confucian emphasis on intellectual fellowship across time and space was emotionally satisfying for him as well. By situating himself within a succession of Confucian paragons who transformed adversity into impassioned creativity, he imbued his individual suffering with collective meaning and assured that his damaged reputation would expand rather than contract with time. To a defender of creative autonomy such as Shi Lu, Confucianism was arguably the most salient and robust mental tool at his disposal to combat the totalitarian impulses of the Cultural Revolution. An indefatigable idealist, like Confucius himself, Shi Lu persisted in asserting his values even when there were no reasonable prospects for success.[7] Confucianism's tradition of bold remonstration gave him the backbone he needed to imagine himself confronting Mao, a task psychologically impossible for most Chinese people. He did not challenge the "emperor" face to face, choosing instead to deposit his admonitions and defiance in art for the benefit of history.

What Shi Lu most desired within the context of the Cultural Revolution was the space from which he could reconsider New China's place in history and his own relationship to politics. As doubt and anger eroded his Mao-centred faith, he summoned not only Confucius, but also the spirit of cosmopolitanism and individualism he had experienced as a youth during the New Culture era. Writings by the seminal New Culture author Lu Xun (whom Shi Lu so revered during his young adulthood that he adopted "Lu" as the second half of his pen name) resurfaced in his consciousness as his hero-worship of Mao lessened. During the early 1960s, he began privately to immerse himself in the study of the arch-individualist painter Shitao, or Daoji (1644-1717), another idol of his youth (and source for the first part of his pen name).[8] Both Lu Xun and Shitao offered native precedents for Shi Lu's fierce drive for independence. Thinking of himself as extending their bold creative legacy fortified his will to resist political pressure and to continue creating self-expressive art. The schizophrenia triggered by his falling away from Mao also played a role in his capacity for shaking loose from previous beliefs and attachments. Mental illness was not simply a symptom of his emotional pain. Schizophrenia imbued him with a special cognitive perspective that allowed him to be unusually self-interpreting and flexible in his thoughts.[9] His enhanced capacity to divorce himself from social expectations and to contemplate himself from a remove transformed him into a political agnostic much sooner than was the case for his contemporaries. By the late Cultural Revolution period, a triumphant but frail Shi Lu had completed an anguished process of pushing aside a secular god and replacing him with his own personal space.

Shi Lu's Refusal to Revise *Fighting in Northern Shaanxi*

Shi Lu's political troubles began in earnest during 1964 when a military official, perhaps the chairman's own mouthpiece, found fault with his 1959 *Fighting in Northern Shaanxi,* a history painting that features Chairman Mao in 1947, during the time in which he led communist troops against Nationalist forces (Figure 2.1).[10] Party organs had commissioned Shi Lu to create a painting on this theme for the newly constructed Museum of Revolutionary History at Tian'anmen Square in honour of the tenth anniversary of the People's Republic. Beijing cultural officials including Cai Ruohong, Hua Junwu, and Wang Zhaowen reviewed his drafts and approved his painting in 1959.[11] Initially, party publications hailed it as a masterpiece. However, in the more radical political climate of 1964, Shi Lu's eccentric choice of positioning the chairman near a Shaanxi cliff edge and turning him sideways so that he stands with his back to the viewer fell under renewed scrutiny. Mao's relatively small size and the fact that only three bodyguards and

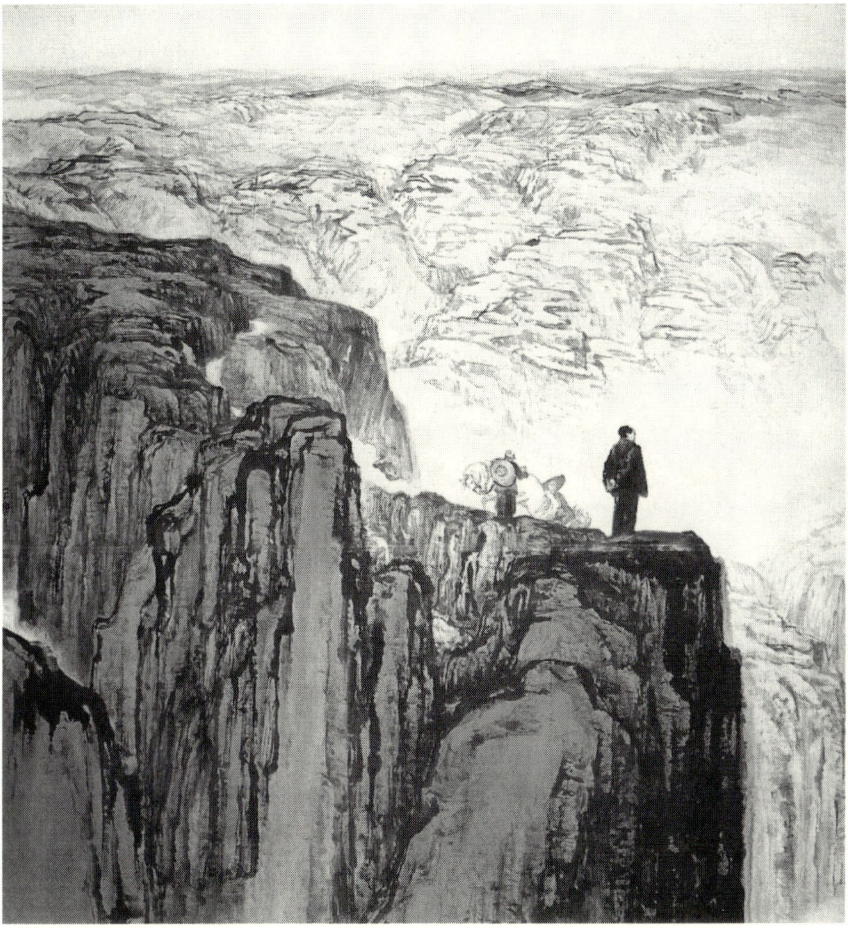

Figure 2.1 Shi Lu, *Fighting in Northern Shaanxi* (1959, detail). The full image measures 238 by 216 centimetres. Julia F. Andrews and Kuiyi Shen, *A Century in Crisis: Modernity and Tradition in the Art of Twentieth-Century China* (New York: Solomon R. Guggenheim Foundation, 1998), Figure 141.

his horse accompany him on the summit became issues rendering the painting politically suspect. According to an official complaint sent to Shi Lu in 1964, a military official suggested that the artist's portrayal made the chairman appear "isolated and at the end of the road."[12] The unfortunate coincidence that the painting dated from 1959, the same year in which then minister of defence Peng Dehuai had famously criticized the chairman's Great Leap Forward policies during the Lushan conference, raised the spectre that it functioned in collusion with Peng's criticism of Mao.[13]

These accusations against Shi Lu's painting should be seen within the larger context of the military's increased role as guardian of the chairman's prestige under Lin Biao, the general whom Mao chose to succeed the ousted Peng Dehuai. By 1964, the military had begun a rigorous inspection of official displays of art in connection with an escalating cult surrounding Mao. Any portrait of China's supreme leader now had to measure up to the exaggerated conventions of deference customary in socialist-realist portraiture of Stalin and Lenin. Shi Lu's portrait was, at least on the face of it, out of tune with these soaring expectations regarding images of Mao. Shi Lu's depiction of Shaanxi's mountain peaks, the endpoint of the famed Long March (1935-36) and cradle of Chinese communism, was not the target of criticism. They were bathed in symbolic red, and the play of sunlight gave them an aura of heroism. But the Great Man of Chinese Communism situated within these vast peaks looked uncomfortably modest in comparison to his magnificent surroundings. Although accusations of hidden subversive content may sound arbitrary to modern readers, the claim that Shi Lu's painting reveals ambivalence toward Chairman Mao's leadership may have validity. Even a fellow artist, a sculptor who shared living quarters with Shi Lu at the time, wondered why the chairman was so small.[14] The highest red peak in the foreground and the rest of the mountain range receding into the distance at the upper left occupy a higher plane than Mao. Not only does he stand virtually alone on the precipice, he faces sideways, with his face partially hidden from the viewer. Moreover, the figures in the painting, including Mao himself, are situated on a descending slope at cliff's edge. No one may be sliding down the hill yet, but their cliff-side perch affords them no stable ground. Mao's horse, with his arched neck and raised foreleg, seems unsettled despite the peasant attending him. Given the eccentric visual quality of this configuration, the official charged with shoring up Mao's reputation, which was flagging due to the disastrous failure of the Great Leap Forward initiative, had grounds for questioning the artist's intentions: was Shi Lu admonishing Chairman Mao to step back from the ledge?

Shi Lu's disaffection from the Great Leap Forward campaign can be inferred from his later writings during and after the Cultural Revolution. He adamantly disagreed with Mao's relentless push toward steel construction and bomb making, imbalanced policies already recognized by 1959 to have contributed to a famine that eventually claimed an estimated 30 million lives. Thus, it is conceivable that he intended his cliff-side imagery to suggest a veiled remonstrance against the chairman's policies, or perhaps his repressed anger unintentionally registered in the work. Although the painting does position Mao in the luminous centre of the national landscape, the vast scale of the mountains cuts him down to human size. Dwarfing Mao in a landscape may have been Shi Lu's way of injecting a cautionary note concerning the danger of treating him like a god. A speech he delivered to the Standing Committee of the Chinese Artists' Association in 1979 confirms the disgust he felt for the cult of Mao and for those who championed it, particularly Mao's wife, Jiang Qing.[15] In 1959, Shi Lu may have viewed his public commission as an opportunity to make a statement about what he saw as the true meaning of China's communist revolution. A veteran cadre, he had spent the late 1950s touring the remote, impoverished regions of Shaanxi Province, sketching its farmers and distinctive geography. He had seen with his own eyes the famine triggered by the chairman's policies. As a participant in the original revolutionary community headquartered at Yan'an during the 1940s, he perhaps felt that his prerogative and duty was to remind the chairman, in the great tradition of a Confucian censor, to live up to his promise: "to serve the people."

One thing that cannot be disputed is the degree to which Shi Lu took the public commission seriously as an opportunity to make a grand statement about Chinese art in the revolutionary era. The aesthetic choices he made in response to this political assignment were ambitious and all his own. Like Shitao, the painter from whom he took half his pen name, Shi Lu believed that a great landscape painting revealed in its brushwork the artist's own emotions and stored experience. According to Shitao's treatise on art (which Shi Lu had studied intensely and would write a sequel to in 1963), the mountains in a painting would not come alive unless they reflected the artist's personal knowledge of actual topography. To prepare for this honoured assignment to paint on behalf of Shaanxi Province, Shi Lu had exhaustively sketched the region's distinctive loess terrain. Although he admired the socialist-realist tradition developed in the Soviet Union, he thought that a reliance on Soviet prototypes for this project would dishonour the national heritage. He hoped to pioneer an entirely new format for socialist realism using brush and ink, one that would be informed by Chinese landscape painting and Tang poetry. Perhaps his fervent desire to create a personal masterpiece drawn from native precedents distracted him from thinking carefully enough about the political risks of adopting such a bold conceptual strategy. Indeed, this painting marked an important breakthrough in his development of a new landscape style. Shi Lu's son suggests that part of the controversy surrounding this painting stemmed from uncertainty regarding whether it should be categorized as a landscape or a figure painting. Shi Lu's masterful portrayal of Shaanxi's mountains argued for the former. However, the presence of such a revered icon within the landscape made it incumbent on the artist to create a quasi-religious aura around the figure. According to this explanation, Shi Lu set out to pay suitable homage to Mao but encountered controversy because he followed an unconventional formal strategy.

According to the 1985 reminiscence of Ma Gaihu, the sculptor mentioned earlier who roomed with the painter during the project, Shi Lu made the key decision while preparing sketches for the painting that he would symbolically represent the "one million strong soldiers" loyal to Mao as features of the mountain landscape.[16] Employing multiple mountain peaks to suggest the presence of the soldiers, rather than literally drawing each one, would render a more dignified, grander conception. In early drafts, he had surrounded Mao with other communist leaders but ultimately decided to portray him alone at the summit (save for a small retinue slightly below) because he thought this would most effectively herald Mao as the centrepiece of China's communist movement. In the final version, Mao's profiled figure shares the mountaintop with a groom attending his horse and an old peasant gazing respectfully up at him. Ma remarked that this triangular arrangement of figures was intended to illustrate both Mao's supreme importance (as the triangle's tallest member) and his indissoluble connection to ordinary people. This interpretation of the painting as a paean to Mao does not necessarily negate the more dangerous meaning placing limits on Mao's authority, as postulated above. Shi Lu's common practice was to conceive paintings in such a way as to invite the viewer to discover a range of possible meanings. Some of his paintings can be shown to present one meaning initially, only to reveal another once a symbolic clue is recognized and decoded.[17]

According to Ma's memoir, Shi Lu postponed painting Mao until he had completed everything else. Throughout the drafting stage, he scrutinized and copied several existing sculptural versions of Mao, but none completely satisfied him. Finally, he asked his friend Ma to make a sculpture of Mao's full body with two hands clasped in back. Shi Lu copied the resulting work numerous times until he had internalized it to such a degree that he could execute it spontaneously without any visual aid. Only after he shut himself off in his studio for several nights and became confident that he could execute the figure perfectly did he undertake to paint it. The final outcome was a virtuoso freehand rendition of the chairman's profile, daringly executed in the "boneless" brushwork of ancient Chinese ink painting!

The retrospective comments of Shi Guo, Shi Lu's son, add another dimension to our understanding of the artist's thoughts regarding the figure of Mao. Shi Guo reports that his father had a specific conception in mind – to represent Mao's inspired presence within the communist movement as analogous to a pagoda. Shi Lu's companion piece to this painting, commissioned at the same time for the Shaanxi hall of the Great Hall of the People and titled *Letting the Horses Drink at the Yan River*, features just such a cliff-side pagoda of roughly the same scale and shape as Mao's figure in the Shaanxi painting. By associating Mao symbolically with a pagoda (particularly the famous Treasure Pagoda overlooking Yan'an), Shi Lu sought to reinforce his central message that Mao's leadership was the beacon and unifying force that gave communist fighters the will to prevail.

On the other hand, the subject matter of this companion painting can also be interpreted as bolstering the more dangerous message of admonishing Mao for failing to put the welfare of the people first. When these two paintings were contemplated and completed in 1959, the rhetoric of the Great Leap Forward campaign encouraged the masses to make steel without respite. In this companion painting to the Mao portrait, Shi Lu chose to represent the very moment when the workhorses serving the revolution are allowed to nourish themselves. Riderless and unsaddled except for one, the horses have been set loose to drink their fill. A Chinese peasant, also at ease, gazes up toward the Yan'an pagoda visible in the distance, tinted red by the sunset and occupying the highest point on the mountain. In this painting, Chairman Mao's presence is implied but not depicted.

Having vested enormous energy and ambition in this commissioned project in honour of the nation's founding, Shi Lu was supremely confident that his landscapes were among the most important of his career and that they deserved the high praise that they initially received. Thus, when a high-ranking military official criticized *Fighting in Northern Shaanxi* in 1964, Shi Lu ignored the complaints. The artist refused to bow to superiors who wished him to modify the work (even though revision was customary practice in the Soviet Union and among Soviet-inspired Chinese oil painters). In response to Shi Lu's unwillingness to modify his portrayal of Mao, Beijing authorities halted production of a catalogue of his works featuring the disputed picture and ordered a recall of any copies already distributed to bookstores. Shi Lu was asked to replace the image with another, but he flatly refused, angrily returning the money he had received for the catalogue's production. The stalemate ended with the removal of his masterpiece *Fighting in Northern Shaanxi* from the Museum of Revolutionary History's exhibition hall.

Connecting with Qu Yuan (1969)

Shi Lu was still wrestling with the rancour he felt regarding this controversy when mental illness, and then the Cultural Revolution, engulfed him. He commented directly on his Cultural Revolution experience in a 1969 lament composed in the ancient style of Qu Yuan's "Encountering Sorrow" *(Li sao)* and specifically invoking "Heavenly Questions" (Tian wen), another poem in the same series. In his archaic-style poem, Shi Lu likened the slander levelled at him by radical Maoists to that directed at Qu Yuan, who was unjustly banished from court and forced to wander in the wilderness in present-day Sichuan until he finally drowned himself in the Miluo River.[18] What makes Shi Lu's retelling of the legend such compelling political theatre is the fact that, when he conceived the poem, he himself was wandering alone in the Sichuan Mountains, having fled his "ox-shed" jail cell during the summer of 1969. Hungry and unkempt, musing aloud about his mistreatment, and contemplating suicide, Shi Lu re-enacted Qu Yuan's story as a vehicle through which to proclaim his continued loyalty and record his inner thoughts. In the reader's retrospective imagining, the curtain rises on an exhausted yet defiant artist-revolutionary alternately cursing and weeping at his Cultural Revolution fate:

VERSES FOR CHANTING BY LAKES, REPAIRING THE SKY
By Shi Lu

(Translation by Shelley Drake Hawks)

1.
Laws blackened, azure sky
Streaked like the arched brow of a painted woman, oh!
Desperate flight ends in green mountains, weeping.
Tears shared among netted fish and turtles, oh!
I'm not ready to descend to the underworld yet.
Why is Qu Yuan distressed to see his native Chu inflamed? oh!
You lost sight of the road to Communism!
Why should my body fill the belly of fish?
I'd be denounced as traitor.
I'll hold back sobs and question heaven.

2.
Climb to the universe's summit, oh!
Peer down at a tiny world,

Horses, orchids: pelted by sand, a landscape alters completely, oh!
Look out over vast heights – enough steps!
The old war horse still enjoys fresh grass, oh!
Why maliciously blow dew from the blossom?

3.
Wishing to shout, "Long live the Chairman!"
Mouth suddenly gagged: a struggle for control, oh!
Now look, who will expel the hoodlums trained in Russia?
I think they are the remnants of Chiang Kaishek's running dogs.
Dirtying the water, turning the fish black,
Toxic hands whip callously until blood flows,
Scoffing at the virtuous life.
I'll keep walking my own path.

4.
Step by step crossing heaven's bridge,
I ask questions, eat wind, drink water –
Which family should I deprive of cooking oil?
Mountain cliff, water's edge – is there no road to follow?
Suppose I fly the body across the sky to ask the sun?
In a myth of bygone days, an archer shoots that fiery light.
I never opposed Heaven or tried to change the star.[19]
I ask myself, does integrity remain?
Parading in my dunce cap, I know within:
This world is not hateful.
Ugliness need not infect the self.
Communist Party members are not black criminals.
Gazing at flowers, the autumn moon, I wonder at the reason,
Maybe old Cang Jie himself could say.[20]

5.
I am luminous as the north star, oh!
Shaking with the wind.
Why not look toward high ground
Where spring wind revitalizes?
Ancient and modern are one.
Behold – the full horizon.

(Shi Lu's postscript)
All day I chanted verse, no dreams,

Feeling a little crazy. Now I know why.
To repair the sky – that was Nu Wa's beautiful story.[21]
I look at spring-autumn-flower-moon as a single moment –
Why trifle over wasted things?[22]

Shi Lu's poem opens with a typically Confucian evocation of a sombre sky mirroring the blackened state of human affairs. Against this vivid backdrop, the anguished poet invites the reader to listen in as he narrates his thoughts. Although the poem is presented as a spontaneous upwelling of grief, in actuality each line has been carefully crafted to distill Shi Lu's emotions, politics, and philosophy. The landscape plays a special function of marking his progression in resolving the classic Confucian dilemma of how a virtuous minister should respond to unjust accusations. As in the original Qu Yuan poem "Encountering Sorrow," the poet's body taxis between the actual landscape of mountains and rivers, where he weeps and paces restlessly, and a cosmic landscape physically associated with the sky. Solving the predicament entails taking a magical journey upward to question legendary heroes and sky authorities. The poet's ultimate aspiration, as stated in the poem's title and its epilogue, is to repair the broken sky, perhaps a reference to finding a way of reversing the damage caused by the Cultural Revolution.

Within the main body of the poem, Shi Lu explains why his reputation has been sullied (assigning blame to the "hoodlums trained in Russia") and announces his continued loyalty to Chairman Mao ("I never opposed Heaven or tried to change the star"). Though he has sunk to the depths of despair, Shi Lu clarifies that he will not take the path of suicide chosen by Qu Yuan and many Cultural Revolution victims. Rather, he will live on stubbornly, communing with the spirit of ancestors. As the poem progresses, he stokes up confidence in himself and his program ("I'll keep walking my own path"). Although he begins the poem with the traditional pose of questioning Heaven – for example, remonstrating with a higher authority – he shifts to a process of finding his own answers by the fourth stanza.

This evolving sense of independence culminates dramatically in the final stanza, when the poet describes himself in vaunted terms as a cosmic exemplar ("I am luminous as the north star").[23] He tempers and humanizes this assertion by characterizing himself as "shaking with the wind." By linking himself with the sky, Shi Lu also suggests that he has finally risen above the strife associated with the terrestrial world to achieve transcendence. He counsels posterity to strive for purity regardless of environment, remarking "Ugliness need not infect the self" and adding "Why not look toward high ground / Where spring wind revitalizes?" The final two lines of the fifth stanza emphasize what would be a constant theme throughout Shi Lu's Cultural Revolution art: the communist age must not be cut off from the larger stream of Chinese history: "Ancient and modern are one." The way to escape narrow thinking and restore one's sense of perspective, Shi Lu's poem suggests, is to think like a landscape painter: climb to an elevated place and look out unimpeded at "the full horizon."

Shi Lu's Qu Yuan–inspired poem stresses his continued loyalty to communism and does not necessarily indicate that he has departed from a Mao-centred faith. A fine poet himself, Mao would have appreciated the elegance of Shi Lu's language and might not have found it offensive had he had the opportunity or inclination to read it. Although Shi Lu's poem shows clear disrespect for extremists like Jiang Qing, whom he held responsible for the catastrophe, his strong identification with a remote ancestor such as Qu Yuan was not necessarily inconsistent with Chinese communist sensibilities. Qu Yuan had been respected even within communist circles during the 1940s and 1950s as a national icon and symbol of Chinese culture's literary greatness. During the Great Leap Forward era, he had even been promoted as an alter ego for Mao, symbolizing the bold critical spirit associated with revolution. Therefore, Shi Lu's adoption of the Qu Yuan persona to remonstrate with the Cultural Revolution would not have been problematic had the old party establishment returned to power. Possibly, he envisioned circulating the poem as a vehicle for persuading some high political authority to reverse extremist policies and remedy the unjust purging of sincere and committed communist officials (including Shi Lu himself).

Although the poem is ostensibly concerned with Shi Lu's loyalty in the face of adversity, a close scrutiny of the poetic narrative does hint at his evolving disaffection. The fact that the "you" in the dramatic line "You lost sight of the road to communism" remains unidentified leaves him open to the accusation that he may be addressing Mao himself. In the fourth stanza, Shi Lu flies across the sky to ask the sun for an explanation. That he can find no requisite authority in his search for answers suggests that the sovereign is not properly minding the shop. This interpretation is supported by a remark made by Shi Lu when he was recaptured by radical authorities following his escape to Sichuan. Questioned about his feelings regarding the chairman, he admitted that he had something critical to say, even about Mao himself. According to his son's memoirs, he criticized Mao for putting his trust in "the new aristocracy," his name for the Cultural Revolution group.[24]

Thirty years before, Shi Lu had fled a privileged upbringing in Sichuan to pursue revolution in Yan'an. Now, in the context of his 1969 escape, he fled the revolution to return to his hometown. His return south must have stirred memories of his childhood in a wealthy landholding family, a class background he had long since renounced. The southern lake region's historic association with suffering poets may also have informed his choice of destination. For two months, he turned back the clock, chanting poetry and surviving on wild vegetables and fruit. When his hunger became desperate, he borrowed corn from peasant households and left a note explaining that he would return with money. Sometimes he performed acupuncture treatment in exchange for food. His bizarre appearance created a commotion among villagers. Local authorities grew concerned about the unusual vagrant in their midst and eventually jailed him, suspecting that he was a Soviet spy. Once his true identity as an escaped "counter-revolutionary" was revealed, the fugitive poet was returned to the custody of the Shaanxi Revolutionary Art Association at the Xi'an Art Academy.

After his return to solitary confinement in the fall of 1969, Shi Lu wrote a self-criticism document in which he aired his doubts about the validity of practically all of Mao's major policy initiatives, including collectivization and the Great Leap Forward steel-making campaign. He expressed his absolute opposition to the Cultural Revolution and stunned his accusers by deftly using Marxist theory to support his assertions.[25] His criticism of Jiang Qing and her art policies was so blatant and uncompromising that authorities felt justified in sentencing him to death. Only the steady appeals of friends and family, who argued that he was still mentally ill, saved him from execution.

A Revised Identity: Indian Spirit-Kings and an Eastern Venus de Milo (1970)

In late 1969, Shi Lu received the welcome news that his "ox-shed" jail was to be closed down and that he could return home to the care of his family until his political case was resolved. Most artists at this time were sent out to the countryside as labourers, but Shi Lu's unstable mental health and the legal claims against him argued for keeping him under the surveillance of workers' groups now controlling the Xi'an Art Association.

Shi Lu seized the opportunity to return to painting. He locked himself in a small storeroom adjacent to the family apartment and refused to allow anyone to enter. Haphazardly scattered about the room were his art supplies and old paintings recently returned to him by workers' groups. When his wife, Min Lisheng, quietly looked in on him from a window, she was shocked to observe him chatting and laughing as if to a friend. Recognizing that his mental condition had worsened, she made an excuse to force her way into his studio, where she was bewildered to discover that Shi Lu was adding new subject matter and inscriptions to the very 1950s-era paintings that had helped establish him as a famous communist artist in China. The images he was revising were the closely observed studies he had made of fellow Third World men and women during the mid-1950s when he had toured Egypt and India under party auspices.

In the aftermath of his experience of persecution, Shi Lu's finely drafted pictures of dignified proletarians from foreign lands underwent a stunning change. As the noted painter Wu Guanzhong remarked upon seeing these works later, their new subject matter "did not belong to India any more."[26] Adding layer upon layer of red and black ink, Shi Lu encircled his old subjects with a new background of blood-red spider webs, menacing snakes, and flying bats. The sky around them is full of ancient symbols evocative of neolithic pottery. Because he left their tranquil, self-confident expressions unchanged, these besieged persons seemed to show remarkable composure despite the dangers encompassing them. He added new inscriptions as well, some of which changed the identity of his subjects: the itinerant Indian monk in Figure 2.2 became a "spirit-king" who could "capture tigers and trap dragons"; an ordinary cart driver became the Greek god Apollo, guiding his chariot toward the sun. These mythical personas created from the raw material of his earlier Indian and Egyptian work constituted Shi Lu's new pantheon of heroes. In fact, he identified so strongly with these "sky people" from Egypt and India that he signed *Indian Spirit King* with a new Indian pen name, Shi Gu Lumanden. To add to the aura of a shrine, he surrounded his subjects with enigmatic inscriptions honouring foreign luminaries including Rabindranath Tagore, Leo Tolstoy, Leonardo da Vinci, Benjamin Franklin, and Thomas Edison. In the example reproduced below (Figure 2.2), the names of Tagore and Tolstoy appear just below the spirit-king's staff or sword.

Like his earlier Qu Yuan poem, Shi Lu's revised paintings offer an opportunity to assess how persecution affected him spiritually. The intense imagery and the agitated brushwork of his additions plainly signal trauma. Given his refusal to modify a single aspect of his Mao Zedong portrait in the 1960s, his decision to drastically alter his previous works during the 1970s is certainly surprising. The impetus for revision was the outgrowth of Shi Lu's wish, declared to his family in late 1969, to "say goodbye to his past" by making a clear demarcation between his pre–Cultural Revolution identity and that of its aftermath. He also destroyed all the personal name-chops he had used on paintings prior to the Cultural Revolution, as part of this self-proclaimed rebirth.

Shi Lu told his family that the revision of his old paintings stemmed from a certain discomfort he felt upon seeing them again and discovering that they no longer seemed "finished." To resolve this newly perceived deficiency, he added lines to the faces and inserted the hidden dangers he now knew to be bedevilling his subjects. Because he believed that his paintings should reflect the inner stuff of his own personality, making a drastic alteration to conform to his current feelings felt perfectly logical as long as it was not imposed on him, as had been the case of the Mao portrait. These revised paintings attest to a fundamental transformation in Shi Lu's worldview. By defacing his own 1950s-era portraits with spontaneous markings akin to graffiti, he disowned the rosy socialist-realist propaganda he had once espoused.

His *Eastern Venus de Milo* conveys a similar message of rupture and transformation (Figure 2.3). This completely new painting was produced in stages, its initial form subjected to a radical revision like his Indian and Egyptian work. Although Shi Lu's children were not normally allowed to observe him painting, he made an exception in this instance, inviting them to watch as he prepared an exquisite fine-lined drawing on silk.[27] Shi Lu's son, Shi Guo, who aspired to be a painter, was astounded by his father's masterful control of the brush as he worked on the goddess' clothes and hair. Originally, the image featured only a female deity against a plain background; there were no inscriptions yet. The family thought it an exceptional creation, evidence that Shi Lu could still paint beautifully despite his many recent setbacks. What he did next, however, horrified them. Some months later, alone in his studio, he poured a bottle of bright red oil-based ink (commonly used for stamp pads) over the work, partially covering the goddess' torso. Shi Lu's wife complained that he had completely ruined the painting by making the goddess seem to float in an "ocean of blood." Not long after, Shi Lu committed another radical act of desecration, scissoring the image into two. When his family asked for an explanation, he said he wanted to give half to his son and half to his daughter. Today, the painting is still severed at the middle. Its two sections must be pushed together if it is to be photographed as one piece.

The work's inscription calls the female deity "Goddess of Beauty," and another inscription at the bottom explains that she is actually an Eastern version of the Venus de Milo. In 1972, after Shi Lu decided to give the painting to his son, he added an inscription at the top, counselling him to "Never marry ugliness. Socialize only with beauty." That he had earlier bathed the Venus in blood and severed her in half suggests a parallel to the brutal assault Shi Lu personally, and art generally, had experienced within

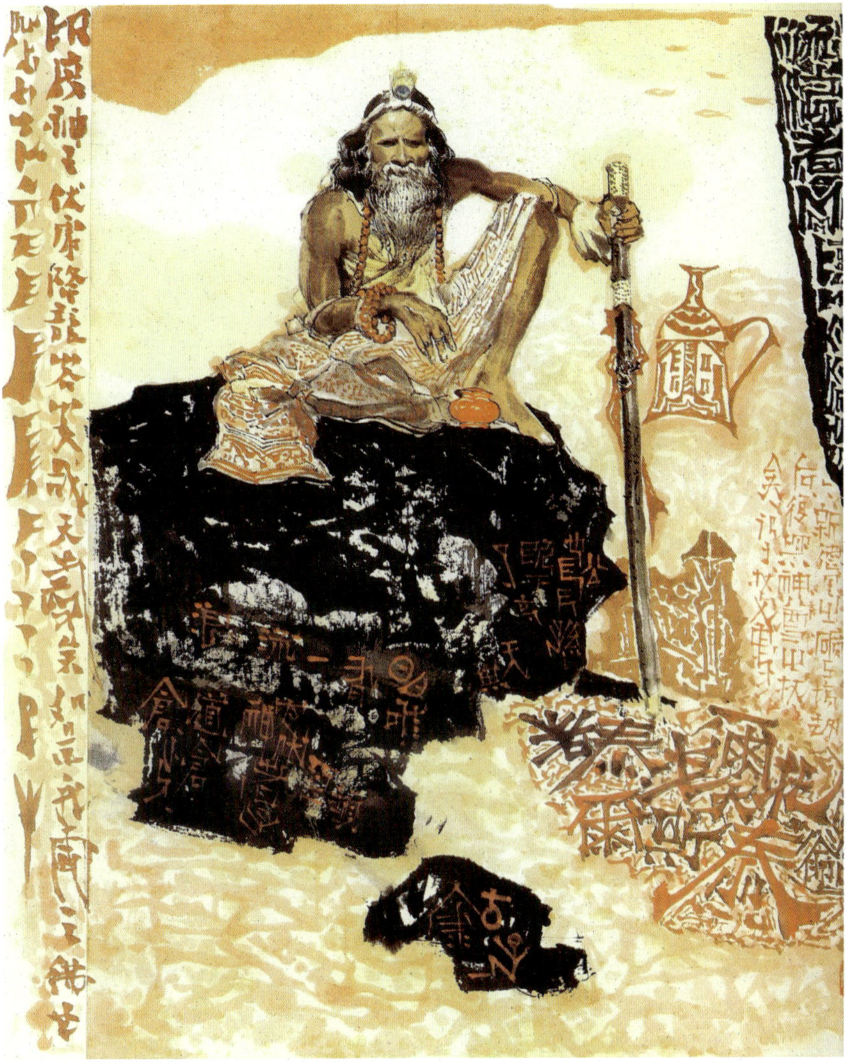

Figure 2.2 **Shi Lu, *Indian Sage-King* (1970 revision of travel sketch drawn on site in India in 1955; inscriptions and other details altering an indigent wanderer into a "spirit king" added in 1970). On the left side, the vertical inscription describes the subject as "Indian spirit-king who captures tigers and traps dragons." The large Chinese characters at the tip of the king's staff (or sword) refer to the Russian author Leo Tolstoy and the Indian poet Rabindranath Tagore.** Wang Yushan and Cai Peixin, eds., *Shi Lu. Zhongguo jin xiandai mingjia huaji* [Shi Lu: Collected paintings by Chinese contemporary masters] (Beijing: People's Art Press, 1996), 180.

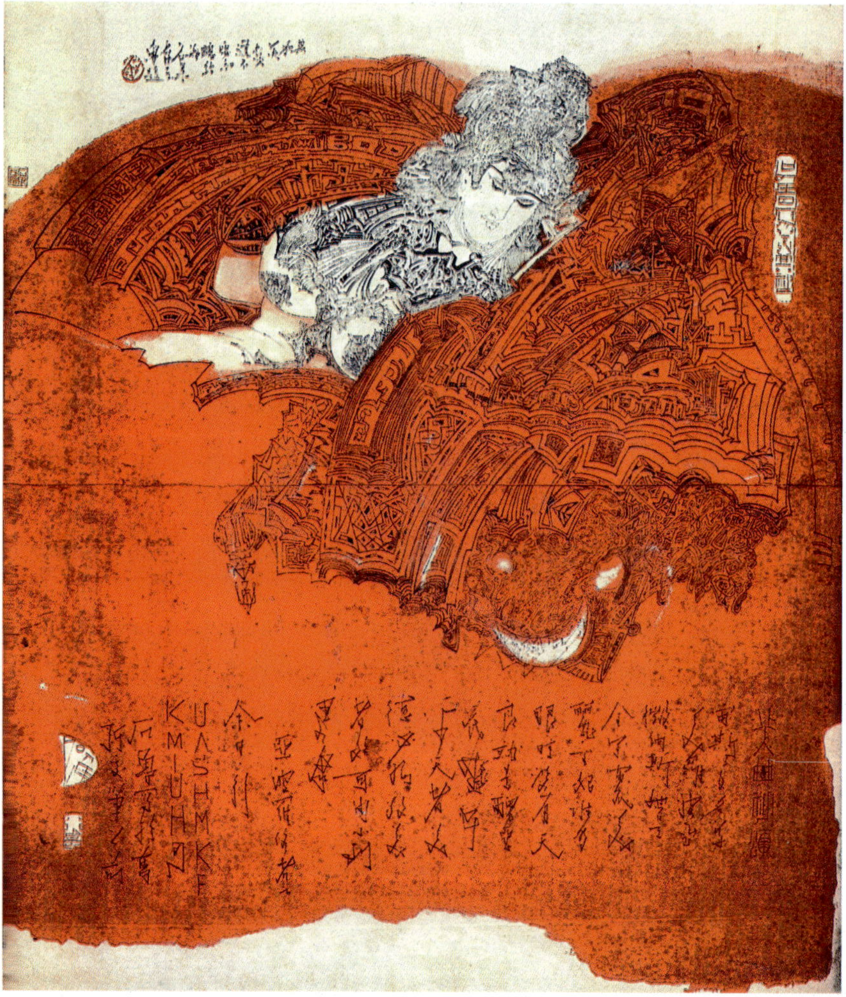

Figure 2.3 Shi Lu, *Eastern Venus de Milo,* alternatively titled *Goddess of Beauty* (1970 ink drawing poured with red ink, inscriptions added c. 1972). The drawing is in two parts, as a result of the artist cutting it with scissors. As a whole, its dimensions are 100 by 90 centimetres. *Shi Lu: A Retrospective* (Hong Kong: Hong Kong Institute for Promotion of Chinese Culture, 1987), Figure 22.

the context of the Cultural Revolution. The goddess retains a divine aura even in her diminished state, conveying Shi Lu's faith in the sustainability of "Beauty" even in the direst of circumstances. The violence he visited on the painting after it was nominally complete, dousing it in red ink and cutting it with scissors, could be seen as a re-enactment of the emotional and physical wounds he received during the Cultural Revolution. According to his son's memoirs, no conflict was more profound for Shi Lu than the sense of betrayal he felt with regard to his former idol. For him, the break with Mao had severe psychological consequences, "as if an axe had cut him into two."[28] *Eastern Venus de Milo* attests to both the severity of Shi Lu's injury and his will to survive the strain.

Although Shi Lu's family was distressed by his apparent disregard for the integrity of what they considered an admirable work, they found that its inscriptions, which he added in about 1972, conveyed a serious message. Buried in the painting's lower inscription is what might be taken as the artist's own Cultural Revolution motto: "Those who respect 'beauty' can transform themselves from smallness to good health." Defining "beauty" as entailing more than physical appearance, he advised his son (to whom he had now dedicated the painting) that beauty was inseparable from virtue. Ugliness was the state of "having no kindness in your eyes." At the conclusion of this inscription, Shi Lu again made reference to his own profound personal transformation, signing it with "Shi Lu just before the switching point between old and new."

Shi Lu's Art as a Product of His Illness

Shi Lu's children remember the brief half-year period from late 1969 to the summer of 1970, when he created his revised paintings and *Eastern Venus de Milo,* as a strange dream-like phase in his life.[29] Until 1987, the family remained reluctant to exhibit these works, for fear that they would be dismissed as the by-products of insanity. The ten or so paintings created during this time possess a surrealistic quality unlike any others in Shi Lu's oeuvre. His tenuous connection with everyday reality after years of incarceration led him to bend his observational powers inward, to visualize a landscape of gods and goddesses, of ancient symbols and crowded inscriptions, as an expression of his own mental turbulence. Not long after he finished *Eastern Venus de Milo* in fact, his illness became so severe that his family convinced party authorities to have him institutionalized for a second time. When he returned home in 1971, he was so heavily sedated that he found it difficult to paint. Determined not to become a "retarded person," he threw away his pills. Once his mind cleared and he began to paint again, he seldom depicted human figures. He developed a more sparing and quiet style of painting and calligraphy focusing on traditional scholarly subjects such as flowers and mountains.

If mental illness is conceived as a condition in which the affected person loses touch with reality, how credible are Shi Lu's "mad" paintings as an indicator of his political opinions? Did illness open a space for him that conferred special vision, or was it a hindrance to his art, rendering it confused and unintelligible? Schizophrenia, in particular, is typically seen as a sensory and cognitive deficiency that robs its subjects of life potential and confines them in a solitary delusional world. How is one to explain, then, that the onset of the disease appears to have had the opposite effect in Shi Lu's case? A plausible argument might be that, *within the context of the Cultural Revolution,* a brain that was internally occupied and impervious to the outside world was actually a healthy orientation. Shi Lu's tangential connection to consensual reality gave him the sense of distance he needed in order to contemplate his situation from a remove and loosen his ties to social conventions. Though his language was at times disorganized and his sensory perceptions distorted, his thinking on political matters became more discerning and candid rather than increasingly confused. Despite his obvious physical and mental challenges, he did not stagnate but continued to accomplish stunning innovation in his artistic and personal development.

The Cultural Revolution, like the Nazi Holocaust or Stalin's reign of terror, was such a dark tunnel in history that persons subjected to its fury would be perfectly justified in going mad or committing suicide.[30] When the extreme situation of the historical context is appreciated, Shi Lu's psychosis appears to be a rather logical response, a type of allergic reaction, to a profound social malady. A true believer in communism, he was set adrift spiritually and emotionally at his betrayal by the leader he had idolized. Schizophrenia aided him in detaching himself from moorings that had proved false. Art enabled him to climb out of the wreckage of a broken ideology to find a new anchor. Mental illness never completely derailed this tortured process of growth; indeed, the unhinging of ties to social conventions, symptomatic of schizophrenia, may have accelerated this transformation.

Shi Lu's behaviour, as described retrospectively by family and friends, as well as his mid-1960s medical diagnosis of schizophrenia, is consistent with so-called atypical psychosis, or brief reactive psychosis, discussed in current medical literature.[31] This milder, less chronic expression of schizophrenia is found primarily in developing areas such as China and Africa, and is said to be characterized by "a dream-like state with slight clouding of consciousness and perplexity."[32] Patients with this version of schizophrenia are thought to recover more quickly and more completely than their Western counterparts. Its onset typically occurs in a sudden burst, usually in response to a blow to self-esteem or another commensurate psychic event. Thus, if Shi Lu had this atypical, benign form of schizophrenia rather than the Western equivalent, his ability to continue writing and painting productively even while ill makes sense. We need not react to him as some of his radical contemporaries did, presuming that he was simply "faking" it all along.

This is not to deny that Shi Lu took advantage of his illness for the extra immunity it gave him to think and behave in an oppositional manner. Clearly, he engaged in play-acting, performing the role of madman as a strategy for protest within the extremely repressive environment of the Cultural Revolution. In his lucid periods, he could draw on his memories of his real psychosis to re-enact madness theatrically. Shi Lu understood himself as part of a romantic tradition of poets and painters who either feigned madness or slipped in and out of genuine insanity in response to political and social evils. At times, he seemed to impersonate the diary-writing madman of Lu Xun's famous short story who shouted at humanity to stop "eating men."[33] Others have described his theatrical madness as reminiscent of Shakespeare's Hamlet or Cervantes' Don Quixote.[34] On such occasions, he "performed" madness rather than suffered from it. By invoking famous characters from literature, he not only connected his predicament to a broader human story but also signalled a discerning audience that he was still capable of exercising choice. Mental illness affected his life and his art, but it was his companion in artistic enterprise rather than an overriding force that robbed him of his capacity to navigate his own destiny.[35]

From both the Cultural Revolution and schizophrenia, Shi Lu harvested a more penetrating knowledge of himself. Suffering wore him down physically and emotionally, but surviving both traumas enhanced his metacognition. Understanding that history had cast him in a far-fetched drama, he would not simply perform a starring role – he would also narrate this bizarre tale for future generations. He emerged from the catastrophe determined to prepare an archive of paintings and poetry capable of transmitting a witness account of both a personal and a national tragedy.

Diary of an Upside-Down Plum

By the time Shi Lu returned from his second hospitalization in late 1971, the political situation had significantly improved. The hypocrisy of the Cultural Revolution had been exposed when Lin Biao, champion of the cult of Mao, died during an attempt to flee to the Soviet Union following the failure of an alleged coup to topple the chairman. Lin Biao was willing to betray Mao in the end, although he was ostensibly Mao's biggest supporter. As the radicals' grip on power lessened, the pragmatists led by Premier Zhou Enlai re-established ascendancy. China's new special relationship with the United States, as a hedge against the Soviet Union, also encouraged policy changes beneficial to artists. In 1972, the Foreign Ministry invited Shi Lu not only to return to teaching art students, but also to produce paintings for display in recently opened foreign embassies and hotels, and for resale in Hong Kong to earn foreign currency. Welcoming this return to respectability, he thrust himself back into the Xi'an art community with great energy. He painted prolifically during this period and acquired an enthusiastic following among young artists who privately respected his innovative style.

Unfortunately, this honeymoon period lasted only until late 1973. At that point, the Cultural Revolution Group led by Mao's wife, Jiang Qing, launched a counteroffensive against Premier Zhou Enlai and his supporters – the Criticizing Lin Biao and Confucius movement, a strained attempt to reaffirm the Cultural Revolution and to forestall Zhou Enlai's efforts to roll it back. Although the premier was not directly named as its target, diminishing his power was in fact one of its key political objectives. The Cultural Revolution Group sought to portray Zhou Enlai's rehabilitation of purged intellectuals and cadres as dangerous backsliding. Radical propaganda warned the populace that modern disciples of Confucius now threatened to undermine China's revolutionary future by advocating a return to feudalism and a restoration of the Confucian rites. For an artist such as Shi Lu, who had been a conspicuous beneficiary of Zhou Enlai's policies, the Criticizing Lin Biao and Confucius movement ushered in yet another phase of incrimination. He was identified as the "number one black painter" in Shaanxi Province; his old friend Zhao Wangyun, who had accompanied him on the Egypt and India tour in 1955, ranked just below him. Authorities organized a group of scholars to examine Shi Lu's paintings and prepare a report detailing the counter-revolutionary content of each one. The 1974 report was prefaced with the following biographical summary accusing Shi Lu of "advocating the road of Confucius and Mencius":

> Shi Lu is the vice-president of the former Xi'an Art Association. He came from a vicious landlord family. He always insisted on a reactionary stance. He was part of the "Wild, Strange, Chaotic and Black" school of painting. He not only created reactionary paintings, but he used his position to advocate a counter-revolutionary art road against Mao Zedong

> thought. During the Cultural Revolution, a lot of people criticized his crimes. Shi Lu responded to this with deep hatred. For several years, he pretended insanity, resisting the investigations of the party and the masses. He continued to secretly make reactionary paintings and poetry. He advocated the road of Confucius and Mencius. He attacked the Proletarian Dictatorship, wishing to bring reactionary ghosts back to life. The contagion spread by these examples of reactionary painting and calligraphy is extremely serious. Businessmen in Macao have paid large sums of money to buy them, and the influence is very bad.[36]

Representatives of the Cultural Revolution Group seized a cache of Shi Lu's works awaiting export in Tianjin and made them the focus of a black painting exhibition in Xi'an.[37] Authorities highlighted one of these – a depiction of blossoming plum branches drooping downward – as an example of the artist's alleged self-pity and unwillingness to accept the bad luck of his fallen status. Only a photograph of the original work survives, but another plum painted by Shi Lu in 1972 conveys its spirit (Figure 2.4). Shi Lu's political enemies mounted a shrill attack on his plum painting as a tool to discredit him.[38] Their interpretation was based on a pun linking the "upside-down plum" of Shi Lu's picture with the phrase "it's a pity" (both phrases are pronounced *"dao mei"*). They had some basis for making this connection: the convention of interpreting downward-pointing plum branches as representing the distressed circumstances of the artist began with the Ming dynasty painter Xu Wei, who famously made this assessment on a fourteenth-century plum blossom painting by Wang Mian. Shi Lu was, in fact, drawing on the plum's established symbolism to signal corrupt political times but not in the simpleminded way that his critics claimed. Indeed, the tone of the poem he wrote on the disparaged painting was not at all self-pitying:

> Snow makes the plum proud;
> Cold makes its blossoms plentiful;
> Slowly dancing in the remaining wind,
> Looking for spring's possibility to grow taller.

Another plum painting Shi Lu produced in late 1973 vigorously defended the plum's dignity and denied the validity of the pun associating it with self-pity or hard luck: "From this horizontal branch, the world looks vast. Don't call it a pitiful flower. It is a *plum* flower."[39]

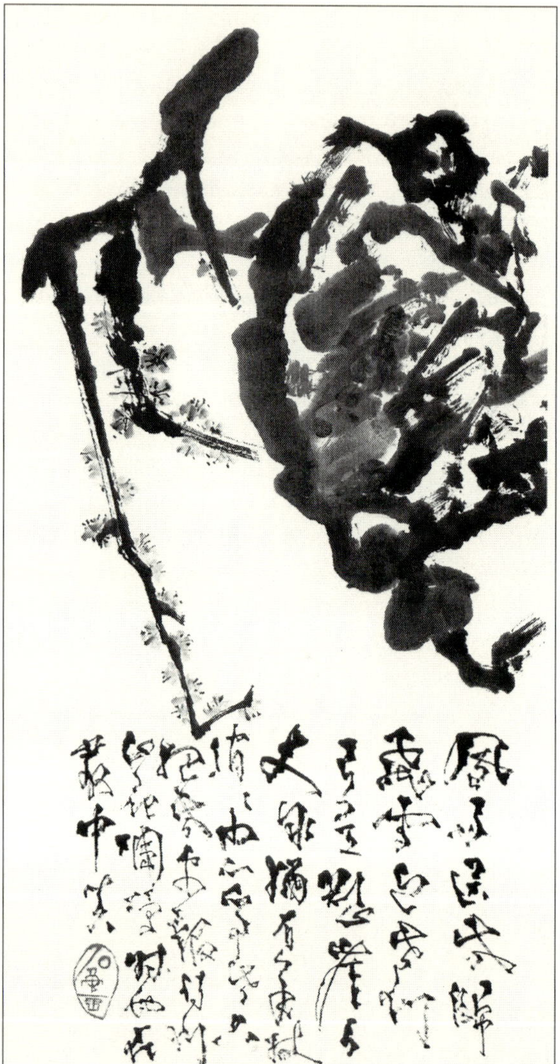

Figure 2.4 **Shi Lu, *Winter Plum Illustration* (1972) inscribed with Chairman Mao's 1961 poem "Winter Plum." The original painting criticized during the black painting exhibition of 1974 was lost. Shi Lu executed another exact copy of it in 1978. The work reproduced here was created around the same time as the repudiated version and also portrays plum blossom branches pointing downward. In it, Shi Lu copied the text of Mao's 1961 poem "Winter Plum" verbatim. On the repudiated version, however, he inscribed his own poem on the same theme as Mao's "Winter Plum."** Yu Yingpo and Liu Jiming, eds., *Shi Lu huaji/Shi Lu hui* [Shi Lu painting collection/Shi Lu drawings] (Beijing: People's Art Press, 2006), 2:330.

Like the hearty plum celebrated in Confucian literature for blossoming in the midst of winter, Shi Lu had accomplished the rare feat of continuing his artistic life in a hostile political climate. His poems on the plum paintings implied that persecution had not extinguished his vision, but rather, sharpened and extended it. Because its red blossoms burst forth even before warm temperatures arrived, the plum was associated in Chinese tradition with the inner strength of a superior scholar who withstands hardship to usher in better times.[40] Drawing on this ancient symbolism, Shi Lu considered the plum a fitting emblem for his own moral toughness and redness – for his revolutionary purity in the face of the Cultural Revolution.

In a telling gesture, he affixed a photograph of the repudiated plum painting to the cover of his private poetry journal. In this treasured upside-down plum diary, he collected poems, sketches, and fables. During the height of the black painting exhibition, fearing that his house would be searched and the diary confiscated, he gave it to a trusted friend for safekeeping. Working on it exclusively at night from 1973 to 1975, he used the diary as the repository for his replies to the claims of detractors. Shi Lu told his son that he considered the poetry inscribed in this diary to be the greatest accomplishment of his later years.[41]

Summoning Confucius Back to the Castle

Within the pages of his plum diary, Shi Lu offered insights into the meaning of one of his most enigmatic revised works, *Indian Fort* (Figure 2.5). The original sketch featured the red sandstone gateway of an ancient rampart built by sixteenth-century Mughal emperors in Old Delhi.[42] Shi Lu produced it on-site in 1955, when he toured India with a delegation of Chinese painters. According to his family, he revised the image in 1970, adding a profusion of details in red and black ink to imbue the ruins of the Indian castle with the aura of a spiritual domain. Precisely when he added the long inscriptions above, beside, and below the castle is not clear. The content of these inscriptions argues for a post-1970 date because the homage to Confucius and the anger vented at the Cultural Revolution Group suggest that Shi Lu was directly responding to the Criticizing Lin Biao and Confucius movement of 1973-74.

In the left-hand inscription in black ink, Shi Lu chastises the current leadership for attempting to cut off China from its ancient history and "publicly expounding lies as if they were truth." Complaining about the ridiculousness of acting as if China has no ancestry, he shouts back at the radical iconoclasts who have no respect for tradition: "Strike down your

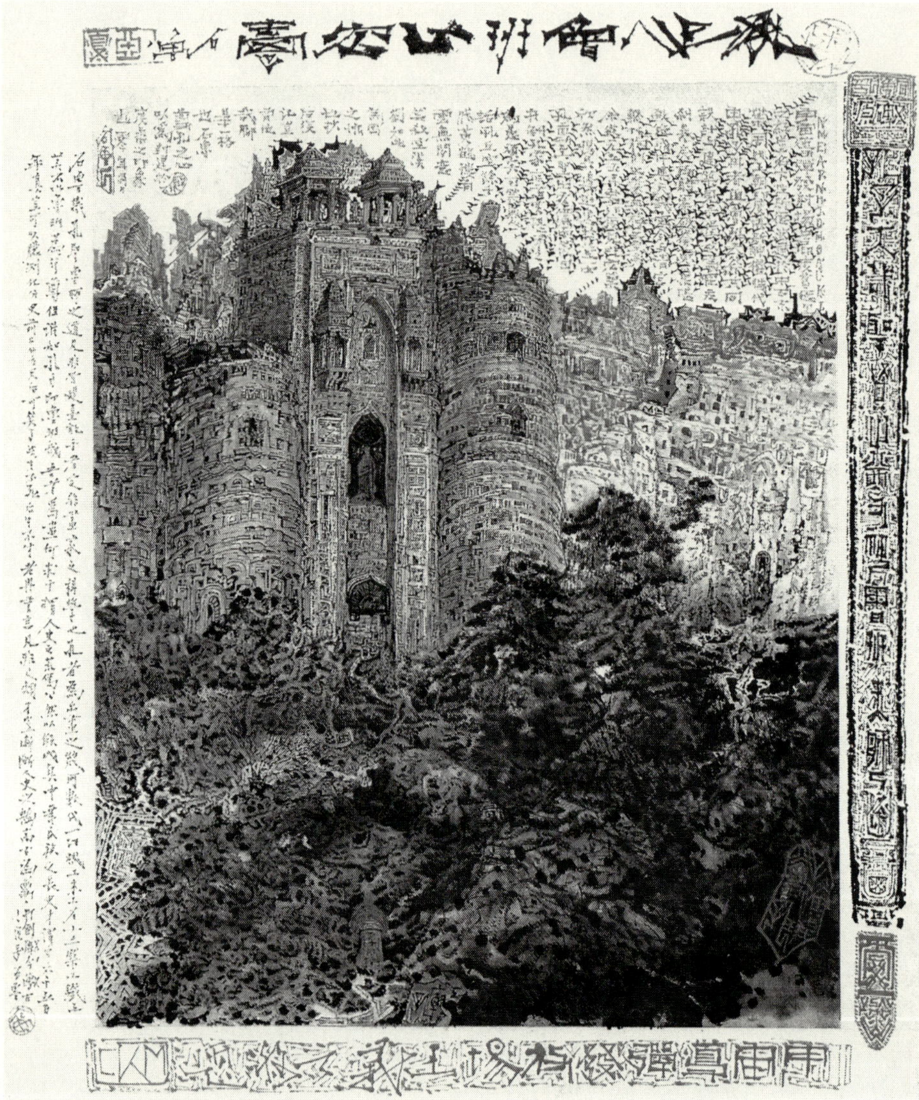

Figure 2.5 ***Indian Fort/Tower to Recognize the Heart of Lu Ban*** **(1970 revision of a 1955 travel sketch on site at Old Fort, Old Delhi; the red and black elements, and inscriptions, were added later, apparently during the Criticizing Lin Biao and Confucius Movement of 1973-74). The latter part of the title is inscribed at the top in large black characters and signed by Shi Lu.** Yu Yingpo and Liu Jiming, eds., *Shi Lu huaji/Shi Lu hui* [Shi Lu painting collection/Shi Lu drawings] (Beijing: People's Art Press, 2006), 2:304.

false slogan: 'Favour the present and slight the ancient!'" Within the same inscription, he bemoans the current restrictions placed on people of talent and suggests that they can find creative outlets other than their chosen fields: "The ones who are good at building are forbidden to build. Those who are not allowed to paint can become scientists. How many know that Confucius is now a painter?"

In the middle of the inscription, Shi Lu elaborates upon his notion that Confucius has a hidden identity by making the surprising claim that the sage is not only a painter, but a carpenter too. He asserts that Confucius and the master carpenter Lu Ban (who, like Confucius, came from the region of Lu and is typically thought of as his contemporary) are actually one and the same. At the top of the painting, in what appears to be the revised image's title, he inscribed "The Vast Tower Recognizing the Heart of Lu Ban." Thus, he has transformed the travel sketch of the Indian fort into a pantheon dedicated to China's most famous philosopher and legendary carpenter, whom history had misconstrued as two different people. In fact, Shi Lu asserts that this combined personality of Confucius and Lu Ban not only made a pilgrimage to the site but actually built the castle itself.

It would be tempting to dismiss the far-fetched claims in the inscriptions as unintelligible and to attribute them to schizophrenia. Certainly, their connections are eccentric and fluid, and the mode of expression is difficult to follow. But reading the long inscriptions on this painting in conjunction with the fable of Confucius that Shi Lu wrote in his diary yields important clues regarding his thoughts when he made these assertions. It is quite possible that Lu Ban was a pseudonym or alter ego for Shi Lu himself. The "Lu" in the two names is expressed with the same Chinese character. By invoking Lu Ban specifically, Shi Lu may have been making a sly joke about the incompetency of the Cultural Revolution–era authorities assigned to condemn his paintings. A common traditional saying "plying the axe in front of Lu Ban" refers to shameless amateurs who display their lack of skill before an acknowledged master.[43] By affiliating his castle with the master craftsman Lu Ban, Shi Lu restored an honoured status to the experts victimized during the Cultural Revolution and scorned those who demeaned them. The apparently nonsensical claims of his inscriptions – that Confucius was a painter who went to India – may be hints that "Confucius" is simply another name for himself. Shi Lu had been pejoratively linked to Confucius during the Criticizing Lin Biao and Confucius movement of 1973-74. Although Confucius never went to India, Shi Lu did, in 1955. Although Confucius did not build the castle, Shi Lu did, at least a version of it on paper.

The Confucius fable in Shi Lu's plum diary makes it clear that Shi Lu and Confucius are meant to shade into one another as a kind of blended personality. Shi Lu explains this affinity with Confucius as based on a similar personality, described variously as one that loves truth-telling, identifies with the common people, and has a romantic vision.[44] His Confucius narrative often departs from historical fact and takes on an unmistakable autobiographical flavour. For example, Confucius becomes a beggar (like Shi Lu, who wandered Sichuan after his 1969 escape) and witnesses scorched fields in the midst of a horrible famine (probably a reference to Shi Lu's 1959 tour of Shaanxi Province at the time of the Great Leap Forward). The image of Confucius, drawn in red and black ink in the plum diary, bears an unmistakable resemblance to Shi Lu's pre–Cultural Revolution appearance (Figure 2.6). Confucius' body is slender like Shi Lu's, and his face is open and gentle. During the Cultural Revolution, Shi Lu was known to dress in a simple white robe evocative of a Confucian scholar in mourning. The conjecture that the image of Confucius is a covert self-portrait is strengthened by the fact that two other sketches in the diary are clear self-portraits: in one, Shi Lu guards a spiritual garden; in the other, he pays homage to poetry on his own gravestone.[45]

In his diary, Shi Lu identifies the drawing of Confucius with a statue he says he discovered on a hill near the Purana Qila (Old Fort) in Old Delhi:

> In 1955 when I went to India, I was captivated by the red fort, a building from ancient times. With excitement I gathered my painting tools and climbed to the top. My spirit felt expansive and yet sad and lonely. I turned my body around and felt a powerful wind from the ancient building blow on my face. My spirit longed to return to its origins. My writings on the subject are muddled like a dream or a puzzle. In a mental haze I saw a kind of spiritual temple. An ancient inscription read something like "Honoured Confucius." The Indian people created a statue of Confucius wearing a tall cap and plain cotton clothing. I saw ancient words inscribed on his sash, so I moved closer to examine them. What a surprise! Amazing! Why did Confucius go to India?[46]

Revising his 1955 *Indian Fort* in 1970, Shi Lu added a statue of Confucius–Lu Ban to the open arch above the ancient gateway. Like many of the spiritual figures in his reworked paintings, it is executed in red, a colour that, for this artist, appears to have been emblematic of bloodshed in defence of revolutionary ideals. On the right side of the image, Shi Lu painted

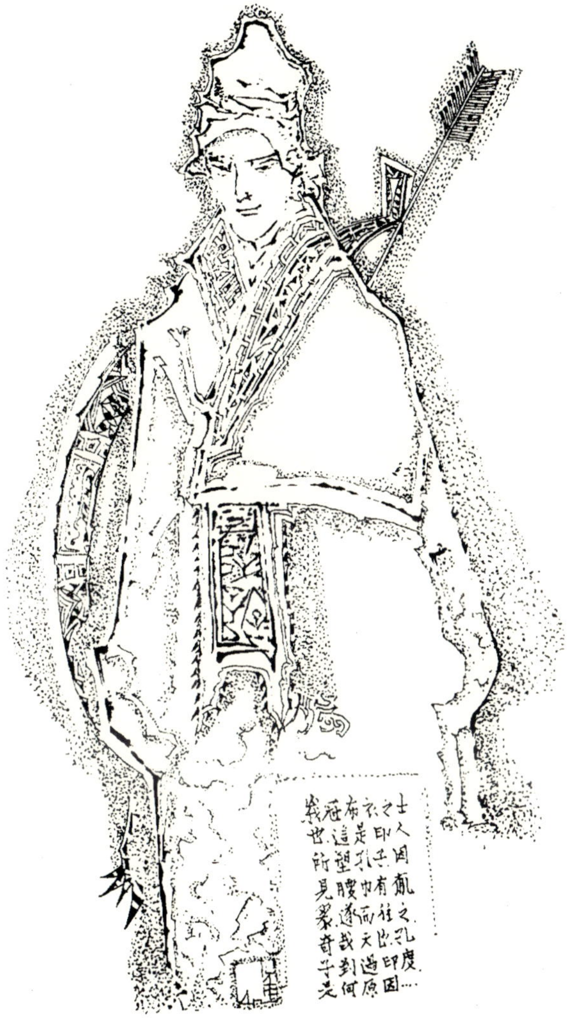

Figure 2.6 Shi Lu, *Confucius* (1974-75). Drawing in red and black ink, a page in Shi Lu's Diary of the Denounced Plum. Author photograph, private collection.

a stone carving in archaic style honouring Confucius and Lu Ban as holy sages. At the bottom, he created another stylized stone carving purportedly inscribed by the ancient calligrapher Wang Xizhi. Playing upon the fact that the cylindrical towers of the fort resemble missiles, Shi Lu cum Wang Xizhi named the castle Cosmos Missile Platform, as if it were the site from which a powerful weapon could be hurled. In likening a castle dedicated to Confucius to a launch pad for a nuclear missile, Shi Lu created a vivid metaphor for implying the power of ethical ideas. Perhaps he was also pointing out the absurdity of Cold War governments, which invested so much effort in bomb making but so little in cultivating the spirit.

Why did Shi Lu associate the ancient Indian fort with such transformative energy? According to his son, he truly did experience an epiphany of sorts during his 1955 trip to India. Visiting ancient ruins and leaving China for the first time in his life sharpened his appreciation for ancient Chinese learning. When he returned home in 1956, he devoted himself to developing new ways to sketch landscapes and people based on Chinese brushwork. In locating his romantic heroes in the India of his imagination during the Cultural Revolution, he may have been influenced by the hero of his youth, the author Lu Xun, whom he had honoured in his choice of pen name. In the opening paragraphs of his famous 1908 essay "On the Power of Mara Poetry," Lu Xun had used India as a focal point for describing the dilemma of ancient civilizations that had become "arid" in recent times.[47] Of course, Lu Xun's commentary on India implied criticism of China too, but he danced around the obvious so skillfully that his commentary acquired an ironic quality rendering it more interesting and effective. According to Lu Xun, "shadow lands" like India lost their splendour as their cultures became "shriveled." However, the voice of the soul, the source of poetry, remained palpable there. They could be regenerated if there were maverick thinkers bold enough to challenge the status quo, in the manner of Mara, the Indian god of destruction. Lu Xun bemoaned the fact that China had not yet produced a Mara poet capable of pushing against ingrained culture with sufficient force to catalyze the old society into evolving into a modern nation. Perhaps Shi Lu was thinking of Lu Xun's essay and imagining himself as a Mara poet when he reworked his old travel sketches to give the Indian figures and terrain a spiritual aura.

The inscriptions he added to *Indian Fort* suggest that he thought of the old structure as a symbol of China's besieged national character. For him, the abandoned ruin must have conjured associations with China's ancient civilization in a state of neglect and disesteem during the Cultural Revolution. In his 1908 manifesto on Mara poetry, Lu Xun had warned that, unless China stopped killing off its Qu Yuans – its truth-telling poets – it would never become vigorous again.[48] In the red-ink inscription above the castle, which is interspersed with flying bats (or crows?), Shi Lu wrote a poem in which he mourned the absence of Confucius:

Funny how no one talks of Confucius any more;
The Yellow Crane Pavilion is now an empty ruin.
White clouds pass by without lingering.
Ridiculous that the Han emperor let it fall vacant.[49]

This poem offers a pointed indictment of what the Cultural Revolution's razing of tradition and disregard for ethics meant for the Chinese nation. Its final line suggests that the founding emperor of the Han dynasty (readable as Mao) is responsible for allowing China's national character to become a hollow shell. As in his Qu Yuan poem, Shi Lu asserts that the artist can play an active role in repairing this barren situation. Through the intervention of his brush and ink, he summoned the spirit of Confucius back to the empty castle. A hollow ruin was revitalized because the artist as carpenter (Lu Ban) restored Confucius' statue to an honoured place within the national temple.

Admonishing Qin Shihuang

Shi Lu's anger toward Mao, hinted at in his painting and poetry, is confirmed within the pages of his private diary written from 1973 to 1975. The fable in which Confucius encounters Qin Shihuang, China's first emperor, dramatically reveals his total break with his romantic idol.[50] Its references to Qin Shihuang clearly applied to Mao, for Mao had consciously identified himself with the emperor since 1958. Although Qin Shihuang had traditionally been viewed negatively for his brutal treatment of scholars and Confucian learning, Mao had attempted to reverse this logic by candidly approving of his actions in burning books and burying scholars. In 1958, speaking to party members, he asked, "What does Qin Shihuang amount to? He buried only four hundred and sixty scholars alive; we have buried forty-six thousand scholars alive. Haven't we killed counter-revolutionary intellectuals? In my debates with some members of the minor democratic parties, I told them: 'You revile us for being Qin Shihuangs, for being dictators. We have always admitted this. It's a pity you didn't go far enough, and we have frequently had to augment what you have said.'"[51]

Mao's decision to launch the Cultural Revolution was consistent with his positive re-evaluation of Qin Shihuang and his affirmation of "revolutionary violence" as a means to destroy class enemies. According to his Marxist-inspired conception, a modern-day burning of books and burying of scholars was a completely justified and urgently required intervention to preserve the proletarian revolution. If reactionary forces were not snuffed out, history would stagnate or slip backward rather than surging ahead.

Shi Lu felt repulsed by the wrong-headed logic and facile justification of violence underpinning Mao's positive evaluation of Qin Shihuang. To exterminate all the intelligent people and bury their knowledge, he protested, was an absurdly short-sighted policy. In his fable, he blended a critique of Mao's frenetic steel-making campaign (the Great Leap Forward of 1958-61) with a discussion of the Qin state's proliferation of iron technology. His fable subtly interweaves the personality of Qin Shihuang with that of Mao to signal that a reference to one entails the other. As narrator of the fable, Shi Lu asserts that Qin Shihuang pursued iron making with such relentless ambition that his face itself turned to iron, robbing him of the humility and humaneness necessary for governing:

> Qin Shihuang made a very big beginning but he did not know how to foster it to the end ... Later he gave a big speech about wanting to control the country. It did not matter that it would cost blood. He became iron-faced, showing no sympathy. This earned him the ridicule of later generations. In a rage he threw (his advisor) Li Si into a big pot. Once he destroyed all the knowledge, Qin devoted everything to ironwork. He became a slave in his heart despite his hatred for slavery. He became iron-hearted. Obsessed with the thought of living a life without rust, even in death Qin Shihuang wanted to be buried in iron ore.[52]

As a young revolutionary at Yan'an, Shi Lu had felt pride to be told that his face was similar to Mao's and had once inscribed a picture of a face resembling Mao's and his own with the boast "This face will explode the twentieth century!"[53] Now his sketch of Qin Shihuang (Figure 2.7) attested to his renunciation of Mao. The two portraits of Confucius and Qin Shihuang in the same diary are sharply differentiated; no one could possibly identify them as depictions of the same person. Qin Shihuang's broad, flat face looks unmistakably like that of the aging Mao. It is not a complimentary portrait! According to its inscription, the emperor's clothes are "tattered," his mouth is "drooling," and "his nose running." He is dreaming of a wildly ambitious iron-making campaign. His robe and face are outlined in black ink, without a trace of revolutionary red. In contrast, the portrait of Confucius is calm and dignified. The sage's robe is made of cotton and outlined in red, an expression of his strong identification with the common people. These contrasting portraits confirm that a once blended revolutionary personality has been divided in two. Shi Lu positioned himself on one side

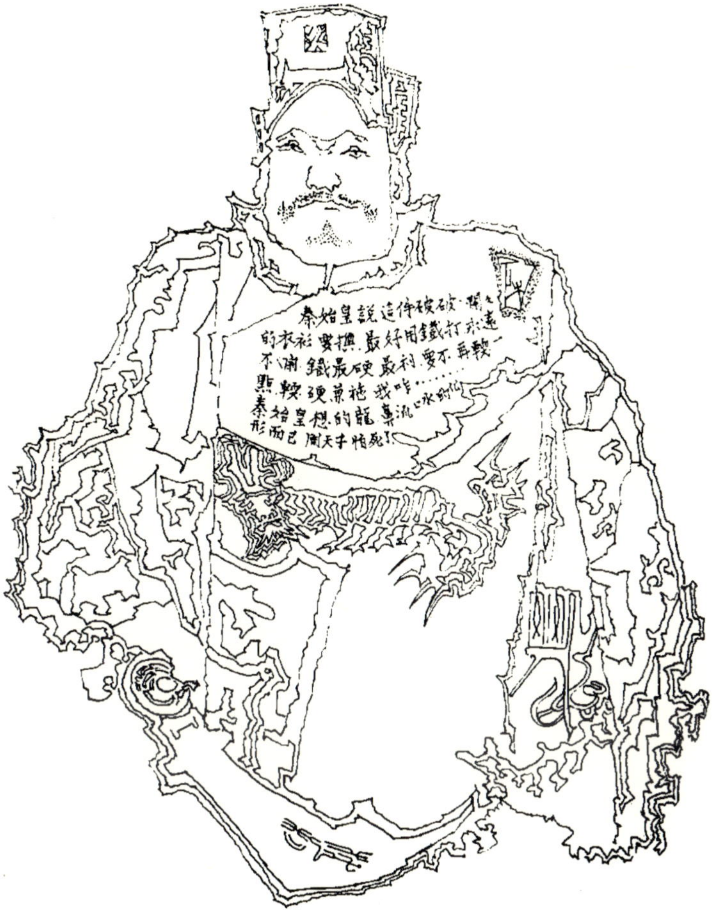

Figure 2.7 Shi Lu, *Qin Shihuang* (1974-75). Drawing in black ink, a page in Shi Lu's Diary of the Denounced Plum. Author photograph, private collection.

of the political schism, declaring his affinity with Confucius and forswearing the ruthless men of action and expediency, Mao Zedong and Qin Shihuang.

In the fable, Confucius tries unsuccessfully to persuade Qin Shihuang to use "the mild, humane way to govern," but the emperor, an earthy man of limited vision, an artisan turned dictator, foolishly relates every problem to iron making. Shi Lu registers special disapproval of the way in which Qin

Shihuang became the "Golden Mouth" for all of society: "Everything he said, all had to follow." The emperor's true agenda is to "shake the nerves" of society so as to bring about a momentous change, but he fails to think his plan through. Had he had been willing "to explore his own shortcomings" and develop a deeper understanding of the country's challenges, he would not have produced so much damage, and history's evaluation of him would be positive. Despite this pointed critique, Shi Lu extends sympathy to the failed emperor: "Who truly understands the sadness of Qin Shihuang?" He also attributes good intentions to him: "He tried to do the right thing but it just turned out wrong."[54]

Even prior to the Cultural Revolution, Shi Lu's Mao-centred faith had eroded around the edges. When *Fighting in Northern Shaanxi* was rejected and persecution ensued, he felt as though an axe had split his revolutionary ideology in two. By the 1970s, his belief in communism had been drastically whittled down to its most cogent, defensible claims and reoriented away from his former idol. At the end of his life, Shi Lu still affirmed the Yan'an communism he once identified with Mao – that is, the promise of an emancipated life and a robust nation more egalitarian than ever before. But now the balancing centre of his ideals was his own expansive personality in a broad and fluid conversation with the world's great thinkers. He spent the remainder of his life pursuing a "self-revolution" in visual art. In his paintings of flowers and mountains, he developed an intensely personal calligraphy style alternating between "lean" and "fat" characters. For viewers who knew of his distressed circumstances, the lean characters suggested analogues for his body, worn thin by suffering; the fat ones were evocative of the wet properties of tears and blood.[55]

During the Cultural Revolution, Shi Lu summoned Confucius back to his worldview as a way to cope with the strain of an identity crisis and as a social corrective for the deficiencies of Maoism. As he slowly excluded Mao from his revolutionary pantheon, the romantic cosmopolitanism of the New Culture era and the ethics nurtured by his Confucian schooling resurfaced. In stubbornly resisting, deeply thinking, and constantly creating throughout his suffering, Shi Lu proved himself a worthy heir to the quest for a fully developed personhood associated in his mind with Shitao, Lu Xun, and Confucius.

PART 2

Artists Remember: Two Memoirs

3
Brushes Are Weapons: An Art School and Its Artists

Shengtian Zheng

An Image from the Past

In May of 1996, *Newsweek* published a painting on its cover to mark the thirtieth anniversary of the Cultural Revolution in China (Figure 3.1).[1] In it, Mao wears an army uniform and a red collar badge. With his hat in one hand and a cigarette in the other, he stands defiant and proud under a rosy sky and in front of a bird's-eye view of China. Behind him, Shanghai, Hangzhou, Jinggang Mountain, and Lushan Mountain can be seen, covered with crowds waving countless red flags. The painting's original title is *Man's World Is Mutable, Seas Become Mulberry Fields: Chairman Mao Inspects the Situation of the Great Proletarian Cultural Revolution in Northern, South-Central, and Eastern China.* The first part of the title is a line from "The People's Liberation Army Captures Nanjing," a poem written by Mao in April 1949.[2]

During the first part of the Cultural Revolution, most artworks, including paintings, posters, sculptures, and political cartoons, were created anonymously and collectively. Personal contribution and credit were not recognized, and thus a work was usually attributed to an organization or a collective rather than to an individual artist. This painting, which is often referred to as *Chairman Mao Inspects Areas South and North of Yangtze River Near Wuhan,* is attributed on its lower right side as having been "provided by the Zhejiang Academy of the Workers, Peasants, and Soldiers." In fact, much of it was my own work!

When I first saw the cover of the Asian edition of *Newsweek,* I was assailed by ineradicable memories. When the Cultural Revolution ended after Mao's death in September 1976, followed by the downfall of the so-called Gang of Four, most artworks produced during its early years were considered meaningless political propaganda and either destroyed or thrown away. My colleagues and I did the same thing in order to release ourselves

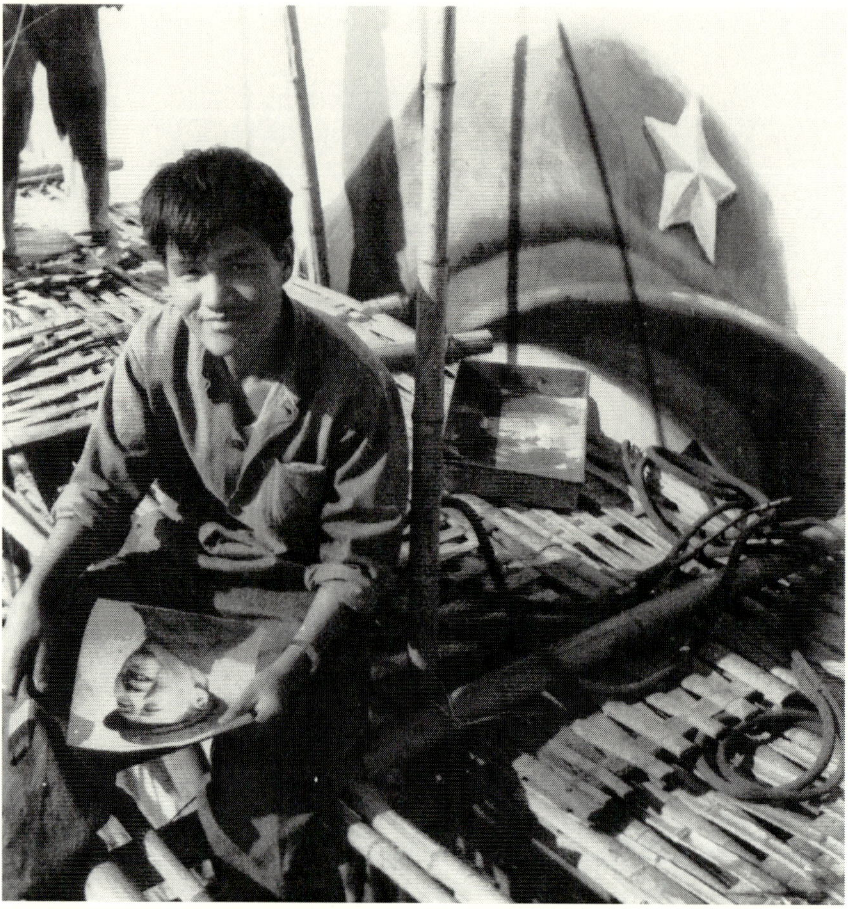

Figure 3.2 Shengtian Zheng at work on a mural portrait of Mao early in the Cultural Revolution. Collection of the author.

from the nightmare. Nobody knew where the original canvas of this oil painting was, and nobody cared.

When the Cultural Revolution began, I was a young teacher working at my alma mater, Zhejiang Academy of Fine Arts in Hangzhou, now the China Academy of Arts (Figure 3.2). The academy was founded in 1928 by Cai Yuanpei, a prominent liberal educator and former president of Beijing University, and the artist Lin Fengmian, a European-trained modernist.[3] It is one of only two prestigious art academies to come directly under the

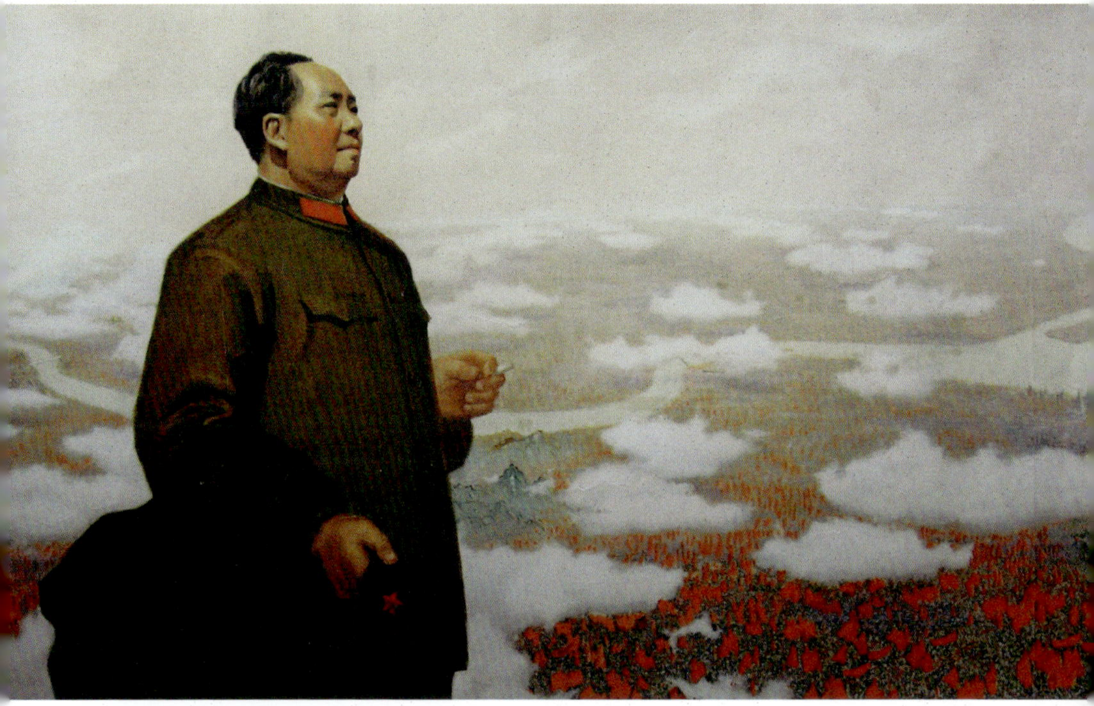

Figure 3.1 *Man's World Is Mutable, Seas Become Mulberry Fields: Chairman Mao Inspects the Situation of the Great Proletarian Cultural Revolution in Northern, South-Central, and Eastern China* (1967). **Oil painting published as a poster, 61.0 by 84.5 centimetres.** Collection of Wang Mingxian, photograph, Howard Ursuliak.

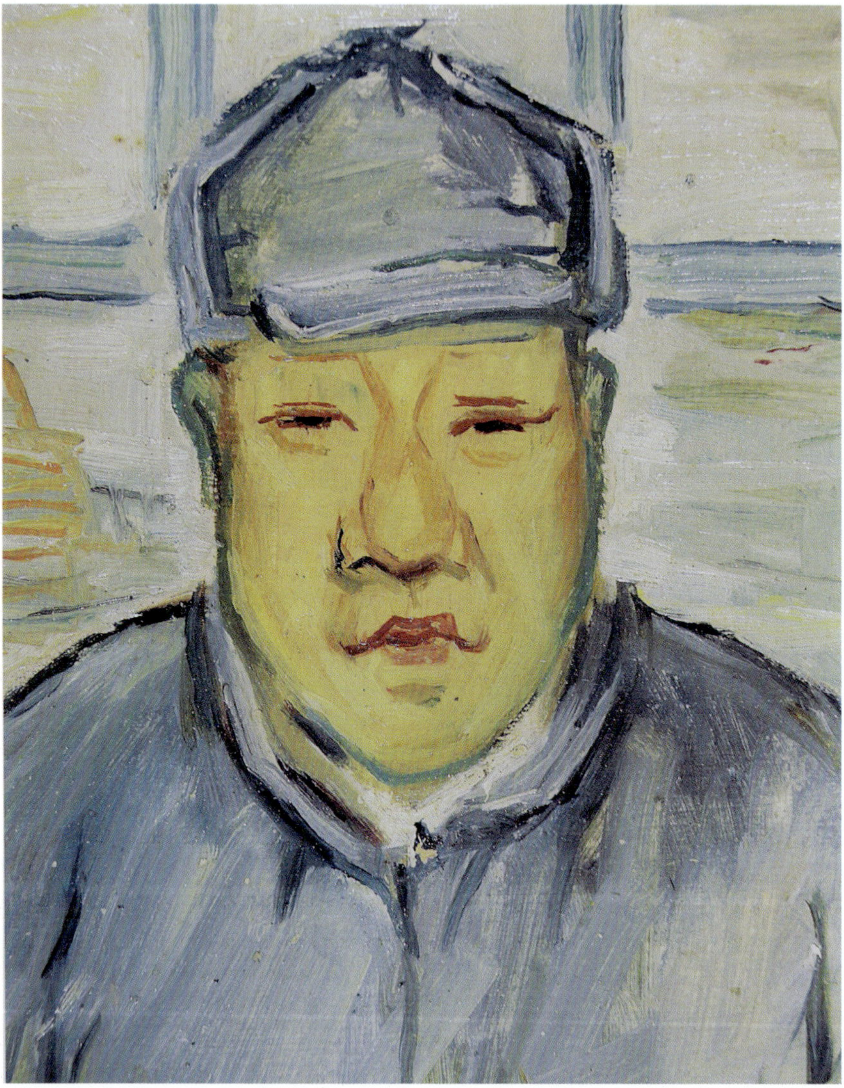

Figure 3.3 Wang Liuqiu, *Labour-Reform Farm Inmate* (n.d.). *Wang Liuqiu, His Art* (Hong Kong: Shen Ping, Lie Muk Lan, The Suang Lan Art Center and Inspiration Art Press, 1990), 29.

jurisdiction of the State Ministry of Culture and is where many of the nation's finest artists have been trained in recent decades.[4] Because of its liberal approach, the academy also has a history of cultivating artistic rebels and revolutionaries that goes back to its earliest days. In 1929, Chen Zhuokun and some schoolmates in Hangzhou organized a group called Xihu yi-ba yi she (Art Society of the Eighteenth at West Lake).[5] Inspired by the famous writer Lu Xun, these young students actively promoted woodcuts as a revolutionary art form and took part in the 1930s left-wing movement in art and literature.[6] Some of the members of this group were arrested by the Guomindang (Nationalist Party) authorities, and one of them, a girl named Yao Fu (Xia Peng), lost her life in jail at the age of twenty-four.

Despite its progressive and revolutionary stance during the first two decades of its history, the Zhejiang Academy was often referred to after 1949 as the base camp of bourgeois liberalization. Lin Fengmian was compelled to leave his teaching position in the early 1950s, and in 1957, during the Anti-rightist Campaign, nearly all of the leaders at the academy were removed for their "anti–Communist Party activities," with Vice-President Mo Pu, Dean Jin Lang, and thirty-two teachers and students labelled "bourgeois rightists."[7] Even during this time, when intellectuals were widely attacked and punished, what happened at the academy was exceptional, "a very rare case in the whole nation."[8]

On 16 May 1966, the Central Committee of the Chinese Communist Party passed the famous "May Sixteenth Directive," a document partially written and edited by Mao that announced the theory, guidelines, and policies for launching the Cultural Revolution. This date is commonly considered to mark the start of the Cultural Revolution in China. In early June, the newly appointed Cultural Revolution Group of the Chinese Communist Party began encouraging students in almost all Chinese universities and schools to walk out of their classes and join in the "revolutionary mass criticism and repudiation" activities. At the Zhejiang Academy, rebel students, along with a few young teachers and workers, formed a radical group called Hongweibing zhandoudui (Red Guard Fighting Force). This group was led by Zhang Yongsheng, a fifth-year student in the Printmaking Department who was from Hanshan, a small town in the neighbouring province of Anhui. He had taken my watercolour class for a year and had never been considered a particularly talented student or a potential leader. Much to the surprise of many teachers, Zhang was to play a key role during the turbulent period of the Cultural Revolution – not only at the school but also at the provincial and national level.

Activism and Persecution

As the head of the campus Red Guards, Zhang Yongsheng successfully networked with radical student organizations from high schools and universities in the city. In the summer of 1966, classes began to be cancelled in schools throughout China, though teachers and staff still received their basic salaries, and students were permitted to stay in the dormitories. On 15 November 1966, Zhang formed Hong San Si (Headquarters of Revolutionary Rebel and Red Guards of Hangzhou). On 30 December, he established Sheng Lian Zong (General Headquarters of the United Rebel Factions) and proceeded to expand his power to other areas in the province.

In early 1967, under Zhang's leadership, Red Guards kidnapped Jiang Hua, the party secretary of Zhejiang Province and a powerful member of the Central Politburo of the Communist Party. Following the example of Shanghai's "January Storm," many violent rallies were organized to attack the current provincial government. The following year, Zhang was officially appointed vice-chairman of the Revolutionary Committee of Zhejiang. He also held the post of chairman of the Revolutionary Committee of the Academy and became one of the most powerful persons in Zhejiang, an important coastal province with a population of 32 million.

Under the leadership of Zhang and his band of rebels, the academy was turned into a living hell for senior professors and school administrators, who were considered enemies of the people and the prime targets of the Cultural Revolution – "ox-demons and snake-spirits." As early as the summer of 1966, a group of students had already picked out a few professors and publicly humiliated them. Writing later for a catalogue of works by the late artist Fang Gangmin, I offered my own eyewitness account of events on campus in those cruel times:

> One summer afternoon in 1966, Professor Fang stepped onto campus with his usual, slightly serious demeanour and a clean outfit. When he reached the staircase at the main building of the Oil Painting Faculty, he was surrounded by a group of hostile and fanatical young red guards who were lying in wait for him. They poured ink and paint all over Mr. Fang, and insolently placed a tall "dunce's cap" on his head. This defenseless old man could only stand in the heat of the sun, as these violent people humiliated him. For Mr. Fang, the ten-year hell of the Cultural Revolution began that day. During this long and painful journey, almost no one of his generation would escape torture and persecution. Some even lost their lives.[9]

One of the victims who did not survive was Pan Tianshou, then president of the academy and one of the most important artists of twentieth-century China.[10] On 6 September 1966, Pan was taken by the Red Guards to an "ox-shed," the detention space where the "ox-demons and snake-spirits" were kept, in his case an old dining hall on campus. His wife, He Yan, was told to take some sheets and a blanket to the ox-shed but was not allowed to see him.[11] The next day, Pan and more than thirty of his colleagues, forced to stand on a truck, dunce caps on their heads and cardboard placards hanging from their necks, were paraded through the streets of Hangzhou in public humiliation. From that rainy day on, without any legal process, President Pan lost his freedom and was frequently taken to all kinds of public rallies where he was unfairly criticized and denounced. This went on until his death five years later.

On 19 May 1968, Mao's wife, Jiang Qing, then referred to as the "standard-bearer of the Cultural Revolution," received Zhang Yongsheng and his deputy Du Yinxin in Beijing.[12] Two other prominent radical leaders, Yao Wenyuan and Chen Boda, accompanied her, as well as Jiang Qing's daughter, Xiao Li, then head of the People's Liberation Army newspaper.[13] Zhang reported to them about the campaign against Pan Tianshou that he had initiated in Hangzhou and showed them a painting by Pan, *Vultures.* Jiang Qing remarked, "Pan Tianshou's paintings are very dark. I don't appreciate them. His vultures are really unpleasant, gloomy and ugly." Yao Wenyuan added, "The darkness and gloominess of his paintings is related to his work as a spy. The grey vultures Pan likes to paint are incarnations of spies."[14]

The charge of "spy" came from an accusation fabricated against Pan by Red Guards. They had found his name in the archives of the former Nationalist government on a "list of personalities in cultural circles who may be recommended to join the Nationalist Party." The list was prepared by Zhang Daofan, the Nationalist Party's chief propaganda officer.[15] Also, because Pan was appointed president of the Zhejiang Academy in 1944 by Chen Li-fu, then minister of education, who was also the head of the Nationalists' right wing C-C clique, Pan was assumed to have been a member of this powerful and secretive group.[16]

Pan's tenuous association with Nationalist power holders brought him the title of "Guomindang cultural spy." At the instigation of the leaders of the Cultural Revolution, the campaign against Pan was raised to a new level. He was not only paraded and criticized on the streets of Hangzhou, but in other cities as well, including his hometown of Ninghai. On 10 March 1969, on the train back from Ninghai, the broken-hearted artist wrote a poem on a cigarette package:

Don't complain the cage is cramped and narrow,
One's heart could be as large as heaven and earth;
Untrue charges can be fabricated and framed up,
And unrighteous judgments have always been around.[17]

These were the last words Pan Tianshou wrote. Convinced he had nothing to hide, he included it in his report to his prison guard. On 5 September 1971, this great artist passed away, wretched and alone, in a local hospital in Hangzhou.

Of course, Pan Tianshou was not the only one whose life was destroyed by the Cultural Revolution. As described in a biography of Pan, the academy campus "became a concentration camp" during the early years of the Cultural Revolution: "Interrogation went on until dawn. Horrendous sounds of torturing, whipping, crying, and screaming were heard all over the campus at midnight. The famous sculptor Xiao Chuanjiu was tragically beaten to death by those rebels in the academy ... Ms. Fei, a female teacher of the academy's high school was subjected to all kinds of tortures. She couldn't stand it any more and hanged herself."[18]

Professor Wang Liuqiu's story is equally sad and shocking. Wang was labelled a rightist and removed from his position as chairman of the Painting Department during the Anti-rightist Campaign in 1957. For almost ten years, he worked as a janitor. When the Cultural Revolution broke out, Wang was forced by Red Guards to move to a tiny, stinking public lavatory, with his bed right beside the toilet. The humiliation and torture the Red Guards inflicted on him was unbelievable. After a couple of months, he could take no more; at great risk, he managed to escape from the campus and fled the city.

Wang was trying to go back to his overseas Chinese family in Thailand, which he had left behind thirty years before. He trudged through reed marshes, climbed mountain trails, and eventually arrived at the bank of the Lancang (Upper Mekong) River in the southwestern province of Yunnan. He tied some basketballs together to make a raft and floated downstream for two days. Hungry and exhausted, he landed on what he thought was the other side of the border. But he was wrong; he was immediately arrested by local police and escorted back to Hangzhou. There he was sentenced to ten years in prison for his attempt to "betray the motherland and go abroad illegally."

In the labour-reform farm, or penitentiary, where he was confined, Wang Liuqiu worked as an assistant for a furniture painter. Amazingly, he was able to make small paintings (approximately ten by sixteen centimetres) in his leisure time, using industrial paints and lacquer. He depicted scenes of the inmates' life and their portraits (Figure 3.3). A group of these paintings, which he called the *Jade Collection,* was preserved by the artist as a valuable record of that unforgettable time.[19]

Artists in Confinement

During the Cultural Revolution, apart from those designated ox-demons and snake-spirits, people were generally divided into three categories. The first were the *zaofanpai* (rebels), who led or participated in radical activities and struggled for and won power in their *danwei* (work units). The second were the *baoshoupai* (conservatives), who, though espousing Mao's cause, often defended the existing authorities and opposed the seizure of power by the rebels. The remainder were the *xiaoyaopai* (non-partisans), who stayed away from the political factions and tried to maintain a private life outside politics. Every person was said to belong to one of these categories, and his or her fate was affected accordingly.

I was labelled a stubborn conservative, even though I had been quite excited when the Cultural Revolution began. Mao's idea of taking a critical approach to the literature and arts of the past, and creating a new culture for working people, sounded very appealing to me. As a young artist, I was dissatisfied with the way in which the art establishment was controlled by a few bureaucrats and old-fashioned senior artists. I believed that the Cultural Revolution would open a new phase for China and the rest of the world. Many of my colleagues shared the same excitement and enthusiasm in the first few months of 1966. I burned my own paintings and writings, and got rid of many of my books on classical Chinese and Western literature. Unfortunately, the Red Guards did not appreciate my self-criticism and revolutionary spirit. They saw me as an incurable sinner who was beyond redemption, since I had been educated under the "capitalist revisionist educational system" for too long. I was not allowed to join the Red Guards or take part in any rebel activities.

When I expressed my disagreement with the excessive violence of the Red Guards, I was arrested by the Red Guard Fighting Force at the beginning of January 1967 and placed in the ox-shed where Pan Tianshou and other "people's enemies" were kept. I was held prisoner there for about three months. We would wake up in the morning, sweep the campus, and then line up to recite Mao's quotations and slogans. Most of time, however, we sat in the room and studied the "Little Red Book" of quotations from Chairman Mao and Cultural Revolution documents. As detainees, we had to criticize and humiliate each other in order to show our willingness to subordinate ourselves to the Red Guards.

Considered too young to be kept in the ox-shed, I was released in April 1967 and appointed to work in the school cafeteria. For a few months, I got up at 2:00 a.m. and cooked a huge vat of rice porridge for hundreds of students. Eventually, I won back my freedom through hard work. I was allowed to go back to my department building and join other members of the "revolutionary masses" for "re-education." Besides reading newspapers and official documents, we did little but sit and talk for most of the time. Painting and other activities considered non-political were not permitted. We felt that there was no reason to get involved in such dangerous affairs.

In the summer of 1967, the situation in many provinces throughout China was characterized by massive confrontation and fighting between various rebel and mass factions. Large-scale battles were fought in Shanghai, Nanjing, Changzhou, Zhengzhou, Shenyang, Chongqing, Changsha, and other major cities. Numerous lives were lost and the system of government collapsed in many places. In the July Twentieth Incident in Wuhan, radical emissaries from Beijing were detained by more conservative commanders at the Wuhan garrison, prompting fears of outright civil war.[20] Mao felt that it was the time to regain control in order to prevent the country from falling into chaos. He took a special trip to cities in north, east, and south-central China in order to inspect the precarious situation. On 7 October 1967, immediately following this unannounced inspection, the Central Committee of the Chinese Communist Party circulated a new instruction from Mao. It called for a ceasefire among opposing mass organizations and stated that "there is no conflict of interest within the working class, and there is no reason to split into irreconcilable groups."[21]

I had been very puzzled since the Red Guard movement began. I had thought the Cultural Revolution was supposed to create a new culture and encourage new ideologies; I thought its purpose was to eliminate the differences between intellectuals and the working class, and to combine the interests and abilities of all sectors of society. The violence unleashed by the Red Guards shocked me. When I was arrested by students one chilly night in the small town of Jiaxing, near Hangzhou, I argued with them; I said, "Beating me can damage my skin and flesh, but not my soul." Their response was to quote from Mao's Little Red Book, a common tactic for winning arguments in those days: "Revolution is not a dinner party, or writing an essay, or painting a picture, or doing embroidery."[22]

During the months spent in detention, I was very distressed and did not understand why I was treated as an enemy. I did not understand how the Cultural Revolution could stir up such hatred among people. Later, the violence increased and bloodshed occurred all over the country. Like many other true believers, I still trusted Mao and thought that these developments went against his intentions. When his new instruction was released – criticizing the use of excessive violence as wrongdoing and calling for unity – I felt a sense of vindication and was filled with hope once again. The instruction stated, "Some became Conservatives and made mistakes. It's just a question of understanding. If someone stands on the wrong side, then steps over to our side, that's all [there is to it] ... The majority of cadres are good, only a very small minority are bad ... We allow cadres to make mistakes, and allow them to correct their mistakes. Don't attack and bring them down once they make a mistake ... We have to tell the heads of revolutionary rebels and young red guards: now is the time they may make some mistakes too."[23]

Everything Mao said sounded so right to me.

A Return to Painting

Around the time that Mao's instruction was released, students and teachers were preparing a new exhibition to salute the Cultural Revolution. For almost a year, nobody had touched their brushes and painting boxes. We never thought we would go back to the studio. As the smoke of gunpowder gradually dispersed on the campuses, Red Guards threw themselves into further feverish action. In October 1967, an exhibition called Long Live the Victory of Chairman Mao's Revolutionary Line was held at the National Art Gallery in Beijing to commemorate the eighteenth anniversary of the People's Republic. This was the first national exhibition since 1966, and some sixteen hundred paintings, posters, sculptures, and crafts were shown, by both amateur and professional artists.[24] The exhibition was an example of this new enthusiasm for producing art, and many similar shows soon followed in other provinces and cities.

After a long period of quarantine, I was allowed to join in the activities of the Fanxiuzu (anti-revisionism group) of the Oil Painting Department in the fall of 1967. Members were busy preparing artworks for the upcoming exhibitions. Of course, all of these had to eulogize Mao. One of our collective products was a series of portraits representing Mao at different ages and in front of various historical sites, such as the Nanhu Lake in Jiaxing close to Shanghai, where the First Congress of the Chinese Communist Party was held in a boat in 1921, and Jinggang Mountain, where Mao established the first revolutionary military base in 1927. I was assigned one of the sixteen planned portraits: Mao's face glowing from the torch lights during the 1945 parade in Yan'an (the Chinese communists' wartime headquarters) celebrating China's victory over Japan in the Second World War.

Teachers felt they were being useful again in the service of the Cultural Revolution, their professional skills needed and valued in order to produce good paintings. Quan Shanshi, a professor who had been trained at the Repin Academy of Fine Arts in Leningrad during the 1950s, suddenly found himself the centre of attention, since many students needed his help to achieve Mao's likeness or the colour balance for their compositions. The completed portraits were published and distributed all over the country.

Now that I had a little more confidence, I started to work out the composition of a new painting of Mao (Figure 3.1). I wanted to depict him as a towering leader, standing high above his country and reviewing it, as a way to symbolize his recent inspection trip and the instruction that had touched me so much. In terms of style, I was still fascinated by Mao's idea of "Combining revolutionary realism and revolutionary romanticism."[25] During my years at the Zhejiang Academy, I had never been satisfied with the strict realistic style that attempted to present a straight copy of reality. Even for a political poster, I felt that more creative imagination was required. Using a horizontal format, I sketched Mao standing on top of the world, clouds flowing around his massive body. I borrowed the Blue and Green style of traditional landscape painting to highlight areas along the south side of the Yangtze River.[26] The whole land was covered with red flags and banners in accord with the slogan "The globe is entirely red!" Everyone liked the idea, and my sketch was readily approved.

Before I started work on the canvas, I was told that it should be produced collaboratively. Two artists were assigned to the team: Zhou Ruiwen, a student and member of the anti-revisionism group, and Xu Junxuan, a teacher who was originally in the conservative group but had later turned against it. Because painting was considered a revolutionary task, it was thought that the people who had a higher revolutionary consciousness should play a major role – painting the most important part of the picture. As a young student, Zhou was given the honour of painting Mao's face. As an "awakened intellectual," Xu was allowed to paint Mao's body. The largest part of the painting – the sky, clouds, and entire background – was left for me, a "bourgeois intellectual" who was still under some measure of surveillance. Despite the large proportion of the total area, the parts I had been assigned to paint were not considered politically important. I was occasionally invited to retouch some colours on Mao's face and body to assist in achieving a realistic likeness.

The finished painting was well received: it was not only shown in the provincial art exhibition of 1968, but was also published in many different formats and distributed widely. It was reproduced on a huge billboard in front of the Shanghai Railway Station and in public areas of many other cities in China. During our 2001 research trip to China to gather material for the Vancouver exhibition, we found the image on posters, calendars, and even printed on metal plates and desktop ornaments in the street markets of Beijing, Shanghai, and Hong Kong.[27]

As the leader of the school, Zhang Yongsheng must have felt proud of the nationwide popularity of this work. On his 1968 trip to Beijing, Zhang took reproductions of this painting, and other works created at the Zhejiang Academy, to show to Jiang Qing and other leaders of the Cultural Revolution. According to the report relayed later to students and teachers, Jiang Qing's response during their 19 May meeting was not favourable. She claimed that the painting did not portray Mao's image correctly. She stated, "People said it's a good painting, a good painting; but if you look at it carefully there are problems. The background is too complicated. [Mao's] chin doesn't look comfortable. The right arm is not well painted."[28] She told Zhang and Du, "There is a painting called *Chairman Mao Goes to Anyuan,* which is extremely good. It brings out Mao's vital spirit."[29] (This painting, by the young artist Liu Chunhua, is discussed by Julia F. Andrews in Chapter 1 and appears as Figure 1.6.)

Only after the end of the Cultural Revolution, when Jiang Qing was arrested and many previously secret documents were released, did I finally realize why she disliked our painting and praised another. *Chairman Mao Goes to Anyuan* portrayed a political message that she approved. Mao's inspection trip and instruction in 1967 targeted the policies of extreme left-wing leaders in China, including those of Jiang Qing herself. Of course, she was not happy with Mao's criticism of her allies and did not want to see a painting that took this criticism as its theme. She preferred *Chairman Mao Goes to Anyuan* because it reproduced a piece of history she herself had fabricated. Denying the leading role of Liu Shaoqi in the early workers' revolutionary movement, Jiang said, "It was Chairman Mao who walked to Anyuan Coal Mine, step by step."[30] Whereas *Chairman Mao Goes to Anyuan* became "the model of 'making foreign things serve China' and opened a new page of art history," our painting quickly disappeared from public view.[31] I learned that an anonymous letter was sent to the Revolutionary Committee of Zhejiang accusing the producers of this painting of being counter-revolutionary enemies. My enthusiasm faded away, and I was not encouraged to participate in other artistic activities for the next few years.

Reversals of Fortune after the Cultural Revolution

By the next year, 1969, the most radical phase of the Cultural Revolution was over. On 7 October 1968, a Workers' Propaganda Team had been sent to the Zhejiang Academy of Fine Arts to replace the Red Guard leadership. In December of 1969, all the students, staff, and teachers were moved from the campus to Chen County, a hilly area east of Hangzhou. The following year, the academy was ordered to relocate again, this time to Tonglu County along the Fuchun River, the same river that, six hundred years earlier, had inspired the artist Huang Gongwang (1269-1354) to create the masterpiece *Fuchun Mountain Dwelling*.[32] However, the members of the academy suffered greatly from these forced relocations; I became ill and was hospitalized for a long time. Zhang Yongsheng gradually lost his power and influence. On 27 July 1975, he was separated from his followers and sent to a small village in Hebei Province.

The year 1976 marked the end of the Cultural Revolution. That October, one month after Mao's death, Jiang Qing and the other members of the Gang of Four were arrested. Zhang Yongsheng was accused of having been a trusted follower of Jiang Qing in Zhejiang Province. One tabloid paper reported that he had agreed to be chosen by Jiang Qing as a prospective son-in-law, through a marriage to her daughter Xiao Li. The authorities spent more than two years investigating his crimes of factionalism and his relationship with Jiang Qing. On 3 April 1979, Zhang, then aged thirty-nine, was sentenced to life imprisonment by the Hangzhou Intermediate People's Court, deprived of his political rights for life. He was denounced as "the chief culprit responsible for unrest throughout Zhejiang Province."[33]

In Professor Ding Shu's article "The Death Toll of the Cultural Revolution Amounts to Two Million," the author lists some of the charges against Zhang: "Zhang Yongsheng, the head of rebel factions of Hangzhou, used armed force to suppress Xiaoshan and Fuyang Counties. [Twenty-seven] were killed in Xiaoshan. Most were tortured and beaten to death after being arrested. [One hundred and thirty-five] were killed in Fuyang. [Three hundred and nineteen] were injured and disabled. More than [twelve hundred] houses were burned down."[34]

After his trial, Zhang was sent to a labour camp in the remote province of Qinghai, not far from the Gobi Desert. His wife divorced him and left China. For many years, nothing was heard from him.[35]

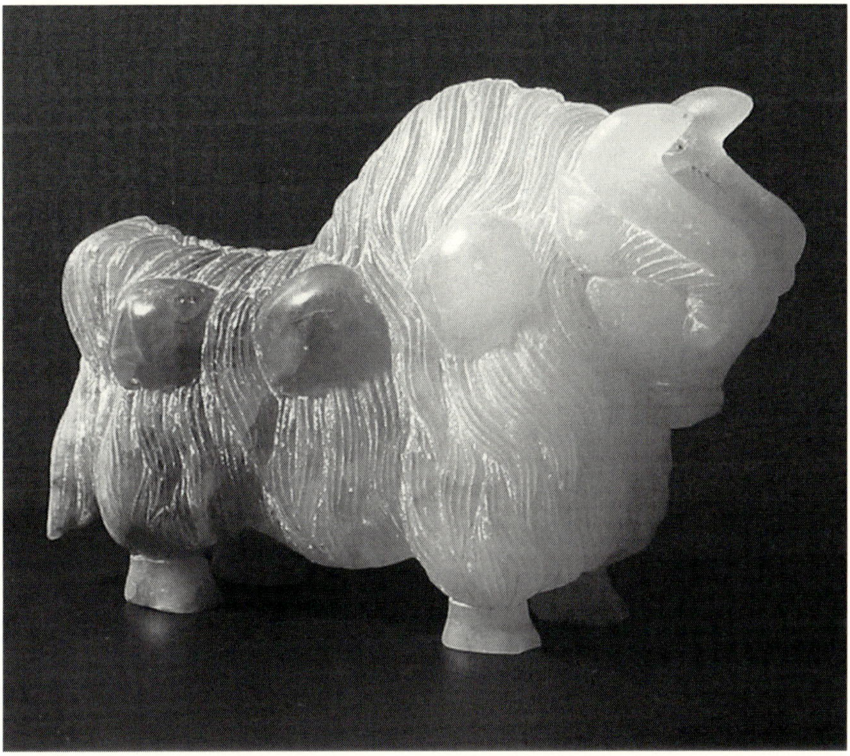

Figure 3.4 *Great Yak.* Jade. This jade sculpture was give to the author in 1994 by the Qinghai Province's delegation to Canada.

In 1994, having moved to Vancouver, I had a chance to receive a high-ranking delegate who was visiting from Qinghai Province. During his visit, Liu Lixun, director of the Foreign Economic Relations and Trade Commission, gave me a small jade carving as a gift and asked me if I could help find a market for this kind of product (Figure 3.4). Made of legendary Kunlun Yu (jade from Kunlun Mountain), this sculpture of a yak demonstrated the skills of a professionally trained artist. When I asked Mr. Liu where it was from, he did not answer directly. He said, "It was produced by prisoners in the labour camp." He continued: "But in the camp there was a very good instructor, Zhang Yongsheng, who graduated from the prestigious Zhejiang Academy of Fine Arts."

What a turn of events! This carving of a yak found its way into my hands in Canada, thousands of miles from China. It brought to mind a slogan that was often heard in art circles during the Cultural Revolution: "Brushes are weapons." Holding brushes was not only a privilege for trusted artists, but also an obligation to serve a revolutionary purpose. Brushes were taken away from many great artists during the Cultural Revolution, destroying their careers and their lives. Brushes were allowed to paint only the propaganda that worshipped Mao. However, almost thirty years later, Zhang Yongsheng, now a political prisoner for his role in the Cultural Revolution, was using a sculpting knife to carve art pieces whose only function was to serve as a market commodity. Nothing could be more ironic than this dramatic change in Zhang Yongsheng's role in history. If *Chairman Mao Goes to Anyuan* can be bought at auction for $1 million (as it was in 1995, making it the most expensive Chinese oil painting sold to that time), and if the sculptures of the *Rent Collection Courtyard* can become the subject of a high-stakes copyright lawsuit (as Britta Erickson describes in Chapter 5), then Zhang's return to the role of artist, his art tools no longer weapons but simply implements, is probably a suitable epilogue for the absurdity that existed in the art world during the Cultural Revolution.[36]

4

When We Were Young: Up to the Mountains, Down to the Villages

Gu Xiong

When I returned to China in the summer of 2001, I found over twenty of my old sketchbooks filled with drawings that I had made during the Cultural Revolution. As I flipped through the pages, memories of my life then, in the countryside, leapt out of the faded images: it was a turbulent time, accompanied by empty loss. Confusion and mindless obedience shaped the fate of a whole generation. But eventually we were able to regain control of our destinies.

From the drawings, details re-emerge that convey my experiences, my emotions, and my thoughts in those days. In my quest for art, I obtained an inner freedom and hope, which is captured in these sketchbooks. It is from these personal, historical, and political perspectives that I will approach the Cultural Revolution in this chapter.

Frenzy

My generation was the first to be born and raised in the People's Republic following the communist victory in 1949 and the third of the three generations described by Julia F. Andrews in Chapter 1 as being harmed by the Cultural Revolution. We were nourished solely by the ideals of revolutionary heroism, and we grew up to become the fanatics of the Cultural Revolution. We were taught to obey the absolute authority of the Communist Party's leader, Chairman Mao Zedong; in the words of Lei Feng, the young soldier who was held up as a martyr and model for us to emulate, we were to become "screws that never rust," constantly in the service of the revolution.

When Mao initiated the Cultural Revolution in 1966, he told the young that "Revolution is no crime, rebellion is justified." (A visual representation of this popular slogan appears as Figure 1.1 in Chapter 1.) The Red Guards were told to smash the old world and break with the influence of tradition and the West. This threw the country into complete disorder. No one was safe: even President Liu Shaoqi was condemned and died in jail. At that time, I had just graduated from elementary school. I joined the revolution enthusiastically and made my contribution by painting portraits of Mao and political propaganda posters.

The Red Guards in my home town of Chongqing, the largest city in Sichuan Province, split into two warring factions in 1967; each was convinced that it was truly loyal to Chairman Mao and that the other was the enemy. Chongqing was the site of some of the fiercest fighting in the entire country, resulting in many fatalities. As night fell on the battles, I sat on a hill, watching the multicoloured glow of bullets travelling over the river. Watching the battles was a favourite pastime of children in those days. In Shaping Park in Chongqing, there is a cemetery for the many Red Guard victims who died at that time, some of whom were barely more than children themselves. My own cousin was shot to death as she hid under a bed in her apartment while two factions fought to control the building; she was only fourteen years old.

Up to the Mountains, Down to the Villages

By 1968, with his opponents crushed, Mao and his supporters had control of the country: all of China was "red." Now that Mao had attained his goal of absolute power, his once beloved Red Guards were of no further use to him, and their factional battles were causing considerable social disruption, so he devised a solution to deal with them. On 22 December 1968, he decreed, "It is very necessary for urban educated youth to go to the countryside and learn from the poor and middle peasants. We must persuade urban cadres and everyone else to send their children who have graduated from middle schools, high schools, and universities to the rural areas. We need to mobilize. Comrades in the countryside should welcome them warmly."[1] In the years that followed, over 17 million young people from the cities were transformed from Red Guards to peasants as a result of Mao's re-education program. I was one of those city youths who grew to adulthood in the villages (Figure 4.1). Our "re-education" took place in some of the most remote regions of rural China, in keeping with the slogan "Up to the mountains, down to the villages," which was the title of a political movement that would last ten years. And we, the youth, holding a framed copy of the celebrated oil painting *Chairman Mao Goes to Anyuan* (Figure 1.6 in Chapter 1), marched toward what we believed would be a path of unity with peasants and workers. Along the way, our individual destinies merged in the larger destiny of a generation (Figure 4.2).

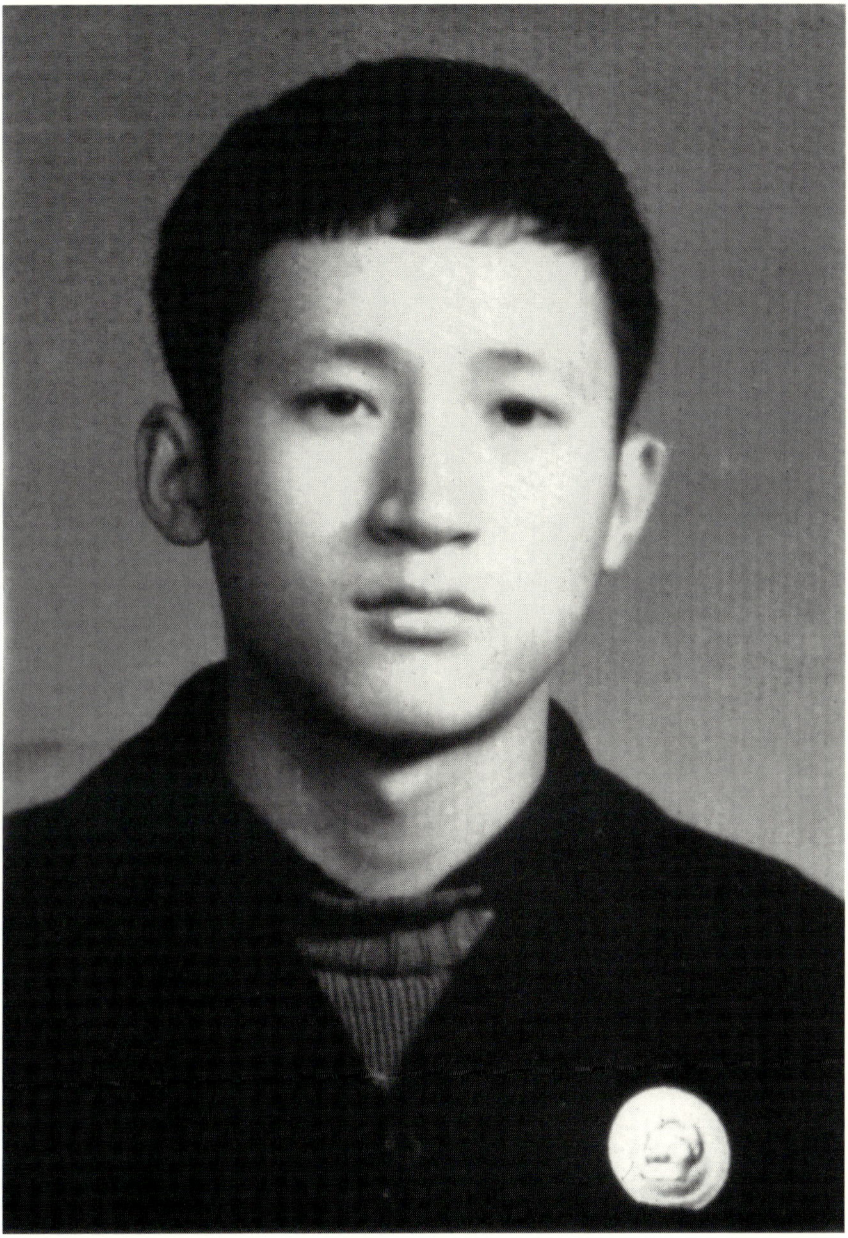

Figure 4.1 Gu Xiong on the eve of his journey to the countryside. Photograph, Ge Luo Shan Photo Studio. Collection of the author.

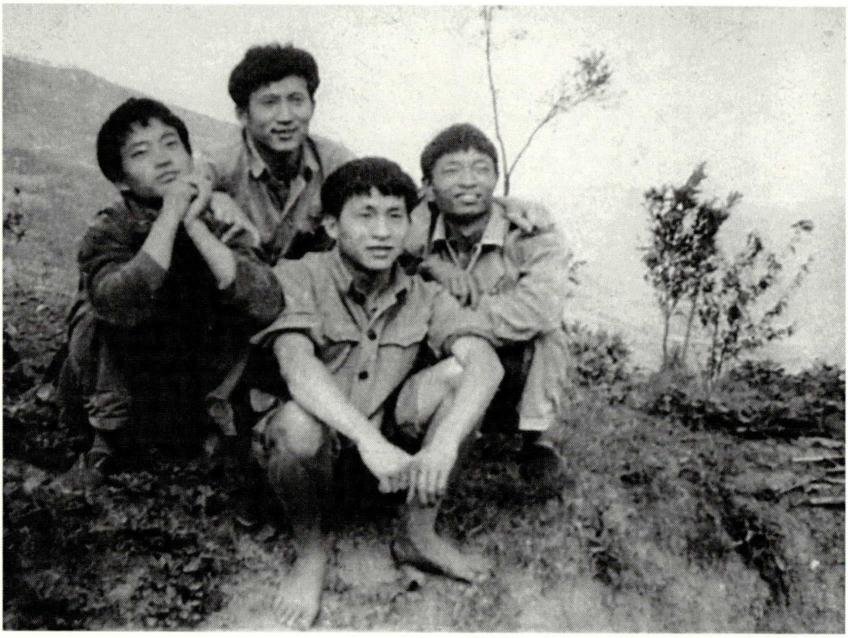

Figure 4.2 Gu Xiong (centre at the back) and friends in the countryside. Photograph, Kwan Lifu. Collection of the author.

With my brother and sister, I went to the countryside, leaving my mother alone at home. It was common for families to be separated like this, with huge numbers of "educated youth" suddenly disappearing from the city. My brother and I were sent to the Daba Mountain Region at the border of Shaanxi and Sichuan Provinces, where I began the entries in my sketchbooks (Figure 4.3). The region had been a base for the Red Army in the 1930s and was one of the most remote, impoverished, and backward areas in China. There were no roads and no electricity; all supplies had to be carried in on foot.

We were sent to a village of one hundred people situated halfway up a mountain. We lived in a courtyard house with six families (Figure 4.4). Every time it rained, the roof would leak. The basic tasks of living were never simple. For example, cooking required gathering fuel, and because most trees had been cut down in the attempt to make steel during the Great Leap Forward (1958-61), we had to climb to the top of the mountains to get tree branches. We walked more than thirty kilometres with over seventy kilograms of fuel on our backs.

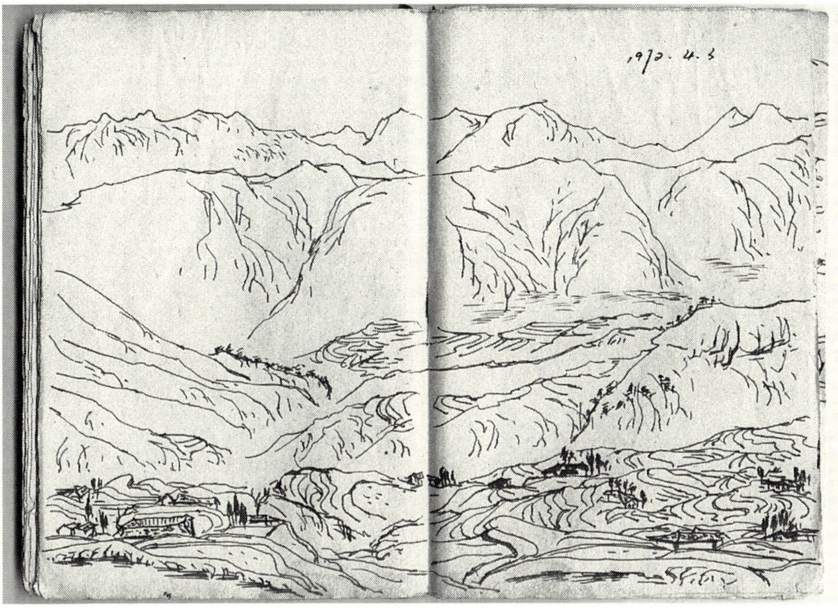

Figure 4.3 Gu Xiong, ***Qingping Village Scene in the Daba Mountains*** **(5 April 1972).** Collection of the author.

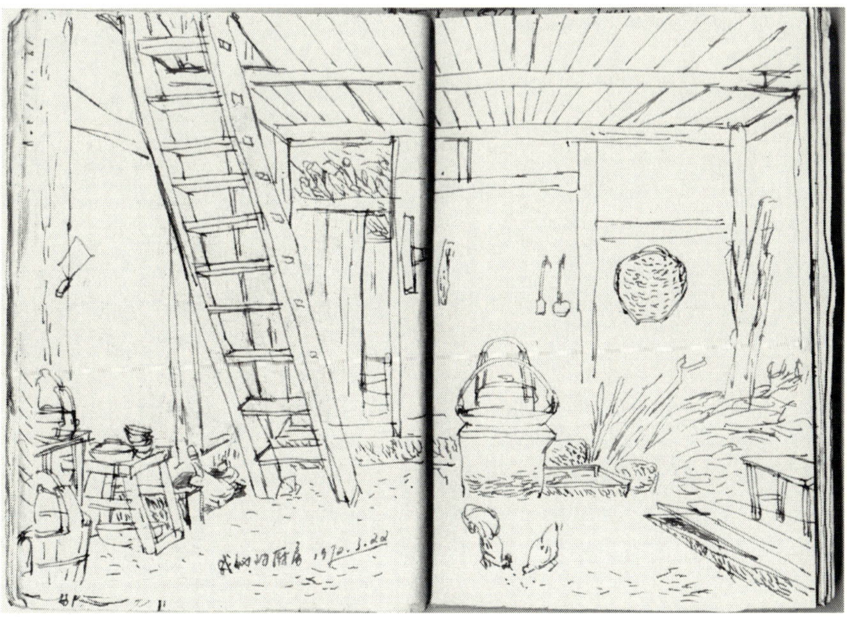

Figure 4.4 Gu Xiong, ***Our Kitchen*** **(23 March 1973).** Collection of the author.

When we first arrived, our only goal was, as a slogan of the day decreed, to "Roll in the mud and gain a red [revolutionary] heart" by performing the dirtiest and hardest tasks. We worked from sunrise to sunset and earned enough work-points for the equivalent of eight *fen* (less than two cents US) in wages. During spring and fall, we worked about twenty hours a day at whatever tasks needed to be performed (Figure 4.5). With scarcely any time for sleep, we would take naps on a bamboo bed by the field. We did not have adequate food, because the old supplies were used up and the new provisions were not yet ready for consumption, so we ate whatever we could find.

In the name of the revolution, thousands of sent-down youth died. For example, in Inner Mongolia, sixty-nine died while trying to put out a wildfire without water or equipment.[2] In Guangdong Province, hundreds drowned after they were ordered to form a human wall in the face of a tsunami.[3] Many of the female youths were raped by local cadres. Many more were falsely accused of crimes by local officials. An entire generation matured in the midst of these tragedies and hardships.

Our revolutionary fervour was chilled by the reality of daily life. Hardship and isolation forced us to question the Cultural Revolution, though we could not express our loss of faith for fear of being branded counter-revolutionary. Critical reflection led to doubt, but it allowed us to rediscover ourselves and the Chinese nation. My sketchbooks are silent witnesses of this larger transformation.

No Leisure Life

Even though the countryside was far removed from the culture and politics of the urban centres, aspects of the political movements still reached the border regions. When not farming, we participated in revolutionary criticism sessions and the production of propaganda. We wrote big-character slogans on houses and rocks, and we painted propaganda images on walls. I knew they were meaningless, but I still did it because it was better than hard physical labour, and we wanted to create the impression that we were good political activists, which we hoped would improve our chances of returning to the city.

There was no cultural life in the countryside. We would write letters and wait eagerly for replies, a process that took a month. We read each letter over and over; they were our connection with the outside world. Once a year, we were allowed to return home to visit our families. This was vitally important: not only were we happy to see our loved ones, but we embraced

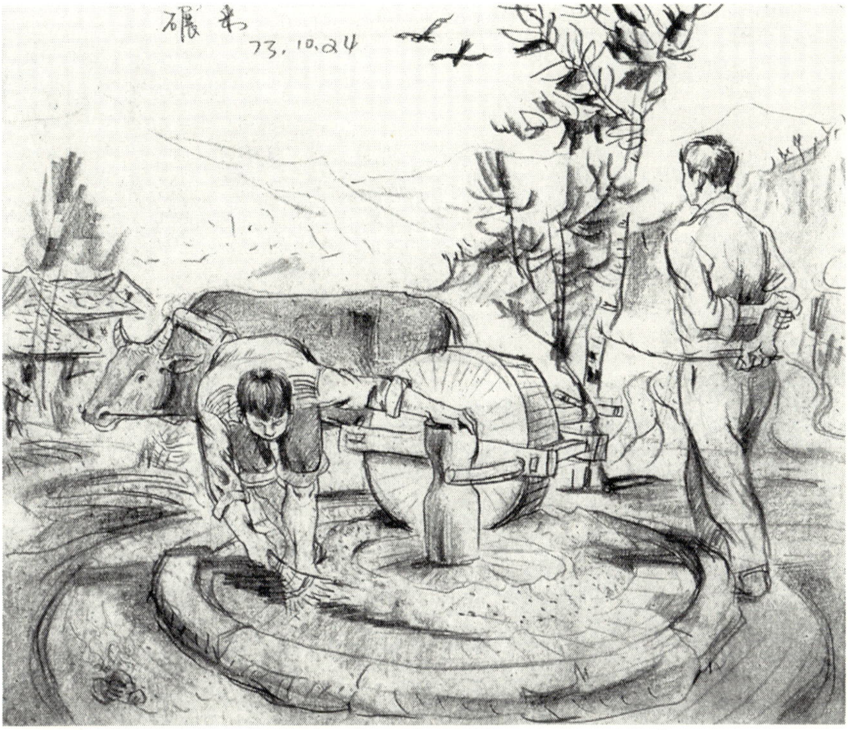

Figure 4.5 **Gu Xiong, *Grinding Grain* (24 October 1973).** Collection of the author.

the opportunity to exchange the harsh rural environment for a civilized urban setting. Until the next trip, those visits provided us with vivid memories to last the entire year. Memories of home – a place we belonged to and longed for – sustained us in our rural exile.

We were lonely, living in a production unit far from friends and family (Figure 4.6). Our favourite pastime was to visit each other; we would gather in groups of ten or twenty to drink and eat, and to forget our troubles. Every two months, the local government organized meetings for educated youths as a way of monitoring them. These meetings were intended as political study programs, but no one was interested; they were simply a way for us to socialize. When we witnessed the older educated youths who had married locals and assimilated completely into rural, peasant life, we saw a bleak future waiting for us. In contrast, when new youths came to our region, our loneliness was eased.

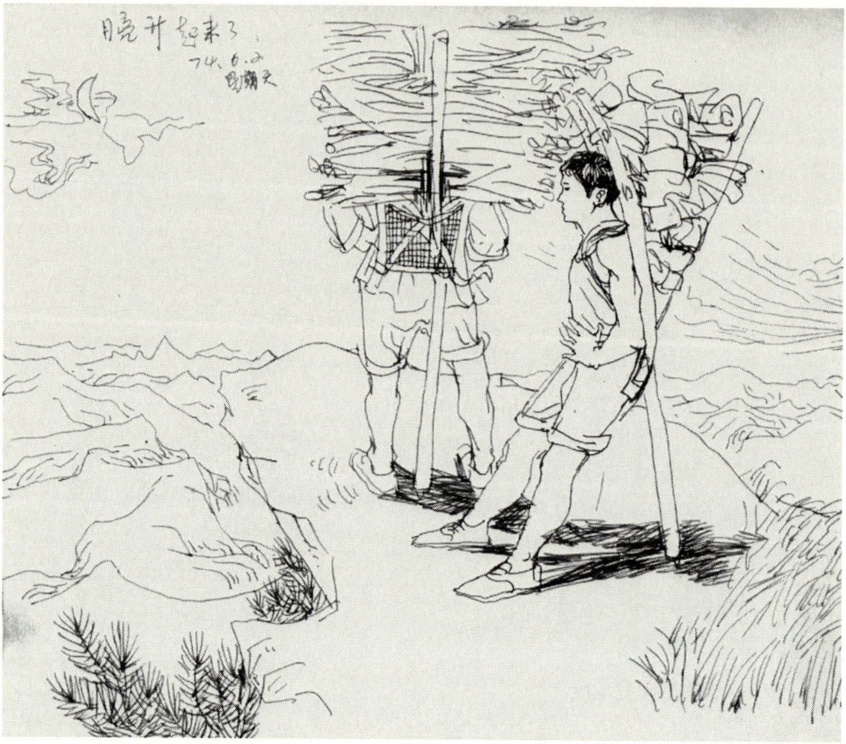

Figure 4.6 **Gu Xiong, *The Moon Is Up* (2 June 1974).** Collection of the author.

Watching movies was a rare event, something that happened once or twice a year. Films were shown outdoors and always at the same location. We were prepared to walk long distances at night to see a film we might already have seen several times (Figure 4.7). Only a very limited number of films were screened in those days, including the Soviet film *Lenin in 1918*. We liked this movie because it showed ten seconds of *Swan Lake* and repeated the Bolshevik promise of "milk and bread." The former revealed the beauty of art and romantic love, whereas the latter reminded us of the irony of our struggle for survival.

Because of the tight controls on culture and art, very few works were performed. Each local region organized its own "Chairman Mao's thought entertainment group" to put on local productions of the model theatrical works selected and promoted by Mao's wife, Jiang Qing. My brother and I joined our regional group, which toured and performed in various villages.

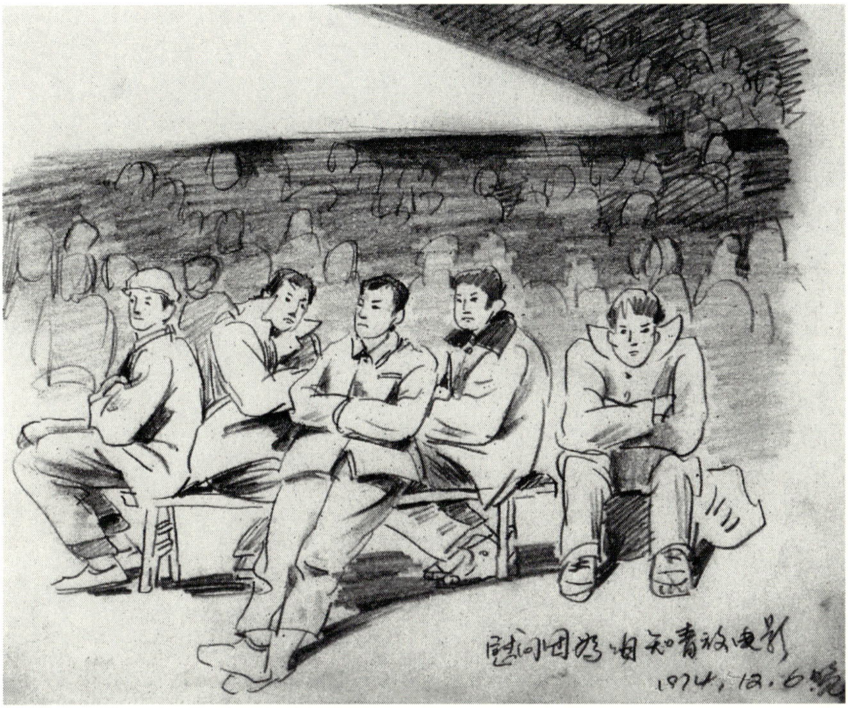

Figure 4.7 Gu Xiong, *The Entertainment Troupe Shows a Movie to the Educated Youth* (6 December 1974, evening). Collection of the author.

Although the peasants knew more than we did about farming, we distinguished ourselves with our superior artistic talent and earned their respect. In addition to these entertainment groups, there were sports teams. I joined the regional basketball training camp because I was tall, though I found it exhausting; sometimes we were so tired that we hardly had the energy to change our clothes. We were always hungry, but we ate well there was meat at every meal – so this was the best possible life at the time.

Though card games were not allowed, we managed to get away with playing them during the little spare time we had. The losers had to stick paper on their face or crawl under tables as a forfeit. We also used the cards to tell our fortunes, while our real future remained uncertain. We were stranded in what seemed a perpetual limbo.

Most novels were banned in the cities, but we experienced more freedom in the countryside. We bought illegal books, which we shared with one another. Unofficial novels were reproduced and distributed in secret. Most were romantic stories and therefore very popular in an age when the word "love" was not spoken even between lovers. One of the most famous of these works of "underground" fiction was Zhang Yang's novel *The Second Handshake (Di'er ci wo shou);* the author was jailed for four years, but his novel was published after the end of the Cultural Revolution.[4]

We were allowed to sing revolutionary songs only, yet the propaganda contained in the lyrics lost the power to inspire us due to the harsh reality of our lives. Instead, we liked singing Western folk songs, and we made copies of these to pass on to our friends. There were also people who composed their own songs; one of these was "The Song of Chongqing," which was written by an unknown educated youth. The songs expressed a longing for home and described our uncertain futures; they were condemned at the time as counter-revolutionary. The composer of "The Song of Nanjing" was sent to jail for ten years.[5]

After a period of farm work, I became a substitute teacher – a common occupation among the educated youth. School conditions were poor: some classrooms had no windows, and students suffered from frostbitten fingers in the winter. They brought their own pots and pans to school to cook for themselves. Despite these hardships, they were honest and I liked their innocence, so I did my best to teach them well. At night, I also taught literacy classes to the peasants; during the day, they taught me farming skills. Through this mutual instruction, the gap between us diminished, and I enjoyed good relations with the peasants and their children.

Theory of Class Origins

During the Cultural Revolution, everyone in China, including members of the educated youth, was distinguished or valued by class origin at birth. Those born into the families of workers, peasants, soldiers, or cadres were from a "red," or revolutionary, background; those born into the families of landlords, capitalists, counter-revolutionaries, and intellectuals were considered to be part of a "black family" and were therefore enemies of the people. This categorization continued from one generation to the next – birth determined one's future. A young man called Yu Luoke wrote an essay criticizing the "Theory of Class Origins," which won widespread support among educated youth. Yu Luoke was subsequently accused of being a counter-revolutionary and executed in 1970 at the age of twenty-seven.[6]

In 1972, the government started to select youth to return to the city to work; however, everyone was subjected to a political background check first,

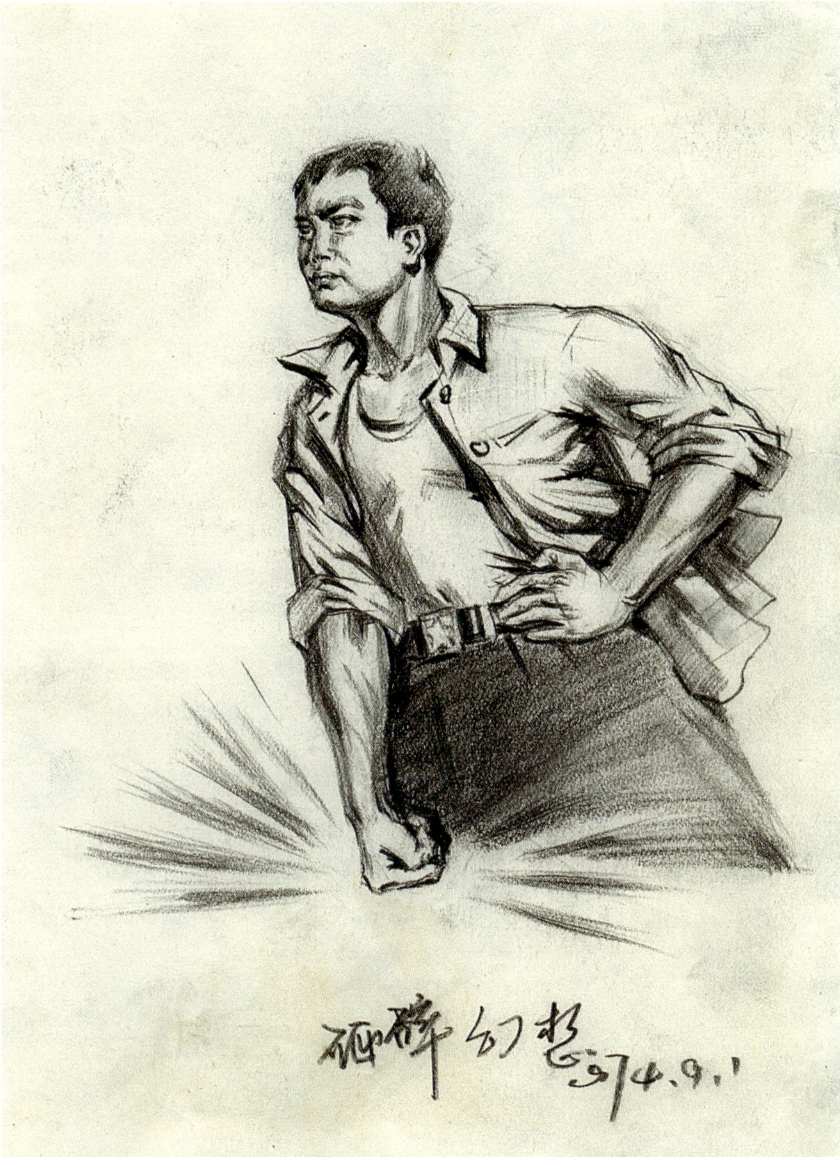

Figure 4.8 Gu Xiong, *Shattering Illusions* (1 September 1974). Collection of the author.

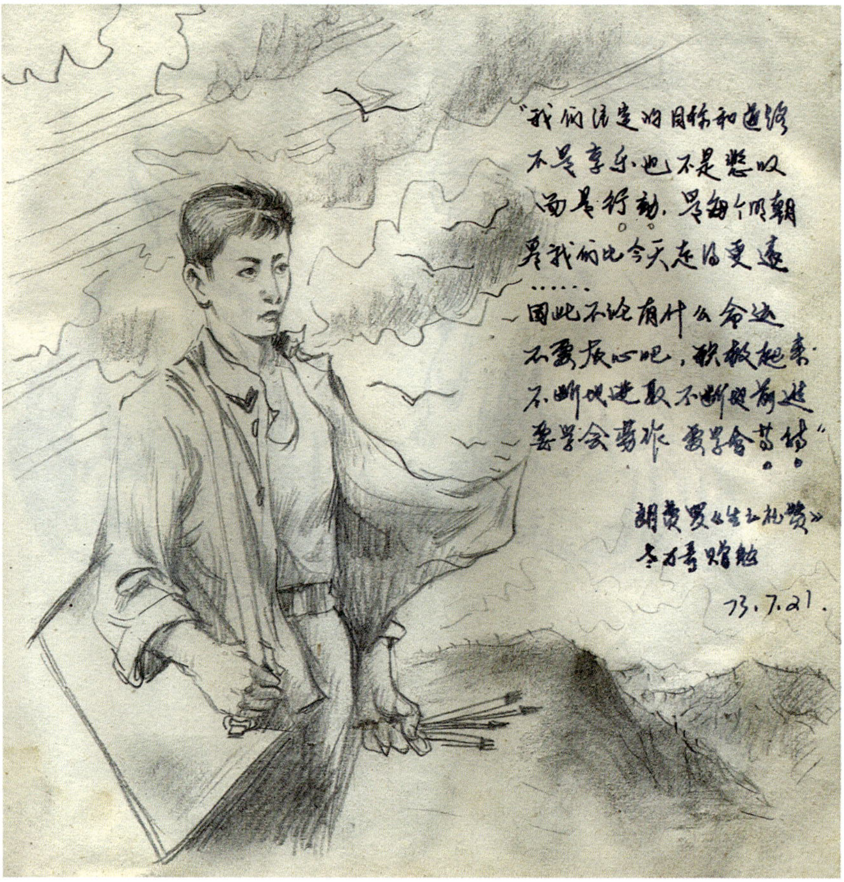

Figure 4.9 Gu Xiong, *From Brother Laowan* (21 July 1973). The inscription is a Chinese translation of two verses from the poem "A Psalm of Life" by Henry Wadsworth Longfellow:

> Not enjoyment, and not sorrow,
> Is our destined end or way;
> But to *act,* that each tomorrow
> Find us farther than today ...
> Let us, then, be up and doing,
> With a heart for any fate;
> Still achieving, still pursuing,
> Learn to labour and to *wait*.

(Words in italics are highlighted in the Chinese translation, not in the original poem.) From Henry Wadsworth Longfellow, *Longfellow's Poetical Works* (London: Frederick Warne, 1880). Collection of the author.

and for those who were born into a so-called black family, like me, there was no chance of going back to the city. In 1957, during the anti-intellectual backlash that followed the Hundred Flowers movement, my father had been accused of being a rightist and a historical counter-revolutionary.[7] He was sent to a labour camp and remained there for thirty years; consequently, my family was discriminated against and stripped of our rights. Children from "black families" had no choice but to stay in the countryside.

Because I drew, played basketball, and worked hard, a number of schools and factories wanted to recruit me, but upon discovering my father's political background, they lost interest – I was rejected by potential employers five times. According to the thinking of the day, it was believed that only 5 percent of all children born into black families could be re-educated. In the beginning, I believed that if I worked hard, I might fit into this category and eventually find my way back to the city. But my dreams were crushed, and I lived with the shame of having been being born into a "black family." My inner feelings and longings surfaced in the white pages of my sketchbooks (Figure 4.8).

Hope

In the midst of this bleak reality, I turned to my art. I started to record my thoughts and experiences through drawing. In the daytime, during work breaks, I would draw other farmers and the landscape. At night, under the light of an oil lamp, I expressed my inner thoughts in drawings. Through these sketches, I began to develop an independent will. My artistic expressions began to shift. According to revolutionary theory, the human body was to be depicted in an idealized manner – "red, smooth, and luminescent" and "tall, robust, and perfect." I eventually abandoned these revolutionary propaganda techniques, which I felt to be hollow and meaningless. Doubts about the revolution, dissatisfaction with the reality of what was happening, and hope for a better future surfaced in my sketches. My sketchbooks reveal a youth's disillusionment with his circumstances and a desire for a different life. This quest expressed in my art symbolized a search for self: these drawings were a form of communication between the outside world and my inner spirit. Eventually, my inner spirit triumphed over the circumstances of my external environment.

Those four long years in the countryside taught me to transform negatives into positives and never to lose hope. In my darkest hours, I remembered my mother's words: "Time will change everything." Years would pass before I realized that her words and my quest for art nourished a spark of hope that I carried with me through this time of disappointment and disillusion (Figure 4.9).

Editor's Postscript

After his years in the village, Gu Xiong was admitted to the Sichuan Arts Institute in 1978, one of the first classes admitted to the academy following the end of the Cultural Revolution. There, he earned bachelor's and master's degrees in fine arts. In 1986, he was the first artist from the People's Republic of China to attend the Artist-in-residence Program at the Banff Centre for the Arts, in Alberta. After returning to China, he became active in the China avant-garde art movement of the late 1980s. He left China in the end of August 1989, going first to Banff Centre and then settling in Vancouver in 1990. Since then, Gu Xiong has become a prominent figure in the Vancouver and Canadian art worlds, exhibiting work in a wide range of media that explores questions of culture and identity. He also teaches in the Department of Art History, Visual Art and Theory at the University of British Columbia, Vancouver.[8]

PART 3

Meanings Then and Now

5
The *Rent Collection Courtyard*, Past and Present

Britta Erickson

In the last analysis, what is the source of all literature and art?
Works of literature and art, as ideological forms, are products of the reflection in the human brain of the life of a given society.

– Mao Zedong, 1942

Thus Mao Zedong, in his 1942 Yan'an Talks, described not only how art is created, but also how it is perceived. The perception of a work of art depends on its reflection in the human brain, filtered through that person's life experience in a given society. Mao continued: "Revolutionary literature and art are the products of the reflection of the life of the people in the brains of revolutionary writers and artists." But what happens to revolutionary art when the artists and audience are no longer revolutionary? What if the meaning or value of a work of art is partly contingent upon the presumed state of mind of the artist and the presumption is incorrect? These questions have arisen in the recent controversy surrounding a Cultural Revolution "model" *(yangban)* sculpture of 1965 – the *Rent Collection Courtyard (Shou zu yuan)* (Figures 5.1 and 5.2).[1]

The prominent contemporary artist Cai Guo-Qiang provoked a heated controversy by copying figures from the *Rent Collection Courtyard* and presenting them, under his own name, at the prestigious forty-eighth Venice Biennale in 1999 under the title *Venice's Rent Collection Courtyard* (Figure 5.3). Throughout his career, Cai has sought to disrupt assumptions about art and culture, often finding highly unorthodox means of doing so: gunpowder, for example, is among his preferred media. His unconventional approach to art was not fully appreciated in China. He left for Japan in 1986 and finally immigrated to New York in 1995; he is now in extremely high demand for exhibitions worldwide. Cai's appropriation of the *Rent Collection Courtyard* and the publicity surrounding it catalyzed a series of events that serve to highlight the extent to which audience expectation plays a role

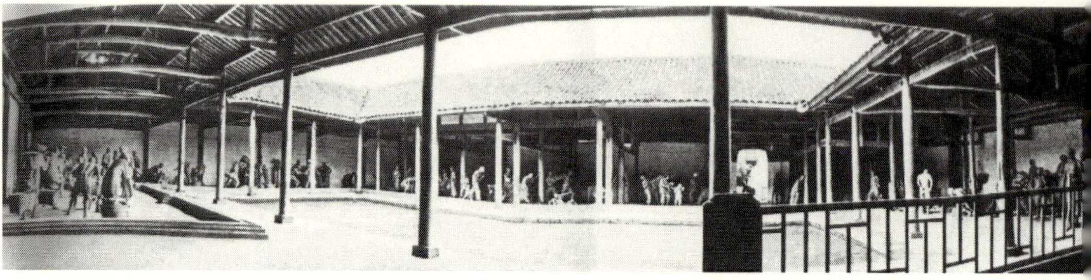

Figure 5.1 Team of sculptors, *Rent Collection Courtyard* (1965). Mixed media installation, overview, Landlord's Courtyard of Oppression Exhibition Hall, Dayi County, Sichuan. Luo Zhongli, ed., *Shou zu yuan qundiao* [The *Rent Collection Courtyard* group of sculptures] (Shijiazhuang: Hebei Fine Arts Publishing House, 2001), 1.

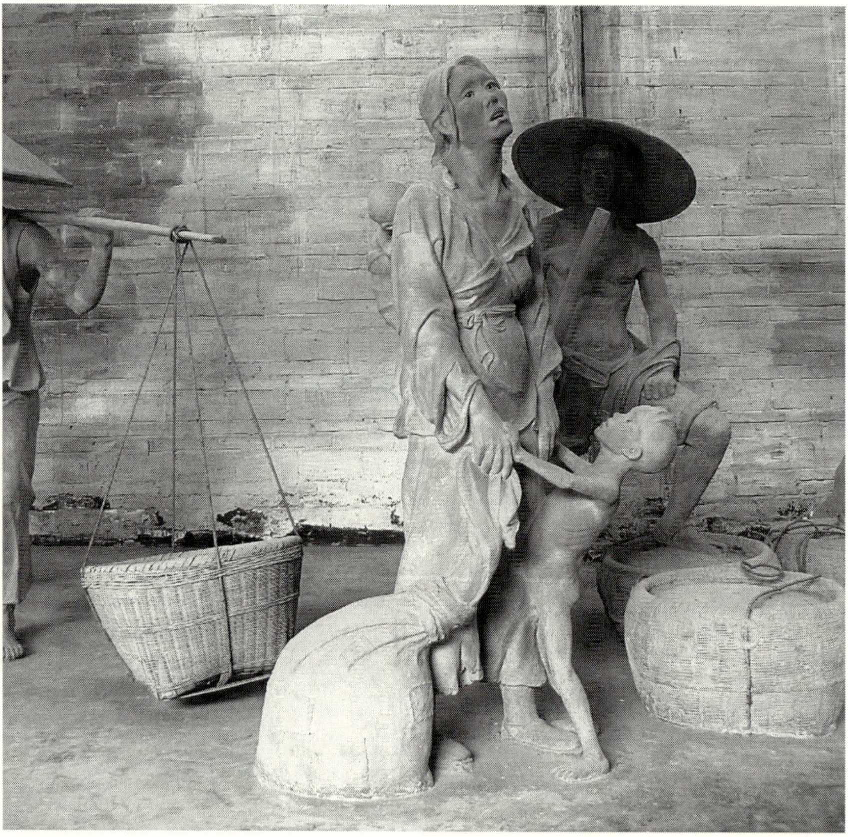

Figure 5.2 Team of sculptors, *Rent Collection Courtyard* (1965). Detail of Part 1: *Bringing the Rent.* Author photograph.

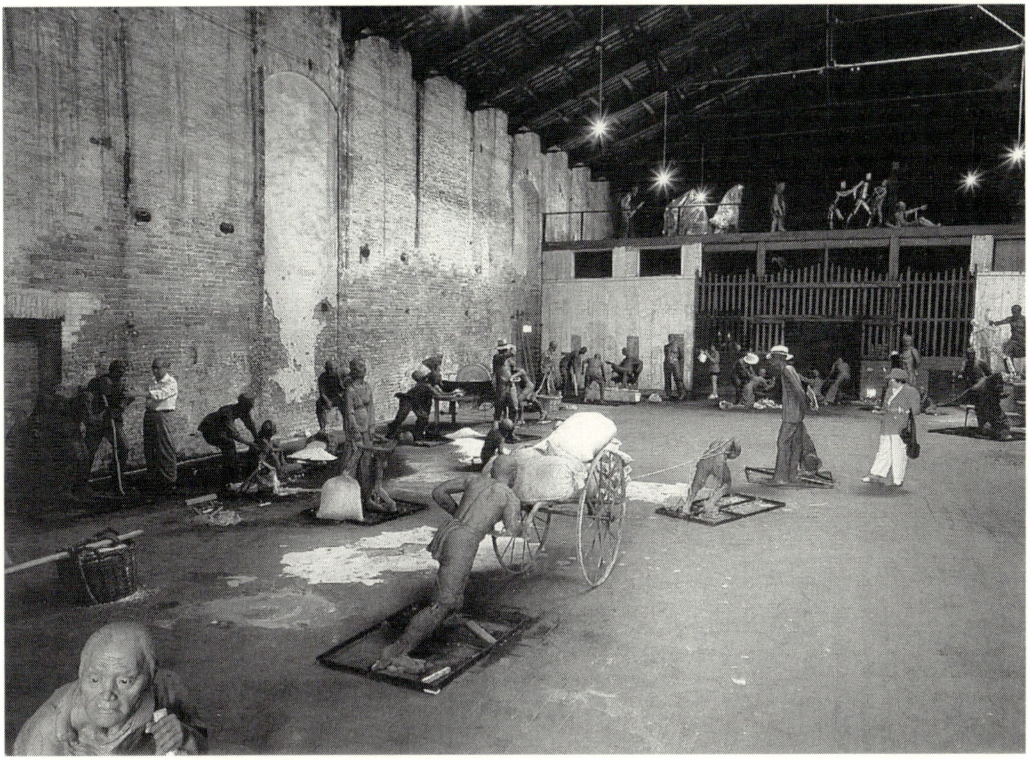

Figure 5.3 Cai Guo-Qiang, *Venice's Rent Collection Courtyard* (1999). Mixed media installation, overview, including *Bringing the Rent,* Arsenale, Venice Biennale, Venice. Photograph, Elio Montanari; courtesy of the artist.

in manufacturing the meaning of a work of art. Just as reception is of paramount importance for Cultural Revolution works, so, too, is reception a key component in the creation of contemporary conceptual art. The difference is that, in China during the 1960s and 1970s, the mode of reception was mandated, but in the late 1990s and beyond, in China and beyond, audience reaction is unconstrained.

Reception was a primary consideration in creating works of art during the Cultural Revolution. It was not enough to produce something attractive or compelling: art was required to serve a higher purpose, acting on the minds of viewers to improve their revolutionary consciousness in some way. As the only sculpture to earn Jiang Qing's highest approval, identified by her as early as February 1966 as a "model" for artists, the *Rent Collection Courtyard* clearly fulfilled this goal.[2]

Ironically, for a work ostensibly representing an extremely well-defined subject, the *Rent Collection Courtyard* and its most recent reproduction have proven fertile soil for an extraordinary array of projected meanings. Clearly, a large-scale publicly exhibited work of art is not solely a work of art: it is also an opportunity for the generation and propagation of rhetoric. From the beginning, the rhetoric around the *Rent Collection Courtyard* has played a role in creating the wider meaning of the piece.

The first definitive version of this set of sculptures was completed in October 1965 at the Landlord's Courtyard of Oppression Exhibition Hall established in the mansion of a former landlord, Liu Wencai, in Anren Town, Dayi County, fifty-two kilometres west of Chengdu. This, the first set of sculptures to bear the title *Rent Collection Courtyard,* consists of a series of 114 life-sized clay figures arranged in tableaux in a courtyard. The landlord, standing with his back to the audience, dispassionately surveys an array of starving peasants unable to pay their rent, mothers carrying babies dressed in rags, and other pathetic figures illustrating the horrors of life under the former feudalistic society (Figure 5.4).

This 1965 version of the *Rent Collection Courtyard* is bracketed by a bewildering parade of both precursors and copies. Prior to exhibiting the 1965 version, the Landlord's Courtyard of Oppression Exhibition Hall had displayed several smaller, less complete sets of sculptures on a similar theme. The first, displayed in October 1960, was composed of life-sized sculpted figures constructed with a wooden interior framework, coloured wax hands, feet, and faces, and real clothes.[3] These were made by people from the exhibition hall's art department, working with local folk artists.[4] In January of the following year, a series of dioramas, *One Hundred Crimes,* composed of small clay (or plaster) figures and illustrating Liu Wencai's supposed crimes against the peasants, was put on display.[5] The dioramas were made by local elementary school teachers.[6] In 1963, a set of midsized figures on the same theme was created for the exhibition hall.[7] Later, the exhibition hall developed the idea of displaying objects employed in the oppression of the peasants (such as wheelbarrows and threshers) and finally arrived at the concept of a grand sculptural installation, integrating tools and life-sized clay sculptures, and arranged to tell the story of rent collection under the control of the feudal landlord Liu Wencai.[8] At this point, the exhibition hall decided to enlist the aid of professional sculptors from the Sichuan Arts Academy. From June to October 1965, workers from the two institutions cooperated to create the first definitive version of the *Rent Collection Courtyard,* constructing the figures with a wooden framework covered by layers

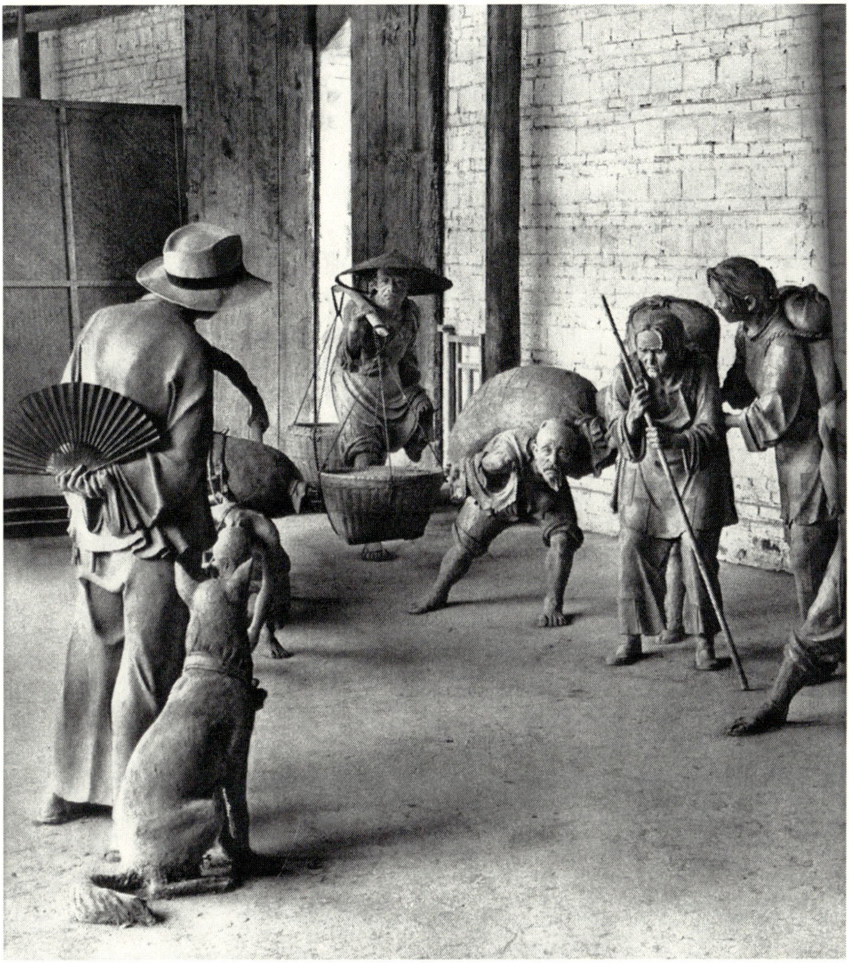

Figure 5.4 Team of sculptors, *Rent Collection Courtyard* (1965). Detail of Part 1: *Bringing the Rent*. The landlord holds a fan and stands with his back to the viewer. *Rent Collection Courtyard: Sculptures of Oppression and Revolt*, 2nd ed. (Beijing: Foreign Languages Press, 1970), n.p.

of straw, clay, and, for the outer layer, clay mixed with cotton; the eyes were made of glass.[9]

In December 1965, a partial copy (featuring more than forty figures) of the *Rent Collection Courtyard* was made in clay and exhibited at the National Art Gallery in Beijing.[10] Those working on this project included artists from the Central Academy of Fine Arts and the Beijing Architectural Artistic

Sculpture Factory, artists from Sichuan who had worked on the original, and others.[11] Because the enormous crowds coming to view the *Rent Collection Courtyard* (eight thousand visitors a day) overwhelmed the gallery, in September 1966 artists from the Central Academy of Fine Arts and the Central Academy of Arts and Crafts, together with Red Guards and three of the original artists, made a complete copy of the installation in clay, to be exhibited in a larger space in Beijing's Forbidden City.[12] Following the injunction of Jiang Qing's ally Kang Sheng that the installation should express a forceful sense of rebellion, the Red Guards made some changes, adding a scene of revolt and bringing the total number of figures to 119.[13] In many other cities, including Guangzhou, Shanghai, Wuhan, Xi'an, and Chongqing, artists created clay copies, working from photographs.[14] As the clay copies were too fragile to travel, in 1967 the China Cultural Development Committee ordered plaster copies to send overseas, made by artists from Beijing, Sichuan, and Shanghai.[15] The government sent a complete set to Albania and a partial set to North Vietnam, these two countries being deemed receptive to the sculpture's message.

Finally, between 1974 and 1978, a copper-plated fibreglass version of the *Rent Collection Courtyard* was created, intended to be even more durable than its plaster counterparts (Figure 5.5). Some of the artists who worked on the original, plus some amateur sculptors as well as students and teachers from the Sichuan Arts Academy Sculpture Department, also worked on this set of 114 figures.[16] In 1987, part of the fibreglass version was exhibited in Toronto and then in Japan.[17] Since it was first shown in China in October 2000, it has been housed in the Art Museum of the Sichuan Arts Academy.

Aside from the ubiquitous statues of Chairman Mao that appeared throughout China during the Cultural Revolution, no other sculpture approached the prominence of the *Rent Collection Courtyard.* As different versions and segments of the sculpture were sent around China and to other socialist countries, the rhetoric surrounding it snowballed. The work was promoted as fulfilling major goals outlined by Mao in his 1942 Yan'an Talks, which stated that art must be part of the revolutionary machine and that, in order for it to function thus, artists must solve the problems of their class stand, attitude, audience, work, and study.[18]

Fundamental to the swift acclaim accorded the *Rent Collection Courtyard* was the perceived attitude of the artists, a facade that had crumbled by 1999. Mao had said, "China's revolutionary writers and artists, writers and artists of promise, must go among the masses; they must for a long period of time unreservedly and wholeheartedly go among the masses of workers,

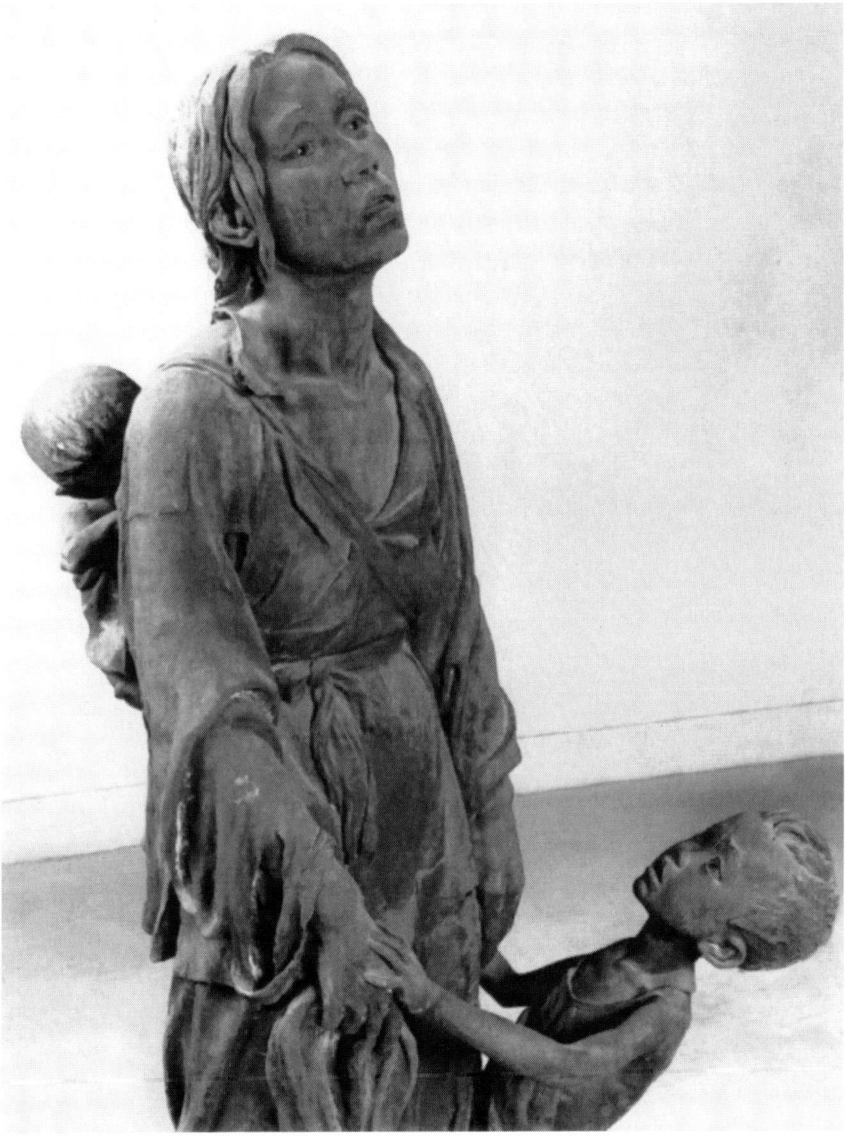

Figure 5.5 Team of sculptors, *Rent Collection Courtyard* (1974-78). Copper-plated fibreglass, detail of Part 1: *Bringing the Rent.* Fei Xinbei, "*Shou zu yuan" qundiao zuopin xuan* [Selected works of the group sculpture *"Rent Collection Courtyard"*] (Chongqing: Art Museum and Sichuan Fine Arts Institute, 2001), 3.

peasants, and soldiers, go into the heat of the struggle, go to the only source, the broadest and richest source, in order to observe, experience, study, and analyse all the different kinds of people, all the classes, all the masses, all the vivid patterns of life and struggle, all the raw materials of literature and art. Only then can they proceed to creative work."[19]

In ideological accord with Mao's pronouncement, a 1967 supplement to the English-language Chinese magazine *China Reconstructs,* called "Rent Collection Courtyard: A Revolution in Sculpture," stated that

> The artists resolutely followed Chairman Mao's instruction that writers and artists must integrate themselves with the workers, peasants, and soldiers and learn from them. They lived and worked in the courtyard where rent had been collected. They created the entire group of figures right among the former tenants of Liu Wencai, now commune members in the neighborhood. The artists first became modest pupils of these former poor and lower-middle peasants, listening attentively to their past sufferings and struggles and consciously trying to learn their noble revolutionary qualities ... Only in this way could they have created works with such strong class feeling.[20]

The artists are described as members of an anonymous team, their identities subsumed within the collective. The *China Reconstructs* supplement, likewise authorless, names none of the artists, merely remarking that "the work was created collectively by eighteen amateur and professional sculptors of Sichuan Province."[21] Similarly, a booklet published on the occasion of a Guangzhou exhibition of a copy of the *Rent Collection Courtyard* names no individual artist involved in producing the sculpture; the booklet itself has no author.[22] In recent years, this cherished anonymity is one of the most significant aspects of the work's public relations facade to fall apart. Details of who created the different versions, and under what circumstances, have become widely available only since the controversy over Cai Guo-Qiang's *Venice's Rent Collection Courtyard.*

At Yan'an (the Chinese communists' wartime headquarters), Mao had called on artists to "conscientiously learn the language of the masses," so that they could work in a language readily comprehensible to the masses while simultaneously raising standards.[23] As he encouraged artists not to be bound by the past, he also told them not to "reject the legacies of the ancients and the foreigners or refuse to learn from them, even though they are the works of the feudal or bourgeois classes."[24] Combining these desiderata, the *Rent Collection Courtyard* artists

> cast aside the rules and conventions followed in making statues with plaster, marble, granite or bronze, and critically adopted the traditional techniques of making clay figures loved by the common folk in China ... The use of black glass for eyes and the treatment of some of the drapery also come from this tradition. On the other hand, they critically took over some of the modern carving techniques that give these figures a greater realism than the ancient clay figures. Their experience serves as an example for other artists in making the past serve the present, making what is foreign serve China.[25]

The *Rent Collection Courtyard* was further praised for epitomizing the socialist-realist mode. Works in this style have the predetermined goal of presenting not everyday reality, but rather reality in a higher and more universal form. The *Rent Collection Courtyard* was billed as showing "the contradiction not only between one landlord and his own tenants but between the landlord class and all peasants."[26] The ultimate achievement of the piece is that it could "play an important role in the socialist education of the viewers, who are reminded never to forget that class enemies still exist and that they must never forget the class struggle."[27] So successful was it in this educational role that it was memorialized in a 1973 poster of *Childhood,* a painting by Jia Xingdong, in which it is viewed by crowds of children. Comments from the public were collected by means of visitors' books and interviews at exhibition sites. The comments cited tend to be either distraught memories of the bad life before the revolution or affirmations of the sculpture's effectiveness in illustrating the righteousness of the revolution. Either way, they confirm the *Rent Collection Courtyard* in its role as an educational tool.

In sum, the *Rent Collection Courtyard* was designated a model sculpture not primarily because of the finished product, but more importantly for the process of its creation and for the interpretive opportunities it subsequently presented. The fact of its existence as a collection of clay (or fibreglass) figures did not suffice for the role of model sculpture.

Following on the success of the *Rent Collection Courtyard,* other socialist-realist sculptural installations were created, featuring life-sized figures in a series of tableaux beginning with scenes of oppression and building to righteous anger and revolt. Such projects include *The Wrath of the Serfs* (1976 or earlier) in the Tibet Museum of Revolution in Lhasa and a series of tableaux at the Three Stones Museum in Tianjin.[28] Both projects had a concrete political objective originating in Beijing. *The Wrath of the Serfs,* created by teachers from the May Seventh College of the Arts in Beijing working with Tibetan artists, consisted of 106 figures portraying the evils of the feudal society in Tibet, billing the Dalai Lama as a despicable land- and slave-owner, and featuring gory scenes of human sacrifice and mutilation.[29] Obviously, the sculptures were intended to justify China's occupation of Tibet by discrediting the previous rulers.

The Three Stones Museum sculptures were designed to meet the needs of Chairman Mao and his closest allies in the shifting factional politics of the early part of the Cultural Revolution. During the mid-1960s, Mao and Vice-Chairman Lin Biao sought to purge the government of moderates and to reassert revolutionary socialist principles. Targeting President Liu Shaoqi as the "number one capitalist-roader," they found an opportunity in Tianjin to equate Liu's policies with capitalist exploitation of workers. In the first half of the twentieth century, Tianjin's Three Stones Street was lined with workshops processing iron. Supposedly as early as 1958, workers established the Three Stones Museum there to memorialize the harsh conditions endured by pre-revolution workers, many of whom were child "bond slaves." In April 1968, Mao and Lin Biao sent People's Liberation Army men to the Three Stones Museum to assist workers in remodelling the museum. In studying Mao's works as a preparatory step for remodelling, the museum workers found it necessary to "wage scathing revolutionary mass criticism of the renegade, hidden traitor and scab Liu Shaoqi's sinister fallacies such as 'exploitation has its merits' and the 'dying out of class struggle.'"[30] The Three Stones Museum was considered an effective site to promote anti–Liu Shaoqi sentiment because of its association with Zhou Yang, who had been a leading figure in cultural and propaganda policy during the 1950s and early 1960s, and was another prominent casualty of the early months of the Cultural Revolution. "At the prompting of the arch-renegade Liu Shaoqi," it was reported, Zhou Yang had "paid several visits to the museum to disrupt it by changing its contents in collaboration with the capitalist-roaders in Tianjin. They attempted to reverse the history of blood and tears and the history of struggle of the Three Stones workers into a tale of how the bourgeoisie had made their fortunes. They prettified the capitalists' course of accumulating wealth through exploitation as achieving prosperity 'through thrift, diligence, and labour,' energetically trumpeting Liu Shaoqi's counter-revolutionary fallacies of 'exploitation has its merits; exploitation is justified' and the like."[31]

Because professional artists were not involved in creating the Three Stones Museum sculptures, their quality was not high; what made them briefly noteworthy was their use as a device to raise political consciousness. The *Rent Collection Courtyard* sculptures were of higher artistic quality and enjoyed wider and longer-lasting fame; however, until Cai Guo-Qiang produced his *Venice's Rent Collection Courtyard,* they too had faded into relative obscurity, taking a place in the history books as representative works of a discredited era of politicized art.

In early 1999, Cai Guo-Qiang commenced work on a reproduction of the *Rent Collection Courtyard* for exhibition at the Venice Biennale. Harald Szeemann, the curator of the exhibition, had long been fascinated by the original *Rent Collection Courtyard:* over twenty-five years before, he had invited China to send it to Europe for inclusion in the 1972 Documenta exhibition in Kassel. Jiang Qing did not deign to respond to the invitation. In preparing for the forty-eighth Venice Biennale, Szeemann reportedly discussed with Cai Guo-Qiang his idea of bringing the *Rent Collection Courtyard* to Europe, planting the idea of recreating the sculpture in Venice.

Directing a crew of Chinese sculptors, one of whom, Long Xuli, had worked on the original *Rent Collection Courtyard,* Cai filled an enormous room in Venice's Arsenale with the activity of recreating the original installation: he emphasized the process of replication rather than the finished product. Visitors to the exhibition saw the sculptors at work, constantly referring to photographs of the 1967 plaster version of the original. They built wire frameworks for most of the figures but completed less than half, filling out the forms with the addition of clay and glass eyes. Cai's installation was awarded the International Golden Lion Prize at the Venice Biennale.

Although both the original and Cai's reproduction received high praise, and the individual figures in the two versions are quite similar, a vast chasm separates the meanings of the two sets of sculptures. The Cultural Revolution *Rent Collection Courtyard* was meant to endure as an educational tool, reminding people of the dismal life under feudalism, acting as a catalyst for people to "speak bitterness," and inspiring revolutionary consciousness. Cai Guo-Qiang co-opted the socialist-realist style for the entertainment of the non-proletarian classes that the original denigrated. Indeed, a visitor to the exhibition, photographed by chance, bore an uncanny resemblance to the landlord (Figure 5.6). The meanings originally accruing to Cai's work include a reading of it as metaphor for the futility of human endeavour, as the clay figures were to be allowed to dry and crumble, falling back into dust.[32] The crumbling sculptures could also imply the failed promise of socialism in China. The awards committee praised the work as questioning the history, function, and the epic of art through temporal and physical contextual isolation. In sardonic response, the Chinese conceptual artist Song Dong created for Cai the Award for Winning Without Making an

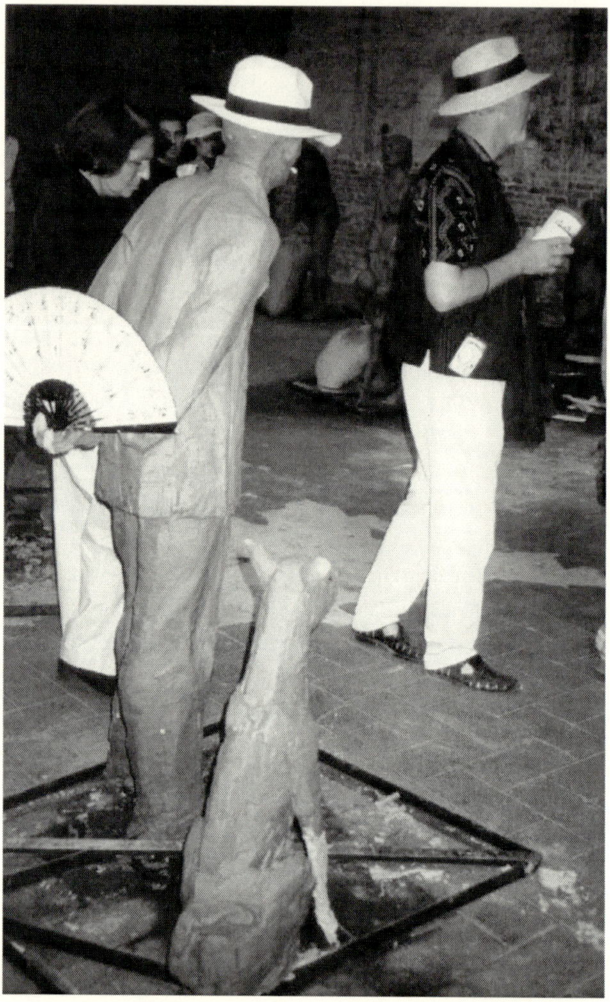

Figure 5.6 Cai Guo-Qiang, *Venice's Rent Collection Courtyard* (1999). Detail of landlord. Author photograph.

Effort, calling it the first award for the original *Rent Collection Courtyard* and posting it on the Internet.

In the months following the opening of the 1999 Venice Biennale, the acclaim Cai Guo-Qiang won with *Venice's Rent Collection Courtyard,* not to mention the prize, acted as a lightning rod for disaffected artists and others in Sichuan and elsewhere in China. Nationalistic resentment compelled

Chinese critics to analyze *Venice's Rent Collection Courtyard* in terms of neo-colonialism. Daozi, a particularly nationalistic art critic from the Sichuan Arts Academy, accused Cai of being a "banana man" (someone who is yellow, or Asian, on the outside and white on the inside) and "using the approaches of postmodern art and his privileges as a green-card artist to ingeniously violate copyright law."[33] Cai, concerned about the vitriol, presented a résumé of his work outside the Shanghai Art Museum, as part of the 2000 Shanghai Biennale. Speaking subsequently to a blasé audience at the 2000 Shanghai Biennale seminar, the critic Wang Nanming declared that "the symbols employed by overseas Chinese artists, including Cai Guo-Qiang, have nothing whatsoever to do with breathing life into today's culture." Furthermore, "by appropriating simple motifs or symbols left behind by tradition, they formulate them into the 'essence' or mark of being Chinese. Such artists strategically seek to carve out a niche in which to survive within the order of the dominant race."[34]

Such nationalistic sentiment, directed against a Chinese artist who, having emigrated, becomes more famous than most of his fellow artists in China, is part of a broader nationalism that includes resentment concerning repeated US attempts to coerce China into upholding international copyright law in regard to computer programs and movies on CD, cheap reproductions of which are readily available on the street in China. The artists who worked on the original *Rent Collection Courtyard* demanded that their work be acknowledged. Factions in Dayi and Chongqing argued over who had produced the authentic original. The Sichuan Arts Academy announced that it would sue Cai for copyright infringement. In Sichuan and Beijing, scholars and critics organized seminars to debate the merits of the lawsuit. The website Tom.com, known for its arts coverage, closely followed the debate, posting scores of letters and documents, including Cai Guo-Qiang's résumé and images of his more important works.[35]

In May 2000, the Sichuan Arts Academy issued a press release declaring its intention to take legal action over copyright infringement: "In as much as China is a signatory member of the Berne Convention, the Sichuan Arts Academy, together with some of the original authors of the work are now filing a lawsuit against the Venice Biennale exhibition, its curator Harald Szeemann, and the artist Cai Guo-Qiang."[36] Working pro bono, the law firm involved, a subsidiary of Xinan Law University, was eager to press forward, seeing an opportunity to gain publicity in the relatively new fields of art law and copyright law; ultimately, however, as the academy concluded, the lawsuit was unfounded.

China's copyright law, passed in 1990, states that a person who creates a work of art owns its copyright. If the work is commissioned, the commissioning party gains the copyright only if this is specified in a contract; otherwise, the copyright remains with the author of the work.[37] The law specifies that "producing or selling a work of fine art where the signature of an artist is counterfeited" infringes copyright law. If the forgery of the signature is done for profit, punishment can include fines and three to seven years in prison.[38]

But most interesting is that, against this vitriolic background, arguments arose over authorship of the original *Rent Collection Courtyard,* including the question of which version counted as the definitive finished product. The Sichuan Arts Academy, in its lawsuit press release, stated, "Using clay for the Dayi Landlord's Courtyard version in 1965 and fibreglass in 1974 – for a reproduction intended for international exhibitions and now part of the Sichuan Arts Academy's Collection – the Academy formed the central force in the collective creation of both projects."[39] In support of its copyright ownership, the academy cited the fact that, in 1974, it had received over 300,000 *yuan* from the Sichuan government to create a better-quality and more durable fibreglass copy that would be available for travel. Following the academy's lawsuit announcement, the museum in Dayi declared the *Rent Collection Courtyard* to be its property and asked the National Copyright Bureau to make a judgment, vowing to take up the lawsuit against Cai if the judgment were in its favour. Meanwhile, documents have been published naming the artists who worked on each version and specifying their status. One of them, Wang Guanyi, wrote a detailed history of the production of the sculpture, and Tom.com published a survey of his career, as if to affirm his worth as an artist and to allow readers to compare his career with that of Cai.[40]

Thus, as Cai was threatened with a lawsuit, the original *Rent Collection Courtyard* became a symbol for forces of China's new nationalism. It also became a focus for individual bids for power and recognition, its authorship hotly contested by both the institutions and individuals involved. If we accept that much of the *Rent Collection Courtyard*'s meaning during the Cultural Revolution was not intrinsic to the work of art, but rather derived from the massive campaigns of political rhetoric surrounding it, how shall we read that piece in the year 2002, when that rhetoric was replaced by new commercialization or nationalism, or otherwise rendered questionable?

Most ironic is the fact that Cai Guo-Qiang's stance more accurately reflects the Cultural Revolution belief that "rebellion is justified" *(zaofan you li)* than does the position of his critics in China, who would jealously guard rights to the work. In recreating the *Rent Collection Courtyard,* Cai actively deconstructed what had been a major Chinese cultural icon, exploring its long uncontested institutionalized meaning while taunting the Western art establishment with a blatant affirmation of the West's preference for Chinese art that "looks Chinese." Times change and audiences change. The question remains, does the work of art change?

6

Hu Xian Peasant Painting: From Revolutionary Icon to Market Commodity

Ralph Croizier

Hu Xian peasant painting was one of the most famous cultural products of the Cultural Revolution; it is also one of the most successful art commodities of the post-Mao new economic era. This chapter will explore how an art form born out of socialist revolutionary fervour became part of a capitalist market economy.

It discusses folk art and politics, ideology and revolution, tradition and commercialization. In some ways, Hu Xian becomes a microcosm of what has happened to the Chinese revolution over the last four decades, touching on broad issues and art's connections to social change, commercialization, and local or national identity in the modern world. But the focus is on one particular rural locale in China, on one extraordinary experiment in mobilizing art from the masses and its ironic results.

The story of Hu Xian peasant painting is best told historically – that is, chronologically. Therefore, we start at the beginning.

Pre-Cultural Revolution Background

Contrary to popular perception, that beginning is not to be found in the Cultural Revolution, although the painters from Hu Xian, a farming district in the Wei River Valley some forty kilometres from the Shaanxi provincial capital of Xi'an, achieved national and international fame during that period. Peasant painting started with the other quintessentially Maoist undertaking, the Great Leap Forward, at the end of the 1950s. That most frantic of mass movements, though centred on production, was an appropriate matrix for a new peasant art because it concentrated on the countryside, and it emphasized popular enthusiasm and the creative power of the masses.

With the nationwide mobilization of peasant labour-power for socialist construction and the formal proclamation of the People's Communes in the summer of 1958, reports of rural production miracles in the cultural sphere, delivered most notably via wall slogans, verses, and paintings, began to appear along with the spectacular figures for grain and backyard steel.[1] The relationship between mass spontaneity and guidance from above is both interesting and important for the subsequent development of peasant painting in the Cultural Revolution era. In its earliest stage, the highly politicized new village art, especially the wall paintings, appears to have been executed mainly by "sent-down" professional artists as part of the popularization and politicization of art following the Anti-rightist Campaign.[2] As the Great Leap's populist fervour mounted, more attention was focused on the creative efforts of the peasant masses themselves; the help they received from professional artists was downplayed, if not ignored.

The party's propaganda line, and the Maoist ideological imperative behind it, claimed that mass enthusiasm released and guided, though not controlled, by the party was the key to instantaneous socialist transformation of the countryside, culturally as well as economically. In a broader sense, it went beyond the particularly Maoist version of building socialism and harked back to Karl Marx's vision in which socialism could unlock the full range of human potential, so that the complete human being would engage in cultural and intellectual, as well as material, production.[3] This humanistic and utopian philosophy might seem a long way removed from the feverish attempts to raise the economic level of the material "forces of production" in China's vast rural hinterland, but Marx looms in the background for the Chinese revolutionaries who saw peasant cultural creation as an asset, not a distraction, for economic construction. Once in power, socialist revolutionaries face the problem of creating a new class art that is not only for the people, but from and by the people. In China, given the country's demographics and the rural history of the revolution, the "people" meant the peasants. The economic catastrophes from the Great Leap Forward's ill-conceived economic measures soon directed attention away from peasant cultural activities and all such utopian visions, but the first faltering steps for encouraging an art by and for the people were taken in the late 1950s. For China, where, more than in most societies, mastery of the writing/painting brush, and thus monopoly of literary/cultural production, had demarcated the basic line between classes, putting brushes in the hands of peasants had truly revolutionary implications. Those implications were crushed in the collapse of the Great Leap Forward, but they would be drawn out more explicitly in Mao's next great revolutionary experiment, the Cultural Revolution.

In 1958, national publicity focused on places such as Pi Xian in northern Jiangsu, or Shu Lu and Chang Li in Hebei, where the initial emphasis on wall painting soon spread to other more portable forms of picture production that could be more widely disseminated and brought to Beijing for exhibition.[4] Even sympathetic commentators at the time noted the crude simplicity of this art, while praising the political enthusiasm behind it. Most of it was indeed crude by any artistic standards, showing lack of preparation in either formal academic or folk art traditions, although certain examples revealed that peasant artists had assimilated some of the techniques of realistic representation that were the favoured style in China's official art system. Mixed with some folk motifs and massive doses of socialist politics, it flourished briefly, generating astounding statistics on quantity of production, but then disappeared almost as completely as the useless pig-iron from backyard steel furnaces when the Great Leap's radical populist line was reversed in the early 1960s.

Hu Xian was at the periphery of this national campaign, provincially significant as one of the more successful localities in Shaanxi Province but not given national publicity. Fortunately, its later prominence created a fuller record for this one *xian* (district, or county) than for any other locale. Those sources show how national and provincial politics interacted with local traditions and local priorities to create a movement that would decline, but not die out, during the 1960s, thus sowing the seeds for its spectacular growth in the 1970s.[5]

The beginnings were quite humble. In 1958, a young graduate from the Xi'an Provincial Art Academy, Chen Shiheng, was sent to the countryside in order to teach the rudiments of drawing and painting to peasants engaged in the zeal of the Great Leap Forward. This was common practice in art academies across China at the time. Apparently, the senior faculty and famous artists escaped the rigours of this Maoist ritual. At first, Chen Shiheng was a self-styled "wandering art peddler" trying to find a district where local cadres would accept his services and, even for brief part-time study, direct some peasants away from the pell-mell construction efforts of the Great Leap. He finally convinced the Hu Xian District leadership to let him teach a class of peasants assembled at one of the district's "backyard steel furnaces."[6] It may have helped, and indicated local interest in promoting peasant art, that a cultural centre *(meishuguan)* already existed there.

From 4 November to 3 December, Chen conducted night classes under the most primitive conditions and with a minimum of supplies. Not surprisingly, given the frantic work pace of the Great Leap Forward, most of his students could not attend class regularly, and he had to make the rounds to their houses and workplaces. Even then, only seven of the original forty finished the "course," and once he left, these too gave up painting. There could hardly have been a more unpromising beginning, although the fact that exhausted peasants showed any interest at all might be an indication of latent potential.

The will to continue the experiment came from above. The Shaanxi Provincial Cultural Bureau took some of the works produced at this initial class for an exhibition of Great Leap Forward art in Xi'an. More importantly, the Hu Xian Party Committee, with much help from the Provincial Art Academy, decided to found a temporary Hu Xian Peasant Art School. In line with the part-work, part-study principle of integrating manual labour and cultural production, it was located where a large number of peasants were gathered, at the Gan Yu reservoir project. The reservoir, built where the Qin Ling Mountains reach the Wei River plains, was one of the lasting accomplishments of the Great Leap Forward. No useless steel or wasted labour there. Similarly, the modest school, first opened in a cowshed, laid a lasting legacy for Hu Xian. It started on 20 December and lasted for eighty-eight days, with the peasants mobilized for reservoir construction participating on a time basis of one-third labour, two-thirds study – not exactly "spare-time" painting. The school was designed to have professional art teachers train a core of peasant painters who could spread the activity throughout the district. For that purpose, district- and commune-level party leadership was willing to spare a modest amount of labour-power, twenty-seven workers from the almost finished reservoir project. When major construction ended at the reservoir site in February, the school moved from the mountains to the Xi'an Cultural Centre in the district seat, closing with an exhibition there.

Some of these early works are preserved in the History Gallery of the Hu Xian Peasant Painting Exhibition Hall, built in Hu Xian County Centre during the mid-1970s.

After the exhibition, the new painters were sent to organize small groups at the "lower level" in the villages, and a Hu Xian Peasant Painters Association was established with district government support. By later Hu Xian peasant-painting standards, the works produced were rather crude or cartoon-like, although some showed clear evidence of formal art training. One interesting example, unpublished but surviving in the collection of the Hu Xian Peasant Painting Exhibition Hall, is a painting of the reservoir site itself. Some of the figures are crudely drawn, and the fixed-point perspective is not altogether convincing, but it is far removed from the flat surface, bright colours, and fully filled composition of traditional folk art. The recession into space, the clearly defined horizon line, and the well-executed texture strokes on the foreground rock face are all signs of help from an artist trained in both modern Western academic and traditional Chinese landscape art, which Chen Shiheng was. How much of this early work came from his hand is impossible to know, but it is worth noting that several of the celebrated peasant painters from the Cultural Revolution years, including the "model female poor peasant painter" Li Fenglan, got their start in this first class.

The Great Leap Forward was over by 1961, and for the next "three bad years" of economic hardship and political restraint, peasant painting in the rest of China went the way of backyard steel furnaces and communal kitchens, abandoned as a failed experiment in rural communism. Why did it survive in Hu Xian?

First, the flat assertion that all the initiatives in teaching peasants to paint had been stillborn needs some qualification.[7] As the economy recovered by the mid-1960s, there were scattered notices of continuing or revived peasant painting from various parts of China, although the exaggerated political and cultural claims of the Great Leap Forward years had disappeared. In Hu Xian, a lull in art activities appears to have occurred during the worst of the recovery, but by 1963, peasant painters were playing a prominent role in the resurgence of political activity associated with the Socialist Education Movement. Training classes were reopened, exhibitions, and even travelling slide shows, were held at the village level as well as in the district centre, and the local authorities convened a number of discussion sessions to share experience and spread the movement. The number of peasant painters grew significantly, with some of the most famous practitioners of the Cultural Revolution era getting their start in these years, although the explosion of numbers waited until the next decade.

What accounts for the survival, or revival, of peasant art in Hu Xian, when it lay moribund in most of rural China during the early 1960s? It has been suggested that the local folk art traditions of Hu Xian, a district in the cultural heartland of imperial China, provided a particularly rich matrix for a new peasant art. This is, at most, part of the story. Folk arts were practised locally: embroidery, paper-cuts, and decorative painting on wooden trousseau boxes. Equally important for the peasants' visual imagery were the ubiquitous New Year's pictures *(nian hua),* although they were not produced locally and had come under increasing pressure to reform their "feudal content."[8] So a reservoir of indigenous skills and imagery did exist in Hu Xian. Nevertheless, compared to other regions, Hu Xian was not particularly rich in folk art traditions, and there was no thriving industry using folk designs as in some of the textile districts of the lower Yangtze Valley. Moreover, the party did not want the new painting to perpetuate folk styles and "backward" ideas. It was to be a new art for a new era. Even if folk spirit and naive enthusiasm were still engaged, the instructors were to teach the peasants "correct scientific" techniques, not folk conventions. The native soil of folk tradition was not irrelevant to the growth of this political transplant, especially in the long run, but it was not the main determinant of Hu Xian's success. That came from the party and from politics.

What made Hu Xian different from most other rural districts was the local party leadership's mobilization of peasant painters to push the Socialist Education Campaign. In particular, they played a key role in the three histories *(san shi)* movement, illustrating the superiority of socialism by drawing on family history, village history, and commune history. The overall ideological point was to recall the bitterness of past life compared to the happy present. It was during this period that the hard core *(gu gan)* of peasant painters was built up that would expand so spectacularly in the later stages of the Cultural Revolution. A sympathetic left-leaning report from the 1980s is essentially correct about the indispensable role of local party leadership: "If there had not been the direct participation of Communist Party secretaries, it would have been difficult for peasant painting to develop. The accomplishments of the peasant painters are inseparable from the warm encouragement of basic-level party organizations."[9] Put simply, the new political campaign in 1963-64 came from party centre, or more precisely, from Mao himself, but special encouragement of peasant painting in that campaign was a local party initiative.

Hu Xian as National Model: The Cultural Revolution, 1966-76

As the leftist tide rose during the prelude to the Cultural Revolution, especially in cultural matters, Hu Xian peasant painters started to transcend the local scene. First, their works were shown at the provincial level and then in Beijing, where they were featured at the "Beijing Asia-Africa Authors' Conference" in January 1966 before bursting onto the exploding political scene in July with a full-page article in *People's Daily (Renmin ribao)* titled "Peasants' Revolutionary Paintings." The national political battles were directly joined to this "unprecedented new art movement inspired by the thought of Mao Zedong" by using it as a vehicle to denounce "bourgeois authorities" for looking down on this new art as "simple," "low class," and "crude."[10] In the two-line struggle (between "Mao Zedong's revolutionary line" and the "revisionist counter-revolutionary line of capitalist restorationists") the peasant painters were putting "art in the service of proletarian politics." The pictures, all of political activity and class struggle, affirmed that role.

Hu Xian peasant painting was thus linked to the Cultural Revolution's political goals right from the start, but the ensuing radical phase of the Cultural Revolution was not conducive to any kind of organized cultural activity. The press forgot about peasant painting for the next few years as organized art activities almost disappeared, with government and party organs initially paralyzed at all levels by the political chaos of the late 1960s. Later official accounts are rather reticent about this period, and Chinese art critics and historians have generally avoided it as still being too hot.[11]

Whatever spontaneous radical activity had erupted then, it left no traces in the official record or in the galleries of the soon-to-be-built Hu Xian Peasant Painting Exhibition Hall. Leftist politics would play a major role in the next phase of Hu Xian peasant painting, but they would be of a more controlled, even manipulative nature – and they would lift this modest-sized *xian* into national and international prominence.

The records of the Cultural Affairs Group in Beijing (the Cultural Revolution replacement for the Ministry of Culture) are not as available as the local records in Hu Xian, so it is impossible to know exactly who at the centre, at what time, decided to resurrect peasant painting as a centrepiece for national art politics. But the general picture is as clear as one of the bright and shiny peasant paintings itself.

By the early 1970s, the newly ascendant leftists in Beijing needed a positive example of Maoist mass cultural production to turn back attempts to restore more conventional ("elitist or bourgeois") educational and cultural policies advocated by moderate political leaders. This deepened into a fiercer, though still coded, struggle for power after the fall of Lin Biao, with the left using the cultural field to promote its radical policies and discredit its "revisionist" opponents. The Criticizing Lin Biao and Confucius movement launched in late 1973 was intended simultaneously to dissociate itself and the Cultural Revolution from the disgraced Lin Biao and oppose restoration of pre–Cultural Revolution policies by moderates under the leadership of Premier Zhou Enlai. Zhou's patronage of the so-called Hotel School, in which famous traditional ink painters decorated hotels and public buildings, drew political attention to the visual arts, which until then had been secondary to Jiang Qing's revolutionary operas and other innovations in the performing arts. This was not the whole story of the early and mid-1970s art wars, but peasant painting provided a perfect alternative to these elitist traditional-style paintings. Not coincidently, Hu Xian's propaganda value shot up as the two-line struggle spread to the visual arts after 1972.

We have traced the pedigree of Hu Xian peasant painting that fitted it for this role in national cultural politics. The immediate local impetus for peasant painting's new national prominence lay in the revival of local training classes by 1970, with renewed recognition and support from the Shaanxi provincial leadership, now functioning again after the disruptions of the Red Guard era. Just as important was the coming to artistic maturity of the cohort of peasant painters trained in and after the Great Leap Forward. Very soon, in the early 1970s, these painters would receive quantities of outside professional help far exceeding anything offered during the Great Leap Forward.

In September 1972, two exemplary peasant painters – Liu Zhide and Li Fenglan – were the first ones from Hu Xian to be brought to the capital, where they attended a conference held in conjunction with the first national art exhibition since the onset of the Cultural Revolution. Li Fenglan's works were included in the exhibition. The next month, Beijing's People's Art Publicity House published its first rather modest album of Hu Xian peasant paintings. Much more lavish publications, and publicity, would soon follow.

As another sign that buttons had been pushed in Beijing, immediately after the 1972 national exhibition, art teachers started pouring into Hu Xian in what was called a Double Uniting (Shuangjiehe) campaign. They came not just from nearby Xi'an, but from Beijing as well, and included such administrative art world big shots as Li Songtao, head of the National Art Gallery in Beijing, Zhang Qiuyuan, party secretary of the Central Academy of Fine Arts, and Gu Yuan, the newly installed head of the academy. Rural Hu Xian warranted more than newly graduated art students now: it had become a proving ground for ideological fitness to lead China's new art world.

Understandably, painting production in Hu Xian shot up in quality, or at least in sophistication of artistic design and draftsmanship, as well as in quantity. By October of 1972, the peasant painters were ready for a large-scale national exhibition at the National Art Gallery, occupying the entire second floor of the newly refurbished building, with a total of 318 works.[12] This was followed by massive publicity in newspapers and magazines, special edition postage stamps, a forty-minute documentary film, and a national tour of eight principal cities, with various regional art publishing houses basing next year's New Year's pictures *(nian hua)* on Hu Xian peasant paintings.

Hu Xian had arrived at the centre of national art and politics, but its appeal expanded beyond the national. Reports of the exhibition commented at great length on the many foreign visitors, over 150 from thirty different countries, and how impressed they were by this proof of the people's artistic talent and zeal. This eagerness for foreign approbation seems rather odd, if we accept the view that the Cultural Revolution and the much-touted national policy of self-reliance *(zili geng sheng)* represented a go-it-alone, turn-your-back-on-the-world spirit. Certainly, China was diplomatically isolated in the early 1970s, but supposedly the world's people were on the side of the Chinese revolution. Then there would be the tentative opening to the capitalist West, with Richard Nixon's visit in 1973 and the carefully controlled stream of foreign visitors that followed. As we have seen, this foreign-policy-determined tourism had repercussions in the art world, with the leftist attack on the Hotel School and a renewed push for Jiang Qing's "three prominences" *(san tuchu)* in painting. Hu Xian peasant painting already gave prominence to the first one, "positive characters." That would be themselves, the industrious socialist peasants who, with some tutoring, could put the spotlight on the second and third prominences, the political activists who carried out Chairman Mao's revolutionary line. The third prominence, "the most heroic character," was perhaps Mao himself or the martyrs to the revolutionary cause. Instead of showing foreign guests old-style "black" landscapes, how much better to let them see real people's art showing the new face of China! Soon after the exhibition in Beijing, groups of foreign visitors started to be taken to Hu Xian.

Partly in order to accommodate and impress them, the district, with outside government support, built a massive Soviet-style neo-classical art gallery on Exhibition Hall Street in the town centre. Started in 1975, it was finished in time for the end of the Cultural Revolution, although visitors eager to see the "real China" outside of the major cities continued to flock there for the next several years. From 1972 to 1983, over thirteen thousand foreigners visited Hu Xian, an easy day trip from Xi'an. Among them were several film crews making documentaries on peasant painting.[13] In the eighties, the tourist flow dropped off, but by then the peasant paintings had served their international function of publicizing Cultural Revolution achievements and, contrary to original intentions, of reintroducing the world to China and peasant China to the world.

That process worked in two ways. Tourists came to Hu Xian; Hu Xian paintings, and a few of the painters, went to foreign countries. It started correctly enough, ideologically, with trips to North Vietnam in 1973 and Albania in 1974. The next year, paintings, but not painters, went to Paris for the 1975 Biennale as China started to showcase the peasant paintings in the West. Back home, the Chinese people could be informed that an unidentified "French reporter" had commented, "After seeing other entries one had the feeling that painting was dead and the only really living painting is in People's China."[14] By 1976-77, exhibitions were travelling to a number of cities in Western Europe and Australia. Finally, going where no peasant painter could have imagined a few years before, a delegation arrived in Washington DC to kick off a twelve-month tour of major American cities. Other paintings went to Europe and, by 1980, even to such far-flung outposts of Western civilization as Victoria, British Columbia.

This foreign dimension to the Hu Xian story is important for China's international relations in the 1970s, but the main plot was still China-centred. We can read the paintings from these years in several ways: by looking at what the critics and publicists said about them at the time (repetitive and ideological though their comments are, they highlight the political agenda); by reading what they said later when the politics of the Cultural Revolution had been rejected, and everything associated with it was suspect; and by looking at the paintings themselves.

We take the contemporary (un)critical discourse first. By 1973, a major propaganda campaign was under way, with all the national media – newspapers, magazines, film, and radio – extolling this visible proof of the power of "Mao Zedong Thought" and the Cultural Revolution's new-born things *(xin sheng shiwu).* The art criticism was superficial, but the ideology closely matched current political struggles. The great artistic achievements of ordinary peasants who were simultaneously engaged in productive labour (only occasionally was it noted that the peasant painters category included "cadres, accountants, local school graduates, and sent-down educated youth") were cited as a direct refutation of Lin Biao's elitism and theories about "special talents."[15] In the mid-1970s, this was the radicals' code for attacking Zhou Enlai and his followers, who put greater stress on formal education and technical knowledge.

In brief, peasant art was enlisted in the left's political cause. That is why the militant rhetoric escalated during the 1970s. It is full of military metaphors: the painters are "troops"; their brushes are "weapons." Newspaper articles often used the word "battle" *(douzheng)* when reviewing the social function of Hu Xian peasant art. It is unclear to what extent the peasant painters were aware of their involvement in these behind-the-scenes power struggles. The model peasant painter and village-level cadre Liu Zhide (the 1974 delegate to Albania) remarked simply, "What the party wants us to paint, we paint."[16] But, in Mao's last years, who spoke for the party?

The national publicity campaign peaked in 1974, with reproduction volumes, films, and postage stamps reinforcing the numerous newspaper articles. By 1975 and early 1976, Hu Xian was still famous but not quite at the centre of the ongoing cultural wars. Then, after the fall of the Gang of Four, the national political agenda changed, and Hu Xian painters faced the tricky task of disassociating themselves from the leftist political line that had appropriated them to its cause. That later discourse, despite its somewhat disingenuous denial of leftist intentions, provides more useful factual information about the first two stages of Hu Xian peasant painting, before and during the Cultural Revolution, than anything published at the time. Somewhat surprisingly, the cadres and artists involved still spoke in a more or less Maoist tone well after that rhetoric was no longer fashionable or politically advantageous. For instance, in 1983, the reporter-turned-historian Jiang Qisheng described in detail the beginnings of Hu Xian painting in order to prove that it had not been one of the Gang of Four's "new-born things." It had been born much earlier, he asserted, under the inspiration of Chairman Mao's teachings.[17]

The Paintings: Folk Art or Political Art?

Several foreign visitors had written enthusiastically about Hu Xian peasant painters from the mid-1970s on, but the first serious critical analysis, based on the paintings themselves rather than field research or casual tourism, came from the art historian Ellen Johnston Laing in a 1984 article titled "Chinese Peasant Painting, 1958-1976: Amateur and Professional."[18] Through stylistic analysis, she demonstrated rather conclusively that the Hu Xian peasant paintings, at least from the 1970s onward, were hardly untutored amateur folk art, as most of the Cultural Revolution publicity claimed. The peasants had been taught by professionals, the sent-down artists noted earlier, and it showed.

This essay can scarcely hope to improve upon the analysis in her now classic article. It has already corroborated her point about professional tutoring from both documentary and oral sources, and it will extend the history of peasant painting beyond 1976. First, however, we take a fresh look at Hu Xian's artistic production during its peak years of the early 1970s in view of our increased knowledge about conditions then and our longer historical perspective on how peasant painting would subsequently evolve.

The key remaining question is not whether, or to what degree, the peasants were tutored. We know they were. More relevant now is the question of how central policy and local conditions mixed, or how formal artistic training interacted with folk art and popular aesthetics.

In her analysis of Hu Xian paintings, Laing detected two modes, or basic sources. The one to which she accorded most attention was formal, professional art, the influence of the imported tutors. This, in turn, had two rather different sides reflecting the basic division in China's professional art establishment. One she called "glossy socialist realism," which was basically nineteenth-century European realism as reshaped by the socialist agenda in the Soviet Union and China. She referred to the other as "textbook Chinese painting," brush and ink painting, with the freer, more personalized, and expressive elements expurgated for political reasons.[19] Differing in origins, the two came closer to fusion in the Cultural Revolution's ideological pressure cooker than they did before or after. Opposed to this dual-natured professional side was folk art. Although the pictorial folk art tradition was rather weak in Hu Xian, the custom of painting decorative designs on trousseau chests being its strongest component, there definitely was a popular visual culture grounded in embroidery, stuffed toys, and the ubiquitous New Year's prints. From the start, a tension existed between the two. The political and artistic tutors of the peasants pushed them toward scientific realism (fixed-point perspective, correct proportions and foreshortening of figures, shading, and shadowing). Their peasant students often adopted these techniques with enthusiasm, but this did not necessarily eradicate traditional folk art influences, not permanently anyway.

Two anecdotes about the famous peasant painter Liu Zhide illustrate the complex and ambivalent relationship between formal and folk art. When his nationally publicized *Old Party Secretary,* a portrait of a veteran party cadre studying Mao's works while taking a break from productive labour, was shown in the provincial capital of Xi'an, some of the professors at Xi'an Provincial Art Academy thought the drawing too smoothly professional to be the work of an uneducated peasant and suggested that it must have been touched up by a trained painter (Figure 6.1). So, to demonstrate his mastery of formal techniques, Liu painted it again, "only better this time."[20] The peasant painter was proud of his professionalism, or, to put it in the correct ideological format, he had demonstrated that, in art, as well as production, the ordinary peasant could master advanced scientific technique. The fact that he was hardly an ordinary peasant was beside the point.

This would seem to indicate that peasants had gladly abandoned folk art conventions, in which few had been trained anyway, for a formal, more realistic art better suited to the new times. But, on another occasion, Liu Zhide turned to a traditional folk aesthetic: asked why he had made the rice shoots in three paddy fields all the same size rather than applying the rules of perspective and making them smaller in the farthest field, he replied, "For our socialist collective economy to paint only two of the seedbeds and leave the other empty, is to empty the superior nature of the collective economy."[21] Correct politics trumped formal art, and "unscientific" folk styles could serve socialism too.

It may therefore be incorrect to speak of a tension between folk and formal art styles, but a sample of other featured paintings from this era shows a wide range along the folk-to-formal spectrum. At one end would be a picture like Liu Zhigui's *Attending Party Class,* based on the formal quasi-academic style of socialist realism (Figure 6.2). The usual bright colours of peasant painting are toned down, perhaps to give the image a little more solemnity as befits the seriousness of the occasion. The formal composition has a semi-circular group of figures focusing attention on the party cadre. The desk forms a strong horizontal to solidify his position, even if it is at the edge of the picture. Most noteworthy is the careful attention to detail in individualizing the faces of the figures – these are separate individuals, each with his or her own expression, but all are united in their adherence to the party line.

Attending Party Class is a standard realist group figure painting with antecedents going back to Soviet socialist realism and the nineteenth-century academic style introduced into the Central Academy of Fine Arts by Xu Beihong at the beginning of the People's Republic. Behind that stands the great neo-classical tradition of solemn, moralistic history paintings such as those produced by Jacques-Louis David at the time of the French Revolution. It has been updated here – as one of Mao's poems suggests, "For truly great heroes look to today" – and the skill level is not quite up to Chinese, let alone French, academic standards. But a grand genre of high art has been transplanted into Hu Xian's fertile soil, with the new moon and hanging ears of corn outside the window lending a rural, folkish touch. The artist, Liu Zhigui, was another of the model painters chosen to represent Hu Xian at exhibitions and tours.

The spread, sometimes gap, between professionalized and cruder, more folkish styles can readily be seen in two face-to-face pages in the Chinese edition of the colour reproduction volume of Hu Xian peasant paintings published in 1974.[22] We also have biographical information on the artist, Zhang Lin, which is illustrative of the local party leadership's role in creating peasant painters. As an elementary school graduate in 1962, he liked to draw traditional figures such as Guan Gong, the god of war. When he and his father came to the district capital to sell traditional window cut-outs for New Year's in 1964, cadres at the cultural centre heard of his talent and called him in for a talk. Encouraged to paint new things instead of old, he produced a serial picture strip and sent it to the cultural centre. Art cadres came to his home to tutor him, and soon he was producing works such as *Helping the Army* and *Herds of Livestock,* which were entered in the 1965

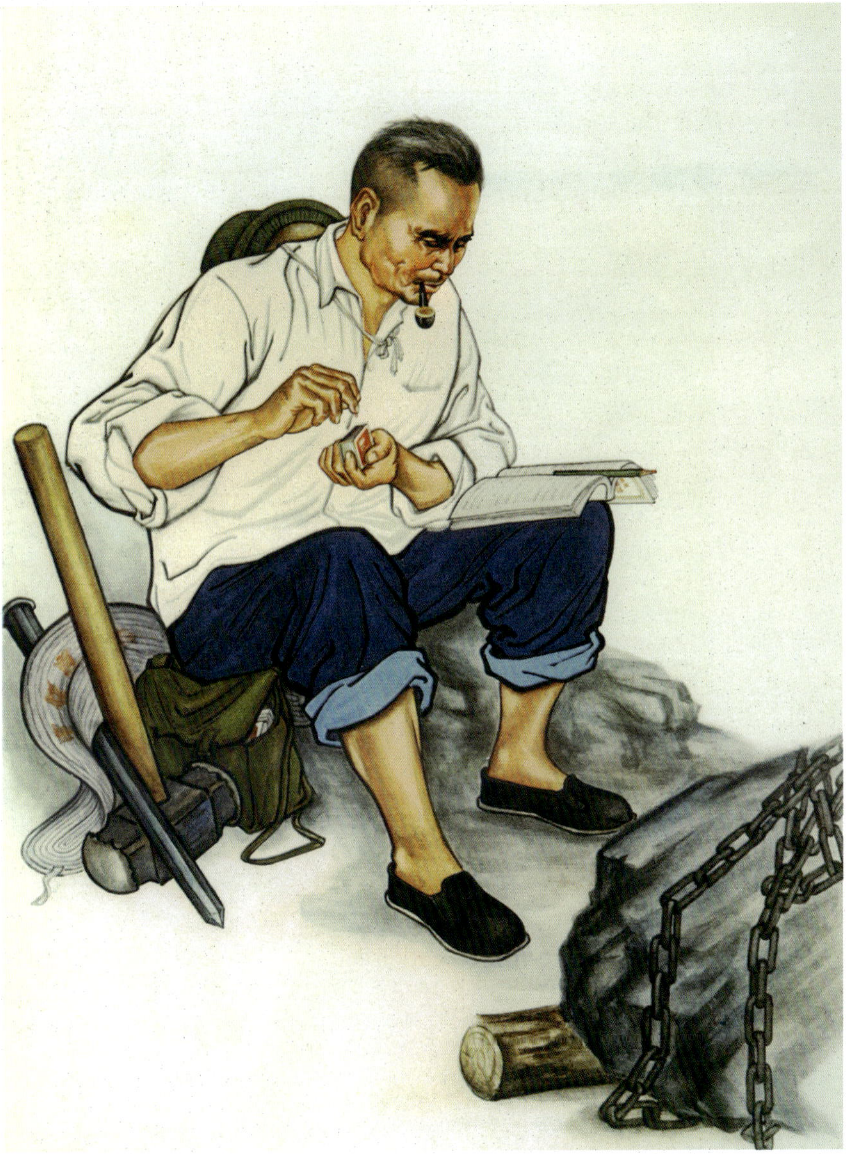

Figure 6.1 Liu Zhide, ***Old Party Secretary*** **(1973).** *Hu Xian nongmin hua xuanji* [A selection of Hu Xian peasant paintings] (Xi'an: Renmin chubanshe, 1974), 3.

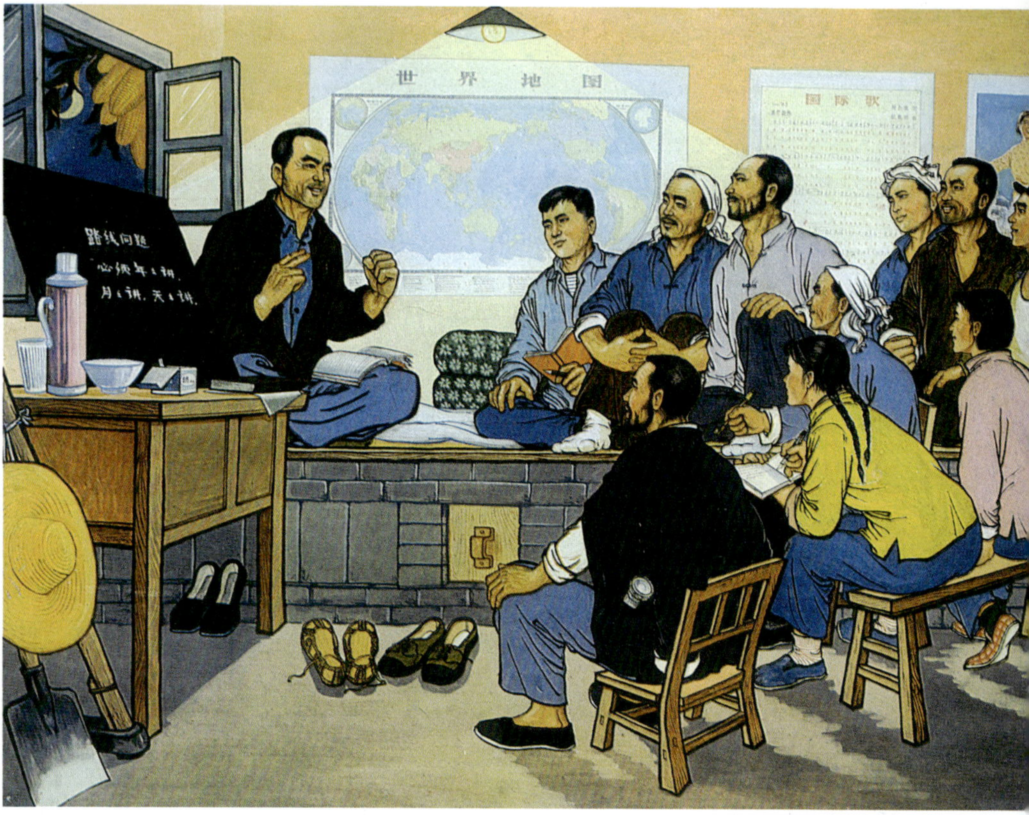

Figure 6.2 Liu Zhigui, ***Attending Party Class*** **(1972-73).** *Hu Xian nongmin hua xuanji* [A selection of Hu Xian peasant paintings] (Xi'an: Renmin chubanshe, 1974), 5.

national exhibition.[23] The originals are no longer available, but two of his works in the reproduction volume show how much peasant painting could change with professional guidance.

The subjects are similar, peasant figures in a courtyard set among a herd of animals, but one, *Herd of Cows and Horses,* is crude, amateurish, and folksy, whereas the other, *Never Stop Being Industrious and Thrifty,* is a sophisticated and well-drawn composition. Presumably, the cruder work is earlier, although neither is dated. The composition in the other comes straight from the academy, with the slightly inverted "V" of the cows and their framed heads framing the central figures. The work also features realistic depth recession, careful modelling of the figures, and skilful light effects. By contrast, *Herd of Cows and Horses* features a simply drawn human figure and a scattering of awkward animals across a flat surface. The appeal presumably is in the simplicity and naivety, but this is not the most effective example of the genre.

The more "folkish" paintings were, and are, much more appealing to Western eyes and, more recently, to Western customers. One of the better-known examples is Bai Tianxue's *Raising Goats* (Figure 6.3). The entire picture surface is covered, in keeping with the *horror vacui* characteristic of most folk art: there is no horizon line, the picture surface is flat, and the goats, arranged in the decorative patterning also typical of folk art, are all the same size regardless of their distance from the viewer. Yet the two herd boys are quite realistically drawn, and their colourful individual shapes stand out in lively fashion against the patterned grass and goats. This is a deceptively simple but actually skilfully composed picture, a rather sophisticated naivety that also indicates familiarity with formal art techniques. The "reserve white" used for the goats (leaving those parts of the paper uncoloured) is a favourite technique of Chinese ink painters, and the overall composition bears a striking similarity to those used by modern Chinese woodcut artists, some of whom had visited Hu Xian.

This combination of folk simplicity and more sophisticated artistic conventions can also be found in the most widely publicized single work of the most widely publicized individual painter from Hu Xian. This is Li Fenglan – another model commune worker of poor peasant background, illiterate until after the revolution and a participant in the first peasant-painting class back in 1959.[24] Her best-known work, *Spring Hoeing,* was repeatedly shown in exhibitions, illustrated articles, and reproduction volumes (Figure 6.4). Laing devoted special attention to this particular image, analyzing the sophisticated semi-circular arrangement of the figures, the subtle integration

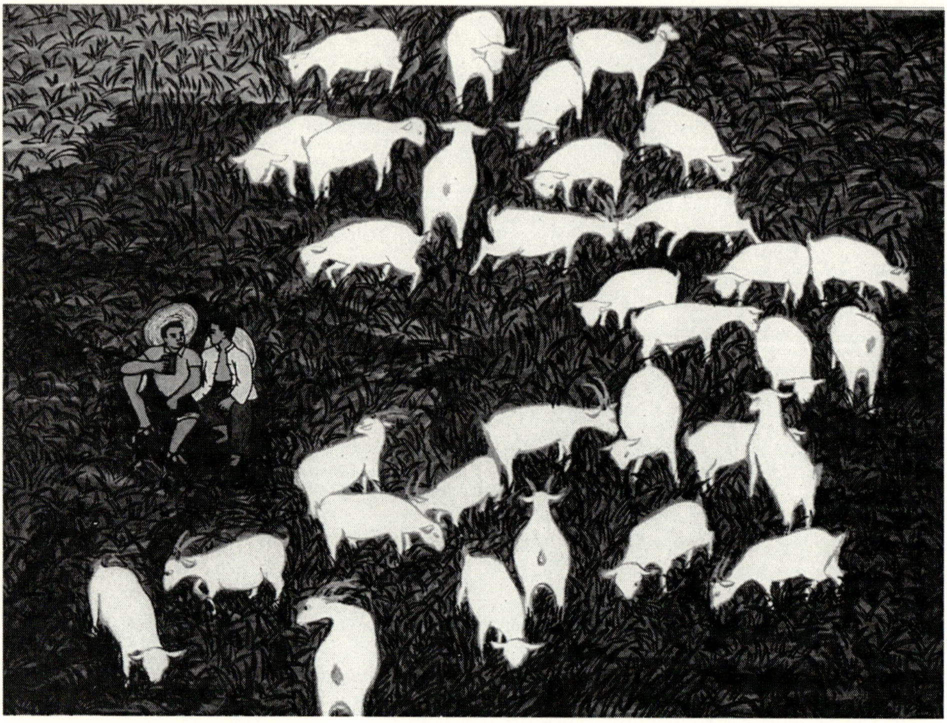

Figure 6.3 **Bai Tianxue, *Raising Goats* (c. 1973).** *Hu Xian nongmin hua xuanji* [A selection of Hu Xian peasant paintings] (Xi'an: Renmin chubanshe, 1974), 47.

of the regular geometric rows and the cloud-like wafting mists (actually sprayed insecticide!), and the finely drawn figures. Comparing it with Li Fenglan's other published works, which are much cruder in design and execution, Laing concluded that it "taxes credibility" to believe that she could have done it unaided.[25]

The purpose of Laing's analysis was to expose the professionalism behind those ostensibly amateur paintings. Here, we are more concerned to note the sometimes harmonious blending of folk and formal art elements, even if in this case the folk art side is much subordinated. It was this combination that gave Hu Xian peasant painting, at its best, an aesthetic appeal beyond the obviously political function. As we shall see, it helps explain how peasant painting survived the collapse of the Cultural Revolution.

Two more examples reinforce this point and show that some real artistic talent emerged out of the peasant-painting classes: first is Dong Zhengyi's *Communal Fish Pond,* which was much admired by foreign viewers

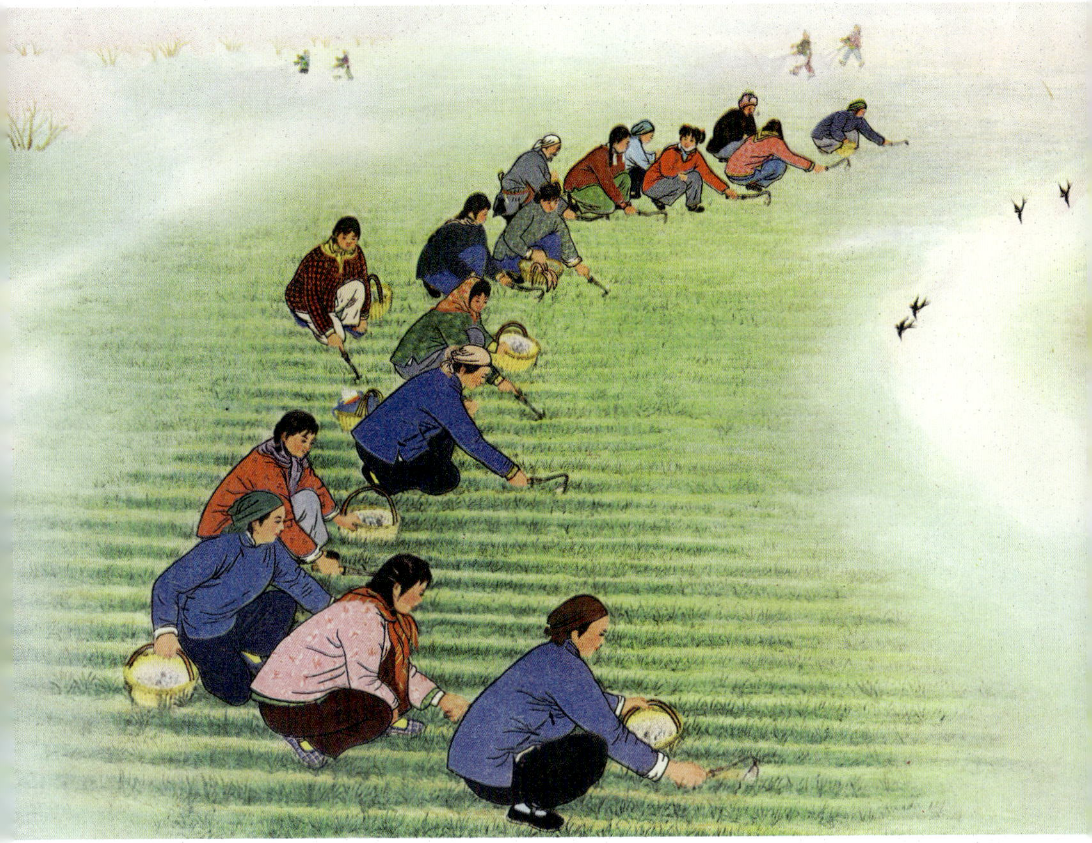

Figure 6.4 Li Fenglan, ***Spring Hoeing*** **(n.d.).**
Hu Xian nongmin hua xuanji [A selection of Hu Xian peasant paintings] (Xi'an: Renmin chubanshe, 1974), 19.

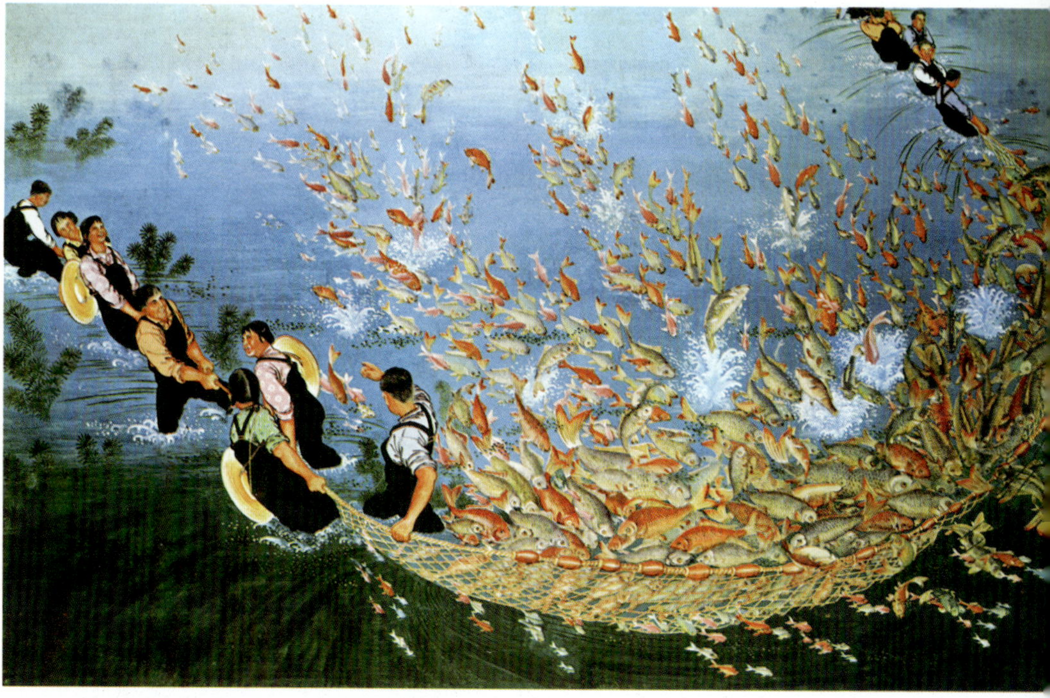

Figure 6.5 Dong Zhengyi, *Communal Fish Pond* (1972). *Hu Xian nongmin hua xuanji* [A selection of Hu Xian peasant paintings] (Xi'an: Renmin chubanshe, 1974), 55.

(Figure 6.5). Laing put it in the glossy category – "technically highly proficient, polished and slick ... compositions based on large, dramatic, sweeping arcs, not an invention of peasant painters." Nor is "an understanding of how to render light and its reflections ... in the shining, glittering, scales on the leaping fish."[26] No doubt, this is a tutored painting. But the folk elements and folk flavour are still strong: bright colours, abundance, and the familiar fish symbol for material plenty. The original was hung in the Shaanxi room of the Great Hall of the People; a second version was given to President Nixon on his China trip.

It is hard to find folk antecedents for Fan Zhihua's *Digging a Well,* but the work does not fit any standard socialist-realist format either (Figure 6.6). The unusual vertiginous perspective and bustling human activity provide the visual impact. Especially during the Cultural Revolution, only a bold professional painter would so daringly deviate from established composition formulae, for distorting realistic representation in this manner was the hallmark of Western modernists, "bourgeois formalists." But a peasant painter had folk art naivety as his defence. Tutored or not, and as one of the original part-time students in 1959, he certainly had been, Fan and his kind

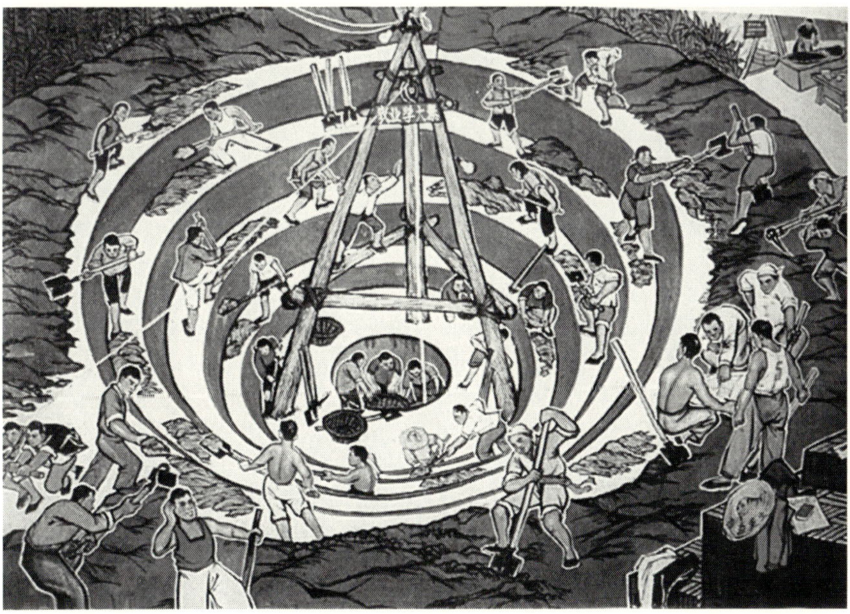

Figure 6.6 Fan Zhihua, *Digging a Well* (n.d.). *Peasant Painting from Huhsien County* (Beijing: People's Fine Arts Publishing House, 1974), 21.

had more leeway for stylistic innovation and experiment than their politically suspect professional teachers. Sometimes this produced visually interesting results.

"Reform" and Beyond: The Business of Painting, 1977-2002

The peak of national publicity for Hu Xian as the focal point of a new popular socialist art was reached before 1976, and the peasant painters seem to have missed close involvement in the last political campaign to "beat back the right deviationist wind," associated with the second purging of Deng Xiaoping. That was indeed fortunate for them because it meant that they were not tarred with the ultra-left brush when the Gang of Four fell from power later in the year. Still, as the political pendulum swung slowly and then rapidly to the right, and the Cultural Revolution and all its "new things" were rejected as "ten years of chaos," the peasant paintings so closely connected with those radical years inevitably fell under suspicion. With Dazhai, the model for collective agriculture exposed as a fraud, Hu Xian was vulnerable too.

But Hu Xian and its painters were able to weather the transition and then reinvent themselves to fit the new era of "reform and opening." Several factors worked in their favour. First, they remained useful for cultural diplomacy as China reopened to the world. More importantly, domestic politics during the 1976-78 interregnum still favoured their kind of art. The Gang of Four was anathema, but Mao Zedong thought and the mass line were still icons used to legitimate party rule. For a time, peasant art continued to be used in political campaigns. In December 1976, Hu Xian painters contributed cartoons to the Smash the Gang of Four campaign. In 1977, they sent fourteen works to the exhibition in Beijing commemorating the thirty-fifth anniversary of Mao's Yan'an Talks. Later, they were enlisted to execute works to popularize science and promote the Four Modernizations.

Like national politics, the accumulation of vested interests in continuing peasant painting, at both the provincial and the local level, worked in their favour. For Shaanxi Province, the paintings meant continued recognition on the national and even international stage. At the district level, not solely local pride, but a substantial infrastructure of painters, art cadres, and administrators at the cultural centre and the large new exhibition hall were involved. The painters now numbered over nineteen hundred, with local painting groups in almost every village.[27] Both cadres and painters had a strong interest in keeping the movement going even as it faded from the centre of national interest, and the stream of foreign visitors started to dry up.

Their most pressing political task was to disassociate from the Cultural Revolution and the Gang of Four. In May 1977, the local government convened a conference and an art show at the exhibition hall with over one thousand works on display. Its announced purpose was "to refute the mistaken view that peasant paintings are a product of the extreme left line."[28] A kind of informal absolution was granted in 1979 when Hua Junwu, the new head of the National Artists Association, visited Hu Xian and declared that "the peasants made no mistakes."[29]

So there were forces at work helping Hu Xian painting to survive as a recognized movement, but the paintings themselves had to change, and, once again, this was not simply a matter of local choice by individual painters. The reformist, no longer left-wing, cultural leadership in Beijing wanted to use peasant painting for more than foreign relations. On the one hand, the leadership wanted it to shift away from its leftist bias to reflect and support the new policies that were changing rural life under Deng Xiaoping. On the other hand, as Deng Xiaoping cracked down on democracy activists and their Western modernism-influenced artistic fellow travellers at the beginning of the 1980s, the party promoted a revival of folk art as a made-in-China solution to the problem of such dubious foreign influences.[30] For this, the Hu Xian model was still useful once the paintings had been cleansed of their Cultural Revolution associations and made more authentically Chinese. In a sense, the new purpose for peasant painting was to validate the party as protector of Chinese national identity in the face of renewed Western cultural inroads. Hu Xian was not necessarily best situated to benefit from this new turn. Its painters had more experience, but also more baggage. Hu Xian's most formidable rival as the leading centre for peasant painting emerged during this period in Jin Shan, a rural district but located within the Greater Shanghai Municipal Region.

The key individual in starting peasant art activity in Jin Shan was Wu Tongzhang, a sent-down art instructor from Shanghai. Initially, without much concern for socialist themes, he guided aspiring peasant painters toward exploring the rich heritage of arts and crafts in that part of China known as Jiangnan (the name translates to south of the [Yangtze] river), especially in textiles and embroidery.[31] Out of this came a more stylized, decorative peasant painting, which stressed "ethnic character" and "folk tradition." With their close involvement in fabric arts, women were especially prominent in the first generation of Jin Shan peasant painters. Cao

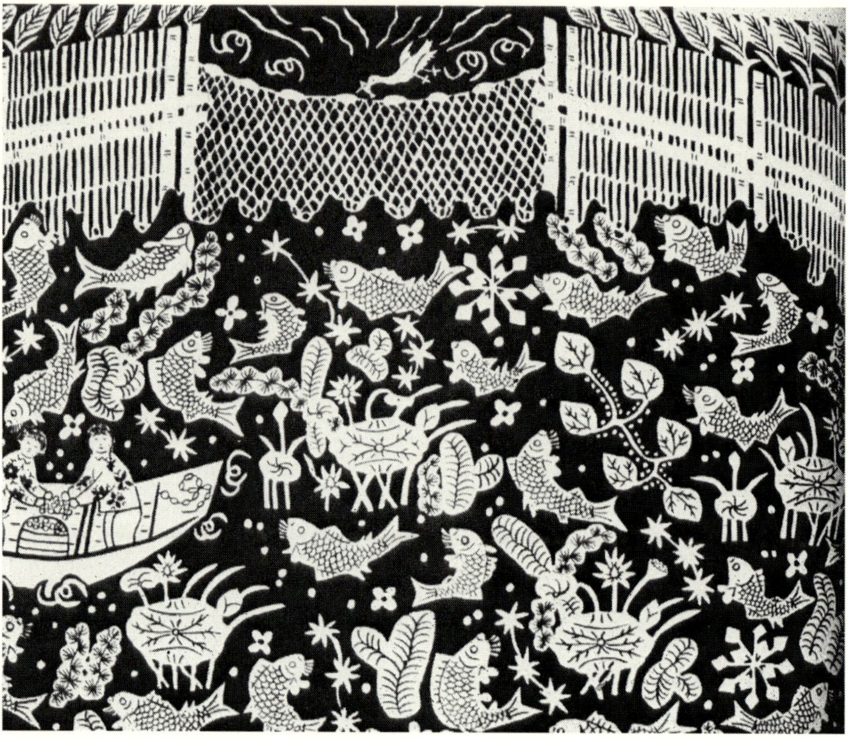

Figure 6.7 Cao Jinying, *Fish Pond* (c. 1982).

Jinying, a middle-aged embroiderer turned painter, for example, produced one of the earliest widely acclaimed works, *Fish Pond* (Figure 6.7). This almost abstract, highly decorative design is a world removed from earlier Hu Xian treatment of the same subject (compare Figure 6.7 with Figure 6.5). The stylized shapes, blue-and-white colour scheme, and overall pattern all come from textile decoration rather than realist painting techniques.

Other works displayed both folk style and the material prosperity of peasant life during the early 1980s. In *Welcome Guests,* a painting by Zhang Xinying, a rather elegant blue-and-white tea set with a bowl of fruit manifests the welcome of the title; the kitchen scene has a traditional stove, beautifully decorated with folk motifs, and the housewife carries in that most common symbol of prosperity, a fish. Very occasionally, modern appliances, a stereo player or a refrigerator, were depicted in such images, but these manifestations of modernity were almost always avoided in order to stress "tradition" and folk character. When, by the mid-1980s, marketing

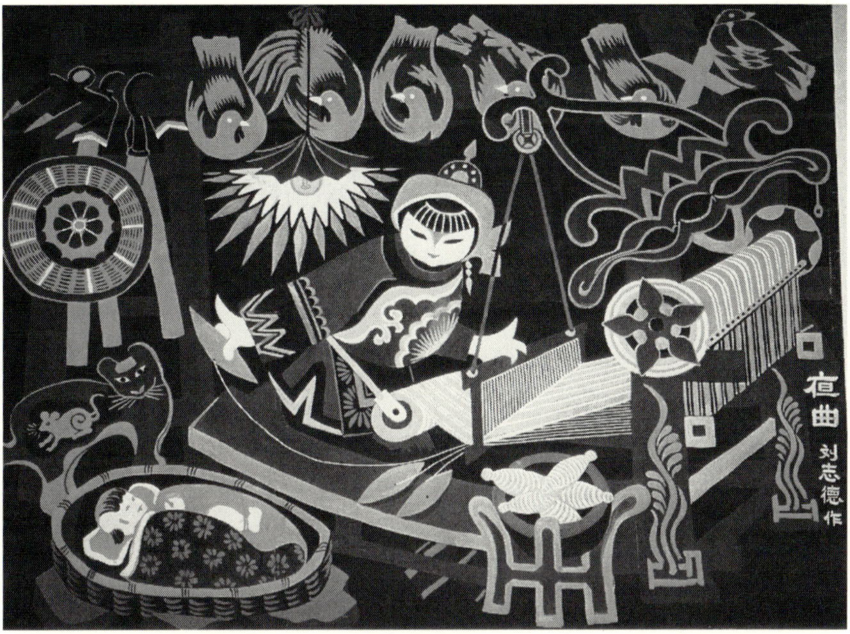

Figure 6.8 Liu Zhide, ***Night Melody*** **(1983).** Author photograph.

opportunities entered into the picture, the symbols of modernity spoiled the folk appeal. At a time when rural material life was changing faster than at any other point in Chinese history, the peasant paintings portrayed an idyllic, eternal China undisturbed by the tensions of change, and certainly undisturbed by the class struggle that had been a central subject for peasant painting a decade earlier.[32]

The newer peasant painting centres of the lower Yangtze Valley, especially Jin Shan, would have considerable influence on Hu Xian as the painters and cadres there tried to adapt to changing times. In some ways, Hu Xian, because of its long-established reputation, still had pride of place in the new Chinese peasant-painting world. So, when a major touring exhibition of contemporary peasant painting was organized in 1984, it was billed as the Hu Xian, Jin Shan, Dong Feng United Peasant Painting Exhibition. But Jin Shan and the eastern seaboard were clearly the trendsetters now, quicker off the mark in exploiting nostalgia for the essential rural China and quicker to market. This trend even won tacit official confirmation. At the 1983 National Peasant Painting Exhibition in Beijing, Hu Xian's entries did no better than second-grade prizes.

These new outside pressures hastened the trend for Hu Xian peasant painting to change itself. A most obvious example was a painting by Liu Zhide, the famous creator of the Cultural Revolution icon *Old Party Secretary.* In 1983, he painted *Night Melody,* a work that, with its flat blue-and-white composition, looks very much like something from Jiangnan (Figure 6.8). A winsome, pink-cheeked young mother weaves into the night as her cherubic infant (only one under the new policy!) gurgles happily in the cradle. A cat straight out of folk art toys looks on. Simple folk art? Hardly. There is a good deal of professional skill and sophistication in its carefully designed artlessness. Furthermore, Liu adopted the traditional Chinese painter's practice of putting signature, title, and artist's seal on the picture, although he labelled it "China Hu Xian Peasant Painting." Why include "China" in the label? Perhaps it reflects a resurgent national pride or, more likely, is an indication that the paintings were no longer addressed solely to an internal audience. Foreigners had admired peasant paintings since the early 1970s, and now, with the tourist trade opening up and economic reform reaching the art world, there was a market for authentic made-in-China paintings.

Jin Shan, strategically located in the outskirts of Shanghai, had led the cultivation of the tourist trade. By the mid-1980s, hotel shops in all the major cities sold peasant works, often regional, but sometimes from famous national peasant-painting centres. With state support for the arts dwindling, and a considerable establishment of cultural cadres and peasant painters to support, Hu Xian could hardly ignore the new reality.

This did not mean that it abandoned regional character in pursuit of either the Jin Shan style or that of other places. Borrowing could occur, as was the case in Liu Zhide's *Night Melody,* though this artist also produced other works that maintained the more usual northwest colours, red and yellow, and drew on local customs. One of Liu's paintings, *Treading on a Big Drum,* has carefully drawn Shaanxi peasants, wearing their characteristic white turbans, exuberantly bouncing on huge festive red drums. Another, more interesting from the viewpoint of local roots for peasant painting, shows a craftsman painting decorative designs on bridal wedding chests. Finally, to take an even more striking example of the return, or rather rediscovery, of native arts and crafts in the early 1980s, Li Fenglan painted *Cloth Tiger,* an image of a characteristic folk toy from the region. All folk character, no political content.

The shift to market was only starting in the 1980s; it went much further during the next decade, with the paintings becoming commodities and the

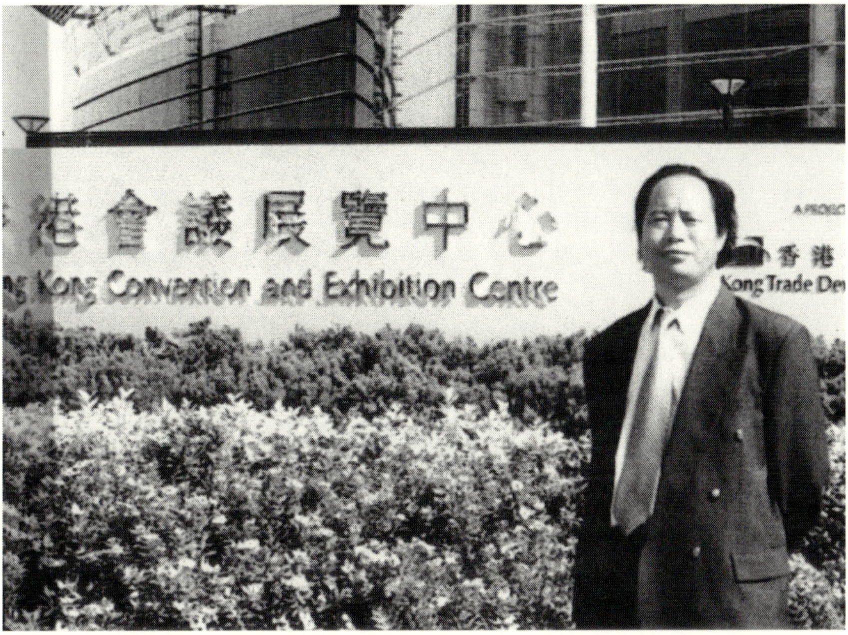

Figure 6.9 Liu Fengtao, an example of the internationally successful new generation of Hu Xian peasant painters, in a business suit during a 1990s visit to Hong Kong. His father was one of the first generation Hu Xian peasant painters. His wife and son are also professional artists. *Huxian nongmin hua zhi Jia Zuopin Ji: Collection of Paintings for Huxian County Farmer Painters Family* (Huxian, 2000), 1.

more successful, or more enterprising, of the peasant painters becoming "independent professional artists," or entrepreneurs. The better-known painters no longer had to "hold the plough in one hand and the painting brush in the other." Of course, the new economic opportunities meant that many former peasants were no longer working the land. Peasant painting was one ticket away from peasant work. Some of the painters, such as Liu Zhide and the veteran art teacher Liu Qunhan (the two are not related), maintained official administrative-teaching positions while painting too. Photographs of the three generations of painters in Liu Qunhan's family demonstrate how far in appearance, in their artistic persona, they have come from their peasant roots (Figures 6.9 and 6.10).

As for the art produced, it is enormously varied in style, content, and quality. The return to folk roots, real and apparent, is a prominent trend. One of the more striking instances of this is the fact that the model peasant

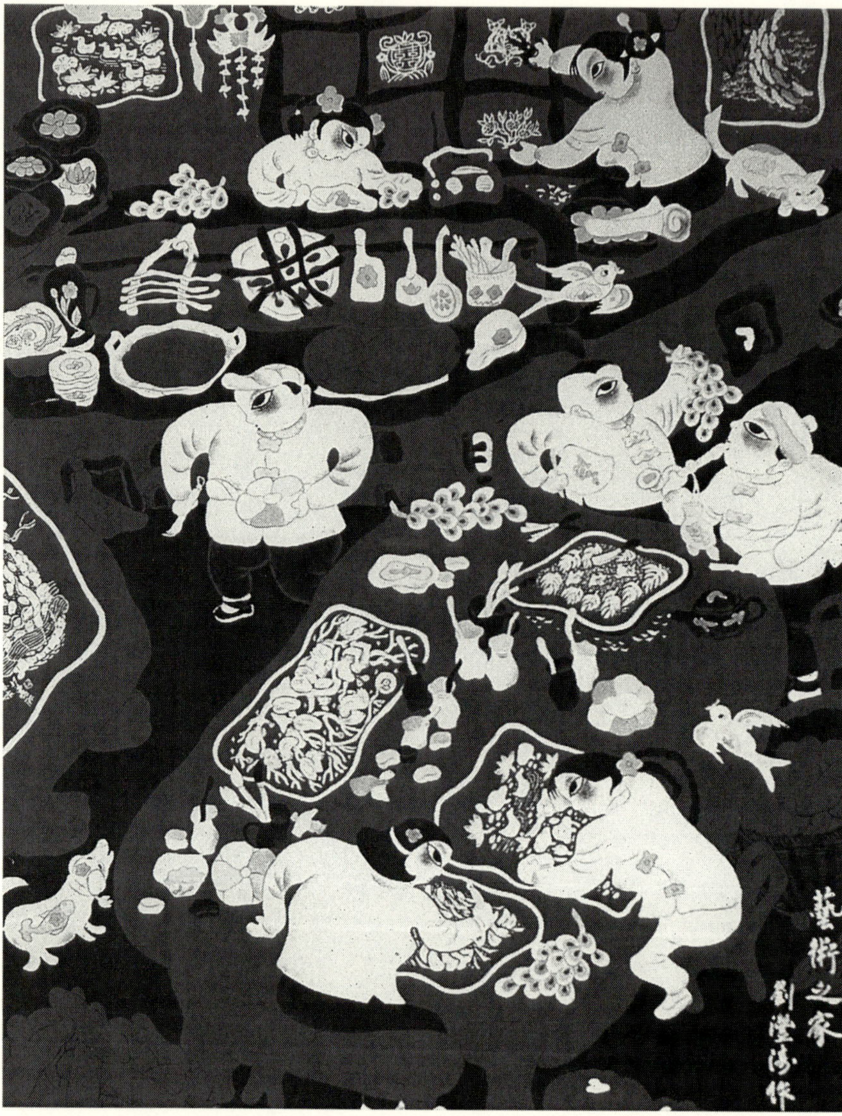

Figure 6.10 Liu Fengtao, *Artistic Family*, n.d. The traditionally dressed peasants in the painting, busy with the pure folk art of paper-cuts, are presumably the artist's family, but the four professional artists in his family are hardly peasants anymore.

painter Li Fenglan put down her brush and turned exclusively to the very traditional folk art of paper-cuts.

In seizing personal and professional opportunities while maintaining ties to the official system, these no-longer peasant painters resembled their urban counterparts in the Chinese art world. But, by the end of the century, the official positions were few in Hu Xian, and the opportunities outside the system were many. This is not to say that most of the painters trained in the Cultural Revolution's short-term schools and village-level painting groups became professionals. It is just that the professionals set the pace and the character of peasant painting now. The total number of painters grew modestly from 1983 to 1994 – according to locally published statistics – from nineteen hundred to twenty-one hundred.[33] Given that the foreign visitor business was dropping off during this period and that state support had greatly diminished, this is an indicator that other factors were sustaining and transforming peasant painting in Hu Xian. Part of that may be due to more spare time or Sunday painters in the villages, thus realizing the original vision of empowering peasants to raise rural cultural levels. However, these kinds of amateur painters, or their influence, are not apparent to the short-term visitor, at least not in the fall of 2001. Nor are such grassroots amateur paintings featured in the official promotional literature. In Hu Xian, commercialization is obviously the main trend. At times, the press speaks of this and worries about loss of quality or reputation. A particularly interesting case emerged in 1997 when, disturbed by the sale of fake Hu Xian paintings in tourist centres across China, the district government began requiring seals of authenticity. There was no indication of how this regulation would be enforced or fake seals and signatures prohibited. A reporter for the national daily paper *Guangming ribao* cautioned buyers to beware.[34] Another index of this unrestrained commercialization was the proliferation of colour printed catalogues, art books, and biographies, which try to enhance the reputation of the paintings as serious, but also very affordable, art. Most of this mini-flood of new publications was privately sponsored by the artists themselves.

Meanwhile, the cavernous Peasant Painting Hall on Exhibition Hall Street continued to show the official face of Hu Xian peasant painting, looking very much like a relic from a bygone age. A week after National Day, in October 2001, it was still festooned with tattered banners and slogans. Inside, the viewer was immediately greeted by mural-sized paintings that had nothing to do with productive labour, much less socialist construction.

Above the table featuring a raised relief model of Hu Xian's topography hung a toy tiger in the painted folk tradition. Nearby was a cosmic creation scene out of Chinese mythology, with folk-toy-like representations of the twelve animals of the Chinese zodiac that faintly recalled the murals from the Beijing airport, controversial in 1979 when the airport was new and Chinese viewers were unaccustomed to anything that differed from socialist art. By the beginning of the twenty-first century, that kind of political correctness was long past, even in this former showplace for socialist art.

The other walls confirmed this. Even pictures of farm activity no longer exalted labour and class struggle. Instead, they showed bucolic peasants in consciously folkish styles that often verged on kitsch. The rest of the building, eight more large galleries, was all fully hung but not nearly so well maintained as the entrance hall. There were no visitors, and the disinterested staff acted as if they neither expected nor wanted any. The front counter offered a number of reproduction volumes and postcards for sale, but there was no obvious push to sell paintings. In short, the exhibition hall had the air of many of China's official museums and memorial halls – a relic from a past that seems more distant than it actually is.

The exhibition hall for a new art had become a somewhat decrepit and neglected museum, the real action in Hu Xian having moved elsewhere, from public institutions to the private realm. On the rapidly spreading suburban outskirts of East Han Village there lay a newly built Peasant Painting Centre that looked more like an American high school gymnasium than anything out of China's recent or traditional architectural heritage. It hosted public functions and visiting official delegations, but also served to promote business and sales for the no-longer-rural villages of the no-longer-peasant painters.

One such painter, Cao Quntang, a published artist who had visited the United States, had a solo exhibition at the painting centre in the fall of 2001. Although his bright, colourful peasant-like pictures covered all four walls of the auditorium-sized room, he spoke little about them and was anxious to show a foreign visitor his more personal work. The hung paintings were just how he made a living: his sketchbooks were his real art, sensitive fine-line drawings he had made on a sketching trip to North Shaanxi and black-and-white woodcuts reminiscent of the great age of modern Chinese woodcuts in the 1930s and 1940s. The subject matter was quintessentially Chinese – the cave houses of the Yan'an area – but it was not peasant art, and it contrasted sharply with what he had on display. He explained that in recent years he had studied drawing and printmaking at the Xi'an Provincial Art

Academy. No more sent-down art instructors. The peasant-turned-artist went to the academy to improve the professional skills of which he was obviously proud.

Cao exemplified how far "peasant painting" had come from the original ideals of Yan'an or Hu Xian, but the real switch to a new era was more apparent in the many family (a euphemism for private) studio-galleries in the brand new, gated, and pretentious housing developments springing up around the town centre as a mini-version of what was happening near China's major cities. One of these was the two-storied home of Pan Xiaoling. Born in 1956, she represents the second, or even third, generation of Hu Xian painters, those who missed the Great Leap Forward and most of the Cultural Revolution. She too had been to America (exhibited in Los Angeles), as well as Singapore and Japan. Her spacious second-story gallery was lined with colourful paintings of varying size and price, from 100 to 300 *yuan*. Volume 2 of her perhaps self-published book featuring reproductions of her work was available at a cheaper price. The paintings in the book and on the wall definitely belonged to the slick and glitzy category, some more realistic than others, some almost insufferably cute. A member of the Provincial Artists Association, she was obviously successful. Production in volume seemed to be a key to that success. In the back of her upstairs gallery, several young women were assiduously "practising," making copy after copy of their "teacher's" works.

This brings us to the all-important market question: who buys them? The number of foreign tourists has dropped off, and the occasional stray academic is not much help. It appears that two new market forces sustained this obvious prosperity for at least some of the Hu Xian peasant painters. First, an internal art market, for both locals and visitors, had arisen in China. Hu Xian paintings, I was told, make good gifts. They were relatively cheap, they had broad popular appeal, and in the complicated negotiation between the private and the public sphere in China, "gift paintings" could hardly be considered a bribe. When the representatives of Chinese "units" (or enterprises?) came to Hu Xian, they bought in quantity. One took home two hundred paintings. The resurgence of nationalism in China, and the new appreciation of ethnic character, even as modernization wipes out most of it, might also have played a role in this recent urbanization of "folk art."

As for the vanished international visitors, global marketing meant that Hu Xian could reach out to its second market – overseas buyers. Some artists have commercial exhibitions and dealers abroad, but e-commerce may be an even more important key to this globalization of the local. Several websites sell "authentic Hu Xian paintings." Finding them is simply a matter of entering "Hu Xian," or even "Chinese peasant painting," on any good search engine.

We conclude this section with a personal footnote to market outreach in the global cyber age. Three months after visiting Hu Xian, the author was at a private ski lodge in Truckee, California, near Lake Tahoe. It was owned by a socially conscious, arts-involved woman physician from the San Francisco Bay area. Apart from family photographs and outdoors paraphernalia, the main decorations on the walls of almost every room were bright, cheerful, and signed Hu Xian peasant paintings. One is reminded of the Cultural Revolution slogan "We have friends [now read 'customers'] all over the world."

Conclusion?

From the above narrative, it should be clear that the history of Hu Xian peasant painting has not come to an end. It lives on, recognizable as the offspring of the revolutionary social-cultural experiment that started in the Great Leap Forward and was pushed to political extremes in the Cultural Revolution. Obviously, it failed to abolish the difference between physical labour and cultural creation. Marx's ideal of every man as philosopher-worker-fisherman-poet was not realized. But more than a few peasants seem to have gotten out of the fields, or out of the kitchen, to find careers in art and business.

We need not dwell on the irony of this outcome in view of the socialist principles that originally motivated the peasant-painting movement. All revolutions fail in their more ambitious radical projects, but they may have some liberating effect on the lives of the masses, or at least change them, sometimes for the better. Without the original radical impulse to put brushes in the hands of peasants, would these successful peasant artists ever have gotten their opportunity? We are talking about a small number here, a successful cottage industry. The more meaningful, and less answerable, question is as follows: what difference has this made to cultural life at the village level in Hu Xian and elsewhere?

The pseudo revival of folk tradition and the successful marketing of it inside and outside China raise one more question about local traditions and globalization. As all modernities and all traditions converge in the global village, or global marketplace, does this lead toward ultimate convergence of styles, values, and socio-economic systems? Are local identities reduced to superficial markers of difference or simply to market commodities? Chinese peasant paintings in a Lake Tahoe ski lodge – quite chic – although another click of the mouse would take us to websites selling Ecuadorian peasant painting, or Native American Indian art, or Tibetan tankas. Interchangeable decor for a world where real difference is disappearing?

Such speculation carries us far beyond Hu Xian, the Cultural Revolution, and the proper scope of this chapter. To end, not with Mao, or with marketing, but with Marx: "Men make their history, but they do not make it as they please; they do not make it under self-selected circumstances."[35] Yes, and Hu Xian painters, men and women both, have made their art under changing historical circumstances, which they could neither foresee nor control. But they have adapted, first to political demands and then to market opportunities. To fully appreciate their art, one needs both a sense of history and a taste for irony.

PART 4

Beyond the Visual Arts

7

Model Theatrical Works and the Remodelling of the Cultural Revolution

Paul Clark

Constructing an understanding of the Cultural Revolution from a distance of four decades presents a challenge. When the culture of the period is mentioned, the eight initial revolutionary model theatrical works *(geming yangbanxi)* come immediately to the minds of both the Chinese who lived through the era and foreign scholars of the period. The five modernized Beijing operas, two full-length ballets, and one symphony that made up these eight works are seen to epitomize Cultural Revolution cultural production. They are symbols of the supposed paucity of cultural activity in that period, captured in the old saw about 800 million people watching eight shows *(bayi ren kan bage xi)*. In most discussions of Cultural Revolution culture, the symphony is ignored and one of the operas, *Raid on the White Tiger Regiment (Qixi Baihutuan)*, overlooked. Other modernized operas of the period (including sung versions of the two model ballets) were later added to the model works and have become part of the generalized image of the Cultural Revolution. Heroic men and women in Chinese Civil War uniforms striking a group pose, nobly gazing toward the certainty of a glorious future under communism, have become a kitsch icon of the era.

This chapter will attempt to construct a more nuanced picture of cultural life in China between 1966 and 1976. Although memory, nostalgia, and mythology place the model theatrical works firmly at centre stage in those ten years, the reality seems to have been somewhat different. As with other aspects of the Cultural Revolution, rhetoric and myth cloud our understanding of the period. The politicians who commandeered the model works for their own purposes, and the artists who performed them, certainly argued vehemently that they were central. Other artists and audiences may well have chosen to differ.

The position of the model theatrical works will be explored by charting the attention devoted to them in the National Day celebrations of early October during the Cultural Revolution decade and in the commemorations

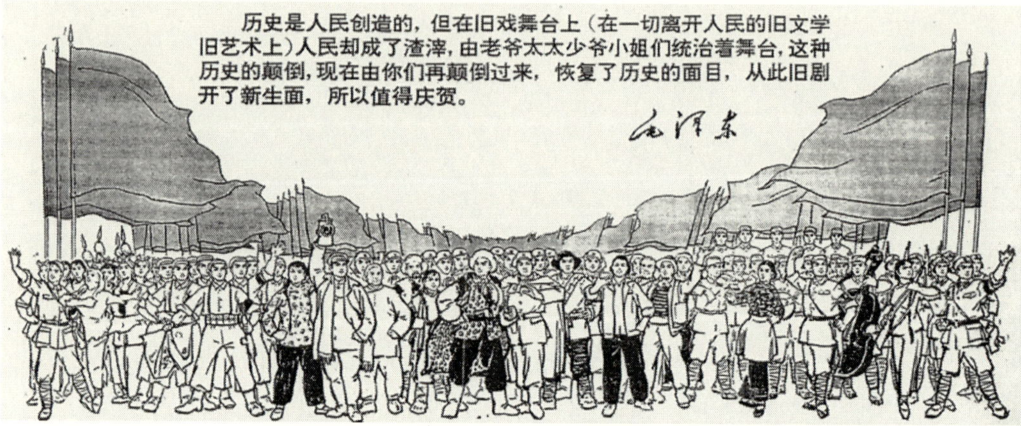

Figure 7.1 **Assembled characters from the model theatrical works. The caption reads, "History is created by the people, but on the old opera stage (in all literature and art that departs from the people), the people became the dregs, and lords, ladies, young masters and young mistresses dominated the stage. Now this reversal of history has itself been reversed, restoring the true face of history. From this point the old opera has been given new life, and this is cause for rejoicing." The reproduced signature is that of Mao Zedong.** *People's Daily*, 15 June 1967.

each May of the anniversary of Mao Zedong's 1942 Yan'an Talks on art and literature. By the 1950s, the Talks had assumed the role of a policy statement on the proper relations between writers, artists, and audiences in communist China. Their twenty-fifth anniversary, in May 1967, was the occasion at which Mao's wife, Jiang Qing, and her allies chose to claim iconic status for the first eight model theatrical works. The five operas were *Taking Tiger Mountain by Strategy (Zhiqu weihushan), The Red Lantern (Hongdengji), Shajiabang* (the title is the name of the place where the action occurs), *On the Docks (Haigang),* and *Raid on the White Tiger Regiment.* The two ballets in the initial eight model theatrical works were *The Red Detachment of Women (Hongse niangzi jun)* and *The White-Haired Girl (Baimao nü);* the next chapter, by Bai Di, offers a reading of these two ballets. Images of the day often group the central heroic characters of the model theatrical works together (Figure 7.1; see also Figure 0.1 of the Introduction, where the characters are arranged around Jiang Qing). The eighth work was a symphonic rendering of *Shajiabang.* May and October commemorations through to 1976 show that, rather than being uniformly important, the model works rose and fell in significance. A misinformed and generalized fixation on them can obscure the subtle fluctuations in their position as models. Contention and disputation ensured that an imagined linear development of their role is misplaced.[1]

Operas on Contemporary Themes

Modernizing the sung dramas or operas of China presented considerable challenges, and models or key works were a favoured means of promoting change. Models could serve both artists, expected to create new-style works, and audiences, urged to show an appreciation for the changes. The conventionality of sung drama in China – well-defined and limited role types, musical motifs and styles associated with particular roles, and limited variation in staging – had always made opera ripe for modernization. But performers and their audiences showed firm resistance, even after 1949, to taking contemporary works seriously. Most such efforts, even after the major shift to modern professionalism and the rise of academic direction in opera training and staging during the 1950s, were greeted with skepticism, if not contempt. The models provided a means of overcoming this resistance to change, both onstage and in the auditorium. A few works, with proper revision and improvement, might achieve a degree of artistic success, thus weakening resistance and paving the way for a broader effort at opera modernization. In the summer of 1964, a trial festival of Beijing operas on contemporary themes held in Beijing provided opera professionals and cultural officials with the opportunity to identify the more promising new operas for elevating to model status. Four of what would become the first five model theatrical operas – the exception was *On the Docks* – were presented in Beijing that summer. Almost three years after the festival, in May of 1967, the five were named as model theatrical works. This occurred a full year after the May Sixteenth Directive of 1966, which marked the official start of the Great Proletarian Cultural Revolution. For works supposedly at the heart of the Cultural Revolution, this was something of a delayed start.

The Eight Models

This is not the place to rehearse the histories of the individual model works. Each of the operas and ballets emerged from the efforts of a considerable range of specialists: actors, writers, musicians, composers, stage directors, choreographers, and set designers, among others. This set them apart from most operas and dance works, which were usually produced in much less resource-rich circumstances. The operas that became model theatrical works were singled out for this attention because they offered the basis, in terms of setting, plot, and characters, for operas that might try to match the appeal of their more familiar Beijing counterparts. This promise of artistic achievement in modernizing Beijing opera fostered high expectations and led to the lavishing of resources of talent, funding, and time on their development and refinement.

In the case of the two ballets, audience appeal was made more likely by the popularity of earlier versions of the stories in different genres. *The White-Haired Girl* had a long Yan'an-derived pedigree as a modern musical drawn from local folktale and the dramatic folk-dance form known as rice-sprout song *(yangge)*. It had been adapted into one of the earliest box-office and artistic successes of the post-1949 film industry. Transformation into a full-length ballet offered an opportunity for its creators to sinicize the dance form, to help ballet put down Chinese roots for the first time. The full-length ballet version of *The White-Haired Girl* had its premiere in May 1964. *The Red Detachment of Women* had also proven its popular appeal as a feature film, released in 1961. This film, directed by Xie Jin, was turned into a ballet by the China Dance-Drama Troupe (Zhongguo wuju tuan) in Beijing. The Shanghai City Dance School (Shanghai shi wudao xuexiao) worked on adapting its story of a young woman in the mountains of the northwest. The ballet version of *The Red Detachment of Women*, focusing on female guerrilla fighters, was first presented publicly in September 1964.[2] Both ballets had thus been in existence for some time before they achieved model status in May 1967.

The eighth of the first model works was the *Shajiabang* symphony. It was somewhat overshadowed during the ten years of its official status as a model theatrical work and has usually been ignored since 1976. It was officially the creation of the Shanghai Symphony Orchestra, which took as its material the model modernized Beijing opera of the same name. A somewhat incestuous hybrid, the symphony featured opera soloists performing arias from the opera *Shajiabang*. The latter had attempted to fuse Chinese and Western instruments, but the sung portions of the symphony were even more unusual, for the singers were accompanied by a full Western orchestra enhanced with some Chinese instruments from the conventional opera orchestra. As with the ballets and modernized operas, the Cultural Revolution innovators conceived the symphony as a model for the further sinicization of Western orchestral music. Such music was already much more familiar to Chinese audiences than ballet or modernized opera. Film scores and radio broadcasts, for example, had made it part of many people's lives. The need for a model to help popularize this performance genre was less pressing, so its model function was less important than that of its seven stablemates. As a hybrid of orchestral music and opera, it was also harder to stage. The first public performance of the *Shajiabang* symphony was on National Day, 1 October 1965, but it was seldom performed thereafter.[3]

The eight model works did not emerge at the same time: some underwent many years of development and refinement, whereas others were relatively new when they were officially identified in May 1967. With the exception of the earlier sung-drama versions of *The White-Haired Girl,* the model theatrical work with the longest pedigree was the opera *Raid on the White Tiger Regiment,* which had first been performed in Shandong in 1957. The first version of *Taking Tiger Mountain by Strategy* had appeared in 1958. Its plot was drawn from an episode in *Tracks in the Snowy Forest (Linhai xueyuan),* a 1957 novel by Qu Bo, and it was further refined after the 1960 appearance of a film based on the novel.[4]

Shajiabang started as a Shanghai opera (Huju) in 1960 with the title *Sparks among the Reeds (Lu dang huozhong). The Red Lantern* could not claim such a lengthy heritage, being based on a 1963 feature film titled *Others Will Follow Us (Zi you houlairen).* At the June-July 1964 Festival of Beijing Operas with Contemporary Themes, several provincial troupes presented their own versions of *The Red Lantern.* In these cases, as with the two ballets, popular success in another genre provided a basis for attempting adaptation into the unfamiliar form of modern-subject Beijing opera. *Taking Tiger Mountain by Strategy* was also presented in Beijing during the summer of 1964.

These works were models, not solely for a new Chinese culture, but also for a new Chinese person. Behaviour, attitudes, and beliefs were to be modelled on those of the heroes in the new works. The self-sacrifice, cooperation, determination to succeed, devotion to the Chinese Communist Party and Chairman Mao, stoicism in adversity, and firm belief in the ultimate triumph of the cause were all model qualities of the men and women placed firmly centre stage in the model operas and ballets. The symphonic work was also hero-centred, though it borrowed this from the *Shajiabang* opera. Audiences watching these works were expected to model their attitudes and actions on those of the heroes.

As other scholars have observed, they were a strange set of heroes. The only one to have a family was Li Yuhe, the railway signalman in *The Red Lantern,* and even that family was a constructed one: he, his daughter, and his mother were all unrelated biologically. The other heroes, singular in determination and achievement, were also all single. In a culture that had privileged the family for two millennia, this new model person was a deliberate effort to repudiate the heroes of the "feudal" past. The central heroes of the model operas and ballets have a substitute family in the form of their comrades-in-arms and a caring and supportive Communist Party. Politics thus takes precedence over biology in moulding a new, modern Chinese person.

The Appeal of the Models

The reasons for the selection of these particular pieces as model theatrical works lie in their content, their artistic success, and the contexts in which they emerged. During the first half of the 1960s, Beijing opera troupes across the nation were working on a long list of new-style works with modern subjects. So why were the five operas named in May 1967 and singled out for that level of promotion? They themselves provide the first part of an answer to this question. Stories of personal bravery and cheeky resourcefulness to fool a seemingly overwhelming enemy have always appealed to readers of popular novels and to storytellers and their audiences. Yang Zirong (hero of *Taking Tiger Mountain by Strategy*) mounting Tiger Mountain disguised as a bandit, resplendent in tiger-skin waistcoat, had much in common with the manly heroes of the novels *Water Margin (Shuihu zhuan)* and *Three Kingdoms (Sanguo zhi yanyi),* and with those of folktales and stories. Yang Zirong appears as one of the panels in the Cultural Revolution triptych presented by Richard King in Chapter 9. Although updated with the addition of a Red Army uniform and a pistol, he also had his antecedents in earlier, more traditional operas. Similarly, the cunning wiles displayed by Sister Aqing, the tea-house proprietress of *Shajiabang,* as she deceives the Japanese and puppet troops while protecting the wounded New Fourth Army soldiers, came straight out of popular fiction or conventional opera.

For Chinese audiences, however, Yang Zirong and Sister Aqing appeared far from familiar: they dressed in a stylized version of appropriate twentieth-century clothing, and they moved and sang in ways that combined the familiar with the new. Yang Zirong mimed the whipping of an imaginary horse as he rode through snowy forests, depicted naturalistically on the stage. Conventional opera was performed on a much plainer set, the standard being a table and two chairs at centre stage. Yang's arias, which were accompanied by Chinese opera and Western musical instruments, mixed different standard melodic styles. Both the singing style and the new-style musical accompaniment had a forceful impact on listeners: it was as if the opera stage had borrowed the conventions of close-up, zoom, and travelling shot from the movie screen. The role of Sister Aqing was also innovative: she sang in ways that opera-goers associated with male, rather than female, roles.

With one exception, the first batch of model operas and ballets were set some years in the past. *On the Docks* was alone in having a close-to-present-day setting, that of Shanghai in the early 1960s. *Raid on the White Tiger Regiment* was set in the early 1950s but at a geographical and cultural distance, in Korea during the Korean War. The other three operas and the two ballets were set in the 1930s and 1940s, during the war against Japan or the Chinese Civil War. Wartime settings offered a degree of excitement that more contemporary stories could not. People watched opera to be taken out of their everyday contexts: modern wartime heroics could serve this purpose as much as the more ancient stories in conventional opera. For many Chinese viewers, *On the Docks* was the least interesting of the model theatrical works; its setting and story were too familiar.[5]

The Patrons

The fact that these pieces ended up as model theatrical works during the Cultural Revolution involved more than the appeal of their exciting plots and heroic characters: they had patrons. The cultural apparatus in China during the early 1960s may have employed millions of people, but, as in other areas of Chinese life, the people who mattered were remarkably few in number. Hierarchy and status had enormous importance: a provincial troupe, earnestly working up a modern-subject opera for presentation at the next experimental performance opportunity in the region or in Beijing, had little hope of making it into the big time. Individual actors, musicians, or backstage talents, however, could well be transferred to the more prestigious troupes in Beijing or Shanghai. Troupes there, with suitably influential political patrons, could draw upon the best of Chinese creative and performing talent. These included musicologists and stage directors of a kind that had rarely been involved in conventional operas.

Most notable among these patrons was Mao's wife, Jiang Qing. Determining the extent of her influence is one of the most difficult aspects about culture during the Cultural Revolution. Emerging in the mid-1960s after twenty years of virtual absence from public life, Jiang Qing was closely associated in Cultural Revolution sources with the creation and promulgation of the model theatrical works. She made a brief address on modernizing opera to the summer 1964 festival at the capital. Her speech was noted in contemporary reports of the festival but was not published until more than three years later (probably substantially rewritten and now titled "On the Revolution in Beijing Opera"), after the official identification of the eight model works.[6] With the start of the Cultural Revolution, Jiang Qing's role in encouraging and, as suggested, even shaping the efforts of opera and ballet specialists was widely praised. She was presented, by her political allies in particular, as practically the godmother or midwife of the model theatrical works.[7]

That image changed after Jiang Qing's arrest in October 1976. Now she was attacked as an impediment to the work of artists who knew better and as a meddler in their efforts to modernize opera and ballet. Little had apparently escaped her jaundiced eye, as she insisted on changes, small and large, to the new versions; she was described as encouraging certain members of the troupes involved to undermine the ideas and experiments of men and women she distrusted or disliked. After 1976, it was suggested, the achievement of the modern-style Beijing operas and China's two answers to *Swan Lake* and *Giselle* had occurred despite, rather than because of, Jiang Qing's involvement in the projects.[8]

These opposite views of Jiang Qing's role in the creation of the model works notwithstanding, there is no disputing her importance in their dissemination as models for a new, modern Chinese culture. To Jiang Qing, politics appears to have been a stage for the acting out of the Manichaean struggle between supporters and opponents of her husband and herself. A self-image as an embattled but noble fighter, dramatized by a sweeping cloak or army greatcoat hung from her shoulders, seems to have grown in the former actress' mind. Her abilities to perform in public appearances before massed Red Guards, aroused at the presence of the wife of Chairman Mao, were obvious. Self-deprecation, emotion, sarcasm, and laughter were all devices she used to disarm her critics. Arrests, mistreatment, internal exile, and home invasions were more destructive means to the same end. Where the interests of the new, modern culture ended and ego took over is a difficult point to establish. But it was Jiang Qing who pushed for the announcement of the eight model theatrical works in May 1967, on the twenty-fifth anniversary of Mao's Yan'an Talks, only a month after she saw *The White-Haired Girl* for the first time.[9]

October 1966: What Was On

The first National Day celebrated during the Cultural Revolution came at a time of considerable political and social upheaval. Examination of the cultural performances offers the chance to establish something of a baseline for pre-model performance culture, less than eight months before their May 1967 promulgation. The *Tianjin Daily (Tianjin ribao)* – the main paper of what, at that time, was China's third-largest city, just ninety kilometres from the capital – offers an extensive advertisement for cultural events around the October 1966 festivities.[10] Covering about one-third of the back page of the issue, the listing gives prominence to several documentary films featuring Chairman Mao meeting Red Guards and others.

Another film playing widely in Tianjin for the 1966 National Day was a documentary on the *Rent Collection Courtyard,* a group of statues created in Sichuan in 1965 as a text for class-struggle education of visitors (it is discussed by Britta Erickson in Chapter 5).[11] As was to become the case for the model theatrical works, filming this huge sculptural ensemble made it accessible to many millions more people than could see it in travelling versions or who could travel themselves to view it in situ, at the former landlord's mansion in the town of Dayi, Sichuan. The documentary was onscreen in twelve venues throughout Tianjin.

Contrary to a frequent claim that all feature films made in China before 1966 were banned from public screening during the Cultural Revolution, the National Day cultural activities that year included several popular films from the 1950s and 1960s.[12] Among a dozen other Chinese and foreign features onscreen that October was *Others Will Follow Us,* the 1963 film whose plot would be retold in the modernized Beijing opera *The Red Lantern.*

The Red Lantern and the operatic version of *Shajiabang* were the only instances of what would make up the model theatrical works announced almost eight months later. *The Red Lantern* was presented by the Tanggu Beijing Opera Troupe and the Tianjin City Beijing Opera Troupe. Performances of *Shajiabang* by the Red Art Soldier Beijing Opera Troupe (Hongyibing jingju tuan) were sold out until 14 October, as were those by the Fighting Opera Troupe (Zhandou). The unavailability of tickets to these two operas in October 1966 indicates their rising importance. Group sales to work units *(danwei),* party and Youth League members, and others help account for some of this, but we should not discount the genuine appeal at this stage of accomplished new-style works.

These two modernized Beijing operas did not enjoy a monopoly on the stage in late 1966, almost half a year after the official start of the Cultural Revolution. Other operas were also available in late October to sung-drama aficionados in Tianjin: for example, the Tianjin Special Region Northern Opera Troupe (Tianjin zhuanqu Pingju tuan) was playing *Jiao Yulu,* an opera based on the story of a real-life model rural party secretary from the early 1960s. Low ticket prices and group concessions indicated difficulty in attracting audiences, in contrast with the sold-out notices for *The Red Lantern* and *Shajiabang* performances.

With the initial Cultural Revolution operatic focus on modernizing Beijing opera, troupes that specialized in other forms of opera had little choice but to attempt new-style Beijing opera or otherwise change their repertoire. The October 1966 listing includes shows by the Tianjin City Shaoxing Opera Troupe (Yueju tuan) vaguely titled as "Songs of Praise *(gesong)* for the Great Leader Chairman Mao; Songs of Praise for the Great Proletarian Cultural Revolution; Songs, Dances and Other Artistic Performances." The former Henan Opera Troupe (Yuju tuan), now going by the name of War of Resistance Song and Dance Ensemble (Kangzhan wengongtuan), offered all seats at thirty *fen* (less than five cents US), students and children half-price, for *Sending Precious Books (Song baoshu), Songs of the Red Guards (Hongweibing zhi ge), and Eulogy for Liu Yingjun (Liu Yingjun zan).* Thus, the skills of the troupe were adapted to presenting work rather different from conventional Henan opera.[13]

Vestiges of other opera styles, however, can be detected in October 1966. The Tianjin City Northern Opera Troupe (Pingju tuan) was offering *Making Revolution Following Chairman Mao Forever (Yongyuan genzhe Mao Zhuxi nao geming).* This was a large-scale performance and sung piece *(da biaoyan chang)* in a style that had become dominant on the eve of the Cultural Revolution. It combined massed singing with group chanting and moving about a stage to create sculpture-like tableaux.[14] The Northern Opera Troupe's other item, however, is more intriguing. Despite its clichéd title, *A Great Joyous Occasion for the Whole People (Quanguo renmin de da xishi),* it is identified in the newspaper advertisement as "Northern opera" (Pingju). This was at a time when modernized Beijing opera is now said to have been the only approved opera form.[15]

Other previously well-established performing groups had also seen a change of repertoire by late 1966. The Tianjin City People's Art Spoken Drama Theatre (known by its abbreviated title Renyi) had become the City Worker-Peasant-Soldier Song and Dance Ensemble. Its members were presumably pleased at least to preserve their status – and access to resources – as a municipal-level artistic group. They were reduced to presenting *Chairman Mao's Red Guards, A Great Happy Occasion for the Whole People*, and *A Fine Son of the People (Renmin de hao erzi).* The plays by Ibsen and the early twentieth-century Chinese dramatist Cao Yu, performed during the 1950s and early 1960s, were long gone for the troupe and its audiences. But the skills of a troupe like this could still be appreciated even in dross, and work units could provide their staff en masse with bulk purchase of tickets.

In a similar vein, the former City Opera School (Xixiao), now the Tianjin City Worker-Peasant-Soldier Art School, had sold out all tickets until 5 October to its enticingly titled *In Praise of Mao Zedong Thought (Gesong Mao Zedong sixiang),* described as a "music, dance, and opera *[xiqu]* variety artistic evening." Like the groups that had reworked conventional Beijing opera into a new form, other groups also put the old vocal art forms to Cultural Revolution purposes. These included the former municipal *quyi* (variety performance) troupe, now the Tianjin City People's Recitation Troupe (Shuochang tuan), which offered a "show of new variety and recitation" *(xin quyi shuochang hui).* Acrobatic performances, always popular with Chinese audiences, were given a new look to better serve Cultural Revolution purposes. The Tianjin Acrobatic Troupe had a program titled *Acrobatic Art Reflecting Real Life (Fanying xianshi shenghuo zaji yishu).*

Apart from casting doubt on the claim that advertising did not exist during the Cultural Revolution, this third-of-a-page schedule of National Day performances and films suggests both narrowness and breadth.[16] A wider range of entertainment options was available to the Tianjin public than might be expected, given the usual statements about the supremacy of the modernized Beijing operas and model ballets. At the same time, the predominance in the Cultural Revolution of praise of Mao Zedong and all his works shows how limited the choices were in terms of content.[17]

Promulgation of the Models

Less than eight months later, on the twenty-fifth anniversary of Mao's Yan'an Talks, the eight model theatrical works were officially disseminated. Media coverage was considerable: the 24 May 1967 issue of *People's Daily (Renmin ribao)* featured a front-page report on the official gathering in Beijing to mark the event. Three major articles filled page 6. Pride of place was given to the speech by Yu Huiyong at the Beijing gathering. Yu, a composer and music teacher by profession, was then forty-one years old and had risen from leadership of the Shanghai Conservatory to membership in the circle of cultural authorities under the Politburo. In Shanghai, he had participated in the creation of *On the Docks,* at which time he had allied himself with Jiang Qing as she took a direct interest in the modernized operas.[18] Having paid standard hyperbolic tribute to Mao and quoted from the Talks, Yu named the five modernized operas as triumphs of Mao Zedong's line on art and literature. Later, he cited in particular *Taking Tiger Mountain by Strategy* and *On the Docks* to illustrate his encomium to Mao's wisdom. In a clever play on the words *shan* (mountain) and *hai* (sea), which were components in the two operas' Chinese titles, he noted that opponents of Mao sneered at the operas as the Cultural Revolution version of the ancient geomantic text *Shanhai jing* (Classic of mountains and seas). Yu praised his patron Jiang Qing for her direct participation in the struggle to produce these two new-style operas.[19]

The other two articles on this page covered the rest of the newly proclaimed model theatrical works: the two ballets and the *Shajiabang* symphony. As in the case of the opera article, they were speeches that had been given at the Yan'an Talks commemorations in Beijing. Praising the ballets as beacon lights of a revolution in dance, well-known ballerina Zhong Runliang contrasted *The Red Detachment of Women* and *The White-Haired Girl* with the old Western *(yang)* ballets of the past. Zhong also singled out Jiang Qing for praise, crediting her with leading the "ballet revolution" in the spring of 1964. Mao's attendance at a performance of *The Red Detachment of Women* in October 1964 was said to have been crucial in encouraging the modernization and sinicization of ballet.

In his speech on the new symphony, Chen Rutang, from the now officially disbanded Central Symphony Orchestra, also emphasized Jiang Qing's support of the project. In January 1964, he reported, she had urged the Central Symphony Orchestra, "Do not take the dead end route of westerners; you should find your own road." The *Shajiabang* symphony was allegedly "worker-peasant-soldier symphonic music." As with the other two speeches delivered that May, Chen contrasted the attitudes of those who criticized the new works with the proletarian determination of their creators to produce art that responded to the Yan'an Talks emphasis on a mass audience.

People's Daily capped the praise for the new, modern works advocated by Jiang Qing with a front-page editorial on 31 May 1967. The large headline used the word "model" *(yangban)*, proclaiming the productions to be "outstanding models of revolutionary literature and art."[20] The text of the editorial helped popularize the term "revolutionary model theatrical works"; in Beijing a week earlier, Zhong Runliang had not used it in his speech commemorating the Yan'an Talks, and Chen Rutang had used it only once. But nationwide reprinting of the editorial and insistent media follow-up indicated that the term "model theatrical works" had arrived. The provincial newspaper *Ningxia Daily*, for example, gave front-page prominence to the editorial, but other coverage of the model theatrical works was hard to find in such newspapers. That May, audiences in Beijing may have enjoyed (or otherwise) live performances of the eight models, but in the provinces, they were still a somewhat distant phenomenon, heard on radio but not seen live.

The association of Jiang Qing with the eight models in the *People's Daily* editorial and other articles created a strong linkage between the woman and the works. Four phrases much used by Mao Zedong were also attached firmly to the model works in the May 1967 editorial and afterwards: "let a hundred flowers bloom; throwing out the old and bringing in the new; making the past serve the present; and making foreign things serve China" *(baihua qifang; tui chen chu xin; gu wei jin yong; yang wei Zhong yong).* These four-character clichés summed up the central role of the model theatrical works in the latest stage of China's cultural modernization project. Far from being some abhorrent rejection of this ongoing twentieth-century project, the Cultural Revolution continued the push though ultimately, perhaps, up a sidetrack.

Spreading the Model Theatrical Works

The importance of these eight model theatrical works should not be underestimated. Once they had been identified as models, they were broadcast with the full resources of Chinese state cultural apparatus. Even in the midst of the Cultural Revolution, when chaos is said to have reigned on the streets, the cultural organs continued to function. The bitter factional battles being waged at all levels do not seem to have disrupted the payment of salaries and the provision of housing, rudimentary health care, and other services to members of these cultural work units. Later, in 1969 and 1970, a large number of cultural organizations were disbanded, but even then at least a proportion of wages appears to have been paid to their former members.

Social and political upheaval did not seem to have hindered the presentation of the model works across the nation. The original opera and ballet troupes (and the Central and Shanghai Symphony Orchestras) spent their time performing the works widely. Despite their iconic status, continuous refinement was carried out on all seven theatrical works (the operas and ballets), with different dated "performances texts" *(yanchu ben)* filling the pages of *People's Daily* and the other national and regional newspapers in the late 1960s and early 1970s. Other, lesser, troupes rehearsed and presented the works locally and had been doing so since before May 1967. By the early 1970s, scores, full libretti, and stage and costume design books had been published for each of the model theatrical works, to facilitate nationwide efforts to duplicate their perfection live onstage. New modern-subject Beijing operas were also created, refined, and popularized.

These works took on a function as models for other performing art. Episodes from the original five operas were retold in other artistic forms: by chanting pairs of performers in *kuaishu* (clappertalk), by storytellers, and even in short spoken dramas without musical accompaniment. Comic books and the retelling of episodes as short fiction took the model stories to younger audiences than would be reached by regular opera.

By the early 1970s, in indirect acknowledgment of the paucity of little more than five operas among the model theatrical works, and in order to revive other types of regional and local musical drama in appropriate revised form, transplanting *(yizhi)* the models became a major focus of the cultural authorities. Hebei clapper opera *(bangzi)* proved one of the easiest opera styles in which to adapt the Beijing originals, as both were northern forms that featured a "hardness" of musical and performing style. Practitioners of softer southern opera forms, less used to martial themes, had more difficulty adapting the Beijing opera originals. However, *Shajiabang* appeared in a Cantonese opera (Yueju) version and in a so-called Uighur opera version. This latter was itself a contemporary invention, emerging after 1949 and based on Uighur folk singing melded with modern musical drama *(geju)*. The Xinjiang versions of *Shajiabang* and *The Red Lantern* offered further evidence of the homogenization of non-Han cultures and the mainstream mass national culture guided from Beijing.[21]

The Importance of the Model Theatrical Works

Assessing the importance of the model theatrical works is made more challenging by the tendency to overgeneralize concerning the Cultural Revolution. The joke about a nation of 800 million watching eight shows, like all good jokes, has a grain of truth to it. But it is also a typical misrepresentation of cultural activity during the period, as could be demonstrated by listing a range of cultural offerings during these ten years, from Red Guard morality plays in 1966-67 to underground song contests among sent-down youths and "misty poems" passed among friends in handwritten copies. Such an overview of the decade is beyond the scope of the present discussion.[22]

Official media treatment of these eight titles offers another way to assess the importance of the model theatrical works. The usual generalizations about them would suggest that they dominated the media, and even the most casual perusal of the pages of *People's Daily* or any provincial newspaper shows that they certainly were granted great prominence. But the attention, I suggest, was not constant. Sporadic intensive coverage was punctuated with periods in which little was mentioned regarding the model operas and ballets.

If the model theatrical works were as dominant in Chinese cultural life as is generally assumed, May commemorations of the Yan'an Talks and National Day celebrations each year could be expected to reflect this. An examination of the May and September-October issues of central and provincial newspapers between 1966 and 1976 suggests the fortunes of the model theatrical works waxed and waned. The changes in the attention accorded them indirectly reflected the relative strength of Jiang Qing and her allies among the Cultural Revolution innovators from year to year. Strident emphasis on models and Cultural Revolution conventionality was not a sign of strength: more often, it was an indicator of the sense of threat felt by this faction at a given time.

The annual commemoration of Mao's Yan'an Talks in May took on greater significance during the mid-1960s. On the eve of the Cultural Revolution, as Mao and his allies began to use the cultural realm as a beachhead in their conflict with their party rivals, marking the Talks assumed more importance in factional politics. With the apparent triumph of this wing of the party in 1966, the annual celebration of the delivery of the Talks was a means to assert the hegemony of Mao and his insurgent allies. The 1966 anniversary, around 23 May, the date in 1942 when Mao had delivered the second of his speeches that made up the Talks, was obscured by more immediate political developments, most notably the issuing of the May Sixteenth Directive by the Central Committee of the Chinese Communist Party, an event that came to be regarded as marking the official start of the Cultural Revolution.

The following May, in 1967, was the occasion for the formal identification of the eight model theatrical works. It was also the twenty-fifth anniversary of the Talks. Prominent articles in *People's Daily, Guangming Daily (Guangming ribao), Liberation Army Daily (Jiefangjun ribao),* and provincial newspapers praised the eight works.

Works Modelled and Ignored

It would be wrong to assume that the model theatrical works, including the eight original pieces and those added later, were consistently at the centre of media attention. Perusal of the pages of provincial newspapers in the last two years of the 1960s suggests a decline in official public interest. In Ningxia, for example, the May 1969 commemorations of Mao's Yan'an Talks seem to have been low-key affairs, without the usual articles or stage stills of model operas and ballets.[23] Even at other times of the year, the unrelenting presentation of the model theatrical works faded somewhat during 1968 and 1969. In the then quasi-official Red Guard newspapers of 1967-68, the absence of much reference to the model theatrical works is also striking.[24] For works that had been in the public eye for half a decade, this was perhaps only natural, if naturalness could be allowed in Chinese public discourse at the time.

Even the model theatrical works apparently needed defending. In the September 1969 issue of the party's theoretical journal *Red Flag (Hongqi),* the pseudonymous writer Zhe Ping spoke of threats to their status as models for the new culture. Under the title "Study the Revolutionary Model Performances, Defend the Revolutionary Model Performances," the article claimed that two kinds of evil persons were actively undermining the models. The first kind came allegedly from landlord and counter-revolutionary backgrounds or had been expelled from opera troupes during their recent cleansing *(qingxi).* Such critics had pieced together *(pincou)* "black" opera troupes to perform the old-style "ghost, pornographic, and traitorous plays." A second, more insidious, type of class enemy had infiltrated amateur song and dance troupes, and ensured that the model performances were presented in ways that damaged them in the eyes of their audiences.[25] If one discounts the Cultural Revolution rhetoric, this report suggests that even the model theatrical works could be tampered with, particularly at a local level, far from centralized control.

Models Defined Onscreen

In 1970, a new development offered a way of refocusing attention on the model theatrical works and of establishing their definitive versions. The release of film versions of the operas and ballets, starting in October 1970, was the most significant step in the spread of the model theatrical works. Until then, most Chinese were familiar with the model operas and ballets through radio broadcasts of arias and music, stage stills reproduced in newspapers and other mass media, and amateur performances organized by work units. Those who had access to television would also have seen parts or all of the operas recorded somewhat crudely at actual theatrical performances. Paradoxically, the filming of the model theatrical works was in the hands of the directors, cinematographers, and others who had been condemned as bourgeois or revisionist only a couple of years earlier. But guidance from outside the studios was strict, with much made after 1976 of Jiang Qing's supposed insistence that *On the Docks* be reshot because the shade of red in

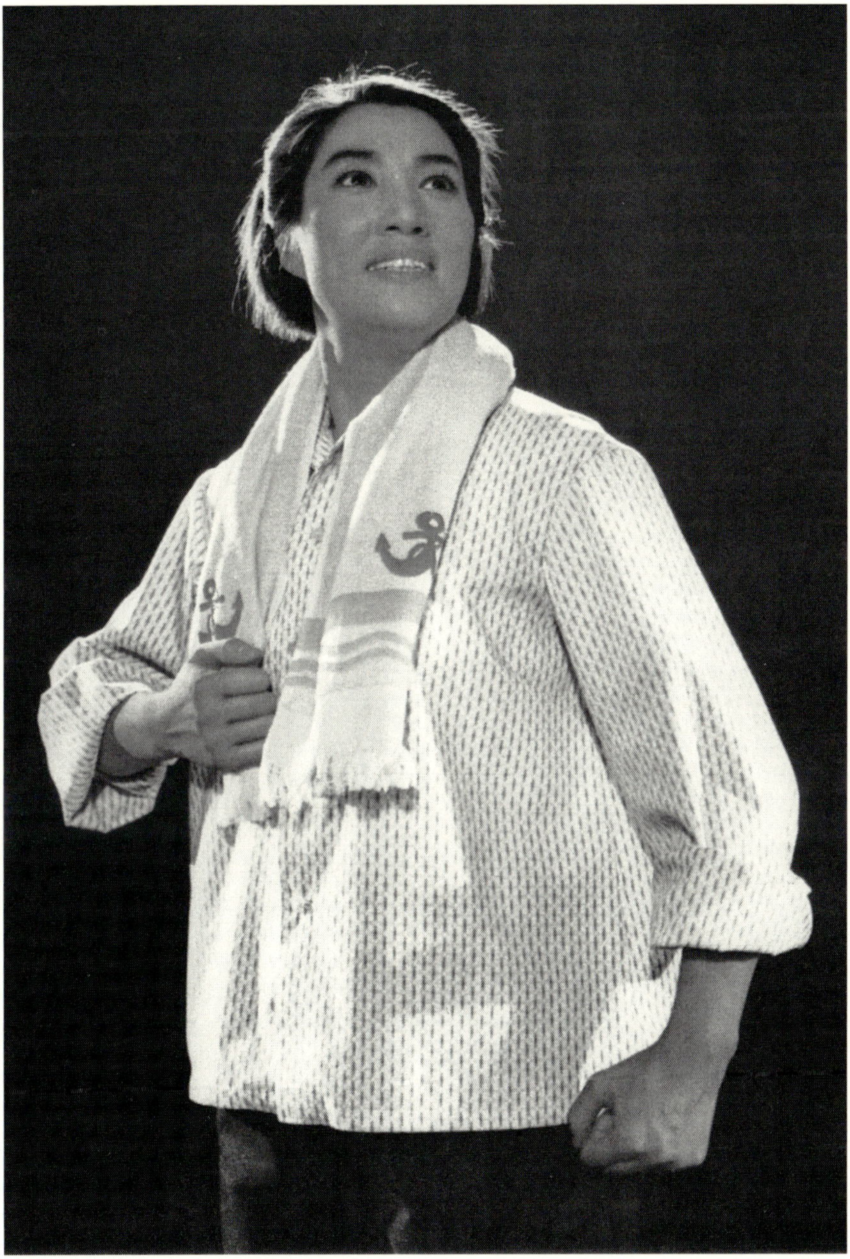

Figure 7.2 **Fang Haizhen, Communist Party branch secretary and heroine of *On the Docks*.**
On the Docks: A Modern Revolutionary Peking Opera (Peking: Foreign Languages Press, 1973).

the heroine's scarf was inappropriate. The illustration here is from the film version as finally released (Figure 7.2).[26]

For Chinese audiences who had had access only to local performances or radio broadcasts of the model works, the release of these films, starting with that of *Taking Tiger Mountain by Strategy* on National Day in 1970, provided the opportunity to see definitive, highly polished versions of the operas and ballets. Access was broadened by the Chinese invention and manufacture of portable 16- and 8.5-millimetre projectors that could be carried, along with electrical generators, by mobile projection teams to relatively remote locations.[27] The filming of the model theatrical works can be said to have guaranteed them a kind of immortality in recollections and reconstructions of the Cultural Revolution. The films, of course, also took these works to audiences around the world, reinforcing the impression of their importance in China.

In their film versions in particular, the model theatrical works served other, non-model functions. For example, certain widely distributed stills of the ballet heroines appealed to the somewhat non-political, baser, desires of many Chinese men. In the mid-1970s, pictures of Wu Qinghua, the determined young woman in *The Red Detachment of Women,* leaping across the stage, legs outstretched in bright red silk "pyjamas," could be seen above many a peasant brick bed *(kang)* or student bunk. A picture of a fierce Wu Qinghua in the same outfit, arms chained high above her head, enjoyed almost equal popularity. *The White-Haired Girl*'s white-pyjama equivalent stills were less common. (For these images, see Figures 8.1 and 8.2 in Chapter 8.)

Models in the New Decade

Ironically, by the time the films achieved general release and helped to set in stone these 1960s model Beijing operas, the range of Chinese opera reaching audiences had begun to widen to include local and regional forms, with great numbers of enthusiastic followers in many parts of the country. The effort started with the so-called transplanting of the Beijing opera into such forms as Hebei clapper opera, Northern opera, and even Cantonese opera. In May 1970, for example, the Ningxia Shaanxi Opera Troupe presented a transplanted Shaanxi opera (Qinqiang) version of *Shajiabang.*[28] The broadening of forms was paralleled by an expansion of the opera repertoire. On National Day in 1972, for example, Tianjin opera fans could watch experimental performances of a new Beijing opera, *Reed Catkin Stockade (Luhua zhai),* and a new Northern opera, *Green Dragon Pond (Qinglong tan).*[29]

But the release of the film versions of the original core model performances gave them a new lease on life. The 1971 commemoration of Mao's Yan'an Talks saw them back at centre stage in media coverage – this time as newly completed films and television documentaries recording stage performances.[30] The attention did not last long – provincial newspapers on the 1972 and 1973 anniversaries of the Talks generally had little to say regarding the model performances and their offshoots.[31]

This absence was a reflection of the times. By the early 1970s, the media were devoting more attention to the broadening of cultural activity that was being officially encouraged. This amounted to overdue acknowledgment of the limitations of an apparently strict diet consisting of model theatrical works and little else. In 1971 and 1972, Mao and Premier Zhou Enlai had both remarked that the range of cultural products available to Chinese audiences was too small.[32] Even though their opinions were not officially published, they became widely known due to the efficiency of the country's unofficial channels of information distribution. The two leaders were merely expressing the attitudes of more ordinary Chinese opera and theatre fans.

After 1973, Chinese audiences could enjoy what passed for a cultural life, even without the model theatrical works. New feature films, not based on the model works, emerged from the studios as they continued the momentum gained from the renewal of production for the films of the model theatrical works. Several of the new films were colour remakes of pre–Cultural Revolution black-and-white features that had been mainstays of holiday screenings in the late 1960s. *Green Pine Ridge* (*Qing song ling,* 1952 and 1973), *Guerrillas on the Plain* (*Pingyuan youjidui,* 1955 and 1974), and *Fighting North and South* (*Nan zheng bei zhan,* 1952 and 1974) were three such films.[33] The attention won from young and old audiences by the children's film *Sparkling Red Star* (*Shanshan de hongxing,* 1974) was an indication of their relief at getting away from the model operas and ballets.[34] Media emphasis on how the new films followed the "three prominences" *(san tuchu)* aesthetic principle of the model operas was a sideshow. Despite an unrelenting concentration on the heroes of the films, audiences were probably pleased that attention no longer centred on Yang Zirong (of *Taking Tiger Mountain by Strategy*), Fang Haizhen (the party secretary in *On the Docks*), and their like, all of them too familiar.

As this suggests, by the mid-1970s, mass cynicism regarding the rhetorical hyperbole surrounding the model theatrical works was widespread.[35] Welcome relief came from non-mainstream Chinese cultures. Minority song and dance, in highly modified reworkings, continued to offer a variety that Han stolidity could not match. The so-called dance-drama *(wuju) Sons and Daughters of the Grasslands (Caoyuan ernü),* for example, took Cultural Revolution full-length dance beyond the two model ballets. Its appeal, which it shared with its animated film predecessor *Heroic Little Sisters of the Grasslands* (*Caoyuan yingxiong xiao jiemei,* 1964), lay in the Mongolian setting, costumes, and choreographic elements.

By this time, any renewed emphasis on the model theatrical works in the media served as a barometer of the rising sense of threat to their cultural authority felt by Jiang Qing and her allies in the cultural apparatus.[36] In May 1974, the residents of Yinchuan, the capital of the Ningxia Muslim Autonomous Region, were treated to a slew of films and live performances of the model operas and ballets.[37] For the May 1975 anniversary of Mao's Yan'an Talks, the newly reconstituted Ministry of Culture, one of the last bastions of the cultural authorities associated with Jiang Qing, organized showings of the films of the model theatrical works in cities and towns across the nation.[38] The massive scale of these screenings was a sign of the weakness of the model works, not of their lasting vigour. Similarly, evidence of a gnawing defensiveness can be detected in a *Guangming ribao* report of an army unit in the Shaanxi military region viewing films of the model works to, as the headline put it, "insist on revolutionary practice in art and literature and criticize the counter-revolutionary crimes of Deng Xiaoping."[39] These soldiers and poor and lower-middle peasants were made of stern stuff, watching a double bill of filmed model works together until after eleven at night. To readers who themselves had probably been organized to watch these films several times, such reports were signs of desperation. Beijing audiences, on the other hand, were treated in May 1975 to an unprecedented number and range of live model opera performances, including several that had been transplanted into forms other than Beijing opera.[40]

Tianjin audiences on National Day in 1975 had a choice of several live performances of extracts from *On the Docks* and a later addition to the model canon, *Azalea Mountain (Dujuanshan).* But these were scheduled with less familiar experimental performances of new short operas.[41] The latter may have been what attracted the curious. In May of the following year, Yinchuan audiences could choose between seventeen opera or dance films, including those of the original eight model works. Curiously, the half-page listing or advertisement for the films provided no details of the times or places of their screenings. It was as if the mere fact that they were apparently being shown together was sufficient.[42]

Expanding the repertoire of modernized Beijing operas was another response to political threat. In 1974, Beijing audiences encountered a relatively new opera from Shanghai, *Boulder Bay (Panshi wan).* Set in 1963 on the southwest coast, it combined a spy story with spectacular stage movements and a hero who actually had a wife. Xie Jin, the eminent filmmaker and experienced director of the films of model works, co-directed a film version in 1976.[43] For many Chinese viewers, *Boulder Bay* was laughable: the surrealism of the scenes, including fighting underwater, took the kitsch qualities of the model operas to new levels of excess.[44] This attempt at modernizing Chinese culture seemed to have reached a dead end.

In the last Cultural Revolution commemoration of Mao's Yan'an Talks, in May 1976, the model theatrical works and their operatic successors seem to have ended up on the sidelines. In Ningxia, for example, two of the seven new feature films on show were short opera adaptations in clapper and Shandong (Luju) styles.[45] On National Day of that year, a subdued occasion three weeks after Mao's death and a week before the arrest of Jiang Qing and some of her closest allies, two of twelve new feature films were operatic. One was an Anhui opera (Huangmei xi); the other, the last of the Cultural Revolution modernized Beijing operas, was *Red Cloud Ridge (Hongyun gang).* As a 1947 story, it was a throwback to the first model works.[46] In 1976, Mao Zedong had been fitfully watching some of the fifty old-style operas that had been filmed that year for his viewing and to preserve the pre–Cultural Revolution opera legacy.[47] This was an ignominious end for the model theatrical works created in his honour, though they survive in memory, on film, in karaoke DVDs, and in occasional stage revivals.

This brief survey of some of the regular public commemorations during the ten years of the Cultural Revolution indicates the need for a careful assessment of cultural production in that era. The works that supposedly lay at the heart of the nation's political and cultural life appear to have had a rather more checkered career. Produced by exceptionally skilled artists and writers, they were closely associated then and now with the group later condemned as the Gang of Four. This tended to give enormous significance to the five operas, the two ballets, the symphony, and the other works added to the model canon, at least in official media. But the close association with a political faction served also to limit the model works, to constrain their effectiveness as creative templates. This meant that their contribution to the ongoing twentieth-century project of modernizing Chinese culture was also limited. But, as efforts in this modern project, they deserve recognition. Achieving a proper assessment of the model theatrical works as art and of the Cultural Revolution in culture requires the kind of reconstruction of actual cultural activity that this chapter has begun to outline.

8

Feminism in the Revolutionary Model Ballets *The White-Haired Girl* and *The Red Detachment of Women*

Bai Di

The revolutionary model theatrical works first appeared on the Chinese cultural scene during the early months of the Cultural Revolution. The term "model theatrical works" was coined to describe a collection of performing art productions revised under the direction of Jiang Qing (1914-91), wife of Communist Party chairman Mao Zedong. The earliest official source proclaiming the existence of the model theatrical works was a 6 December 1966 news report in the newspaper *People's Daily* titled "Carrying Out Chairman Mao's Line on Literature and Art: Brilliant Models." A short editorial on the same page celebrated the birth and significance of these works: "Since 1964, under the brilliant radiance of Chairman Mao's line on literature and art, the high tide of revolutionary reform in the fields of Beijing opera, of ballet, and of symphonic music has swelled. The revolutionary model theatre has been created, which consists of five Beijing operas: *Shajiabang, The Red Lantern, Taking Tiger Mountain by Strategy, On the Docks, Raid on the White Tiger Regiment;* two ballet dramas: *The White-Haired Girl, The Red Detachment of Women,* and the symphony *Shajiabang*."[1]

A 16 July 1967 news report from the government-run Xinhua News Agency (Xinhuashe) incorporated an official tone in the evaluation of the model theatrical works:

> The eight model theatrical works have prominently propagated the shining Mao Zedong thought and prominently eulogized the workers, peasants, and soldiers who are the masters of history. Threading through all the plays is Chairman Mao's revolutionary line on art and literature, which stresses that literature serve the workers, peasants, and soldiers, as well as proletarian politics. Model theatrical works embody the correct guiding principle of "letting one hundred flowers bloom" *[baihua qifang]*, "throwing out the old and bringing in the new" *[tui chen chu xin]*, and "making the past serve the present and foreign things serve China" *[gu wei jin yong, yang wei zhong yong]*.[2]

Over the course of the Cultural Revolution, the term "model theatrical work" became a common designation for any Beijing opera or ballet that exhibited the exemplary qualities of the original eight. The celebrity of the *Shajiabang* symphony, which was not a theatrical piece in the first place, soon faded, and more popular newcomers, such as the Beijing operas *Azalea Mountain* and *Song of the Dragon River*, took its place as models.

The model works dominated the Chinese cultural scene throughout the Cultural Revolution decade. From 1966 to 1976, they were adapted into various local theatrical forms to make them accessible to regional audiences. The Chinese Communist Party's political campaign titled Singing Model Operas, Becoming a Revolutionary (Chang yangbanxi, zuo geming ren), which used literature and art to indoctrinate the Chinese people in its standardized view of revolutionary history and class struggle, as well as in its moral and ethical principles, was arguably the most successful of this type.[3]

In the years immediately following the Cultural Revolution to the mid-1990s, the model theatrical works were generally regarded, both inside and outside China, as the dead end of the Communist Party's political and ideological appropriation of art, a process that had begun with Mao Zedong's 1942 "Talks at the Yan'an Forum on Literature and Art" (hereafter Yan'an Talks).[4] The Cultural Revolution itself was condemned by its critics as "artless, sterile, without depth, without truth, and without reality."[5] Given this assessment, it was not seen as deserving a place in the history of modern Chinese literature. Characteristic of this line of thinking is Joseph S.M. Lau and Howard Goldblatt's *The Columbia Anthology of Modern Chinese Literature,* which skips the Cultural Revolution period completely.[6] Generally speaking, Western scholarship on the model theatrical works, whether descriptive or analytical, has fallen into two similarly limited types. The first, as represented by Walter Meserve, views the model theatre primarily in terms of its political context and consequently assumes that it had scant literary or dramatic value. The second kind of scholarship analyzes the literary-artistic value in the model theatrical works and largely restricts itself to form. This approach focuses on how the works were constructed as popular art and how they were a product of the Communist Party's manipulation of mass performing art and popular culture. Bonnie S. McDougall's "Writers and Performers, Their Works, and Their Audiences, in the First Three Decades," which examines the period 1949-79, is one such study.[7] In either case, when the model theatrical works are viewed solely as propaganda, or as an artistic weapon used for propagandistic purposes, their texts are seldom approached outside of the confinement of anti-Maoist interpretation.

After the end of the Cultural Revolution, critics in the People's Republic of China attacked the model theatrical works out of a shared sense of righteous opposition to what they saw as the evil products of a political and cultural disaster. In their view, the sole reason for the existence of these works was to serve and satisfy Jiang Qing's personal ambition. They perceived the model works exclusively in terms of their political context, or as a part of that political context.[8] The works were regarded not solely as the product of political turmoil, but also as being partially responsible for that turmoil. As the core of Cultural Revolution literary "propaganda," they have been ignored and thrown into critical oblivion. In Chen Sihe's highly regarded *A History of Contemporary Chinese Literature,* published in 1999, the model works are mentioned in one paragraph as being responsible for a "malignant effect" *(elie yingxiang)* in Chinese literary creativity.[9] Although these Chinese and Western critics may agree on the worthlessness, or even the harmfulness, of the Cultural Revolution model theatre, they differ regarding its place in the longer course of Chinese cultural history. Western scholars usually see the model works as the final outcome of Mao's Yan'an Talks and accept that Jiang Qing's line on literature and art met Mao's requirements; Chinese scholars, on the other hand, seldom admit that the works represent a continuation of Mao's literary policy.[10] Rather, they present the works as having deviated from the party's literary tradition.[11]

This chapter is a critical intervention that attempts to redefine the model theatrical works by looking at the definitive texts of the two model ballets: *The White-Haired Girl* and *The Red Detachment of Women.*[12] A study of the texts themselves, it takes neither anti-Mao nor anti–Jiang Qing sentiment as its theoretical starting-point. Its goal is to reach a fresh understanding of the position of the model theatrical works in the cultural history of the People's Republic of China, as well as to recognize their significance in subverting the hegemonic party ideology. To achieve this end, it liberates the reading of model theatre from the political shackles that have hampered exploration of the cultural incongruity of the model works within the Chinese Communist Party's literary tradition. This incongruity, I argue, arises from the model theatrical works' radical and thoroughgoing disruption of Chinese gender construction. Through close readings of the texts, I propose that, in its cultural essence, model theatre is feminist. Its feminism lies in its systematic construction of the heroic images of women against the background of Communist Party history, and of these women's strategic appropriation of class and political identities in order to escape from subordinate gender roles. Within a discourse of class struggle, model theatre creates a feminist utopia where androgyny, "the only social form in which we [women] can live freely," is very much prevalent.[13] The feminism embedded in these works, which stresses degendering, sets them apart from canonical party literature and accounts for their oft-noted and reviled extremes in character portraiture.[14]

My rereading of model theatre so as to elucidate and understand its disruption of Chinese gender construction is also a direct response to a troubling social phenomenon – the current trend in post-Mao China to re-establish clear gender roles. In feminist gender theories, gender is a complex notion. Unlike naturally attributed sex, it is situationally derived. Learning to behave in accordance with one's gender identity is an indispensable stage in the early development of all men and women. The process of acquiring a gender identity is one of learning how a girl/woman or boy/man should feel, think, and act in a social setting. Feminist gender theories make it clear that dissolving rigid gender roles is a task of primary importance to women's liberation. Such gender-based feminist theories have been instrumental in developing my own conceptualizing of model theatre as feminist. During the current economic reform and fervent globalization drive, official publications in China argue that the "responsibility system" and labour efficiency considerations justify women's return to the kitchen, where they will resume the role of "virtuous wife and good mother."[15] As Emily Honig and Gail Hershatter observe in their study of Chinese women in the early eighties, "Public discussion in the 1980s was shaped by a decisive rejection of the experiences of the Cultural Revolution. The fervour and enthusiasm with which women beautified themselves, the widespread support for moving women back into 'suitable' lines of work, the discussions of womanly virtues in the press, must all be understood in part as a reaction to Cultural Revolution norms."[16]

If this widely recognized trend in which Chinese women return to their traditional gender roles is indeed a backlash against the degendered image of women as "holding up half the sky," stressed during the Cultural Revolution period, that degendering deserves closer critical attention. If we are to understand the redomestication and regendering of women that is occurring as China transforms itself into a capitalist economy, we need to examine women's images of the Cultural Revolution. In other words, what is it about the Cultural Revolution that stands so starkly as the antithesis to the current regendering of women?

The White-Haired Girl

The original drama *The White-Haired Girl,* on which the Cultural Revolution model ballet was based, was first produced in 1945 by a group of the

Communist Party's "workers in the arts" following the policies outlined by Mao Zedong in his Yan'an Talks. The popular legend, or dramatized reality, underlying *The White-Haired Girl* was explained by one of its original writers, He Jingzhi. He recalled that, during the early 1940s, stories regarding a "white-haired goddess" were making the rounds in the northwestern part of Hebei Province, then under the control of the communist Eighth Route Army. The white-haired goddess turned out to be a poor peasant woman who had lost her family and was living in the wilderness like an animal. She would emerge from her hiding place at night to search for food. People who encountered her thought she was a ghost. The Eighth Route Army found her and resettled her in her village. The drama *The White-Haired Girl* was said to be based on this ostensibly true story. The American journalist Jack Belden saw the play when he visited Pengcheng, in the area of Henan Province controlled by the Eighth Route Army, during the spring of 1947. According to his vivid account,

> "[The] White-haired Woman" was a tragic melodrama. The heroine of the play is the daughter of a tenant farmer. Seized by the dog legs of the landlord when her father cannot pay his New Year's debts, she is forced to become a maidservant in the landlord's home. There she is constantly beaten by the landlord's wife, a devout, but humorous old Buddhist, and finally raped on a dark night by the landlord's son. Made pregnant, she threatens to reveal her shame to the whole village. The landlord's son, who is about to be married, and the dog legs bind up the girl, throw her in a closet and make ready to murder her. An old woman servant, who many years ago had been brought to the landlord's home under much the same circumstances, releases the girl who flees in the night. The landlord's son and the dog legs pursue her into the mountains. Wailing a defiant song, the girl evades capture by taking refuge in a rocky glen where she gives birth to a baby, her hair turning white in the process. She is adopted by guerrillas who eventually free her home village and bring the landlord's son before a Speak Bitterness Meeting. The villagers debate what to do with the son. The boy, showing repentance, however, is beaten. The land is divided, the girl gets her share and even the landlord his.[17]

In 1951, a musical film version of *The White-Haired Girl* appeared, directed by Wang Bin and Shui Hua. Its plot is set in the latter half of the 1930s and relates the tragic story of a poor peasant girl named Xi'er. Her father, Yang Bailao, works for the vicious landlord Huang Shiren. Unable to pay his grain rent and an accumulated cash debt, Yang is forced in his confusion and bewilderment to sign a contract, promising to give his daughter to the Huang family as payment. Yang then commits suicide, whereupon Xi'er is forcibly taken away by the Huang family. Wang Dachun, her betrothed, runs away and joins the communist Eighth Route Army. Xi'er is treated cruelly by the Huang family and is raped by Huang Shiren. Seven months later, after she has become pregnant, Huang decides to sell her to a brothel; she had expected that he would marry her. On learning Huang's scheme at his wedding, Xi'er escapes from his household and flees to the wild mountains, where she gives birth to his child, who later dies. For more than two years, Xi'er exists like an animal in a mountain cave, avoiding human contact. This hard life, and the lack of salt in her diet, turns her hair completely white. The villagers who encounter her take her to be an apparition. Finally, a detachment of the Eighth Route Army led by Wang Dachun comes to her rescue. The village is liberated, the landlord is executed. Xi'er marries Dachun, and they live happily ever after. Considered a masterpiece of socialist realism, this 1951 film version vividly brought out the Chinese Communist Party's didactic message that "the old society forced human beings to turn into ghosts; the new society changes ghosts back into human beings."[18]

The first post–Cultural Revolution critique of the film was by Meng Yue, in her 1993 article "'*The White-Haired Girl*' and the Historical Complexity of Yan'an Literature."[19] In her reading of the text, Meng Yue goes beyond previous studies of *The White-Haired Girl,* which were trapped in narrow political frameworks. Building a three-stage historiography of *The White-Haired Girl,* Meng insightfully draws out the hidden cultural similarities between the Communist Party's class-struggle rhetoric and traditional Chinese popular value systems. She demonstrates how the Communist Party appropriates the popular tradition to attain a popular legitimacy that serves its own political ends. In the party's literary discourse, class is less a socio-economic concept than a moral one. The concept of class struggle, as Meng argues, is a direct adaptation of the traditional popular discourse of the struggle between the moral and the immoral. The disturbance of the moral order causes injustice and is the reason for social conflicts, which are presented as class struggle in Communist Party rhetoric.

The popular ideal of social and familial harmony presented in *The White-Haired Girl* permeates, for example, the relationships between father and daughter, and between the betrothed couple Xi'er and Wang Dachun. These relationships are naturally moral, for they represent the ideal familial relations. The landlord, on the other hand, is cruel and evil. An outsider to these harmonious relations, he breaks in, destroying the moral ideal. Thus, he is construed as a symbol of anti-order or disorder. A line demarcating classes is drawn, and he becomes a class enemy. Meng Yue concludes that the political discourse of class and class struggle in the Yan'an Talks, as embodied in *The White-Haired Girl,* is grounded in the traditional "popular moral order" *(minjian lunli zhixu).*[20]

However, her account of *The White-Haired Girl* stops short of examining the nature of the traditional popular moral order and social justice. If we dissect the concept of moral justice, we will discover that it is not, as is so often asserted, an impartial "adjustment of conflicting claims."[21] I would argue that, essentially speaking, this "popular moral order" is built upon, and reflects, the traditional Chinese notion of value. The traditional value system is an ideological derivation of China's traditional sex-gender system.

William Galston makes very explicit the logic of a rightfully or justifiably distributive understanding of justice. Justice, he says, "involves an ensemble of possession," which means that justice is not a mere abstract concept. It has a material base, and thus "justice concerns the proper pattern of the allocation of entities" among people in any given society. Every society has its own pattern of distributing properties, the violation of which will be considered unjust. Galston further clarifies that "the domain of entities may include objects, qualities, positions within a system, or even human beings."[22]

Galston's explanation of the nature of justice is very much in line with Gayle Rubin's thesis that patriarchal society has been built upon the traffic in women. My synthesis of these two theses reveals that the concept of social moral justice built upon the so-called morally proper distribution of benefit and wealth among society's members has been primarily constructed on the fair distribution of women by men. Women and their bodies are a part of social wealth. The justice system has a set of rules to guarantee the fair transaction and rightful possession of women. People tend to presume that the proper sphere for this distribution is the family unit. Thus, by perceiving kinship and marital relations as intrinsically fair and natural, they neglect issues of justice within families and therefore neglect the issue of gender inequality. In the film *The White-Haired Girl,* Xi'er is a key figure in the plot, but she is not its agent. The story is not structured around her, but around the ownership of her. Her father assumes his right and authority to trade her as a form of payment to his landlord; the landlord violates him by depriving him of his paternal authority over his daughter. The guilt that drives Yang Bailao to suicide comes from his despair regarding his failure as a father – including the inability to give his daughter in marriage: he has failed to live up to his contract with Wang Dachun. Thus, his suicide is not solely a reaction to social injustice: it is also a symbolic necessity in terms of his social-gender identity. The father plays a key role in this dramatic conflict over Xi'er; first, he fails to protect his daughter, and second, he fails to honour his arrangement with Wang Dachun.

Wang Dachun's loss of Xi'er is more central to the narrative structure than is Yang Bailao's. That his claim over Xi'er is frustrated means not only he has lost his love (possession), but more importantly, that he has lost his manhood, a development that nonetheless contributes to his transformation into a hero. His resentment toward Huang causes him to leave his native village to join the Communist Party. After years in the army, he returns home and settles his account with Huang, regaining possession of Xi'er. Wang gets back what is rightfully his, and justice is restored. The morally sound class wins the class struggle. Huang is a symbol of injustice that stems from his interference in the relationship between father and daughter, and between fiancé and fiancée; his rape of Xi'er is the ultimate violation of moral justice.

So, in the narrative structure, Xi'er's body becomes the carrier of social justice, the trigger of intense social conflict, and a site on which the discourse of class struggle is constructed. Indeed, the fight over the control of a woman's body and sexuality is enacted in the drama as a fierce class struggle.

The Cultural Revolution ballet version of *The White-Haired Girl* made its Beijing debut on 30 April 1966, for the May Day celebration. After more than two years of continuous revision and rehearsal under the direct guidance of Jiang Qing, it was acclaimed a model theatrical work for revolutionizing the foreign art form of ballet (Figure 8.1).[23] It keeps close to the original storyline, but the plot is much thinner and the characters more abstract. The most obvious change is that Yang Bailao does not commit suicide: instead, in the spirit of revolt, he fights against his oppressors and is beaten to death. Similarly, Xi'er is transformed into an embodiment of hatred, the spirit of revenge. She is treated cruelly but is not sexually assaulted. Wang Dachun's significance fades, and he becomes just another young man of Xi'er's class with no romantic attachment to her. In the epilogue, Xi'er picks up a gun and joins the ranks of the Eighth Route Army to carry on the eternal revolution of the proletariat. In doing so, she becomes a symbol of that class.

The simplification of the story, the "overpoliticization" of the theme, and particularly the abstraction of the characters reveal the most dynamic concept contained in the ballet: class is the only social category within

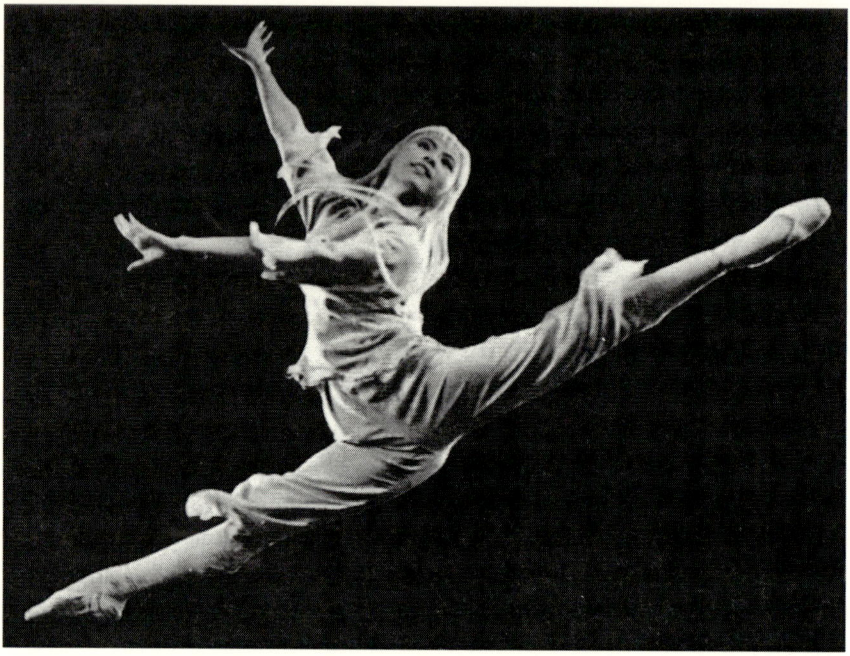

Figure 8.1 Xi'er, the White-Haired Girl. Cover image from Lois Wheeler Snow, *China on Stage: An American Actress in the People's Republic* (New York: Vintage Books, 1973).

which people function. The class discourse overwhelms and replaces "non-politicized ethical concepts, moral principles," and consequently "the entertainment value."[24] Class discourse coercively eliminates the authoritative status of traditional popular culture in the earlier versions. As argued above, social, ethical, and moral values belong to the domain of the sex-gender system. A close comparison of the original and ballet versions reveals that the traditional kinship relations have been eliminated in the latter. What is more dynamic is that class replaces the gender/sexual theme. Xi'er's previous vulnerability as a woman, a body, disappears. Her rape and pregnancy are excised. Sexual or simply romantic elements are eliminated. Xi'er is no longer a betrothed daughter to be raped, a mother giving birth to a child to die, or a ghost waiting to be liberated. When a woman is disassociated from her sexualized body and the gendered functions derived from her body, she becomes a potential agent. She is not a daughter, not a wife, not a mother, not a sex object, not an object of male desire. Woman as agent means the destruction of an active/passive heterosexual division of labour in the narrative structure of the play. Thus, it "disrupts the preexisting patterns of fascination of pleasure," which have been built upon the sexualizing and victimizing of women. And deconstruction of pleasure is a radical weapon for feminism.[25]

The Red Detachment of Women

The ballet *The Red Detachment of Women* reiterates the basic theme of *The White-Haired Girl:* how a poor peasant's daughter becomes a staunch communist. Whereas the ballet version of *The White-Haired Girl* dissolves familial relations, thus allowing a woman to become an active agent, *The Red Detachment of Women* endeavours to present the ideal situation for a girl's maturation into social adulthood. One of the most popular of the model theatrical works, *The Red Detachment of Women* constitutes a perfect model of experimentation in its combination of a foreign art form with Communist Party ideology. It was revised from a 1961 film of the same title directed by Xie Jin. As its title suggests, it deals with two overlapping themes, that of class struggle – red represents the proletarian class – and that of women's liberation. The plot, set in the 1930s when China was under Nationalist rule, focuses on Wu Qinghua, the daughter of a poor peasant. Enslaved as a bondmaid in the household of the evil landlord Nanbatian (southern tyrant), she is viciously beaten by the landlord and his "running dogs" (followers) and tries several times to escape. Finally, with the help of her friends, she succeeds in running away and subsequently encounters a man who turns out to be Hong Changqing, a political commissar in the Red Army. He shows great sympathy toward her and directs her to the camp of a Red Women's Fighting Force. Wu Qinghua's search for home and for liberation, for her utopian dreams, is fulfilled when she finally has found the red flag of the army: "Red flag? Wu stares at the rippling banner with deep emotion." Dressed in red, "Wu staggers forward and presses it against her cheek. Tears roll down her face. 'Red flag, oh, red flag, today I've found you!'"[26] Joining the army marks a new life for her. Tempered by class struggle, full of fire and blood, Wu Qinghua finally becomes a conscious proletarian soldier and eventually the party representative with the women's detachment.

For the most part, the characterization of Wu Qinghua resembles that of Xi'er in *The White-Haired Girl. The Red Detachment of Women* reflects a high level of feminist intervention in the artistic creation of a communist woman. Wu Qinghua is one of the labouring people who have suffered bitterly in the old society. Her suffering at the hands of the landlord is portrayed as a collective experience shared by other peasant women who are always at her side. Consequently, she has an instinctive drive to fight back.

The ballet is meant to "depict her resistance and struggles."[27] From the beginning, Wu Qinghua emits a fighting spirit. While chained to a post so that she cannot run away from the landlord's household, she "stood with chest and head high; her eyes blazing with hatred. If only she could smash the bloody shackles which bound her and wreck the lair of these man-eating beasts!"[28] Her strong class feeling often makes her forget painful injuries, urging her to fight the tyrant to the end (Figure 8.2).

Unlike *The White-Haired Girl*, however, *The Red Detachment of Women* does not let Wu's militancy and fighting spirit go unexamined. In the former, Xi'er's class hatred is treated as a liberating drive that prompts her to join the revolutionary army, whereas in the latter, Wu's rashness and impetuosity as a revolutionary soldier are criticized and repudiated. The plot presents the twisted path that a woman soldier takes to become socially and politically mature.

After Wu joins the Red Army, she is sent on a scouting mission into the landlord's headquarters, where she comes upon the hateful man. Unable to control herself, she shoots him, thus prematurely giving her comrades the signal to attack. Although victorious in the ensuing skirmish, the detachment fails to capture the landlord, who, though wounded, makes his escape. To discipline Wu for her rashness, her pistol is taken away; she reclaims it only when she realizes that the revolution involves much more than simply settling personal scores.

The character development of the heroine suggests that mere aggressiveness does not necessarily lead to liberation. Her desire to fight against her class enemies is instinctive and immature. Simply joining the revolutionary army does not automatically make Wu Qinghua a mature revolutionary fighter; this sort of maturity is gained only after overcoming narrow individualism. After Wu is criticized for not being a conscious proletarian soldier, she realizes that "only by emancipating all humankind can the proletariat achieve its own final emancipation."[29] She vows that she will devote her life to fighting for the liberation of humankind. From this point on, she is redeemed, and in future struggles and battles, she maintains proper discipline. The Red Army soon liberates all the oppressed peasants, and Wu personally kills the landlord (Figure 8.3) and succeeds the dead hero Hong Changqing as party representative.

The main theme of the ballet is revealed through Wu's process of political maturation: women's true emancipation can be achieved only by taking part in the class struggle led by the Communist Party. Individuals must sacrifice themselves for the good of the communist cause. With many thousands

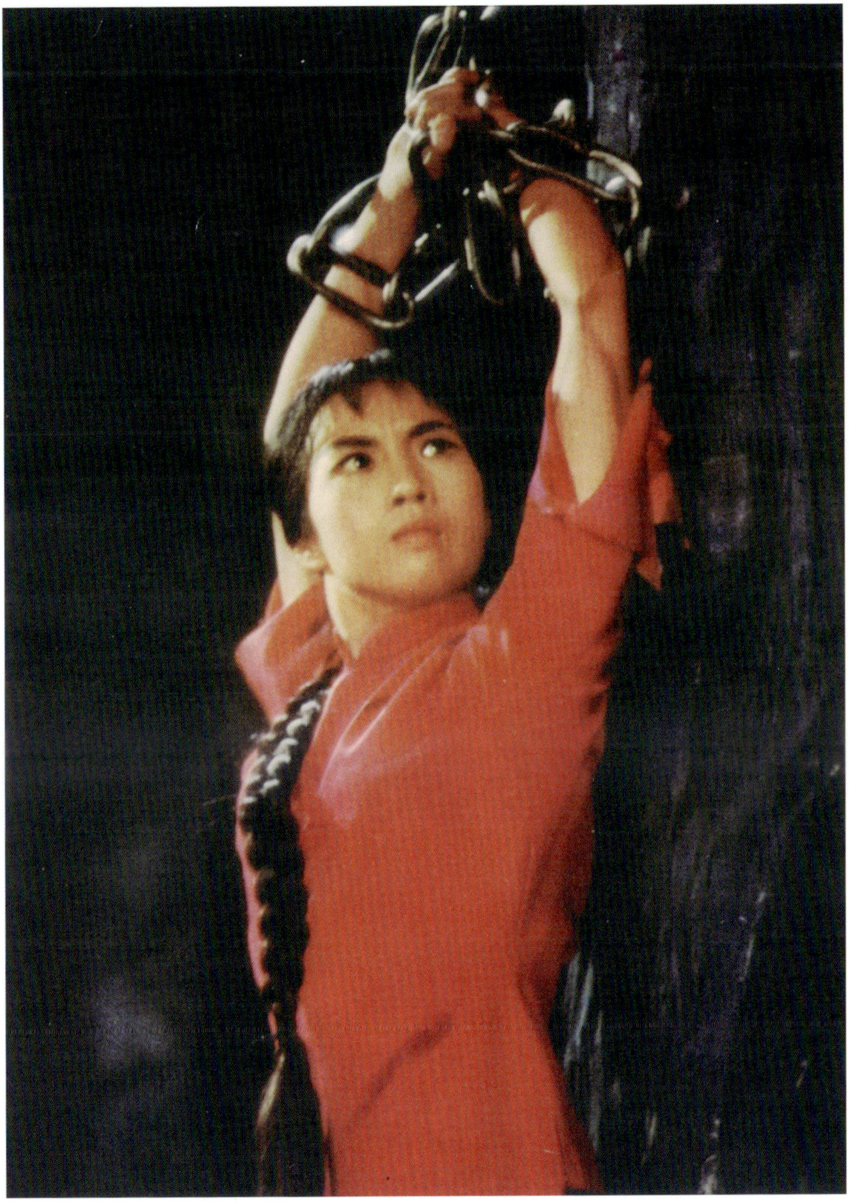

Figure 8.2 The slave-girl Wu Qinghua in chains in the landlord's dungeon; from the prologue to the ballet of *The Red Detachment of Women.* *The Red Detachment of Women: A Modern Revolutionary Ballet* (Beijing: Foreign Language Press, 1972), colour illustrations between pages 78 and 79.

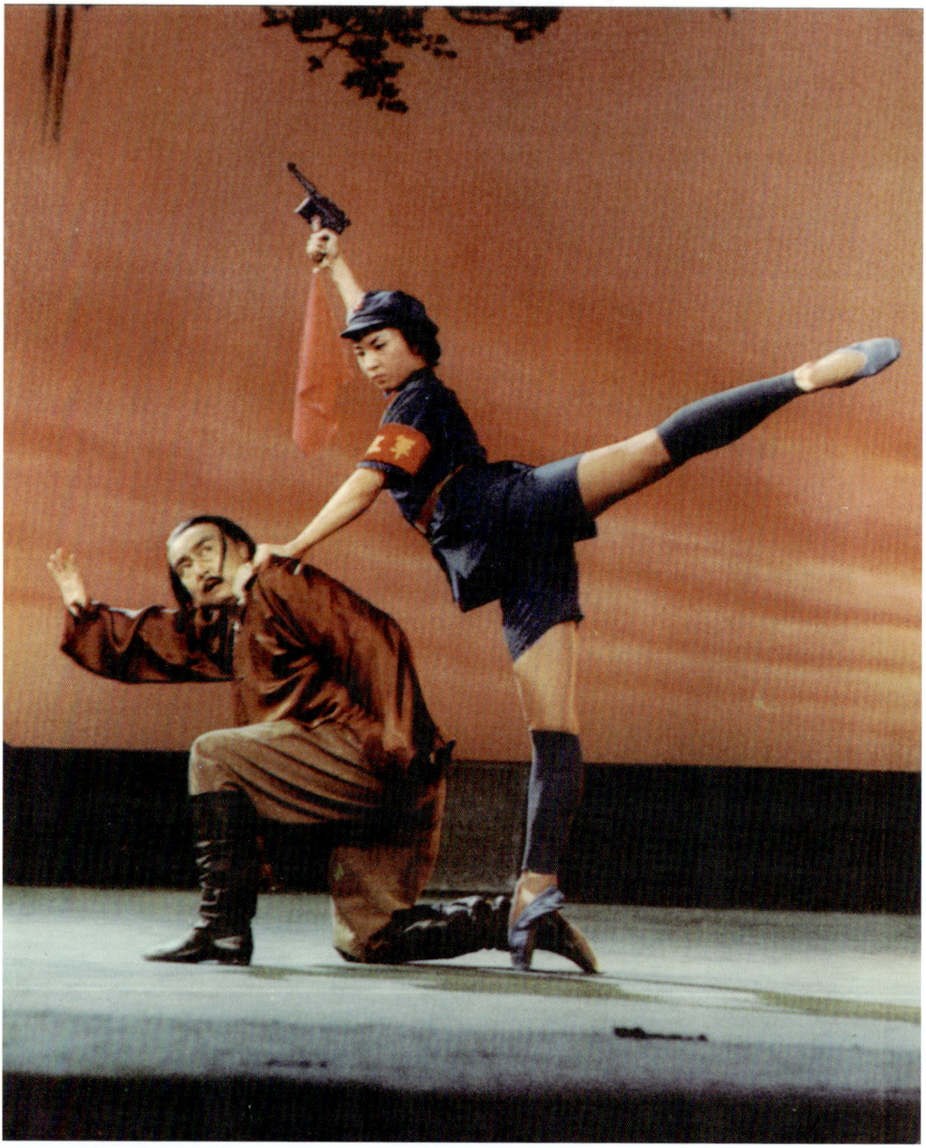

Figure 8.3 **Wu Qinghua, now a member of the Red Detachment, overcomes the landlord in combat; from the final scene of *The Red Detachment of Women.*** *The Red Detachment of Women*: *A Modern Revolutionary Ballet* (Beijing: Foreign Language Press, 1972), colour illustrations between pages 78 and 79.

of self-sacrificing fighters, the cause will win in the end, benefiting both women and the working class.

Hong Changqing, the political commissar, is portrayed as politically "perfect," in contrast to Wu's naivety. When he is finally captured, following Wu's disciplinary faux pas, he demonstrates courage and heroism as he is burned to death by his class enemies. Something of a Christ figure, he dies in order to inspire his followers.

This part of the plot and presentation in the ballet is most problematic for my feminist hermeneutics. The paradigm of the party liberating women is certainly dominant here. On the surface, it seems that *The Red Detachment of Women* endorses the party's role in women's emancipation. My argument here is that, since ideology is socially and culturally determined, Chinese feminism in the 1970s could not escape from the social discourse in which it was enmeshed. If women are to enter into the political realm, they must undergo a degendering process – they must abandon socialized pettiness, naivety, and the focus on the self to be recognized as politically mature. Only when socially constricted attributes of femininity are eliminated can women be treated as mature adults. The party directs them into the public and political arena, and allows them to act as its representatives alongside their male counterparts. This image of the party is an ideal one for women, because they are not asked to be revolutionaries and wives at the same time, as the Communist Party did in reality.

The text's subversive feminist nature is also evident when the party's liberation of women portrayed in the ballet is set against the original cinematic version of the story. The ballet omits an important storyline and an important female character from the original.

The film contains two storylines.[30] One focuses on the main character, Wu Qionghua (her name was slightly modified in the ballet), a slave-girl whose master is about to sell her to a brothel.[31] With the help of a handsome man who later turns out to be a party representative, she manages to escape from the cell in which she is being held. The romantic attraction between the two grows as the story progresses.

The second plot follows Hong Lian, a woman clad in men's clothes, whom Wu Qionghua meets on her way to the red base areas. Hong Lian dresses as a man because she is afraid of sexual assault. She confesses to Wu that she is about to leave her in-laws to escape to the red base areas. Because of a long-ago arranged marriage, she has been forced to marry a wooden figure symbolizing the dead boy who was to have been her husband. She shows the figure to Wu Qionghua: "This is my husband ... I got married when I was ten years old. Since then, I have been sleeping with his wooden corpse for ten years. Do I still count as a live woman?"[32] Both women – Wu Qionghua, suffering from physical and sexual oppression, and Hong Lian, afflicted due to an arranged marriage – escape their unfortunate circumstances and leave for the red base. It is there that Hong Lian unites with her admirer of many years, Feng Agui; she marries him and later gives birth to a girl. In the red base areas ruled by the Communist Party, Hong Lian abandons her "male disguise" and becomes a woman again. In the cinematic version of the story, a variety of motivations drive women to join the revolution, one of which is a happy marriage. And, like *The White-Haired Girl, The Red Detachment of Women* depicts women's oppression in a way that is problematic.

Gender theory tells us that one of the reasons for women's social subordination is that their sexuality differs from that of men. When women are viewed primarily as sexual and sexually subordinate, they are not liberated. The issue here is not that women should not be represented as claiming their sexual freedom, only that before they do so, they must first destroy the traditional concept of female sexual stereotypes. They must break the shackles of these stereotypes to free themselves. Hong Lian's liberation, as the film shows, lies in the sexual realm, in the form of choosing her own husband. Hong Lian represents the ideal liberated woman as portrayed in the Communist Party platform: that is, the liberated woman is both revolutionary and feminine. The party saves Hong Lian from the inhuman treatment resulting from her arranged marriage. In return, she becomes the wife of a revolutionary and the mother of a future revolutionary. However, the revolutionary wife and mother Hong Lian does not appear in the ballet. Jiang Qing was directly responsible for deleting her, citing her "plainness of character" as the reason for doing so; for Jiang Qing, Hong Lian could not represent revolutionary women.[33] The omission of this character from the ballet is a direct statement that clearly defines the relationship between the party and women. *The Red Detachment of Women* describes liberation for women in both public and political spheres but not in reformed kinship or reformed marriage. Overall, the party was in favour of the redomestication of women, as illustrated in the film version.

In order to better understand the significance of the omission of Hong Lian, it is worthwhile to introduce Marxist literary theorist Pierre Macherey's "symptomatic" approach to the literary text, which seeks to disclose what "lack[s]" in the work. For Macherey, a text consists of two parts: the explicit, which is what it says, and the implicit, which is what it cannot say or does not like to say. "The explicit requires the implicit," according to Macherey.

That is, "in order to say something, there are other things which must not be said."[34] He continues to explain that "speech eventually has nothing to tell us. We investigate the silence, for it is the silence that is doing the speaking."[35] "Meaning," he continues, "is in the relation between the implicit and the explicit."[36]

In the ballet version of *The Red Detachment of Women,* Wu Qinghua's maturation under the guidance of the party is an example of the explicit, whereas the omission of Hong Lian's story serves as the implicit. According to Macherey's dialectic, the omitted, the unarticulated, becomes the valuable means of detecting that which threatens and undermines the text's overt project. By removing Hong Lian from the original story, the ballet interrogates the Communist Party's ideology of women's liberation by avoiding a direct challenge to that ideology. Whereas the party's work in the political emancipation of women is recognized and praised, its role in perpetuating women's gender identity as wives and mothers is the unsaid text.

To reveal the unsaid in texts is an important function of feminist readings. The unsaid might be thought of as an unspoken subtext "which by its very telling silence, interrogates and undermines what is represented by the dominant message of the text."[37] To undo Hong Lian's story is to interrogate the social context of the Chinese Communist Party's women's liberation platform.

Both model ballets represent women's appropriation of the political and historical moments when the overarching class discourse provided an opportunity for them to escape the social constructs of womanhood. For women, class-struggle discourse, like the nationalist and humanist salvation discourses of the early modern era, opens a venue for their long-desired liberation from socially derogative categories of femininity. In a sense, class struggle is a shelter that facilitates women's flight from their designated home and hearth. As a result, they are freed from their gendered obligations as daughters, wives, and mothers. They become heroes in the public arena where all social values reside. Thus, the model theatrical works present an idealized fantasy, a feminist utopia. They suggest at the same time both "the grandeur of striving to reach 'the good place' [*eutopia* in Greek] and the futility of searching for 'no place' *[outopia].*"[38]

Surprisingly, from the 1990s to the present, China has experienced a renewed popular interest in the model theatrical works. As "red classics" *(hongse jingdian),* new productions of *The Red Lantern, Shajiabang,* and the two ballets have been commercial successes in spite of their obviously outdated political messages. In celebrations of National Day on 1 October, and on the 1 July anniversary of the founding of the Communist Party, selections from these plays are regular encores. In July of 2004, the Poly Theatre in Beijing ran *The Red Detachment of Women* for a week to capacity audiences. The renewed popularity of the model theatrical works has arguably been responsible for their new and serious rereadings in both Chinese and Western academia. Beijing University professor Hong Zicheng has called this the recanonization of the model theatrical works.[39] How this recanonization will affect the general re-evaluation of modern Chinese literature remains a question. However, the women's utopia observed in the model ballets and operas may partially explain the renewed and abiding popularity of the model theatrical works.

9

Fantasies of Battle: Making the Militant Hero Prominent

Richard King

This concluding chapter offers a Cultural Revolution triptych: three images, drawn from the visual, performing, and literary arts that present, in each case, an exemplary hero ready for literal or metaphorical battle. The unnamed factory worker in the painting *Steady as a Rock (Dizhu),* Yang Zirong of the model theatrical work *Taking Tiger Mountain by Strategy (Zhiqu weihushan),* and Ji Changchun from the amateur writer Duan Ruixia's debut story "Not Just One of the Audience" (Tebie guanzhong) present examples of those heroic images whose production was to become the "basic duty" of the arts in the mid-1970s.[1] The three figures, all mature men, and the works in which they appear, exemplify the concern, even obsession, with battle-readiness that pervades the arts of the Cultural Revolution decade: the heroes of revolutionary art, like the real-life proletarians they were designed to inspire, were constantly alert to the ever-present danger of enemy attack, preserving the mindset of battle even when, or perhaps especially when, no war was taking place.[2]

Seizing the Capitalist-Roader's Microphone

The painting *Steady as a Rock,* the first of the three panels in our triptych, was reproduced in the May 1976 issue of the Shanghai literary magazine *Zhaoxia* (Morning clouds) (Figure 9.1). This special edition *(zhuanji)* of the journal subsequently condemned as a "Gang [of Four] publication" *(bang-kan)* was in celebration of the thirty-fourth anniversary of Mao's Yan'an Talks, which a lead article creatively updated to meet the needs of the current propaganda initiative, the struggle against capitalist-roaders *(zouzipai).*[3] Deng Xiaoping, condemned openly following his dismissal in the wake of the 5 April suppression of Tian'anmen Square demonstrations mourning Premier Zhou Enlai, is named in the article as the representative of those in administrative positions who sought to dampen popular enthusiasm for the

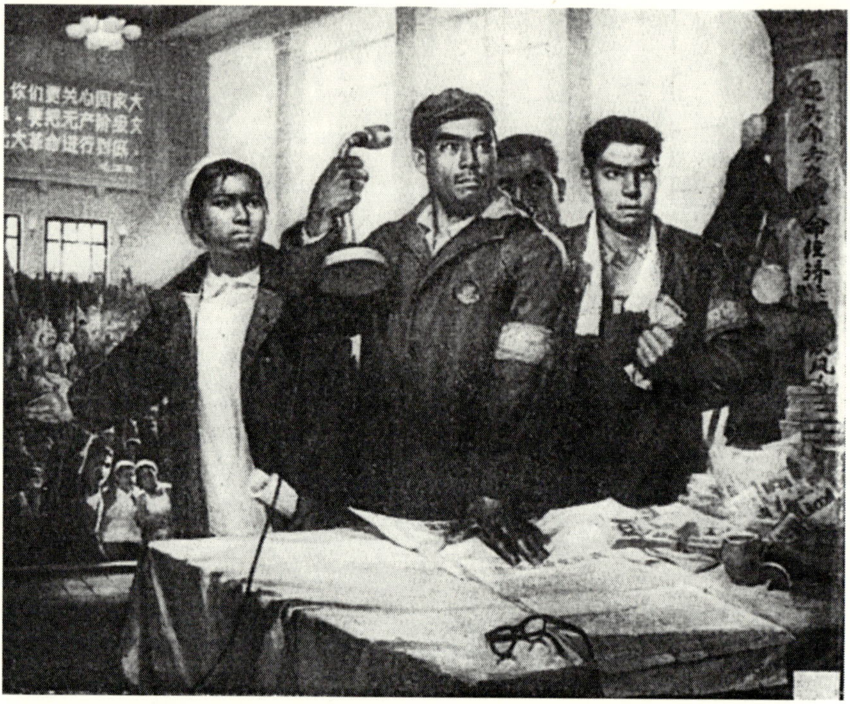

Figure 9.1 **Qingdao Workers' Fine Arts Creation Collective, with Jiang Baoxing in charge of the brush, *Steady as a Rock*.** *Zhaoxia* (May 1976), inside back cover facing page 80.

innovations of the Cultural Revolution and to replace them with bureaucratic management and subservience to the West.[4] This issue represents the Shanghai radical/Gang of Four faction's version of the current stage in its intensifying struggle with the forces that rivalled it for state power during the last year of the Cultural Revolution; a final article calls on artists to "strive to portray the images of proletarian heroes in battle with capitalist-roaders."[5] *Steady as a Rock* illustrates just such a battle.

The painting is set in the assembly hall of a factory, where a mass meeting is under way. At a crucial juncture, members of the revolutionary proletariat have stepped up to become masters of the stage (as had the heroes of the model theatrical works) and now strike dramatic poses in the foreground. The central figure, a powerful worker with the large hands and bushy eyebrows characteristic of proletarian images in socialist-realist art, has claimed ownership of the microphone that symbolizes the power to communicate and command, and now glowers defiantly at the person who must, a moment ago, have been monopolizing the factory's public-address system to convey capitalist-roader ideology. This hero is a mature man, perhaps in his early thirties, the somewhat anachronistic Mao-button above his heart suggesting that he might be a former Red Guard leader returning a decade later to attack for the second time a manager condemned in the mid-1960s but restored to office following the 1973 reinstatement of Deng Xiaoping. To either side of the central figure, slightly behind and slightly below, stand young workers, one male and one female, their faces stern and their eyes likewise set on the former master of the factory's communications technology. The young man, whose strong hand crushes what may be the text of the speech cut short by their intervention, appears to be from the shop floor; the young woman, gesturing back to her co-workers, wears the white bonnet and overall of a canteen worker. A fourth figure stands, slightly lower again, in the shadow of the hero and the young male worker. Behind them, the audience below the stage, illuminated by shafts of light from the windows to its left, is united with the central group in its seizure of power – one man raises a fist, and other members of the workforce look on attentively. Above them all, at the back of the hall, is displayed one of the oracular utterances attributed to Mao and released at intervals to support the course that the revolution was taking in the final months of his life.[6] A female worker pastes up a slogan (unfortunately illegible in the *Zhaoxia* reproduction) at the far right of the picture.

And the capitalist-roader himself? Forced back from the table at which he had been sitting to deliver his speech and out of our view, he is nonetheless clearly identified as an intellectual by the glasses he has left behind. We can easily picture him as he cowers at the back of the stage, a middle-aged man (as fictional capitalist-roaders almost invariably are) dressed for the office rather than the shop floor, squinting despairingly up at the resolute proletarians who have snatched away his microphone and his power. And we can confidently predict the scene to come: a booming voice shouting "Comrades!" echoes over the public-address system, the current condemnation of capitalist-roaders is delivered impromptu, and the meeting that had been called to listen to a tedious litany of production targets and bureaucratic orders ends instead with resounding (though soon to be disappointed) calls for the long life of both Chairman Mao and the Cultural Revolution.

Steady as a Rock captures the spirit of the campaign against Deng Xiaoping and the capitalist-roaders in the hectic spring and summer of 1976: proletarian leaders emerging, inspired by the thoughts and recent utterances of

Mao, to lead the masses in overthrowing the social and economic policies espoused by those who would oppose the Great Leader. From the reading of the picture above, and from the name supplied for its creators, composition would appear to have followed the approved three-in-one *(sanjiehe)* method for cultural production, with leadership supplying the political line to be portrayed, the masses (in this case the Qingdao Workers' Fine Arts Creation Collective) devising the scenario, and a better-than-competent specialist painter (whose name is given as Jiang Baoxing) wielding the brush *(zhibi)*.[7]

The composition of the painting is likewise exemplary, an object lesson in the creative principle of the three prominences *(san tuchu)*. This formulation, attributed to Jiang Qing, was associated with the extensive process of transforming Beijing operas composed on modern themes during the late 1950s and early 1960s into the revolutionary model theatrical works *(geming yangbanxi)* intended to spearhead an unprecedented proletarian aesthetic. In 1968, Yu Huiyong, composer of the *yangbanxi* version of at least one of the operas, later leader of a major writing group promoting the arts of the Cultural Revolution, and minister of culture at its end, explained the concept of the three prominences: "Of all characters, give prominence to positive characters, of positive characters give prominence to heroic characters, of heroic characters give prominence to the most important one, i.e., the central character."[8]

Everything in the painting is as it should be: the characters are disposed in a pyramidal structure, the central hero dominating the action, the secondary heroic figures supporting him on either side, the masses well back and in agreement, and the class enemy banished from his position of authority and represented only by the emblem of his myopia.

Purifying the Martial Hero

The exact timing of the formulation of the three prominences, and their authorship, is open to question. Jiang Qing told her American biographer Roxanne Witke that she had explained the idea to her ally, Shanghai mayor Ke Qingshi, "during the prelude to the Cultural Revolution."[9] A more recent book on the model theatrical works attributes only one prominence to her, the focus on the central heroic figure, claiming the remaining two for Yu Huiyong.[10] Jiang Qing's own prominence within the circle of artists and administrators who worked with her on the operas might explain Yu's reluctance to claim anything but reflected glory whatever his contribution; the creation of the model works was to be Jiang Qing's personal triumph, "every word and every phrase, every tone and every beat, soaked through with the heart's blood of Comrade Jiang Qing."[11]

Reports on Jiang Qing's leadership of the revolution in Beijing opera, a process dated from her participation in, and speech at, a 1964 festival of operas on contemporary themes, and her own comments to Roxanne Witke, invariably stress the pains she took to increase the dominance of the central figures, moulding them into her ideal of Cultural Revolution proletarian heroism.[12] The heroes were to be given "the best music, the best singing, the most forceful gestures, and the most important positions onstage."[13] Where previous versions of the operas had allowed their protagonists to be scruffy or unkempt, the heroes were to be smartened up, presenting a dignified image even in the most perilous of circumstances. In the film versions of the model theatrical works, and the still photographs that accompany the texts, their centrality is emphasized by their position onscreen and the manner in which they are lit, above lesser heroic figures, with the villains, even those in positions of considerable power, dark-lit and crouching.

The most extensively revised of the operas was *Taking Tiger Mountain by Strategy,* one of the original group of eight model theatrical works and also the most celebrated and successful of them. Jiang Qing's lengthy involvement in its reform is the source of the Cultural Revolution cliché about perfectionism: "ten years to hone one opera" *(shinian mo yi xi).*[14] Discussion of the process here will concentrate on what reports from the period identify as the key element: the transformation of the hero Yang Zirong.

Taking Tiger Mountain is the stage adaptation of the most exciting episode in Qu Bo's 1957 military romance *Tracks in the Snowy Forest (Linhai xueyuan),* which recounts the exploits of a small Red Army detachment behind enemy lines in the latter years of the Civil War of 1945-49.[15] Based on the adventures of a real-life military unit, the story features an indulgent self-portrait of the author as the detachment's commander, the "brilliant, handsome young officer" Shao Jianbo.[16] However, as Robert Hegel has demonstrated, the novel also draws heavily on an earlier narrative tradition for its values, characterization, and incident.[17] For example, Yang Zirong's killing of a tiger is an updated socialist version of Wu Song's memorable barehanded tiger-killing exploit in Chapter 23 of *Outlaws of the Marsh (Shuihuzhuan).*[18] In the Tiger Mountain episode, Yang Zirong, the detachment's scout, poses as an outlaw in order to infiltrate the mountain stronghold of a bandit tyrant affiliated to the Nationalist side and smuggles in his comrades while the bandits are drunkenly celebrating their leader's birthday.

The suitability of this portion of the novel for adaptation into opera was immediately recognized by members of the Shanghai Beijing Opera Company, and a first version was performed in September 1958; a revised version was played for Jiang Qing in December 1963 or January 1964 and presented at the 1964 festival of Beijing opera on contemporary themes.[19]

The novel, and earlier versions of the opera, present Yang as a swashbuckling hero whose bandit impersonation included (mildly) racy stories and coarse manners. Though Yang is a communist of proletarian origins, his pre-model incarnations also had some of the air of the traditional *haohan* (bold fellow), rough and jocular as well as earnest and dedicated. In the interests of Jiang Qing's notions of revolutionary purity, if at the expense of realistic portrayal, Yang's language, rakish behaviour, posture, and clothing were smartened up, and his heroics were placed firmly in the context of loyalty not to his commander and comrades, but to the Communist Party and its chairman. An article written by (or ghostwritten for) the Shanghai Opera Company troupe that performed the model version of the opera expressed this in the evocatively unrestrained English of the official translation: "While delineating his [Yang's] indomitable courage and soaring spirit, we also give expression to the steadiness and poise, the sagacity and alertness in his make-up. The description of these facets rests firmly on one essential point, the soul of the hero Yang Zirong, and that is 'the morning sun in his heart' – a red heart that is infinitely loyal to Chairman Mao and his thought ... Without Mao Zedong thought, Yang Zirong would certainly be reduced to a nincompoop, a vulgar and miserable mountebank."[20]

Comparison of a single incident from *Tracks in the Snowy Forest* with its counterpart in the model version of *Taking Tiger Mountain by Strategy* illustrates the transformation of Yang Zirong. It comes as Yang, volunteering to impersonate a bandit and infiltrate the bandits' Tiger Mountain stronghold, outlines to his commanding officer his qualifications to complete the mission. In the novel, the officer is the idealized Shao Jianbo, and the character in earlier versions of the opera retained that name; however, in the revision process toward the *yangbanxi,* the officer's role was weakened to avoid detracting attention from Yang Zirong, and the name Shao Jianbo was dropped in favour of the impersonal "chief of staff" *(canmouzhang).* Yang's initial three arguments are the same in both the novel and the *yangbanxi* versions: he possesses a map coveted by the tyrant, he is familiar with bandit slang, and he can act the part convincingly. However, a subtle difference occurs in his final point, and thereafter the conversation takes a very different turn. In the novel, the scene reads as follows:

"Fourth ..." Yang Zirong paused briefly, his eyes flashing stern and resolute, ... "I have faith in my heartfelt loyalty to the party and the people."

"You think these things will guarantee victory?"

"Yes! That's what I believe."

"You're wrong!" Jianbo looked sternly at the resolute Yang Zirong and argued with him for the first time in their many years as comrades-in-arms. "Those four advantages are enough to infiltrate the enemy camp. They can only help you crawl into the enemy's belly. That isn't the main problem today; the key is how you can carry out the work when you're in his belly."[21]

In the model opera, Yang Zirong describes the final prerequisite for his success as "the most important," and the chief of staff goes on to identify it:

"That is a Liberation armyman's heartfelt loyalty to the party and Chairman Mao!"

Yang Zirong: "Chief of staff, you understand me!"

Chief of staff: "Old Yang, this is no ordinary task!"

Yang Zirong: "Chief of staff!

(Sings) A communist always heeds the party's call,
And takes on his shoulders the heaviest tasks.
Resolved to break the shackles of a thousand years,
And release a spring of eternal joy for the people.

Well I know there's danger in this journey,
But the more dangerous it is, the more I go forward.
No matter how the storm clouds may change,
Revolutionary wisdom will triumph over nature.

With the determination of the Foolish Old Man
who moved mountains,
I will surmount all obstacles and perils.
My red heart, like a flame,
Will forge the sharp blade that slays the stubborn foe!"[22]

Yang's loyalty to the people in the novel has been replaced in the model theatrical work by loyalty to Mao, and that loyalty is not an individual trait, but typical of communist soldiery. The implicit role model for Yang's plan is no longer drawn from traditional narrative (the monkey-king Sun Wukong,

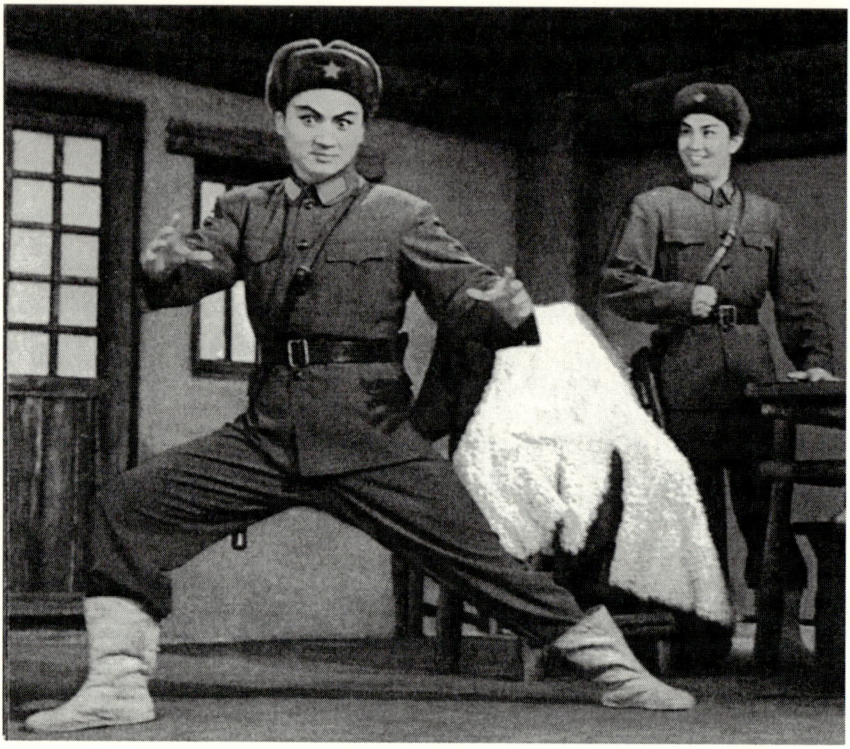

Figure 9.2 Yang Zirong, hero of *Taking Tiger Mountain by Strategy* (detail). From the performance edition of the opera. *Zhiqu Weihushan [Taking Tiger Mountain by Strategy]* (Beijing: Renmin chubanshe, 1970), 86.

whose magical abilities allowed him to crawl into an enemy's belly), but from Mao's writing – in the third of his constantly read essays *(laosanpian),* he used the Foolish Old Man as a parable.[23] Finally, it is inconceivable that the model Yang, as a prominent central hero, could be contradicted by his commanding officer: profession of loyalty to Mao is sure to win any argument, and anyway, the hero is never wrong. So, whereas the novel's Yang is required to elaborate on his plan, the operatic Yang launches into an aria about the battle-readiness of the communist. The bold and resourceful subordinate of *Tracks in the Snowy Forest* has become, thanks to opera reform and the three prominences, a "scout hero of the Chinese Liberation Army armed with the revolutionary courage of the revolutionary proletariat."[24]

The dashing figure of the Beijing opera star Tong Xiangling as Yang Zirong, vowing to outwit the bandits and bring about a famous victory, is the second panel of our Cultural Revolution triptych (Figure 9.2). Even more splendid in the tiger-skin waistcoat and fur-lined greatcoat he wears for his bandit impersonation in the later scenes, Yang is the embodiment of revolutionary romanticism, and the opera is a fantasy of battle and victory.[25] Warfare, with the forces of virtue united against a known and hated foe, is the ideal setting for glamorous heroism, and the task was made easier for the creators and adapters of *Taking Tiger Mountain* by the highly romantic nature of the source material, Qu Bo's novel *Tracks in the Snowy Forest.* Most of the model theatrical works are similarly set in times of battle (the Civil War against the Nationalists, patriotic resistance to the invading Japanese, or confrontation with the United States in Korea), and their heroes share the characteristics of the warrior. Ellen Judd characterizes the quality of the heroes of the model theatrical works as "action on the human world in the form of powerful moral-political leadership ... in the dual form of vanquishing enemies and leading their own people."[26] In dramas with a civilian setting, heroes are also called upon to detect class enemies and, when required, to battle nature, most notably in the scene from *Song of the Dragon River* in which the heroine, party secretary Jiang Shuiying, leads her fellow peasant activists into flood waters to form a human wall.[27] The lesser heroic figures cannot accomplish these feats: in warfare, they are apt to be impetuous; they may be outsmarted by a clever enemy; and they cannot be relied on to rally others to their cause.[28] The three prominences system essentially breaks down at the level of the secondary hero and is rarely tested in the case of the mere "positive characters"; the principal hero alone can win the battle. The three prominences work best in visual images such as the painting with which this chapter began and tableaux from the model theatrical works; in the texts of the opera, and more so in the fiction derived from them, the pursuit of prominence is focused on a single heroic image and largely ignores the lower strata.

Winning the Technological Battle

The model theatrical works were designed to be models both for social behaviour and for all other artistic and literary endeavours; testimonies were written attesting to their transformative power over the lives of members of their audience, and the operas were commended to a new generation of fiction writers when journal publication resumed in the early 1970s after a five-year hiatus.[29] Many of these new writers were amateurs schooled in factory study groups and guided in their creative ventures by party representatives and professional authors. One of the most celebrated was the young Shanghai electronics worker Duan Ruixia, whose brief literary career was launched in 1973 with the story "Not Just One of the Audience."[30] It was acclaimed by the literary establishment of the time, and in a 1976 Fudan University textbook on creative writing, it is the only contemporary work extensively cited as an exemplary short story.[31]

The story focuses on the relationship between life and art, life represented by the electronics industry in which the author worked and art by Mao's Yan'an Talks and the opera *Taking Tiger Mountain.* As it begins, preparations are under way for a performance of the opera to celebrate the thirtieth anniversary (in May 1972) of the Talks. The hero Ji Changchun (whose given name advises the reader that he is "always youthful"), a demobilized soldier now working in electronic product development, decides to improve the opera company's amplification system, so that audiences can enjoy the opera with minimal distortion. To test the equipment, Ji has the young actor playing Yang Zirong sing the central section of the aria quoted above: "Well I know there's danger in this journey, but the more dangerous it is, the more I go forward." The actor delivers a spirited rendition and credits an incident recounted by the senior performer of the role for inspiring him, though he is not given the chance to elaborate. The factory's senior technician Su Qi ("Su" as in "Soviet," a sign of his respect for foreign products) is reluctant to guarantee the specifications Ji proposes, believing Chinese technology to be insufficiently sophisticated for the task. The factory's workers are inspired by Ji's cause and his determination to surpass all expectations, and the improvements are successfully made. The senior actor reveals that his playing of the scout hero was transformed after he took part in a naval exercise in which Ji Changchun, then still in the military, climbed a mast in a storm to repair his ship's radar equipment, injuring his hand in the process. Su confesses to past reluctance to take on technological challenges, and the actors propose that the factory's amateur journalist (the narrator) write up the story.

The author emphasizes the symbiosis between the heroes onstage and the heroes for whom they perform: the singers' convincing rendition of the very words in Yang's aria that so inspire Ji Changchun result indirectly from Ji's own heroism. Ji is the opera hero transposed to the author's environment: in an article describing the creative process that resulted in the final text, Duan Ruixia reveals that to create his story's hero, he began by asking himself the question "if Yang Zirong were at our factory, what would he be like?"[32]

There are, as Duan admits, no Tiger Mountains to be taken at the factory where Ji Changchun works; furthermore, May 1973, when the story first appeared, was a relatively quiet period in the political ferment of the Cultural Revolution: the campaign against Lin Biao had little effect on the world of the arts, and the Communist Party's tenth conference was still three months away. Following that conference, the Chinese media, especially Shanghai journals such as *Zhaoxia* and *Study and Criticism (Xuexi yu pipan),* which were closely associated with the radical faction, engaged relentlessly in the hunt for capitalist-roaders, a reflection of the power struggle taking place at the centre between the group later condemned as the Gang of Four and its rivals for state power – Zhou Enlai, Deng Xiaoping, and those who, following the party conference, had been restored to positions of authority with Deng.[33] In later works, Duan Ruixia's pen would also be put to partisan service in this cause.[34] However, in "Not Just One of the Audience," there is no enemy; the foot-dragging technician Su, who might have been portrayed as a capitalist-roader had the story been written a year later, is a comrade to be won over. Yet, for all the unanimity of the workforce, and its common purpose with the opera troupe, a spirit of warfare pervades the story; the vocabulary of battle is everywhere. Thus, as we observe Ji Changchun performing morning calisthenics, the narrator remarks, "Though he had been demobilized for quite a few years, he still maintained the practices of the military in his lifestyle. Ideologically, he had never forgotten that he was a warrior. Warrior! That was a title to make a man proud! The purpose for his existence was battle, and as he lived he would carry on revolution, and fight bravely for communism."[35]

As he discusses the improvement of the sound system with Su, Ji also couches it in military terms: "Old Su, my background is as a soldier, and the words in my belly are like bullets in a gun-barrel ... What we are faced with is not a normal product development task, but a battle to protect Chairman Mao's revolutionary line in the arts."[36]

The need for battle-readiness in times of peace is most clearly expressed in the extended flashback to the naval exercise in which Ji and the senior actor in the role of Yang meet for the first time. The actor relates his attempts to dissuade Ji from risking his life by climbing the mast during a storm:

> "'It's dangerous!' Without thinking, I restrained him.
>
> "'This is war! Don't you realize?' He was just wearing a vest, and all his muscles were tensed like iron, his words rattling on the deck like lumps of iron.
>
> "'But this is just an exercise,' I said.
>
> "'Exercise?' His eyes were like daggers pointed at me. 'Comrade, you're an actor. When you're onstage, can you play the hero properly if you think you're only acting out a part?'"[37]

This moment, as Ji prepares to risk his life in battle even though there is no war, provides the third panel in our Cultural Revolution triptych.

To emphasize the connection between Ji Changchun and Yang Zirong, the actor's narrative includes tiger references as he concludes the flashback with his description of Ji's injury, recalling both Tiger Mountain and Yang's tiger-killing on his way to meet the bandits. After the two men clasp hands, the actor remarks, "I looked down: along the *hukou* [tiger's mouth, the portion of the hand between thumb and forefinger] of my right hand was a patch of vivid red blood. This was the blood of a hero! The tempest had lacerated his *hukou,* but it had not even slightly affected his heroic *hudan* [tiger's gall, courage]!"[38]

Ji Changchun's view of life as battle, and his readiness to go on the attack *(jingong),* is singled out for praise in the Fudan textbook for aspiring authors: "In portraying this heroic figure, the author has kept a firm grip on Ji Changchun's particular quality, of daring to go on the attack, having the courage to go on the attack, and being good at going on the attack in real life."[39]

The character of the hero, the aspect of the story most admired by contemporary commentators, was also the major emphasis as the young worker-writer's advisors helped him through the process of revising his story to its final form. Early versions (including a third draft published in an industry literary magazine) had featured a young worker who accompanies Ji to the first performance and through whose eyes much of the action is seen; they also contained much detail on the technical improvements made to the sound system. Both the young worker and the technical detail were later perceived to be "burdens" *(baofu)* and jettisoned. The three prominences are cited to justify the removal of the young worker, since the lesser character is seen to have got in the way of the portrayal of the hero.[40] As in the operas, and elsewhere in the literature of the Cultural Revolution, the three prominences turn out to be almost exclusively concerned with the fabrication of model heroes for audiences to emulate.

Thus, the unnamed proletarian seizing the microphone from a capitalist-roader and Yang Zirong volunteering to infiltrate Tiger Mountain are joined by the warrior/factory worker Ji Changchun, fully prepared for battle in a military exercise, in a triptych of images of heroes in three different artistic forms, all constructed according to the three prominences formula of the day, ready to defend the Cultural Revolution version of communism and its leader with their last breath. The events that followed the death of Mao – the arrest and vilification of his supporters and the shutting-down of radical journals such as *Zhaoxia* – showed that the spirit of war so feverishly cultivated in the final months of the Cultural Revolution did not exist outside the polemical and artistic works that promoted it; far from springing to the defence of the radicals who had been responsible for producing these heroic images, the masses appear to have been more than content with their downfall. The battle-readiness of the heroes of the 1970s turns out to have been a fantasy played out in the media and the minds of those who controlled them, evaporating the instant that the real battle was joined.

Notes

Preface

1 The exhibition was assembled by the gallery's curator Scott Watson; the Vancouver-based artist, scholar, and independent curator Shengtian Zheng; and the mainland art historian Yan Shanchun. From Vancouver, the exhibition travelled to the Power Plant Contemporary Art Gallery in Toronto and then on to Winnipeg at the Plug In Institute of Contemporary Art. The catalogue for the exhibition is Scott Watson and Zheng Shengtian, eds., *The Art of the Great Proletarian Cultural Revolution 1966-1976* (Vancouver: Morris and Helen Belkin Art Gallery, 2002).

Introduction

1 Yan Jiaqi and Gao Gao, *Turbulent Decade: A History of the Cultural Revolution,* trans. and ed. D.W.Y. Kwok (Honolulu: University of Hawai'i Press, 1996); Roderick MacFarquhar and Michael Schoenhals, *Mao's Last Revolution* (Cambridge, MA: Bellknap Press of Harvard University Press, 2006); Paul Clark, *The Chinese Cultural Revolution: A History* (New York: Cambridge University Press, 2008).

2 For a study that does examine one of the visual arts of the Cultural Revolution – propaganda posters – and the political and social messages conveyed by them, see Harriet Evans and Stephanie Donald, eds., *Picturing Power in the People's Republic of China: Posters of the Cultural Revolution* (London: Rowan and Littlefield, 1999).

3 Li Zhisui, *The Private Life of Chairman Mao,* trans. Tai Hung-chao, with the editorial assistance of Anne F. Thurston (New York: Random House, 1994); Jung Chang and Jon Halliday, *Mao: The Unknown Story* (New York: Knopf, 2005).

4 Mao Zedong, "Talks at the Yan'an Forum on Literature and Art," in *Modern Chinese Literary Thought: Writings on Literature, 1893-1945,* ed. Kirk A. Denton (Stanford: Stanford University Press, 1996), 458-84.

5 Yao Wenyuan, "Ping xin bian lishiju *Hai Rui ba guan*" [Criticism of the recent historical drama *Hai Rui Dismissed from Office*], *Wenhuibao* [Cultural gazette], 10 November 1965. A translation of the opera appears in Clive Ansley, *The Heresy of Wu Han: His Play "Hai Rui's Dismissal" and Its Role in China's Cultural Revolution* (Toronto: University of Toronto Press, 1971).

6 D.W. Fokkema, *Report from Peking* (Montreal and Kingston: McGill-Queen's University Press, 1972), 48.

7 Yu Huiyong, "Yu Huiyong tongzhi de jianghua" [Speech by Comrade Yu Huiyong], *Hongqi* [Red flag], May 1967, 47. Unless otherwise indicated, all translations are our own. Yu Huiyong became minister of culture in the Cultural Revolution following involvement as a musician with the model theatrical works. Qian Haoliang, the star of the opera *Hongdengji* (The red lantern), made much the same point regarding Jiang Qing to her American biographer Roxanne Witke. Witke, *Comrade Chiang Ch'ing* (Boston: Little, Brown, 1977), 414.

8 *Quotations from Chairman Mao Tse-tung* (Beijing: Foreign Languages Press, 1967), 288.

9 For a translation of the *Renmin ribao* editorial of 1 June 1966, see "Sweep Away All Monsters," *Peking Review* 23 (23 June 1966): 3-5.

10 Much of this section is derived from Wang Mingxian, "The Fine Arts Movement of the Red Guards" (paper presented at the conference "Cultural Production and the Cultural Revolution," Vancouver, 22 March 2002).

11 Yan and Gao, *Turbulent Decade*, 431-32.

12 Witke, *Comrade Chiang Ch'ing*, 380, 413.

13 Words by Eugene Pottier (1871), music by Pierre Degeyter (1888).

Chapter 1: The Art of the Cultural Revolution

1 Zhang Shaoxia and Li Xiaoshan, *Zhongguo xiandai huihuashi* [A history of painting in modern China] (Nanjing: Jiangsu Art Press, 1986), 287. Unless otherwise indicated, all translations are my own.

2 Hong Yung Lee has argued that the Cultural Revolution can "be best described as Mao's attempt to resolve the basic contradictions between the egalitarian view of Marxism and the elitist tendencies of Leninist organizational principles." Lee, *The Politics of the Chinese Cultural Revolution: A Case Study* (Berkeley: University of California Press, 1978), 3. R. Keith Schoppa has more recently characterized the Great Proletarian Cultural Revolution as a "Death Dance." Schoppa, *Revolution and Its Past: Identities and Change in Modern Chinese History* (Upper Saddle River, NJ: Prentice Hall, 2002), 340.

3 For more on the art of the Cultural Revolution, see Ellen Johnston Laing, *The Winking Owl: Art in the People's Republic of China* (Berkeley: University of California Press, 1988); Julia F. Andrews, *Painters and Politics in the People's Republic of China, 1949-1979* (Berkeley: University of California Press, 1994); Zou Yuejin, *Xin Zhongguo meishu shi* [History of the art of New China] (Changsha: Hunan meishu chubanshe, 2002); and Wang Mingxian and Yan Shanchun, *Xin Zhongguo meishu tu shi, 1966-1976: The Art History of the People's Republic of China, 1966-1976* (Beijing: China Youth Press, 2000).

4 Andrews, *Painters and Politics*, 317, quoting *Meishu fenglei* [Art storm] 3 (1967), as reproduced in *Red Guard Publications (Hongweibing ziliao)*, vol. 15 (Washington,

DC: Center for Chinese Research Materials, Association of Research Libraries, n.d.). It is now known that five issues of *Meishu fenglei* were published between June and September 1967.

5 Byung-joon Ahn, *Chinese Politics and the Cultural Revolution: Dynamics of Policy Processes* (Seattle: University of Washington Press, 1976), 210-11, 313-16.

6 Andrews, *Painters and Politics,* 317; Yan Jiaqi and Gao Gao, *Turbulent Decade: A History of the Cultural Revolution,* trans. and ed. D.W.Y. Kwok (Honolulu: University of Hawai'i Press, 1996), 41; *Meishu fenglei* 3 (1967).

7 Ahn, *Chinese Politics,* 219-20.

8 Maurice Meisner, *Mao's China: A History of the People's Republic* (New York: Free Press, 1977), 314. This event was commemorated by many Red Guard paintings. An excellent example rendered Mao in the traditional medium of ink and colour on Chinese paper with his writing brush raised to execute his *dazibao.* The work is in the standard socialist realist manner taught at the Central Academy of Fine Arts and China's other major art academies, and is, ironically, closely related to the styles of the teachers who would soon be condemned. See *China Reconstructs* 2, 1968, front cover.

9 Meisner, 313.

10 Laing, *The Winking Owl,* 63-64. Laing cites attacks on Qi Baishi, Huang Binhong, Jiang Feng, Shao Yu, Wo Zha, Huang Miaozi, Ye Qianyu, Zhang Ding, Hu Kao, Zhang Guangyu, Zhang Zhengyu, Yu Feng, Ding Cong, Wu Zuoren, Guo Weiqu, Pan Tianshou, and Chen Banding.

11 *People's Daily,* 11 January 1967, as summarized in *China News Items from the Press* (Hong Kong: Regional Information Office, 1967), no. 154, 4-5 (CNFP).

12 Other key images of the movement were the model theatrical works, developed under Jiang Qing's supervision, and propaganda photographs. See Jiang Qing's own photographs, published under her pseudonym Jun Ling, in *China Pictorial,* July-August 1971, 3, 22-23, 41.

13 A colour photograph of Mount Jinggang Red Guards making a room-sized poster appears in *China Pictorial,* November 1967, 16. Groups bearing this name were found at other institutions, including Qinghua University, Beijing Normal University, and the Beijing Conservatory of Music. See Lee, *The Politics of the Chinese Cultural Revolution,* 210-12, 215-17.

14 An excellent discussion of the debate, with emphasis on the pro-bloodlines faction, may be found in Yan Jiaqi and Gao Gao, *Turbulent Decade: A History of the Cultural Revolution,* trans. and ed. D.W.Y. Kwok (Honolulu: University of Hawai'i Press, 1996), 102-6. Also, Hong Yung Lee analyzes the complex political undercurrents to the debate regarding class origin, in *The Politics of the Chinese Cultural Revolution,* 68-84. In Chinese, the couplet is "Laozi yingxiong, er haohan; laozi fandong, er hundan." Translation modified from Lee, *The Politics of the Chinese Cultural Revolution,* 72.

15 *Sing Tao Daily,* 16 November 1966, as summarized in CNFP, 1966, no. 147, 6-7.

16 Meisner, *Mao's China,* 316; Ahn, *Chinese Politics,* 228.

17 The collection of Wang Mingxian, part of which was shown at the University of British Columbia in the exhibition that inspired this volume, includes Red Guard periodicals from other Beijing arts groups, such as *Art War Gazette (Meishu zhanbao).*

18 Andrews, *Painters and Politics,* 325-28, citing *Meishu fenglei* [Art storm] 1 (1967): 1. Others include Chinese Artists' Association Red Rebel Group, Chinese Art Research Centre Cultural Revolution Delegates Small Group, People's Art Press Little Red Soldiers Armed Struggle Corps, People's Art Press Prairie Fire, Central Academy of Fine Arts Sculpture Creation Studio Ten Thousand Mountains Red Corps, and so forth.

19 Andrews, *Painters and Politics,* 328, citing *Meishu fenglei* 1 (1967).

20 Ibid.

21 Ibid.

22 Andrews, *Painters and Politics,* 329, citing *Meishu fenglei* 2 (1967).

23 Ibid.

24 Andrews, *Painters and Politics,* 331-32.

25 Reproduced in CNFP, 1967, no. 160, 5.

26 *South China Morning Post,* 24 February 1967, as reproduced in CNFP, 1967, no. 159. The report is attributed to the Beijing correspondent of the Japanese journal *Sankei Shinbun.*

27 The work has been widely reproduced in the West. See Chi Hsin, *Teng Hsiao-ping: A Political Biography* (Hong Kong: Cosmos Books, 1978); see also Rius and Friends, *Mao for Beginners* (New York: Pantheon Books, 1980).

28 The version reproduced here was given to Weng Rulan by Nathan Sivin, who received it free with a book purchase.

29 Stanley Karnow, *Mao and China: Inside China's Cultural Revolution* (New York: Penguin Books, 1984), 242; Union Research Institute, *CCP Documents of the Great Proletarian Cultural Revolution, 1966-1967* (Hong Kong: Union Press, n.d.), 31-32.

30 Karnow describes a Red Guard inquisition on 10 April 1966, at which she was forced to wear the infamous garments. Karnow, *Mao and China,* 326-31.

31 See Yan Jiaqi and Gao Gao's discussion of the United Action Committee (Liandong, referred to in the translated version as the Coordinated Action Committee), in *Turbulent Decade,* 105-19.

32 Karnow, *Mao and China,* 257-58.

33 Yan and Gao, *Turbulent Decade,* 101.

34 "Art That Serves Proletarian Politics," *China Reconstructs,* February 1968, 25.

35 Ibid., 18-20, 25. Also see Laing, *The Winking Owl,* 65.

36 Laing has thoroughly studied the political significance of this work. Laing, *The Winking Owl,* 67-70.

37 A photograph of this peculiar spectacle, which took place at the Beijing Foreign Languages Printing Press, was reproduced on the back cover of *China Reconstructs,* October 1968. Liu's painting appears on the front cover of the same issue.

38 For Jin Shangyi's 1966 *Chairman Mao at Lu Shan,* see *China Pictorial,* July 1967, front cover.

39 Meisner, *Mao's China,* 335.

40 Gifted urban children were privileged to attend Children's Palaces, where they were given specialized instruction in the arts at after-school and weekend programs. In Shanghai, they were organized by district. The one attended by Xu was founded by Sun Yat-sen's widow, Song Qingling, and was considered the best in the city.

41 According to an official who served as her subordinate from 1970 to 1976, she was a relative of Mao's translator. She was more commonly believed to be a niece of Mao, as reported in Laing, *The Winking Owl,* 73.

42 Zhang's meeting with Jiang Qing and Yao Wenyuan, which occurred on 19 May 1968, criticized traditionalist ink painter and academy director Pan Tianshou and the previous Zhejiang Academy of Fine Arts administration. Some publications referred to a Gang of Four in the art world consisting of Wang Mantian, Zhang Yongsheng, Jiang Qing, and Yao Wenyuan. See Song Zhongyuan, ed., *Yishu yaolan* [The cradle of arts] (Hangzhou: Zhejiang Academy of Fine Arts Publishing House, 1988), 36, and Laing, *The Winking Owl,* 64n38. Pan Tianshou did not survive the Cultural Revolution, and Zhang was imprisoned after Jiang Qing's demise.

43 *Meishu* [Fine arts], 1 (1976): 24-25.

44 Published in English as *The New Generation.* See *China Pictorial,* 1972, 35.

45 Shen Jiawei, "Suzao fanxiu qianshao de yingxiong xing-xiang – youhua *'Wei women weida zuguo zhangang'* chuangzuo guocheng" [Modelling the heroic image of the anti-revisionist advance guard – The process of creating the oil painting "*Standing Guard for Our Great Motherland*"], *Meishu ziliao* [Art materials], July 1975, 32-36.

46 Ibid., 34.

47 "Xuexi 'san tuchu' chuangzuo yuanze – buduan tigao chuangzuo ziliang" [Study the creative principle of the "three prominences" – Ceaselessly raise creative standards], *Meishu ziliao,* October 1973, 34-35. According to Laing, who first discussed the three prominences as applied to painting, the earliest articulation of the theory appeared in 1968. Laing, *The Winking Owl,* 72. For more on the three prominences and a reading of a painting in this manner, see Chapter 9 of this volume.

48 For a reproduction, see Kuiyi Shen, ed., *Word and Meaning: Six Contemporary Chinese Artists* (Buffalo: Center for the Arts, University at Buffalo, 2000), 18.

Chapter 2: Summoning Confucius

1 On biographical details in this paragraph and throughout the chapter, see the excellent memoir by the artist's son, Shi Guo, *Shi Lu hua lun* [A discussion of Shi Lu's painting] (Zhengzhou: Henan People's Press, 1999), 5. Shi Lu's daughter, Shi Dan, and his friend and fellow artist Ye Jian, have also published authoritative commentary on Shi Lu's life and art. Shi Dan, *Shi Lu, Zhongguo minghuajia quanji* [Shi Lu: Collected works of famous Chinese painters] (Hebei: Hebei Educational Press, 2003); Ye Jian, "Art Is Valued for Its Originality – An Account of the Chinese Eccentric Painter – Shi Lu," in *Shi Lu shuhua ji* [Shi Lu collected calligraphy and painting], ed. Mao Junyan (Beijing: Renmin meishu chubanshe, 1990), 90-99. Valuable new

material has been collected in Ye Jian and Shi Dan, eds., *Shi Lu yishu wenji* [Shi Lu's art-related literary works] (Xi'an: Shaanxi People's Art Press, 2003).

2 For more details on these controversies, see Shelley Drake Hawks, "'Painting by Candlelight' during the Cultural Revolution: Defending Autonomy and Expertise under Maoist Rule (1949-1976)" (PhD diss., Brown University, 2003). I am presently working on a volume for publication titled *Garden of My Name: Painters' Stories of Resistance during China's Cultural Revolution.* The fallout from a romantic involvement with a student further complicated Shi Lu's relations with his wife and his work unit. See Li Shinan, *Kuang ge dang ku – ji Shi Lu* [A mad song in place of crying – Remembering Shi Lu] (Zhengzhou: Henan People's Press, 1997), 162-63. Li Shinan was an aspiring young artist who became Shi Lu's private student during the 1970s. His memoir offers another insider perspective on Shi Lu's Cultural Revolution years.

3 Ibid., 1-5.

4 These include Ding Cong, Li Keran, Li Kuchan, Huang Yongyu, and Feng Zikai. For another notable example of private resistance, see the "Prison Notes" written by Mu Xin during his solitary confinement in 1971-72 and published in *The Art of Mu Xin: Landscapes and Prison Notes* (New Haven: Yale University Art Gallery, 2001).

5 The phrase "burning books and burying scholars alive" is commonly used to describe the atrocities committed during Qin Shihuang's reign. In 213 BCE, Qin Shihuang ordered privately owned Confucian classics to be burned, and a year afterward, had more than 460 scholars buried alive in a mass grave. Later scholars condemned Qin Shihuang's tyranny, but Chairman Mao championed a reappraisal, arguing that his actions were necessary in order to push history forward. For more background on controversies surrounding Qin Shihuang, see Li Yu-ning, ed., *The First Emperor of China: The Politics of Historiography* (White Plains: International Arts and Sciences Press, 1975).

6 On remonstrating courage, see William Theodore de Bary, *Asian Values and Human Rights: A Confucian Communitarian Perspective* (Cambridge, MA: Harvard University Press, 1998), 19-21.

7 John Berthrong describes Confucius as follows: "Here is a man, who, in his own words, knows he will not always be successful, but keeps on trying because he can do no other." Berthrong, *Transformations of the Confucian Way* (Boulder, CO: Westview Press, 1998), 22.

8 Shi Lu so admired Shitao's treatise on art, *Hua Yu Lu* (Notes on painting), that he wrote a kind of sequel to it titled *Xue Hua Lu* (Notes on the study of painting) while on sick leave in 1963. Although the original text was lost when his home was raided during the Cultural Revolution, parts of his treatise were preserved and distributed in the form of criticism materials published by his opponents to show proof of his errors in thought. A more complete, authoritative version of *Xue Hua Lu,* prepared from the notebook of one of Shi Lu's students, is published in Ye and Shi, *Shi Lu yishu wenji,* 147-69. On Shitao's *Hua Yu Lu,* see Jonathan Hay, *Shitao: Painting and Modernity in Early Qing China* (Cambridge: Cambridge University Press, 2001), 272-81; and Chou Ju-hsi, "In Quest of the Primordial Line: The Genesis and Content

of Tao-chi's *Hua-yu-lu*" (PhD diss., Princeton University, 1970). Shitao's influence on Shi Lu is also discussed in the author's work in progress *Garden of My Name.*

9 See Louis A. Sass, *Madness and Modernism: Insanity in the Light of Modern Art, Literature, and Thought* (Cambridge, MA: Harvard University Press, 1992); and Arthur Kleinman and Joan Kleinman, "How Bodies Remember: Social Memory and Bodily Experience of Criticism, Resistance, and Delegitimation Following China's Cultural Revolution," *New Literary History* 25 (1994): 707-23.

10 This work appears on the cover of Julia F. Andrews, *Painters and Politics in the People's Republic of China, 1949-1979* (Berkeley: University of California Press, 1994). Andrews insightfully discusses it on pages 236-38. Visually stunning and monumental in scale, it was also exhibited in New York during the landmark Guggenheim Museum show of 1998. See Julia F. Andrews and Kuiyi Shen, *A Century in Crisis: Modernity and Tradition in the Art of Twentieth-Century China* (New York: Guggenheim Museum, 1998), Figure 141; Andrews and Shen describe the work on page 231. The author saw the painting when it was exhibited in New York.

11 For Shi Lu's discussion of the approval process, see his "Meishujia bixu yao mei" [Artists must honour beauty], notes from a speech delivered on 9 March 1979 to the Standing Committee of the Chinese Artists' Association, in Ye and Shi, *Shi Lu yishu wenji,* 305.

12 Li, *Kuang ge dang ku,* 5.

13 On the Lushan conference, see Roderick MacFarquhar, *The Origins of the Cultural Revolution,* vol. 2, *The Great Leap Forward* (New York: Columbia University Press, 1983), 187-251.

14 Ma Gaihu, "Zhuiyi Shi Lu tongzhi chuangzuo *'Zhuanzhan Shaanbei'* de qingkuang" [Recalling the situation surrounding Comrade Shi Lu's creating *"Fighting in Northern Shaanxi"*], special supplement memorializing Shi Lu, *Meishu Tongxun* (25 August 1985): 59-60. Of course, human figures are typically depicted on a small scale in traditional Chinese landscape paintings.

15 Shi, "Meishujia bixu yao mei," in Ye and Shi, *Shi Lu yishu wenji,* 304-6.

16 Ma, "Zhuiyi Shi Lu tongzhi chuangzuo *'Zhuanzhan Shaanbei'* de qingkuang," 59-60.

17 During the early 1960s, Shi Lu was one of the leading voices insisting upon the need to leave room for the imagination in painting. One of the themes discussed in a review of his work was his preference for rich content that invited viewers to reach conclusions on their own. Hua Hsia, "The Paintings of Shi Lu," *Chinese Literature,* January 1962, 91-97.

18 The poem "Heavenly Questions," popularly attributed to Qu Yuan, is translated in Qu Yuan, *Ch'u Tz'u: Songs of the South,* trans. David Hawkes (Oxford: Clarendon, 1959), 45-58. Qu Yuan (340-278 BC), minister of the Kingdom of Chu, was slandered by another courtier and sent into exile by his king. While in exile, the grieving poet-official composed laments before eventually committing suicide. Lionized for maintaining his loyalty and inner strength despite his unjust banishment, he is one of Chinese tradition's most enduring heroes. In the first and fourth stanzas of his own poem, Shi Lu refers to questioning heaven, thus explicitly relating his work to Qu

Yuan's "Heavenly Questions." I would like to acknowledge Fusheng Wu's assistance in explaining specific linkages between Shi Lu's poem and those of Qu Yuan.

19 According to ancient Chinese legend, Yi the Archer rescued humanity by shooting down all but one of the sun god's nine unruly sons, who had refused to leave the sky and were scorching the earth. Subsequently, the sun god grew angry at the loss of so many of his sons and banished Yi and his wife to earth. In one version of the story, Yi attempts to usurp the Xia dynasty. Shi Lu's assertion that he never "tried to change the star" attests to his loyalty to the Communist Party.

20 Cang Jie is a legendary figure known as the inventor of Chinese characters.

21 Nu Wa was a mythological healing goddess and benefactor of humanity. According to legend, she repaired the sky after two quarrelling gods knocked over its supporting pillar.

22 Some years after he initially composed this poem, Shi Lu recorded it in his private diary, c. 1973-75. The poetry diary is in a private collection. Unless otherwise indicated, all translations are my own. I would like to acknowledge the assistance of Fusheng Wu, Peihui Wang, and Susan Edwards Richmond, among others, for advice on my translation.

23 Confucius likened a virtuous ruler to the pole star, "which commands the homage of the multitude of stars without leaving its place." *Confucius: The Analects,* Book 2.1, trans. D.C. Lau (New York: Penguin Books, 1979), 63.

24 Shi Lu's behaviour following his recapture is discussed in Shi, *Shi Lu hua lun,* 30. In characterizing radical Maoists as a "new aristocracy," Shi Lu may have been influenced by post-Stalin critiques of the communist system voiced by Milovan Djilas and others. See Djilas, *The New Class: An Analysis of the Communist System* (New York: Praeger Perspectives, 1958).

25 Shi Lu wrote this confession statement, dated 14 December 1969, at a time when he was under considerable pressure to admit to political crimes in order to be released. However, the tone in which he registered his doubts and opposition to radical Maoist policies does seem to have an air of authenticity.

26 Wu Guanzhong, "Shi Lu de 'qiang' ji qita" [Shi Lu's "operatic tune" and other matters], *Meishu* [Fine arts] 9 (September 1983): 42. For Shi Lu's revised paintings, see Liu Xilin, "Shi Lu de lucheng yu yishu feng shen" [Shi Lu's travels and the spirit of his artistic style], in *Shi Lu. Zhongguo jin xiandai mingjia huaji* [Shi Lu: Collected paintings by Chinese contemporary masters], ed. Wang Yushan and Cai Peixin (Beijing: People's Art Press, 1996), 142-43, 177-84.

27 On Shi Guo's memories regarding this painting, see Shi Guo, "Shi Lu hua *'Meidianshen'* ji" [Remembering Shi Lu's painting the *"Goddess of Beauty"*], *Rongbaozhai* 10 (1999): 289-93.

28 Shi, *Shi Lu hua lun,* 21.

29 Shi, *Shi Lu, Zhongguo minghuajia quanji,* 148-62. See also Shi, "Shi Lu hua *'Meidianshen'* ji," 291.

30 On the Cultural Revolution in relation to the Holocaust, see Vera Schwarcz, "The Burden of Memory: The Cultural Revolution and the Holocaust," *China Information*

(Leiden) 11, 1 (Summer 1996): 1-13. On the Holocaust as a circumstance justifying mental illness, see Peter Kramer, "There's Nothing Deep about Depression," *New York Times Magazine,* 17 April 2005, 53.

31 My appreciation to Arthur Kleinman of Harvard University for broadening my understanding of schizophrenia. On brief reactive psychosis, see Sass, *Madness and Modernism,* 359-61. On schizophrenia, works consulted include E. Fuller Torey, *Surviving Schizophrenia* (New York: Harper Collins, 2001); Daniel C. Javitt and Joseph T. Coyle, "Decoding Schizophrenia," *Scientific American,* January 2004, 48-55.

32 This description comes from the International Classification of Diseases, 9th rev., printed in American Psychiatric Association, *Diagnostic and Statistical Manual of Mental Disorders,* 3rd ed. (Washington, DC: American Psychiatric Press, 1980), Appendix D, 417, quoted in Sass, *Madness and Modernism,* 360.

33 Lu Xun's "Diary of a Madman" is collected in *Selected Works of Lu Xun,* trans. Yang Hsien-yi and Gladys Yang (1960; repr., Beijing: Foreign Languages Press, 1978).

34 On Shi Lu's resemblance to Hamlet, see Wang Zhaowen's preface titled "Zai zai tansuo" [Yet again, explore], in *Shi Lu zuopin xuanji* [Selected works of Shi Lu], ed. Ping Ye (Beijing: People's Art Press, 1983), 2-3. According to Shi Guo, Shi Lu reminded people of Don Quixote when he paced the courtyard of the Xi'an Art Academy holding a paddle and accompanied by his loyal sidekick, a small yellow dog. Shi, *Shi Lu hua lun,* 37.

35 Plato defined madness as occurring when the rational soul no longer serves as the "charioteer" of the self. Sass, *Madness and Modernism,* 1, 70-71.

36 Ad hoc Study Group of Ancient Literary Scholars and Marxist Theorists Organized by the Criticize Reactionary Painter Shi Lu Task Force, "Pipan fandong huajia Shi Lu" [Criticize the reactionary painter Shi Lu] (Shaanxi Province Internal Party Document, 6 June 1974), 1-2. Mencius lived roughly a century and a half after Confucius and is generally regarded as the second-most important philosopher in the Confucian tradition. See also Andrews, *Painters and Politics,* 296.

37 On the Xi'an black painting exhibition, see Ye Jian, "Yongxin xian'e de yichang naoju" [An intentionally evil drama], *Meishu* 5 (May 1978): 14-16, 35-36. Ye's essay is also reproduced in Shui Tianzhong and Lang Shaojun, *Ershi shijizhong zhongguo meishu wenxuan* [Selections from twentieth-century Chinese art literature], vol. 2 (Shanghai: Shanghai Calligraphy and Painting Publishing, 1999), 260-68. See also Joan Lebold Cohen, *The New Chinese Painting, 1949-1986* (New York: Harry N. Abrams, 1987), 19-23, 120-24; Ellen Johnston Laing, *The Winking Owl: Art in the People's Republic of China* (Berkeley: University of California Press, 1988), 81-89; Jerome Silbergeld and Gong Jisui, *Contradictions: Artistic Life, the Socialist State, and the Chinese Painter, Li Huasheng* (Seattle: University of Washington Press, 1993), 41, 122, 129; and Eugene Yuejin Wang, "The Winking Owl: Visual Effect and Its Art Historical Thick Description," *Critical Inquiry* 26, 3 (Spring 2000): 435-73.

38 In 1978, Shi Lu repainted an exact copy of the lost plum painting criticized during the black painting exhibition. For a reproduction of this plum painting, see Miao Fanzu, "Zuiren dianfeng" [Drunken man mountain peak], *Jiaodian,* August 1996, 40. For a

transcript of the painting's inscription, see Ye, "Yongxin xian'e de yichang naoju," 16. See also Chuang Shen, "Some Remarks concerning Shi Lu's Art of Painting," in *Collector's Choice: The Genius of Shi Lu* (Hong Kong: Cat Street Galleries, 1994), 53-54, 58. I would like to acknowledge the assistance of Professor Maggie Bickford of Brown University in interpreting the iconography of the plum's downward-pointing branches.

39 Chuang, "Some Remarks," 54, 58 (emphasis added).

40 Maggie Bickford, *Ink Plum: The Making of a Chinese Scholar-Painting Genre* (Cambridge: Cambridge University Press, 1996); see also Maggie Bickford, *Bones of Jade, Soul of Ice: The Flowering Plum in Chinese Art* (New Haven: Yale University Art Gallery, 1985).

41 The diary was the successor to an earlier one begun by Shi Lu when he was in the ox-shed jail at the Xi'an Art Academy; it was discovered and confiscated by political authorities. According to Shi Guo, the Qu Yuan poem discussed above was transcribed from memory by Shi Lu in both the earlier and later diaries. I have seen only the later diary. Information from the author's 2004 interviews with Shi Guo.

42 For Shi Lu's original sketch of the Old Fort (Purana Qila), see *Meishu* 4 (April 1956): 36.

43 The expression originates with a scornful scholar who had grown frustrated at the inferior verse inscribed by amateur poets on the tomb of the great Tang dynasty poet Li Po (701-62). Peter T. Morris, *Chinese Sayings* (Taipei: Longmen Shudian, 1981), 226-27.

44 See Shi Lu's descriptions of Confucius, and his discussion of similar aspects in himself, in Ye and Shi, *Shi Lu yishu wenji,* 211, 199-200. Shi Lu's inscription on his drawing of Confucius speaks of the sage as strongly identified with the common people.

45 The two self-portraits appear in ibid., 261, 262.

46 Ibid., 209.

47 Lu Xun prefaced his essay with a quotation from Friedrich Nietzsche. His admiration (and that of Shi Lu) for rebel poets is influenced by Nietzsche's concept of godlike men who defy convention to live passionately and dangerously. For a translation of Lu Xun's "On the Power of Mara Poetry," see *Modern Chinese Literary Thought: Writings on Literature, 1893-1945,* ed. Kirk A. Denton (Stanford: Stanford University Press, 1996), 96-109.

48 In this famous line concluding the essay, Lu Xun expressed a deep empathy with Qu Yuan as an emblem of the creative individual, "a warrior of the spirit." On Lu Xun's "antitraditional use of Qu Yuan," see Laurence A. Schneider, *A Madman of Ch'u: The Chinese Myth of Loyalty and Dissent* (Berkeley: University of California Press, 1980), 92.

49 Author's translation from the painting's inscription. This poem also appears in Shi Lu's fable about Confucius and Qin Shihuang (discussed below), although the last line differs there. Ye and Shi, *Shi Lu yishu wenji,* 215-16. The published version does not include the pointed line about the Han emperor.

50 The fable appears in ibid., 197-216.

51 Translation from Li Yu-ning, *The First Emperor of China: The Politics of Historiography* (White Plains: International Arts and Sciences Press, 1975), 1.

52 Ye and Shi, *Shi Lu yishu wenji,* 204.
53 Miao, "Zuiren dianfeng," 39.
54 Ye and Shi, *Shi Lu yishu wenji,* 214, 204, 199.
55 For example, on a painting of a horizontally growing plum (Figure 51 in Hawks, "'Painting by Candlelight'"), Shi Lu inscribed, "From the frigid river and autumn moon grows self-clarity." His calligraphy style juxtaposes two thick black characters (frigid river) with two wiry, thin, almost transparent characters (autumn moon).

Chapter 3: Brushes Are Weapons

1 The painting appeared in the Asian edition of *Newsweek.* The author was alerted to it by a reprint in a Hong Kong *Open Magazine,* June 1996.
2 In the official translation, the poem reads, in its entirety,

> Over Zhong Mountain swept a storm, headlong,
> Our mighty army, a million strong, has crossed the Great River.
> The city, a tiger crouching, a dragon curling, outshining its ancient glory;
> In heroic triumph heaven and earth have been overturned.
> With power and to spare we must pursue the tottering foe
> And not ape Xiang Yu the conqueror seeking idle fame.
> Were Nature sentient, she too would pass from youth to age,
> But man's world is mutable, seas become mulberry fields.

See Mao Tse-tung, *Poems* (Beijing: Foreign Languages Press, 1976), 25.
3 Lin Fengmian (1900-91) was the founding president of the Zhejiang Art Academy from 1928 to 1938.
4 The other is the Central Academy of Fine Arts in Beijing.
5 "Eighteenth" refers to the year 1929, which marked the eighteenth year of the Republic of China. In 1930, the group split up. The more radical members called themselves Yi-ba yi she (Art Society of the Eighteenth), omitting the Xihu (West Lake).
6 Lu Xun (1881-1936), the great Chinese writer and leader of the May 4 New Culture Movement, joined the Chinese Left-Wing Writers' Federation after moving to Shanghai. He believed that woodcuts would serve a wider audience than did the traditional art forms and would create a new direction for art. He published and introduced art books by European and Soviet artists, and encouraged young Chinese artists to combine woodcut techniques with traditional methods. Lu Xun even invited (and translated for) a Japanese printer, Uchiyama, to teach a workshop in Shanghai for the Art Society of the Eighteenth.
7 Mo Pu (1915-96) was vice-president of the Zhejiang Academy in the 1950s and president from 1980 to 1983, after the Cultural Revolution.
8 Song Zhongyuan, ed., *Yishu yaolan* [The cradle of arts] (Hangzhou: Zhejiang Academy of Fine Arts Publishing House, 1988), 32. Unless otherwise indicated, all translations are my own.

9 Zheng Shengtian, *Fang Gangmin* (Vancouver: Asia Pacific Art Promotion, 1996), 25. Fang Gangmin (1906-84) studied in France; he was a professor at the Zhejiang Academy from 1930 to 1940 and from 1958 until his death.

10 Pan Tianshou (1897-1971) was president of the Zhejiang Academy from 1944 to 1947 and from 1957 until his detention in 1966.

11 Lu Xin, *Pan Tianshou* (Beijing: China's Youth Publishing House, 1997), 356-87. Lu Xin was the director of the Pan Tianshou Memorial Museum; his book *Pan Tianshou* contains a detailed account of Pan's imprisonment from 1966 to 1970.

12 Du Yinxin, then a young teacher in the Chinese Painting Department of the academy, was also the deputy commander of Hong San Si (Headquarters of Revolutionary Rebel and Red Guards of Hangzhou).

13 Yao Wenyuan (1931-2005) was a writer in Shanghai and a member of the Gang of Four during the Cultural Revolution. Arrested in October 1976 and sentenced to twenty years' imprisonment, he was released on 5 October 1996. Chen Boda (1904-89) was one of the most important interpreters of Mao's thought and a member of the Standing Committee of the Politburo during the Cultural Revolution. After 1976, he was tried as a collaborator with the Gang of Four and was sentenced to eighteen years in prison but was soon released due to his ill health. Xiao Li, also named Li Na, the daughter of Jiang Qing and Mao, graduated from Peking University in 1965. She was appointed as the editor-in-chief of *Jiefangjun bao* (People's Liberation Army News), the official newspaper of the People's Liberation Army, at the beginning of the Cultural Revolution.

14 *Wuxian fengguang zai xianfeng: Jiang Qing tongzhi guanyu wenyi geming de jianghua* [On perilous peaks dwells beauty in her infinite variety: Speeches on the Cultural and Artistic Revolution by Comrade Jiang Qing] (n.p., 1969).

15 Lu, *Pan Tianshou*, 366.

16 Chen Li-fu (1899-2001) was a strident anti-communist Guomindang (Nationalist Party) member. Chen and his brother Chen Kuo-fu are known for founding the C-C clique, which led the party through its formative years on the mainland. Educated in the United States, Chen was also Guomindang leader Chiang Kai-shek's secretary at twenty-seven, before being appointed party secretary general.

17 Lu, *Pan Tianshou*, 378.

18 Ibid., 365.

19 Wang Liuqiu (1919-) graduated from the Art Department of Lu Xun Academy of Arts and Literature in Yan'an in 1945. After his release from the labour camp, he was reappointed as the dean of painting.

20 On 20 July 1967, two of the leading left-wing figures of the Cultural Revolution, Wang Li and Qi Benyu, were arrested by anti-rebel People's Liberation Army troops in Wuhan.

21 Zheng Qian and Han Gang, *Wannian suiyue – 1956 nian hou de Mao Zedong* [The later years – Mao Zedong after 1956] (Beijing: Chinese Youth Publishing House, 1993), 459.

22 *Quotations from Chairman Mao Tse-tung* (Beijing: Foreign Languages Press, 1967), 11. The quotation is from Mao's 1927 *Report on an Investigation of the Peasant Movement in Hunan*, in *Selected Works of Mao Tse-tung* (Peking: Foreign Languages Press, 1965), 1: 28.

23 Translated in Zheng and Han, *Wannian suiyue*, 459-60.

24 Wang Mingxian and Yan Shanchun, *Xin Zhongguo meishu tu shi, 1966-1976: The Art History of the People's Republic of China, 1966-1976* (Beijing: China Youth Press, 2000), 12-16.

25 This slogan, which first appeared in 1958, required that writers and artists apply the principle of combining objective reality with revolutionary idealism in their artwork.

26 The Blue and Green style of Chinese traditional landscape painting uses mainly the mineral colours, such as azurite and green made from malachite.

27 In 1999 and 2001, I travelled to China twice with Scott Watson, the director of the Morris and Helen Belkin Art Gallery at the University of British Columbia, in order to view the public and private collections of Cultural Revolution artworks in preparation for the exhibition The Art of the Great Proletarian Cultural Revolution, held at UBC from 22 March to 25 August 2002.

28 *Wuxian fengguang zai xianfeng*, 109.

29 Ibid., 109-10.

30 Both Mao Zedong and Liu Shaoqi were involved with the Anyuan mining workers' movement in the 1920s. The argument focused on which of them played the leading role in organizing the uprising of 1922. During the Cultural Revolution, Jiang Qing and her followers claimed that Mao was the true leader, while Liu was blamed as an enemy and traitor of the Communist Party. See Wang and Yan, *Xin Zhongguo meishu tu shi, 1966-1976*, 57, 67.

31 Ibid., 65.

32 Huang Gongwang was a famous landscape painter of the Yuan dynasty.

33 Yang Mu, '*Wenge' chuangjiang feng shen bang* [Pathbreakers of the Cultural Revolution] (Beijing: Tuanjie Press, 1993).

34 Ding Shu, "The Death Toll of the Cultural Revolution Amounts to Two Million," (n.d.), http://www.boxun.com/hero/dings/39_1.shtml.

35 After serving more than twenty-five years in the labour camp, Zhang was eventually released and returned to Hangzhou.

36 The sale price of *Chairman Mao Goes to Anyuan* was 6.05 million *yuan*, just over $1 million Canadian at that time.

Chapter 4: When We Were Young

1 Quoted in Gu Hongzhang and Hu Mengzhou, eds., *Zhongguo zhishi qingnian shang shan xia siang shi mo* [The Chinese educated youth (going) up to the mountains, down to the villages, from beginning to end] (Beijing: Zhongguo jiancha chubanshe, 1996), 104-5. Unless otherwise indicated, all translations are my own.

2 Liu Xiaomeng, et al., *Zhongguo zhiqing shidian* [Record of Chinese educated youth] (Chengdu: Sichuan People's Publishing House, 1995), 649.

3 Wang Mingjian, *Shangshan xiaxiang: shanshi nian* [Up to the mountains, down to the villages: Thirty years] (Beijing: Guangming chubanshe, 1998), 90.

4 Liu Xiaomeng, et al., *Zhongguo zhiqing shidian,* 621.

5 Ibid., 615.

6 Ibid., 757.

7 The Hundred Flowers movement was launched by Mao in 1956 with an invitation to criticize the Communist Party's management of the state. Those who dared to respond were quickly condemned as "rightists," and large numbers were imprisoned and ostracized. For more on this movement, see Richard King, "The Hundred Flowers," in *The Columbia Companion to Modern East Asian Literature,* ed. Joshua S. Mostow (New York: Columbia University Press, 2003), 76-80.

8 For more on Gu Xiong's career, see Mary Christene Lucas, "Negotiations of Identity: The Life and Art of Gu Xiong" (master's thesis, Department of History in Art, University of Victoria, 2002).

Chapter 5: The *Rent Collection Courtyard, Past and Present*

1 The epigraph is from Mao Zedong, *Talks at the Yenan Forum on Literature and Art,* 3rd ed., 2nd rev. trans. (Beijing: Foreign Languages Press, 1967), 18. My thanks to Feng Bin, director of the Art Museum of the Sichuan Fine Arts Institute, for his invaluable and enthusiastic help with my research for this essay.

2 Julia F. Andrews, *Painters and Politics in the People's Republic of China, 1949-1979* (Berkeley: University of California Press, 1994), 317.

3 The following three texts describe this early set of sculptures, with minor disagreements regarding details: Wang Guanyi, "*'Shou zu yuan'* chuangzuo huiyi lu" [Record of reminiscences of the creation of the "*Rent Collection Courtyard*"], in Luo Zhongli, ed., *Shou zu yuan qundiao* [The *Rent Collection Courtyard* group of sculptures] (Shijiazhuang: Hebei Fine Arts Publishing House, 2001), 1-15; on the debate surrounding the Museum of Liu [Wencai]'s Courtyard of Oppression, see "*Guanyu Shou zu yuan* zhu zuo quan wenti de chenshu cailiao" [Salient data regarding questions assessing the work, the *Rent Collection Courtyard*], c. 2000, http://www.tom.com, accessed September 2000; page now discontinued; Zhangfu Zhangde, "Shi zai zheli ningshi – daxing nisu *Shou zu yuan* de fengyu cheng" [History is on view here – the trials and tribulations of China's large-scale clay sculpture, the *Rent Collection Courtyard*], c. 2000, http://www.tom.com, accessed September 2000; page now discontinued.

4 Wang, "*'Shou zu yuan'* chuangzuo huiyi lu," 1.

5 Ibid. Museum of Liu [Wencai]'s Courtyard of Oppression, "Chenshu cailiao."

6 Wang, "*'Shou zu yuan'* chuangzuo huiyi lu," 1.

7 Ibid. (According to Wang Guanyi, these were life-sized and coloured.) See also Museum of Liu [Wencai]'s Courtyard of Oppression, "Chenshu cailiao."

8 Wang, "'*Shou zu yuan*' chuangzuo huiyi lu," 1.

9 Ibid. Museum of Liu [Wencai]'s Courtyard of Oppression, "Chenshu cailiao."

10 Wang, "'*Shou zu yuan*' chuangzuo huiyi lu," 11.

11 Ibid.

12 Ibid., 12.

13 Li Lang, "Wo ceng paishe guo '*Shou zu yuan*'" [I photographed the *"Rent Collection Courtyard"*], *Observers Monthly* (Hong Kong), September 1980, 49.

14 *"Shou zu yuan" nisu zhanlan* [*The "Rent Collection Courtyard"* clay sculpture exhibition] (Guangzhou: Guangzhou Culture Bureau/Guangzhou Culture Garden, 1967). Private correspondence between the author and Feng Bin, 8 December 2002.

15 Wang, "'*Shou zu yuan*' chuangzuo huiyi lu," 14.

16 Fei Xinbei, *"Shou zu yuan" qundiao zuopin xuan* [Selected works of the group sculpture *"Rent Collection Courtyard"*] (Chongqing: Art Museum and Sichuan Fine Arts Institute, 2001), 1.

17 Wang, "'*Shou zu yuan*' chuangzuo huiyi lu," 15.

18 Mao, *Talks at the Yenan Forum,* 2.

19 Ibid., 19.

20 "Rent Collection Courtyard: A Revolution in Sculpture," supplement, *China Reconstructs* (Beijing), 1967, 2.

21 Ibid., 1.

22 *"Shou zu yuan" nisu zhanlan.*

23 Mao, *Talks at the Yenan Forum,* 6.

24 Ibid., 18.

25 "Rent Collection Courtyard," supplement, *China Reconstructs,* 3.

26 Ibid., 2.

27 Ibid.

28 Additional clay sculpture groups include *In Praise of the Red Guards* (life-sized) and *Family Histories of the Air Force Fighters* (three hundred life-sized statues), both of which are reproduced in *China Reconstructs,* February 1968; others were created at Datong, Fushun, and the Mentougou Mines (the latter were reproduced in *Chinese Literature,* September 1969).

29 "*The Wrath of the Serfs:* Old Tibet in Sculpture," *China Reconstructs,* March 1976, 33-36.

30 "A History of Blood and Tears: On the Art Works of the Three Stones Museum in Tientsin," *Chinese Literature,* November-December 1969, 140.

31 Ibid., 139.

32 Although Cai intended the sculptures to disintegrate, many survived. Riddled with extensive cracks, they have been preserved in Nove, a small Italian town famed for its ceramics expertise.

33 Li Luming and Daozi, "Jiaoban 'Weinisi'" [Edition to order: "Venice"], *Shijue* [Vision] 21, 5 (May 2000): 63. Erik Eckholm, "Expatriate Artist Updates Maoist Icon and Angers Old Guard," *New York Times,* 17 August 2000, E-1, E-6.

34 Wang Nanming, "The Shanghai Art Museum Should Not Become a Market Stall in China for Western Hegemonism – A Paper Delivered at the 2000 Shanghai Biennale" (Shanghai, November 2000). For an edited version of this paper, see Wang, "The Shanghai Art Museum Should Not Become a Market Stall in China for Western Hegemonism," in *Chinese Art at the Crossroads: Between Past and Future, Between East and West,* ed. Wu Hung (Hong Kong: New Art Media, 2001), 265-68.

35 Materials relevant to the *Rent Collection Courtyard* debate are no longer online at Tom.com.

36 Sichuan Fine Arts Institute (also translated as Sichuan Academy of Fine Arts), "The *Rent Collection Courtyard* Copyright Breached Overseas: Sichuan Academy of Fine Arts Sues *Venice Biennale*," press release, 20 May 2000. Press release translated by Robert Bernell. See Britta Erickson, "The *Rent Collection Courtyard* Copyright Breached Overseas: Sichuan Academy of Fine Arts Sues *Venice Biennale*," in *Chinese Art at the Crossroads: Between Past and Future, Between East and West,* ed. Wu Hung (Hong Kong: New Art Media, 2001), 52-55.

37 Zhou Lin, "Chinalaw Web: Art Law in China," 25 June 1998, at http://www.qis.net/chinalaw/prcartlaw.htm, accessed 23 January 2002; page now discontinued.

38 Ibid.

39 Sichuan Fine Arts Institute, "The *Rent Collection Courtyard* Copyright Breached Overseas," press release.

40 Wang, "'*Shou zu yuan*' chuangzuo huiyi lu," 1-15.

Chapter 6: Hu Xian Peasant Painting

1 Huang Dingjun, "Hubei sheng gong-nong yeyu meishu huodong de xin mianmao" [The new face of Hubei worker-peasant part-time art activity], *Meishu* [Fine arts] (May 1958): 35-37. Other issues of *Meishu,* the foremost art journal in China, contained similarly enthusiastic reports through 1958 and early 1959. In English, see Ko Lu, "Art: New Peasant Paintings," *Peking Review,* 23 September 1958, 18; for more details and pictures, consult Ko Lu, "Peasants Speak through Pictures," *China Reconstructs,* July 1959, 19.

2 "Wenhua shangshan, xiaxiang, mianmao gaiguan" [Culture climbs the mountain, goes to the countryside, and its face is transformed], *Meishu* (June 1958): 6. The eminent woodcut artist Gu Yuan published a small book illustrating the simplified, but hardly folk art, drawings he used as models in the village where he worked in 1958. Gu, *Nongcun bihua fanben* [A textbook of models for village wall paintings] (Tianjin: Tianjin meishu chubanshe, 1959).

3 As Marx and Friedrich Engels explained, "For as soon as labour is distributed, each man has a particular, exclusive sphere of activity, which is forced upon him and from which he cannot escape. He is a hunter, a fisherman, a shepherd, or a critic, and must remain so if he does not want to lose his means of livelihood; while in communist society, where nobody has one exclusive sphere of activity but each can become

accomplished in any branch he wishes, society regulates the general production and thus makes it possible for me to do one thing to-day and another to-morrow, to hunt in the morning, fish in the afternoon, rear cattle in the evening, criticize after dinner, just as I have a mind, without ever becoming hunter, fisherman, shepherd, or critic." Marx and Engels, *The German Ideology* (New York: International Publishers, 1939), 23.

4 Pi Xian peasant painters had an exhibition in Beijing during the summer of 1958. Wang Chaowen, "Wall Paintings by Peasant Artists," *Chinese Literature,* January 1958, 194-98. Both Hebei and Jiangsu Provinces produced small reproduction volumes of provincial peasant paintings: *Hebei nongcun bihua* [Hebei village wall paintings] (Hebei: Hebei meishu chubanshe, 1959); *Subei nongcun bihua ji* [A collection of village wall paintings from northern Jiangsu] (Shanghai: Renmin meishu chubanshe, 1958).

5 The most useful compilation of sources and memoirs recently published in Beijing for the Hu Xian Committee of the Shaanxi Provincial People's Consultative Conference is Duan Jingli, ed., *Hu Xian nongmin hua chunqiu* [Annals of Hu Xian peasant painting] (Beijing: Zhongguo dang'an chubanshe, 1999).

6 In this collection, Chen Shiheng tells his story as "Recollections of Hu Xian Peasant Art School." Other essays in this volume also recount the early years of painting in Hu Xian. Chen Shiheng, "Hu Xian nongmin hua xuexiao huiyi" [Recollections of Hu Xian Peasant Art School] in ibid., 127-52.

7 Although Michael Sullivan's remark that "peasants were too bitterly disillusioned – often too hungry – to think about painting" is justified, it ignores the survivals that popped up in China's foreign-language publications once the worst years of the early 1960s were over, but without the extravagant claims of the Great Leap Forward period. See, for example, "Folk Artists: Peasant Women's Exhibition," *Peking Review,* 26 June 1964, 64; "All China Workers and Peasants Amateur Art Exhibition," *Chinese Literature,* July 1965, 105-6; and "Art by Workers and Peasants," *China Reconstructs,* September 1965, 41. The above quote is from Sullivan, *Art and Artists in Twentieth Century China* (Berkeley: University of California Press, 1996), 148.

8 For a discussion of *nian hua* in the early years of the People's Republic, see James A. Flath, "Printing Culture in Rural North China" (PhD diss., Department of History, University of British Columbia, 2000). Flath's subsequent book deals admirably with the history of *nian hua* from the late nineteenth century to the founding of the People's Republic, including Communist Party attempts to appropriate folk art for revolutionary art in the Yan'an period, but omits anything after 1950. Flath, *The Cult of Happiness: Nianhua, Art, and History in Rural North China* (Vancouver: UBC Press, 2004).

9 Jiang Qisheng, "Hu Xian nongmin hua de lishi he jingyan diaocha baogao" [An investigative report on the history and experience of Hu Xian peasant painting], in Duan, *Hu Xian nongmin hua chunqiu,* 52. Unless otherwise indicated, all translations are my own.

10 There is a convenient record of Hu Xian's growing recognition. See "Hu Xian nongmin hua da shi ji" [A record of major events in Hu Xian peasant painting], in Duan, *Hu Xian nongmin hua chunqiu,* 380-404. The *Renmin ribao* article of 26 July 1966 shows four paintings and a serial picture strip.

11 An exception is Wang Mingxian and Yan Shanchun, *Xin Zhongguo meishu tu shi, 1966-1976: The Art History of the People's Republic of China, 1966-1976* (Beijing: China Youth Press, 2000). But its section on Hu Xian peasant painting is a simple narrative with extensive quotations from contemporary publicity and no critical judgments of its own. In this case, the extensive citing of foreigners' uncritical opinions might no longer be intended as justification for Chinese art policies and their results but rather, as one suspects the whole book to be, subtle postmodern irony with the shadows of Maoist platitudes as the butt of the joke. Or is the joke on those gullible foreigners, both then and now, taken in by the hype about new Chinese art? A sign inside the foyer of the Peasant Painting Exhibition Hall, seen by the author in October 2001, simply stated the following under the heading Record of Major Events: "1967-1969 'Cultural Revolution' chaos. Peasant painters' activities were seriously disturbed by the (political) movement: one portion of peasant painting creators engaged in activities such as 'Parade of Clowns' (Denunciation of cadres) and 'Criticize Black Painting' (aimed at professional artists) harming a portion of the provincial and city specialists who were concerned with peasant painting."

12 The Beijing exhibition is reviewed and extravagantly praised in Zhang Nan, "Lai zi gongnong hua gongnong" [Paintings of workers and peasants by workers and peasants]," *Renmin ribao* [People's daily], 5 December 1972, 4.

13 Ding Jitang, "Fudao nongmin hua huodong de yixie benhui" [Leading and guiding peasant-painting activities: Several observations from practice] (Paper presented at the national conference on peasant painting, Beijing, 1983), 2.

14 Quoted in Wang and Yan, *Xin Zhongguo meishu tu shi, 1966-1976,* 116.

15 For a collection of this "art criticism" from the national press, see *Hu Xian nongmin hua lian wen zi* [Collection of articles on Hu Xian peasant paintings] (Beijing: Renmin meishu chubanshe, 1975).

16 Narrated in confidence in private conversation with the author by an artist intimately involved with the Hu Xian peasant painting at its heyday.

17 Jiang, "Hu Xian nongmin hua de lishi he jingyan diaocha baogao," 5.

18 A good example of the foreign-visitor genre is S. Marie Carson, "Dialogue on the Peasant Art of Huhsien," *Eastern Horizon* (May 1974): 7. Contrast this with the later critical analysis by Ellen Johnston Laing, "Chinese Peasant Painting, 1958-1976: Amateur and Professional," *Art International* 28, 1 (January-March 1984): 2-12, 40, 48, 64.

19 Laing, "Chinese Peasant Painting," 8-9.

20 Related in Jiang, "Hu Xian nongmin hua de lishi he jingyan diaocha baogao," 35.

21 Quoted in ibid., 42.

22 *Hu Xian nongmin hua xuanji* [A selection of Hu Xian peasant paintings] (Xi'an: Renmin chubanshe, 1974), 48-49.

23 Jiang, "Hu Xian nongmin hua de lishi he jingyan diaocha baogao," 49.
24 Li Fenglan, "How I Began to Paint the Countryside," *China Reconstructs*, January 1974, 21-23.
25 Laing, "Chinese Peasant Painting," 9-10.
26 Ibid., 8-9.
27 The figure is from Ding, "Fudao nongmin hua huodong de yixie benhui."
28 Duan, *Hu Xian nongmin hua chunqiu*, 387-88.
29 Conversation with Liu Zhide in Huxian, 30 May 2001.
30 Joan Lebold Cohen, "Abstract Art Out and Folk Art In as China Readjusts Its Political Line," *Asian Wall Street Journal*, 15 April 1981.
31 An early account, by Wu Tongzhang himself, is "Jinshan nongmin hua de yishu daolu" [The artistic road of Jin Shan peasant painting], *Meishu* (August 1982): 40-46. For a beautifully illustrated but uninformative update, see the picture book *Jin Shan nongmin hua* [Jin Shan peasant painting] (Shanghai: Pictorial Publishing House, 1999).
32 The catalogue for a 1984 national exhibition of peasant paintings showed works from various localities. Politics had disappeared from the art criticism, which stressed "local colour and national style," and above all the material prosperity created by the dismantling of collectivized agriculture. As the catalogue's preface put it, "When the year is abundant, the people's hearts are happy; when the people's hearts are happy, their brushes are busy." *Zhongguo nongmin hua* [Chinese peasant paintings] (Beijing: Renmin meishu chubanshe, 1984), n.p.
33 The 1983 figure is from Ding, "Fudao nongmin hua huodong de yixie benhui," 1. The 1994 figure, given in the preface to Duan, *Hu Xian nongmin hua chunqiu*, 1-3, was reported in the posted "introduction" on the wall of the Peasant Painting Exhibition Hall in October 2001.
34 Wang Shu, "Gangyin wei nongmin hua zhengming shengfen" [Seals for proving the identity of peasant paintings], *Guangming ribao* [Guangming daily], 30 May 1997, 2.
35 Karl Marx, *The Eighteenth Brumaire of Louis Napoleon* (New York: International Publishers, 1963), 15.

Chapter 7: Model Theatrical Works

1 This chapter is drawn from research for my *The Chinese Cultural Revolution: A History* (New York: Cambridge University Press, 2008).
2 Jiang Zuhui, "Xinwei de huiyi: wuju *'Hongse niangzi jun'* de chuangzuo licheng" [Bitter memories: The creation of the ballet *"The Red Detachment of Women"*], *Wudao* [Dance], November 1987, 22-23.
3 See a long report on its creation published in the Red Guard newspaper *Beijing gongshe* [Beijing Commune], 18 May 1967, 3, and reproduced in Song Yongyi, ed., *Xinbian Hongweibing ziliao* [New materials on the Red Guards] (Oakton, VA: Center for Chinese Research Materials, 1999), 359-60.
4 Robert Hegel discusses the adaptation of Qu Bo's novel to the stage in "Making the Past Serve the Present in Fiction and Drama: From the Yan'an Forum to the Cultural

Revolution," in *Popular Chinese Literature and Performing Arts in the People's Republic of China, 1949-1979,* ed. Bonnie S. McDougall (Berkeley: University of California Press, 1984), 197-223.

5 *Song of the Dragon River (Longjiang song),* another new opera often grouped with the models, also has a modern setting. It focuses on a female party secretary who leads peasants in overcoming drought.

6 Jiang Qing, "Tan Jingju geming" [On the revolution in Beijing opera], *Hongqi* [Red flag], June 1967, 25-27.

7 For a typical example, see Tian Wen and Xin Xiao, "Zan jingju geming shi nian" [In praise of ten years of the revolution in Beijing opera], *Tianjin wenyi* [Tianjin literature and art], August 1974, 24-27; see also Yin Chengzong, "Yi Jiang Qing tongzhi wei guanghui bangyang, zuo yongyuan zhongyu Mao zhuxi de geming wenyi zhanshi" [Taking Jiang Qing as a glorious example, be a revolutionary cultural soldier always loyal to Chairman Mao], *Guangming ribao,* 6 July 1968, 2.

8 See, for example, "Jiang Qing shi pohuai wuju *'Baimao nü'* de zuiku huoshou: geming xiandai wuju *'Baimao nü'* diaocha baogao" [Jiang Qing is the worst culprit in wrecking the ballet *"The White-Haired Girl":* Report on an investigation into *"The White-Haired Girl"*], *Wudao,* March 1977, 7-10, 21.

9 Ibid., 2, 9.

10 A half page of advertisements and performance listings in *Tianjin ribao,* 2 October 1966, 6.

11 The 118-metre-long sculptural suite comprised 114 human figures, 21 of which were negative characters. It had been created between June and October 1965 by a group at the Sichuan Arts Academy (Sichuan meishu yuan): see Chen Lüsheng, *Xin Zhongguo meishu shi, 1949-1966* [New China's art history, 1949-1966] (Beijing: Zhongguo qingnian chubanshe, 2000), 314-21.

12 For a typically ambiguous statement about seventeen years of films not being in distribution, see Ma Shijun, "Woguo dianying faxing fangying gongzuo de huigu yu zhanwang" [A look back and forwards for China's film distribution work], in *Zhonghua renmin gongheguo dianying shiye sanshiwu nian, 1949-1984* [Thirty-five years of the film industry in the People's Republic of China, 1949-1984], ed. Zhongguo dianyingjia xiehui dianyingshi yanjiubu (Beijing: Zhongguo dianying chubanshe, 1985), 340.

13 The third item, *Liu Yingjun zan,* may have been presented in Henan opera style. Liu Yingjun was a revolutionary martyr and model soldier who died in March 1966. *Sending Precious Books* was presumably a tableau involving taking the works, sayings, or calligraphy of Mao Zedong to a deprived group anxious to study them.

14 The exemplar of this kind of performance was *The East Is Red (Dongfang hong),* first staged in 1965 and filmed that year for nationwide distribution.

15 The same page offers further evidence of the dominance of the Beijing opera form. The schedule for Hebei Television included the following: at 2:00 p.m. Beijing opera, a segment of indeterminate length (but probably no more than one hour) followed at 7:00 p.m. by *Country Club (Nongcun julebu),* an educational program for farmers;

on 2 October at 10:00 a.m. and 1:10 p.m., Tianjin Television scheduled unspecified Beijing opera. What these Beijing opera programs consisted of is unclear, though presumably they were confined to the new, modernized works at a time when no full-length television or film versions are known to have been recorded.

16 Yu Hong and Deng Zhengqiang, *Zhongguo dangdai guanggao shi* [History of contemporary Chinese advertising] (Changsha: Hunan kexue jishu chubanshe, 2000), 10. Yu Hong and Deng Zhengqiang indicate that vestiges of advertising enterprises survived through the Cultural Revolution.

17 The same third of a page as the performance listings in *Tianjin ribao,* 2 October 1966, also includes classified-style listings of name changes of several factories in the city. For example, the Tianjin City Social Welfare *(shehui fuli)* Number Two Paper Product Factory was to be known after 1 October as the Tianjin City East Wind Printing and Paper Product Factory.

18 For a description of the life of Yu Huiyong, who became minister of culture in the mid-1970s and committed suicide at age fifty-two in 1977, see Dai Jiafang, *Zou xiang huimie: 'Wen'ge' wenhuabu zhang Yu Huiyong chenfu lu* [Approaching extermination: The ups and downs of Yu Huiyong, Cultural Revolution minister of culture] (Beijing: Guangming ribao chubanshe, 1994). See also Richard Kraus, "Arts Policies of the Cultural Revolution: The Rise and Fall of Culture Minister Yu Huiyong," in *New Perspectives on the Cultural Revolution,* ed. William A. Joseph, Christine P.W. Wong, and David Zweig (Cambridge, MA: Council on East Asian Studies/Harvard University, 1991), 219-41.

19 "Jingju geming shi Mao Zedong sixiang de weida shengli" [The revolution in Beijing opera is a glorious victory for Mao Zedong thought], *Renmin ribao* [People's daily], 24 May 1967, 6.

20 The editorial was reprinted nationwide: see, for example, "Geming wenyi de youxiu yangban" [Outstanding models of revolutionary literature and art], *Hongse dianxun* [Red dispatch], 31 May 1967, 1. *Hongse dianxun* was the Cultural Revolution name of *Ningxia ribao.* Unless otherwise indicated, all translations are my own.

21 On the Uighur *Shajiabang,* see the lengthy article "Guanyu Weiwu'eryu geju *Shajiabang* de chaungzuo" [On the making of the Uighur *Shajiabang*], *Renmin ribao,* 29 May 1975, 2. On the Yueju (Cantonese opera) version of *Shajiabang,* see Bell Yung, "Model Opera as Model: From *Shajiabang* to *Sagabong,*" in McDougall, *Popular Chinese Literature and Performing Arts,* 144-64.

22 The extraordinary work of Yang Jian in charting unofficial activity during the period is noteworthy: see, for example, his *Wenhua da geming zhong de dixia wenxue* [Underground literature during the Cultural Revolution] (Beijing: Chaohua chubanshe, 1993).

23 *Ningxia ribao,* 25 May 1969, 4.

24 See, for example, the 27 May 1967 issue of *Dongfang hong* [The East is red], published by the Beijing gongye daxue (Beijing Industrial University), where the anniversary of Mao's Yan'an Talks is celebrated without mention of the model works. *Dongfang hong,* 14 June 1968, 2, shows a similar unexpected absence. Both are reprinted in Song, *Xinbian Hongweibing ziliao,* 703-4 and 1388.

25 Zhe Ping [pseud.], "Xuexi geming yangbanxi, baowei geming yangbanxi" [Study the revolutionary model performances, defend the revolutionary model performances], *Hongqi,* 30 September 1969, 37-40, especially 39.

26 For a detailed account of the making of these films, see Zhai Jiannong, *Hongse wangshi: 1966-1976 nian de Zhongguo dianying* [Red past: Chinese film 1966-1976] (Beijing: Taihai chubanshe, 2001), 64-184. So-called television documentary versions *(dianshi pingmu fuzhi)* of *The Red Lantern, Taking Tiger Mountain by Strategy,* and *The White-Haired Girl* were available in 1970, although work on the film version of *Taking Tiger Mountain by Strategy* had started in the autumn of 1968.

27 The smaller projector began production in 1968. Yang Haizhou, *Zhongguo dianying wuzi chanye xitong lishi bian nianji* [Chronological history of the Chinese film product manufacturing system] (Beijing: Zhongguo dianying chubanshe, 1998), 267.

28 See advertisement in *Ningxia ribao,* 20 May 1970, 4. The listing of the Yan'an Talks commemoration performances included several pre–Cultural Revolution feature films, among them the so-called *Three Fights (San zhan), Mine Warfare* (*Dilei zhan,* 1962), *Tunnel Warfare* (*Didao zhan,* 1965), and the old favourite *Fighting North and South* (*Nan zheng bei zhan,* 1952 and 1974).

29 See the listing in *Tianjin ribao,* 1 October 1972, 4.

30 See, for example, the listing in *Ningxia ribao,* 23 May 1971, 4. The stills of *Shajiabang* and *The White-Haired Girl* are labelled as from a television film and a television documentary respectively. Due to the new availability of the model films, commemorations in Ningxia did not include the showing of old pre–Cultural Revolution films, as had been usual in the preceding years.

31 For example, the listings of performances in *Ningxia ribao,* 1 May 1972, 1; *Ningxia ribao,* 16 May 1972, 1-3; and the paper's May 1973 issues give full coverage to the Talks but seem to ignore the model performances.

32 See, for example, Gao Yilong and Li Xiao, eds., *Zhongguo xiqu xiandaixi shi* [History of modern-subject Chinese opera] (Shanghai: Shanghai wenhua chubanshe, 1999), 313.

33 For production and plot details, see Zhongguo dianying ziliaoguan, Zhongguo yishu yanjiu yuan dianying yanjiusuo, eds., *Zhongguo yishu yingpian bianmu, 1949-1979* [Catalogue of Chinese art films, 1949-1979] (Beijing: Wenhua yishu chubanshe, 1982), 976, 989, and 992-93. To enhance the impact of the battle scenes, the third film was made in wide-screen format, unlike any of the model performance film versions.

34 The film's appeal was enhanced by two songs that became highly popular across China.

35 This statement is based on the author's personal observation as a student in Beijing from October 1974 to July 1976.

36 Jiang Qing's criticism of two 1975 films, *Haixia* (the title is the name of the central character) and *The Pioneers (Chuangye),* was symptomatic of her awareness that she was increasingly isolated in the rivalry between political factions. For a brief discussion of her criticisms and Mao's dismissal of them, see Paul Clark, *Chinese Cinema:*

Culture and Politics since 1949 (Cambridge, MA: Cambridge University Press, 1987), 143-44.

37 See advertisements in *Ningxia ribao,* 1 May 1974, 4; and *Ningxia ribao,* 2 May 1974, 3. These performances were for May Day, though they extended through the month in commemoration of Mao's Yan'an Talks.

38 See the Xinhua News Agency report of this reprinted in "Wenhua bu zai quanguo chengxiang juban geming yanbanxi yingpian huiying he zai gongchang, nongcun juban gongren hua, nongmin hua xunhui zhanlan" [Ministry of Culture holds revolutionary model performance film screenings nationwide in cities and towns, and holds worker and peasant painting touring exhibitions in factories and villages], *Ningxia ribao,* 22 May 1975, 1. Among other new films screened were celluloid versions of the dance-dramas *Sons and Daughters of the Grasslands (Caoyuan ernü)* and *Song of Yimeng (Yimeng song).*

39 "Jianchi wenyi geming shijian, pipan Deng Xiaoping fandong zuixing" [Maintain the practice of revolution in the arts, condemn Deng Xiaoping's reactionary crimes], *Guangming ribao,* 13 May 1976, 2.

40 See the full-page listing/advertisement in *Renmin ribao,* 15 May 1975, 6.

41 See listings in *Tianjin ribao,* 30 September 1975, 4.

42 *Ningxia ribao,* 14 May 1976, 4.

43 Zhongguo dianying ziliaoguan, Zhongguo yishu yanjiu yuan dianying yanjiusuo, *Zhongguo yishu yingpian bianmu,* 1090-91. On the opera, see Gao and Li, *Zhongguo xiqu xiandaixi shi,* 311-13.

44 A Beijing audience at a spring 1976 live performance that I attended laughed out loud at several points.

45 *Ningxia ribao,* 4 May 1976, 5.

46 See listings in *Renmin ribao,* 29 September 1976, 6. In Tianjin, extracts of the model operas, performed for only three days, were part of the restrained commemorations. See listing in *Tianjin ribao,* 30 September 1976, 4.

47 For listings of such films, over half those in production during 1976, see Zhongguo dianying ziliaoguan, Zhongguo yishu yanjiu yuan dianying yanjiusuo, *Zhongguo yishu yingpian bianmu,* 1039-120.

Chapter 8: Feminism in the Revolutionary Model Ballets

1 "Jiang Mao zhuxi de wenyi luxian jinxing daodi: guanghui de yangban" [Carrying out Chairman Mao's line on literature and art: Brilliant models], *Renmin ribao* [People's Daily], 6 December 1966. Unless otherwise indicated, all translations are my own.

2 "Gu wei jin yong, yang wei zhong yong, ping ba ge yangban xi" [Making the past serve the present and foreign things serve China, a critique of the eight model theatrical works], Xinhua News Agency (Xinhuashe), 16 July 1967.

3 The party had already successfully used literature and art as weapons to serve its political agenda. The *yangge* (rice-sprout song) movement in Yan'an during the 1940s and the *xin minge* (new folk songs) movement in the late 1950s are examples.

4 For an English translation of the Yan'an Talks, see Mao Zedong, "Talks at the Yan'an Forum on Literature and Art," in *Modern Chinese Literary Thought: Writings on Literature, 1893-1945*, ed. Kirk A. Denton (Stanford: Stanford University Press, 1996), 458-84.

5 Walter Meserve, *Modern Drama from Communist China* (New York: New York University Press, 1970), 1.

6 Joseph S.M. Lau and Howard Goldblatt, eds., *The Columbia Anthology of Modern Chinese Literature* (New York: Columbia University Press, 1995).

7 Bonnie S. McDougall, "Writers and Performers, Their Works, and Their Audiences, in the First Three Decades," in *Popular Chinese Literature and Performing Arts in the People's Republic of China, 1949-1979*, ed. Bonnie S. McDougall (Berkeley: University of California Press, 1984), 269-304.

8 The opinion of Yan Jiaqi and Gao Gao is representative in this regard: "She [Jiang Qing] made great efforts to expand her influence in the ideological and the cultural field with the help of the Beijing opera reform. She waved the banner of the 'eight model dramas,' which were also the result of the Beijing opera reform, hoping that people would gather around her banner and elevate her to the throne as the future queen of China." In Yan and Gao, *Turbulent Decade: A History of the Cultural Revolution*, trans. and ed. D.W.Y. Kwok (Honolulu: University of Hawai'i Press, 1996), 400.

9 Chen Sihe, *Zhongguo dangdai wenxue shi* [A history of contemporary Chinese literature] (Shanghai: Fudan daxue chubanshe, 1999), 165.

10 Yu-sun Chou, "Change and Continuity in Communist Chinese Policy on Literature and Art," *Issues and Studies* 22, 9 (September 1986): 18.

11 See *Zhongguo dangdai wenxue shi* [A history of contemporary Chinese literature] (Fuzhou: Fujian renmin chubanshe, 1982); and Wang Huazao, Chen Yuanzheng, and Cao liusheng, eds., *Zhongguo dangdai wenxue jianshi* [A brief history of contemporary Chinese literature] (Changsha: Hunan renmin chubanshe, 1985).

12 "*The Red Detachment of Women*," and "*The White-Haired Girl*," in *Five Chinese Communist Plays*, ed. Martin Ebon (New York: John Day, 1975).

13 Monique Wittig, *Straight Mind and Other Essays* (Boston: Beacon Press, 1992), 53.

14 Many of the model theatrical works have feminist concerns. *The White-Haired Girl*, *The Red Detachment of Women*, *The Red Lantern*, and *Taking Tiger Mountain by Strategy* feature daughters who become revolutionaries, and *Shajiabang*, *Azalea Mountain*, *On the Docks*, and *Song of the Dragon River* focus on degendered communist women.

15 Xiaorong Li, "Gender Inequality in China and Cultural Relativism," in *Women, Culture, and Development*, ed. Martha Nussbaum and Jonathan Glover (Oxford: Clarendon Press, 1995), 411. Li also points out that the change in media images of women is buttressed by the social reality of increased gender disparity. For instance, he notes that the traditional business of selling women for marriage is being revived: "In 1990 alone, 18,692 cases were investigated by the authorities." Also, the nation's educational system has accorded "first priority to males"; as a result, "illiterates" and "school dropouts have been mainly female" (408).

16 Emily Honig and Gail Hershatter, *Personal Voices: Chinese Women in the 1980's* (Stanford: Stanford University Press, 1988), 7.

17 Jack Belden, *China Shakes the World* (New York and London: Monthly Review Press, 1970), 209-10.

18 Meng Yue, "'*Baimao nü*' yu Yan'an wenxue de lishi fuzaxing" ["*The White-Haired Girl*" and the historical complexity of Yan'an literature], *Jintian* [Today] 1 (1993): 177.

19 Ibid., 171-88.

20 Ibid., 177.

21 This is one of the definitions of "justice" in *Webster's New Collegiate Dictionary.*

22 William Galston, *Justice and the Human Good* (Chicago: University of Chicago Press, 1980), 112.

23 "Yang wei zhong yong, geming baleiwu 'bai maonü'" [Making foreign things serve China, the revolutionary ballet *The White-Haired Girl*], *Guangming ribao* [Guangming daily], 30 March 1966, 3.

24 Meng, "'*Baimao nü*' yu Yan'an wenxue de lishi fuzaxing," 186.

25 Laura Mulvey, *Visual and Other Pleasures* (Bloomington: Indiana University Press, 1989), 20.

26 Ebon, *Five Chinese Communist Plays,* 137.

27 Ibid., 126.

28 Ibid., 130.

29 Ibid., 141.

30 For an analysis of the film, see Robert Chi, "*The Red Detachment of Women:* Resenting, Regendering, Remembering," in *Chinese Films in Focus: 25 New Takes,* ed. Chris Berry (London: British Film Institute, 2003), 152-59.

31 The main character in the original version has the very feminine name of Qionghua, which means "beautiful jade flower." In the model ballet, it was changed to Qinghua, a gender-neutral name with a lofty meaning that could be read as "purifying China."

32 *Zhongguo dianying juben xuanji* [Selected scripts of Chinese films] (Beijing: Zhongguo dianying chubanshe, 1963), 104.

33 For a discussion of Jiang Qing's directives on the ballet dance-drama *The Red Detachment of Women,* see Chung Hua-min, *Jiang Qing zhengzhuan* [A true biography of Jiang Qing] (Hong Kong: Union Research Institute, 1967), 109.

34 Pierre Macherey, *A Theory of Literary Production* (New York: Routledge, 1989), 85.

35 Ibid., 86.

36 Ibid., 87.

37 Lynne Pearce et al., eds., *Feminist Readings/Feminists Reading* (London: Prentice Hall, 1996), 190.

38 Maurice Meisner, *Marxism, Maoism and Utopianism* (Madison: University of Wisconsin Press, 1982), 3.

39 Hong Zicheng, *Zhongguo dangdai wenxue shi* [A history of contemporary Chinese literature] (Beijing: Beijing daxue chubanshe, 1999), 194.

Chapter 9: Fantasies of Battle

1 Qingdao Workers' Fine Arts Creation Collective, with Jiang Baoxing in charge of the brush, *"Dizhu" [Steady as a Rock], Zhaoxia* [Morning clouds] 5 (May 1976): inside back cover facing page 80. Dizhu is a rocky island in the Yellow River. The painting's title comes from the *chengyu* (proverb) *"Dizhu zhongliu"* (Dizhu stands in the centre of the stream), which has the implied meaning "stand firm, act as a mainstay." Shanghai Jingjutuan *Zhiqu Weihushan* juzu, *Zhiqu Weihushan* (Beijing: Renmin chubanshe, 1970), performance edition; for the English translation, see *Taking Tiger Mountain by Strategy* Group of the Peking Opera Troupe of Shanghai, *Taking Tiger Mountain by Strategy* (Beijing: Foreign Language Press, 1971). Duan Ruixia, "Tebie guanzhong," first published in *Zhaoxia, Shanghai wenyi congkan* [Shanghai literary anthologies] 1 (1973), 1-17, and reprinted in *Shanghai duanpian xiaoshuo xuan 1971.1-1973.12* [Selected Shanghai short stories, January 1971-December 1973] (Shanghai: Renmin chubanshe, 1974), 225-42 (this is the edition cited in later notes); for an English translation, see Duan Ruixia, "Not Just One of the Audience," *Chinese Literature,* September 1973, 51-64. Chu Lan, "Suzao wuchanjieji yingxiong dianxing shi shehuizhuyi wenyi de genben renwu" [Portraying typical proletarian heroes is the basic task of socialist art], *Renmin ribao* [People's daily], 15 June 1974, reprinted in *Tan "san tuchu" chuangzuo yuanze* [On the creative principle of the "three prominences"] (Taiyuan: Shanxi renmin chubanshe, 1974), 23-30.

2 The compulsive search for enemies that characterizes Cultural Revolution writing is discussed in Andrew G. Walder, "Cultural Revolution Radicalism: Variations on a Stalinist Theme," in *New Perspectives on the Cultural Revolution,* ed. William A. Joseph, Christine P.W. Wong, and David Zweig (Cambridge, MA: Council on East Asian Studies/Harvard University, 1991), 41-61.

3 Sang Cheng, "Ping 'Sirenbang' de bangkan *Zhaoxia*" [Critique of the "Gang of Four's" gang publication *Zhaoxia*], *Shanghai wenyi* [Shanghai arts] 1 (October 1977): 80-86. *Shanghai wenyi,* retitled *Shanghai wenxue* (Shanghai literature) from January 1979, replaced *Zhaoxia* as the city's premier literary journal.

4 Ren Xu, "Wenyi chuangzuo yao wei gugong wuchan-jieji zhuanzheng fuwu" [Artistic creation must serve the consolidation of the dictatorship of the proletariat], *Zhaoxia* 5 (May 1976): 3-5.

5 Ji Zheng, "Nuli suzao yu zouzipai douzheng de wuchanjieji yingxiong xianxiang" [Strive to portray images of proletarian heroes battling capitalist-roaders], *Zhaoxia* 5 (May 1976): 78-80. Unless otherwise indicated, all translations are my own.

6 In this case, "We must be concerned with the affairs of the nation, and carry out the Great Proletarian Cultural Revolution to the end."

7 Jiang Baoxing was admitted to the Central Academy of Fine Arts in Beijing to study painting in the early 1950s, following service in the People's Liberation Army during the Civil War that saw him wounded in the left arm. After graduation, he was

assigned to the Qingdao Workers' Cultural Palace, where he was for many years art instructor and head of propaganda. In 1992, he was transferred to head the newly established Qingdao Oil Painting Institute. He died of cancer around 1997. I am most grateful to this volume's co-editor Shengtian Zheng, formerly of the Zhejiang Academy of Fine Arts in Hangzhou and now an independent curator and artist, for providing this information on Jiang.

8 For more on Yu Huiyong, see Richard Kraus, "Arts Policies of the Cultural Revolution: The Rise and Fall of Culture Minister Yu Huiyong," in Joseph, Wong, and Zweig, *New Perspectives on the Cultural Revolution,* 219-41. Yu's opera was *Haigang* (On the docks) and his writing group Chu Lan. I have not seen the original of Yu's comment, said to date from 23 May 1968 in "a Shanghai publication." It is quoted in Wenhuabu pipanzu [Ministry of Culture Criticism Group], "Ping 'san tuchu'" [Criticism of the "three prominences"], *Renmin ribao,* 18 May 1977, reprinted as the title essay in *Ping "san tuchu"* (n.p.: Guizhou renmin chubanshe, 1978), 1-13.

9 Roxanne Witke, *Comrade Chiang Ch'ing* (Boston: Little, Brown, 1977), 420.

10 Gu Baozi, *Yangbanxi chutai neimu* [Inside story of the staging of the model theatrical works] (Beijing: Zhonghua gong-shang lianhe chubanshe, 1994), 191-92.

11 Yu Huiyong, "Yu Huiyong tongzhi de jianghua" [Speech by Comrade Yu Huiyong], *Hongqi* [Red flag], May 1967, 47. Qian Haoliang, star of the opera *Hongdengji* (The red lantern), said much the same to Roxanne Witke, as reported in *Comrade Chiang Ch'ing,* 414.

12 Jiang Qing, "Tan Jingju geming" [On the revolution in Beijing opera], *Hongqi,* June 1967, 25-27; there is a report on the festival, and the major speeches (not including Jiang Qing's, which remained unpublished until 1967), in "Peking Opera Festival," *Peking Review,* 12 June 1964, 3-4. For an example of Jiang Qing's ideal, see her comments on the portrayal of Li Yuhe, hero of *The Red Lantern,* in Witke, *Comrade Chiang Ch'ing,* 410.

13 Qian Haoliang, "Suzao gaoda de wuchanjieji yingxiong xingxiang" [Portray mighty proletarian heroic images], *Hongqi,* May 1967, 68. The article refers specifically to Qian Haoliang's role as Li Yuhe.

14 Fang Yun, *Geming yangbanxi zhaji* [Notes on revolutionary model theatrical works] (Shanghai: Renmin chubanshe, 1974), 21; Fang Yun claims that the revision process actually took more than eleven years. See also Kirk A. Denton, "The Revision of the Model Opera *Zhi-qu Wei Hu Shan:* The Formation of a Myth" (master's thesis, University of Toronto, 1983).

15 Qu Bo, *Linhai xueyuan* (Beijing: Renmin wenxue chubanshe, 1957), reprinted 1977; for an English translation, see Ch'u Po (Qu Bo), *Tracks in the Snowy Forest,* trans. Sidney Shapiro (Beijing: Foreign Languages Press, 1962), reprinted 1978. The Tiger Mountain episode is spread between Chapters 13 and 21, 170-304 in the Chinese text, 171-300 in the translation.

16 Qu, *Linhai xueyuan,* 1; Ch'u, *Tracks,* 1.

17 Robert E. Hegel, "Making the Past Serve the Present in Fiction and Drama: From the Yan'an Forum to the Cultural Revolution," in *Popular Chinese Literature and*

Performing Arts in the People's Republic of China, 1949-1979, ed. Bonnie S. McDougall (Berkeley: University of California Press, 1984), 197-223.

18 Ibid., 214-15.

19 Dai Jiafang, *Yangbanxi de fengfeng-yuyu: Jiang Qing, yangbanxi ji neimu* [Stresses and storms around the model performances: Jiang Qing, model performances and the inside story] (Beijing: Zhishi chubanshe, 1995), 61-63. This book also has a section on *Taking Tiger Mountain*'s star Tong Xiangling and his involvement with the opera (313-28).

20 Shanghai Jingjutuan *Zhiqu Weihushan* juzu [Group performing *Taking Tiger Mountain by Strategy* at the Shanghai Beijing Opera Company], "Nuli suzao yingxiong renwu de guangrong xingxiang – dui suzao Yang Zirong yingxiong xianxiang de yixie tihui" [Strive to create the brilliant images of proletarian heroes – Impressions on the creation of the heroic image of Yang Zirong] *Hongqi,* November 1969, 62-71; reprinted in *Jingju geming shinian* [Ten years of revolution in Beijing opera] (Beijing: Renmin chubanshe, 1975), 64; translated as "Strive to Create the Brilliant Images of Proletarian Heroes – Impressions on the Creation of the Heroic Image of Yang Tzu-jung," *Peking Review,* 26 December 1969, 36. For the sake of consistency in romanization, I have changed "Tzu-jung" to the *pinyin* "Zirong" in the passage quoted.

21 Qu, *Linhai xueyuan,* 178. Shapiro's translation omits the reference to "the enemy's belly."

22 Shanghai Jingjutuan, *Zhiqu Weihushan,* 30-31; music for Yang's aria, 136-38. Knowledge of bandit slang and the ability to act the bandit, separate conditions in the novel, are combined in the opera; thus the final condition is the third, as opposed to the fourth in *Tracks.*

23 Mao Zedong, "Yugong yi shan" [The foolish old man who removed the mountains], in *Mao Zedong xuanji* [Selected works of Mao Zedong] (Beijing: Renmin chubanshe, 1968), 3:1001-4; translated as "The Foolish Old Man Who Removed the Mountains," in Mao Tse-tung, *Selected Works of Mao Tse-tung* (Beijing: Foreign Languages Press, 1967), 3:271-74. The original story is from the *Liezi.*

24 Shanghai Jingjutuan, "Nuli suzao yingxiong renwu," 63.

25 Yang's costumes are illustrated on 289-91 of the performance edition of Shanghai Jingjutuan, *Zhiqu Weihushan.* The first illustration is of the military uniform in which he volunteers for his mission; the other two show his bandit disguise.

26 Ellen R. Judd, "Dramas of Passion: Heroism in the Cultural Revolution's Model Operas," in Joseph, Wong, and Zweig, *New Perspectives on the Cultural Revolution,* 271.

27 *"Longjiang song" ["Song of the Dragon River"],* in *Geming yangbanxi juben huibian* [Collected libretti of revolutionary model works] (Beijing: Renmin wenxue chubanshe, 1974), 345-402; translated as *Song of the Dragon River* (Beijing: Foreign Languages Press, 1972). The incident cited appears at the end of scene 5, 374 of the Chinese text and 22 in the translation.

28 I have discussed the shared characteristics of the different strata in the three prominences system in "A Shattered Mirror: The Literature of the Cultural Revolution" (PhD diss., University of British Columbia, 1984), 115-26.

29 See, for example, the title essay in *Yizhi changdao gongchanzhuyi* [Singing all the way to communism] (Shanghai: Renmin chubanshe, 1975), 1-23, which reports on the activities of spare-time singers of *yangbanxi* selections.

30 For more on Duan Ruixia's career, and analysis of a later and more controversial story, see Richard King, "A Fiction Revealing Collusion: Allegory and Evasion in the Mid-1970s," *Modern Chinese Literature* 10, 1-2 (1998): 71-90. Duan's 1973-76 publications are listed in a note on 74.

31 *Wenxue chuangzuo* [Creative writing] (Shanghai: Fudan Daxue zhongwenxi, 1976). The section on the composition of the short story is on 99-107, and the examples given are works by Lu Xun and "Not Just One of the Audience." The only other contemporary story mentioned (once) is Hao Ran's "Yidan shui" (Two buckets of water).

32 Duan Ruixia, "Zuo weida shidai douzheng shenghuo de jiluyuan" [Being a recorder of the life of struggle of the age], in *Duanpian xiaoshuo xuandu* [Selected short stories] (Shenyang: Liaoning Daxue, n.d. [1976?]), 92. This collection also includes adulatory essays that first appeared in *Xuexi yu pipan* and the Shanghai daily newspaper *Wenhuibao.*

33 See John Gardner, "*Study and Criticism:* The Voice of Shanghai Radicalism," in *Shanghai: Revolution and Development in an Asian Metropolis,* ed. Christopher Howe (Cambridge: Cambridge University Press, 1981), 326-47.

34 See King, "A Fiction Revealing Collusion."

35 Duan, "Tebie guanzhong," 229.

36 Ibid., 233. The first part of the passage quoted does not appear in the *Chinese Literature* translation.

37 Ibid., 238.

38 Ibid.

39 *Wenxue chuangzuo,* 101.

40 Duan, "Zuo weida shidai douzheng shenghuo de jiluyuan," 88-93.

Bibliography

Ahn, Byung-joon. *Chinese Politics and the Cultural Revolution: Dynamics of Policy Processes.* Seattle: University of Washington Press, 1976.

"All China Workers and Peasants Amateur Art Exhibition." *Chinese Literature,* July 1965.

Andrews, Julia F. *Painters and Politics in the People's Republic of China, 1949-1979.* Berkeley: University of California Press, 1994.

Andrews, Julia F., and Kuiyi Shen. *A Century in Crisis: Modernity and Tradition in the Art of Twentieth-Century China.* New York: Guggenheim Museum, 1998.

Ansley, Clive. *The Heresy of Wu Han: His Play "Hai Rui's Dismissal" and Its Role in China's Cultural Revolution.* Toronto: University of Toronto Press, 1971.

"Art by Workers and Peasants." *China Reconstructs,* September 1965.

"Art That Serves Proletarian Politics." *China Reconstructs,* February 1968.

"Baimao nü" ["The White-Haired Girl"]. Wudao [Dance], March 1977.

Beijing gongshe [Beijing Commune], 18 May 1967. Reproduced in *Xinbian Hongweibing ziliao* [New materials on the Red Guards], ed. Song Yongyi, 359-60. Oakton, VA: Center for Chinese Research Materials, 1999.

Belden, Jack. *China Shakes the World.* New York and London: Monthly Review Press, 1970.

Berthrong, John. *Transformations of the Confucian Way.* Boulder, CO: Westview Press, 1998.

Bickford, Maggie. *Bones of Jade, Soul of Ice: The Flowering Plum in Chinese Art.* New Haven: Yale University Art Gallery, 1985.

–. *Ink Plum: The Making of a Chinese Scholar-Painting Genre.* Cambridge: Cambridge University Press, 1996.

Carson, S. Marie. "Dialogue on the Peasant Art of Huhsien." *Eastern Horizon,* May 1974.

Chang, Jung, and Jon Halliday. *Mao: The Unknown Story.* New York: Knopf, 2005.

Chen Lüsheng. *Xin Zhongguo meishu shi, 1949-1966* [New China's art history, 1949-1966]. Beijing: Zhongguo qingnian chubanshe, 2000.

Chen Sihe. *Zhongguo dangdai wenxue shi* [A history of contemporary Chinese literature]. Shanghai: Fudan daxue chubanshe, 1999.

Chi Hsin. *Teng Hsiao-ping: A Political Biography.* Hong Kong: Cosmos Books, 1978.

China News Items from the Press. Hong Kong: Regional Information Office, 1966, 1967.

Chou, Yu-sun. "Change and Continuity in Communist Chinese Policy on Literature and Art." *Issues and Studies* 22, 9 (September 1986): 13-27.

Chu Lan. "Suzao wuchanjieji yingxiong dianxing shi shehuizhuyi wenyi de genben renwu" [Portraying typical proletarian heroes is the basic task of socialist art]. *Renmin ribao* [People's daily], 15 June 1974.

Chuang Shen. "Some Remarks concerning Shi Lu's Art of Painting." In *Collectors' Choice: The Genius of Shi Lu,* 51-60. Hong Kong: Cat Street Galleries, 1994.

Chung Hua-min. *Jiang Qing zhengzhuan* [A true biography of Jiang Qing]. Hong Kong: Union Research Institute, 1967.

Clark, Paul. *Chinese Cinema: Culture and Politics since 1949.* New York: Cambridge University Press, 1987.

–. *The Chinese Cultural Revolution: A History.* New York: Cambridge University Press, 2008.

Cohen, Joan Lebold. "Abstract Art Out and Folk Art In as China Readjusts Its Political Line." *Asian Wall Street Journal,* 15 April 1981.

Confucius: The Analects. Book 2.1. Translated by D.C. Lau. New York: Penguin Books, 1979.

Dai Jiafang. *Yangbanxi de fengfeng-yuyu: Jiang Qing, yangbanxi ji neimu* [Stresses and storms around the model performances: Jiang Qing, model performances and the inside story]. Beijing: Zhishi chubanshe, 1995.

–. *Zou xiang huimie: 'Wen'ge' wenhuabu zhang Yu Huiyong chenfu lu* [Approaching extermination: The ups and downs of Yu Huiyong, Cultural Revolution minister of culture]. Beijing: Guangming ribao chubanshe, 1994.

de Bary, William Theodore. *Asian Values and Human Rights: A Confucian Communitarian Perspective.* Cambridge, MA: Harvard University Press, 1998.

Denton, Kirk A., ed. *Modern Chinese Literary Thought: Writings on Literature, 1893-1945.* Stanford: Stanford University Press, 1996.

–. "The Revision of the Model Opera *Zhi-qu Wei Hu Shan:* The Formation of a Myth." Master's thesis, University of Toronto, 1983.

Ding Jitang. "Fudao nongmin hua huodong de yixie benhui" [Leading and guiding peasant-painting activities: Several observations from practice]. Paper presented at the national conference on peasant painting, Beijing, 1983.

Djilas, Milovan. *The New Class: An Analysis of the Communist System.* New York: Praeger Perspectives, 1958.

Duan Jingli, ed. *Hu Xian nongmin hua chunqiu* [Annals of Hu Xian peasant painting]. Beijing: Zhongguo dang'an chubanshe, 1999.

Duan Ruixia. "Not Just One of the Audience." *Chinese Literature,* September 1973.

–. "Tebie guanzhong" [Not just one of the audience]. *Zhaoxia, Shanghai wenyi congkan* [Morning clouds, Shanghai literary anthologies] 1. Shanghai: Shanghai renmin chubanshe, 1973. Reprinted in *Shanghai duanpian xiaoshuo xuan*

1971.1-1973.12 [Selected Shanghai short stories, January 1971-December 1973], 225-42. Shanghai: Renmin chubanshe, 1974.

–. "Zuo weida shidai douzheng shenghuo de jiluyuan" [Being a recorder of the life of struggle of a great age]. In *Duanpian xiaoshuo xuandu* [Selected short stories], 86-95. Shenyang: Liaoning Daxue, n.d.

Ebon, Martin, ed. *Five Chinese Communist Plays.* New York: John Day, 1975.

Eckholm, Erik. "Expatriate Artist Updates Maoist Icon and Angers Old Guard." *New York Times,* 17 August 2000.

Evans, Harriet, and Stephanie Donald, eds. *Picturing Power in the People's Republic of China: Posters of the Cultural Revolution.* London: Rowan and Littlefield, 1999.

Fang Yun. *Geming yangbanxi zhaji* [Notes on revolutionary model performances]. Shanghai: Renmin chubanshe, 1974.

Fei Xinbei. *"Shou zu yuan" qundiao zuopin xuan* [Selected works of the group sculpture *"Rent Collection Courtyard"*]. Chongqing: Art Museum and Sichuan Fine Arts Institute, 2001.

Flath, James A. *The Cult of Happiness: Nianhua, Art, and History in Rural North China.* Vancouver: UBC Press, 2004.

–. "Printing Culture in Rural North China." PhD diss., Department of History, University of British Columbia, 2000.

Fokkema, D.W. *Report from Peking.* Montreal and Kingston: McGill-Queen's University Press, 1972.

"Folk Artists: Peasant Women's Exhibition." *Peking Review,* 26 June 1964.

Galston, William. *Justice and the Human Good.* Chicago: University of Chicago Press, 1980.

Gao Yilong, and Li Xiao, eds. *Zhongguo xiqu xiandaixi shi* [History of modern-subject Chinese opera]. Shanghai: Shanghai wenhua chubanshe, 1999.

Gardner, John. "*Study and Criticism:* The Voice of Shanghai Radicalism." In *Shanghai: Revolution and Development in an Asian Metropolis,* ed. Christopher Howe, 326-47. Cambridge: Cambridge University Press, 1981.

Gu Baozi. *Yangbanxi chutai neimu* [Inside story of the staging of the model theatrical works]. Beijing: Zhonghua gong-shang lianhe chubanshe, 1994.

Gu Hongzhang, and Hu Mengzhou, eds. *Zhongguo zhishi qingnian shang shan xia siang shi mo* [The Chinese educated youth (going) up to the mountains, down to the villages, from beginning to end]. Beijing: Zhongguo jiancha chubanshe, 1996.

Gu Yuan. *Nongcun bihua fanben* [A textbook of models for village wall paintings]. Tianjin: Tianjin meishu chubanshe, 1959.

"Guanyu Weiwu'eryu geju *Shajiabang* de chuangzuo" [On the making of the Uighur *Shajiabang*]. *Renmin ribao* [People's daily], 29 May 1975, 2.

Hebei nongcun bihua [Hebei village wall paintings]. Hebei: Hebei meishu chubanshe, 1959.

"A History of Blood and Tears: On the Art Works of the Three Stones Museum in Tientsin." *Chinese Literature,* November-December 1969.

Hong Yung Lee. *The Politics of the Chinese Cultural Revolution: A Case Study.* Berkeley: University of California Press, 1978.

Hong Zicheng. *Zhongguo dangdai wenxue shi* [A history of contemporary Chinese literature]. Beijing: Beijing daxue chubanshe, 1999.

Honig, Emily, and Gail Hershatter. *Personal Voices: Chinese Women in the 1980's.* Stanford: Stanford University Press, 1988.

Howe, Christopher, ed. *Shanghai: Revolution and Development in an Asian Metropolis.* Cambridge: Cambridge University Press, 1981.

Hu Xian nongmin hua lian wen zi [Collection of articles on Hu Xian peasant paintings]. Beijing: Renmin meishu chubanshe, 1975.

Hu Xian nongmin hua xuanji [A selection of Hu Xian peasant paintings]. Xi'an: Renmin chubanshe, 1974.

Huang Dingjun. "Hubei sheng gong-nong yeyu meishu huodong de xin mianmao" [The new face of Hubei worker-peasant part-time art activity]. *Meishu* [Fine arts] (May 1958): 35-37.

"In Praise of the Red Guards" and *"Family Histories of the Air Force Fighters." China Reconstructs,* February 1968.

Javitt, Daniel C., and Joseph T. Coyle. "Decoding Schizophrenia." *Scientific American,* January 2004.

Ji Zheng. "Nuli suzao yu zouzipai douzheng de wuchanjieji yingxiong xianxiang" [Strive to portray images of proletarian heroes battling capitalist-roaders]. *Zhaoxia* [Morning clouds] 5 (May 1976): 78-80.

Jiang Qing. "Tan Jingju geming" [On the revolution in Beijing opera]. *Hongqi* [Red flag], June 1967, 25-27.

Jiang Qisheng. "Hu Xian nongmin hua de lishi he jingyan diaocha baogao" [An investigative report on the history and experience of Hu Xian peasant painting]. In *Hu Xian nongmin hua chunqiu* [Annals of Hu Xian peasant painting], ed. Duan Jingli, 50-57. Beijing: Zhongguo dang'an chubanshe, 1999.

Jiang Zuhui. "Xinwei de huiyi: wuju '*Hongse niangzi jun*' de chuangzuo licheng" [Bitter memories: The creation of the ballet *"The Red Detachment of Women"*]. *Wudao* [Dance], November 1987, 22-23.

Jin Shan nongmin hua [Jin Shan peasant painting]. Shanghai: Pictorial Publishing House, 1999.

"Jingju geming shi Mao Zedong sixiang de weida shengli" [The revolution in Beijing opera is a glorious victory for Mao Zedong thought]. *Renmin ribao* [People's daily], 24 May 1967.

Jingju geming shinian [Ten years of revolution in Beijing opera]. Beijing: Renmin chubanshe, 1975.

Joseph, William A., Christine P.W. Wong, and David Zweig, eds. *New Perspectives on the Cultural Revolution.* Cambridge, MA: Council on East Asian Studies/Harvard University, 1991.

Judd, Ellen R. "Dramas of Passion: Heroism in the Cultural Revolution's Model Operas." In *New Perspectives on the Cultural Revolution,* ed. William A. Joseph,

Christine P.W. Wong, and David Zweig, 265-82. Cambridge, MA: Harvard University Press, 1991.

Karnow, Stanley. *Mao and China: Inside China's Cultural Revolution.* New York: Penguin Books, 1984.

King, Richard. "A Fiction Revealing Collusion: Allegory and Evasion in the Mid-1970s." *Modern Chinese Literature* 10, 1-2 (1998): 71-90.

–. "The Hundred Flowers." In *The Columbia Companion to Modern East Asian Literature,* ed. Joshua S. Mostow, 76-80. New York: Columbia University Press, 2003.

–. "A Shattered Mirror: The Literature of the Cultural Revolution." PhD diss., University of British Columbia, 1984.

Kleinman, Arthur, and Joan Kleinman. "How Bodies Remember: Social Memory and Bodily Experience of Criticism, Resistance, and Delegitimation Following China's Cultural Revolution." *New Literary History* 25 (1994): 707-23.

Ko Lu. "Art: New Peasant Paintings." *Peking Review,* 23 September 1958.

–. "Peasants Speak through Pictures." *China Reconstructs,* July 1959.

Kramer, Peter. "There's Nothing Deep about Depression." *New York Times Magazine,* 17 April 2005.

Kraus, Richard. "Arts Policies of the Cultural Revolution: The Rise and Fall of Culture Minister Yu Huiyong." In *New Perspectives on the Cultural Revolution,* ed. William A. Joseph, Christine P.W. Wong, and David Zweig, 219-41. Cambridge, MA: Harvard University Press, 1991.

Laing, Ellen Johnston. "Chinese Peasant Painting, 1958-1976: Amateur and Professional." *Art International* 28, 1 (January-March 1984): 2-12, 40, 48, 64.

–. *The Winking Owl: Art in the People's Republic of China.* Berkeley: University of California Press, 1988.

Lau, Joseph S.M., and Howard Goldblatt, eds. *The Columbia Anthology of Modern Chinese Literature.* New York: Columbia University Press, 1995.

Lee, Hong Yung. *The Politics of the Chinese Cultural Revolution: A Case Study.* Berkeley: University of California Press, 1978.

Li Fenglan. "How I Began to Paint the Countryside." *China Reconstructs,* January 1974, 21-23.

Li Lang. "Wo ceng paishe guo *'Shou zu yuan.'*" [I photographed the *"Rent Collection Courtyard"*]. *Observers Monthly* (Hong Kong), September 1980.

Li Luming, and Daozi. "Jiaoban 'Weinisi'" [Edition to order: "Venice"]. *Shijue* [Vision], May 2000.

Li Shinan. *Kuang ge dang ku – ji Shi Lu* [A mad song in place of crying – Remembering Shi Lu]. Zhengzhou: Henan People's Press, 1997.

Li Xiaorong. "Gender Inequality in China and Cultural Relativism." In *Women, Culture, and Development,* ed. Martha Nussbaum and Jonathan Glover, 407-25. Oxford: Clarendon Press, 1995.

Li Yu-ning. *The First Emperor of China: The Politics of Historiography.* White Plains: International Arts and Sciences Press, 1975.

Li Zhisui. *The Private Life of Chairman Mao.* Translated by Tai Hung-chao, with the editorial assistance of Anne F. Thurston. New York: Random House, 1994.

Liu Xiaomeng, and Ding Yizhuang. *Zhongguo zhiqing shidian* [Record of Chinese educated youth]. Chengdu: Sichuan People's Publishing House, 1995.

Longfellow, Henry Wadsworth. *Longfellow's Poetical Works.* London: Frederick Warne, 1880.

"Longjiang song" ["Song of the Dragon River"]. In *Geming yangbanxi juben huibian* [Collected libretti of revolutionary model works], 305-402. Beijing: Renmin wenxue chubanshe, 1974.

Lu Xin. *Pan Tianshou.* Beijing: China's Youth Publishing House, 1997.

Lu Xun. "Diary of a Madman." In *Selected Works of Lu Xun.* Translated by Yang Hsien-yi and Gladys Yang. 1960. Reprint, Beijing: Foreign Languages Press, 1978.

Lucas, Mary Christene. "Negotiations of Identity: The Life and Art of Gu Xiong." Master's thesis, Department of History in Art, University of Victoria, 2002.

Luo Zhongli, ed. *Shou zu yuan qundiao* [The *Rent Collection Courtyard* group of sculptures]. Shijiazhuang: Hebei Fine Arts Publishing House, 2001.

Ma Gaihu. "Zhuiyi Shi Lu tongzhi chuangzuo *'Zhuanzhan Shaanbei'* de qingkuang" [Recalling the situation surrounding Comrade Shi Lu's creating *"Fighting in Northern Shaanxi"*]. Special supplement memorializing Shi Lu, *Meishu Tongxun* (25 August 1985): 59-60.

Ma Shijun. "Woguo dianying faxing fangying gongzuo de huigu yu zhanwang" [A look back and forwards for China's film distribution work]. In *Zhonghua renmin gongheguo dianying shiye sanshiwu nian, 1949-1984* [Thirty-five years of the film industry in the People's Republic of China, 1949-1984], ed. Zhongguo dianyingjia xiehui dianyingshi yanjiubu [China Film Association Film History Research Office], 334-48. Beijing: Zhongguo dianying chubanshe, 1985.

MacFarquhar, Roderick, and Michael Schoenhals. *Mao's Last Revolution.* Cambridge, MA: Bellknap Press of Harvard University Press, 2006.

Macherey, Pierre. *A Theory of Literary Production.* New York: Routledge, 1989.

Mao Tse-tung [Mao Zedong]. "The Foolish Old Man Who Removed the Mountains." In *Selected Works of Mao Tse-tung.* Vol. 3, 271-74. Beijing: Foreign Languages Press, 1967.

–. *Poems.* Beijing: Foreign Languages Press, 1976.

–. "Yugong yi shan" [The foolish old man who removed the mountains]. In *Mao Zedong xuanji* [Selected works of Mao Zedong]. Vol. 3, 1001-4. Beijing: Renmin chubanshe, 1968.

Mao Zedong. "Talks at the Yan'an Forum on Literature and Art." In *Modern Chinese Literary Thought: Writings on Literature, 1893-1945,* ed. Kirk A. Denton, 458-84. Stanford: Stanford University Press, 1996.

Marx, Karl, and Friedrich Engels. *The German Ideology.* New York: International Publishers, 1939.

McDougall, Bonnie S., ed. *Popular Chinese Literature and Performing Arts in the People's Republic of China, 1949-1979.* Berkeley: University of California Press, 1984.

Meisner, Maurice. *Mao's China: A History of the People's Republic.* New York: Free Press, 1977.

–. *Marxism, Maoism and Utopianism.* Madison: University of Wisconsin Press, 1982.

Meng Yue. "*'Baimao nü'* yu Yan'an wenxue de lishi fuzaxing" [*"The White-Haired Girl"* and the historical complexity of Yan'an literature]. *Jintian* [Today] 1 (1993): 171-88.

Meserve, Walter. *Modern Drama from Communist China.* New York: New York University Press, 1970.

Miao Fanzu. "Zuiren dianfeng" [Drunken man mountain peak], *Jiaodian,* August 1996.

Mills, Sara, and Lynne Pearce, eds. *Feminist Readings/Feminists Reading.* London: Prentice Hall, 1996.

Morris, Peter T. *Chinese Sayings.* Taipei: Longmen Shudian, 1981.

Mu Xin. *The Art of Mu Xin: Landscapes and Prison Notes.* New Haven: Yale University Art Gallery, 2001.

Mulvey, Laura. *Visual and Other Pleasures.* Bloomington: Indiana University Press, 1989.

"Nongmin de Geming Hua" [Peasants' revolutionary paintings]. *Renmin ribao* [People's daily], 21 June 1966, 6.

Nussbaum, Martha, and Jonathan Glover, eds. *Women, Culture, and Development.* Oxford: Clarendon Press, 1995.

Peasant Paintings from Huhsien County. Beijing: People's Fine Art Publishing House, 1974.

Ping 'san tuchu' [Criticism of the "three prominences"]. N.p.: Guizhou renmin chubanshe, 1978.

"Pipan fandong huajia Shi Lu" [Criticize the reactionary painter Shi Lu]. Shaanxi Province internal party document, 6 June 1974.

Qian Haoliang. "Suzao gaoda de wuchanjieji yingxiong xingxiang" [Portray mighty proletarian heroic images], *Hongqi* [Red flag], May 1967.

Qu Bo. *Linhai xueyuan* [Tracks in the snowy forest]. Beijing: Renmin wenxue chubanshe, 1957.

–. (Ch'u Po.) *Tracks in the Snowy Forest.* Translated by Sidney Shapiro. Beijing: Foreign Languages Press, 1962.

Qu Yuan. *Ch'u Tz'u: Songs of the South.* Translated by David Hawkes. Oxford: Clarendon, 1959.

Quotations from Chairman Mao Tse-tung. Beijing: Foreign Languages Press, 1967.

Ren Xu. "Wenyi chuangzuo yao wei gugong wuchan-jieji zhuanzheng fuwu" [Artistic creation must serve the consolidation of the dictatorship of the proletariat]. *Zhaoxia* [Morning clouds] 5 (May 1976): 3-5.

Rius and Friends. *Mao for Beginners.* New York: Pantheon Books, 1980.

Sang Cheng. "Ping 'Sirenbang' de bangkan *Zhaoxia*" [Critique of the "Gang of Four's" gang publication *Zhaoxia*]. *Shanghai wenyi* [Shanghai arts] 1 (October 1977): 80-86.

Sass, Louis A. *Madness and Modernism: Insanity in the Light of Modern Art, Literature, and Thought.* Cambridge, MA: Harvard University Press, 1992.

Schneider, Laurence A. *A Madman of Ch'u: The Chinese Myth of Loyalty and Dissent.* Berkeley: University of California Press, 1980.

Schoppa, R. Keith. *Revolution and Its Past: Identities and Change in Modern Chinese History.* Upper Saddle River, NJ: Prentice Hall, 2002.

Schwarcz, Vera. "The Burden of Memory: The Cultural Revolution and the Holocaust." *China Information* (Leiden) 11, 1 (Summer 1996): 1-13.

Shanghai Jingjutuan *Zhiqu Weihushan* juzu [Group performing *Taking Tiger Mountain by Strategy* at the Shanghai Beijing Opera Company]. "Nuli suzao yingxiong renwu de guangrong xingxiang – dui suzao Yang Zirong yingxiong xianxiang de yixie tihui" [Strive to create the brilliant images of proletarian heroes – Impressions on the creation of the heroic image of Yang Zirong] *Hongqi* [Red flag], November 1969.

–. *Zhiqu Weihushan [Taking Tiger Mountain by Strategy]* (performance edition). Beijing: Renmin chubanshe, 1970.

Shen Jiawei. "Suzao fanxiu qianshao de yingxiong xing-xiang – youhua *'Wei women weida zuguo zhangang'* chuangzuo guocheng" [Modelling the heroic image of the anti-revisionist advance guard – The process of creating the oil painting *"Standing Guard for Our Great Motherland"*]. *Meishu ziliao* [Art materials], July 1975.

Shen Kuiyi, ed. *Word and Meaning: Six Contemporary Chinese Artists.* Buffalo: Center for the Arts, University at Buffalo, 2000.

Shi Dan. *Shi Lu, Zhongguo minghuajia quanji* [Shi Lu: Collected works of famous Chinese painters]. Hebei: Hebei Educational Press, 2003.

Shi Guo. *Shi Lu hua lun* [A discussion of Shi Lu's painting]. Zhengzhou: Henan People's Press, 1999.

–."Shi Lu hua *'Meidianshen'* ji" [Remembering Shi Lu's painting the *"Goddess of Beauty"*], *Rongbaozhai* 10 (1999): 289-93.

Silbergeld, Jerome, and Gong Jisui. *Contradictions: Artistic Life, the Socialist State, and the Chinese Painter, Li Huasheng.* Seattle: University of Washington Press, 1993.

Song of the Dragon River. Beijing: Foreign Languages Press, 1972.

Song Yongyi, ed. *Xinbian Hongweibing ziliao* [New materials on the Red Guards]. Oakton, VA: Center for Chinese Research Materials, 1999.

Song Zhongyuan, ed. *Yishu yaolan* [The cradle of arts]. Hangzhou: Zhejiang Academy of Fine Arts Publishing House, 1988.

"Strive to Create the Brilliant Images of Proletarian Heroes – Impressions on the Creation of the Heroic Image of Yang Tzu-jung." *Peking Review,* 26 December 1969.

Subei nongcun bihua ji [A collection of village wall paintings from northern Jiangsu]. Shanghai: Renmin meishu chubanshe, 1958.

Sullivan, Michael. *Art and Artists in Twentieth Century China.* Berkeley: University of California Press, 1996.

Tan "san tuchu" chuangzuo yuanze [On the creative principle of the "three prominences"]. Taiyuan: Shanxi renmin chubanshe, 1974.

Tian Wen, and Xin Xiao. "Zan Jingju geming shi nian" [In praise of ten years of the revolution in Beijing opera]. *Tianjin wenyi* [Tianjin literature and art], August 1974.

Torey, E. Fuller. *Surviving Schizophrenia.* New York: Harper Collins, 2001.

Union Research Institute. *CCP Documents of the Great Proletarian Cultural Revolution, 1966-1967.* Hong Kong: Union Press, n.d.

Wang Chaowen. "Wall Paintings by Peasant Artists." *Chinese Literature,* January 1958.

Wang, Eugene Yuejin. "The Winking Owl: Visual Effect and Its Art Historical Thick Description." *Critical Inquiry* 26, 3 (Spring 2000): 435-73.

Wang Mingjian. *Shangshan Xiaxiang: Sanshi Nian* [Up to the mountains, down to the villages: Thirty years]. Beijing: Guangming chubanshe, 1998.

Wang Mingxian. "The Fine Arts Movement of the Red Guards." Paper presented at the conference "Cultural Production and the Cultural Revolution," Vancouver, BC, 22-23 March 2002.

Wang Mingxian, and Yan Shanchun. *Xin Zhongguo meishu tu shi 1966-1976* [Illustrated history of the art of New China 1966-1976]. Beijing: China Youth Press, 2000.

Wang Nanming. "The Shanghai Art Museum Should Not Become a Market Stall in China for Western Hegemonism." In *Chinese Art at the Crossroads: Between Past and Future, Between East and West,* ed. Wu Hung, 265-68. Hong Kong: New Art Media, 2001.

Wang Shu. "Gangyin wei nongmin hua zhengming shengfen" [Seals for proving the identity of peasant paintings]. *Guangming ribao* [Guangming daily], 30 May 1997.

Watson, Scott, and Zheng Shengtian, eds. *The Art of the Great Proletarian Cultural Revolution 1966-1977.* Vancouver: Morris and Helen Belkin Art Gallery, 2002.

"Wenhua shangshan, xiaxiang, mianmao gaiguan" [Culture climbs the mountain, goes to the countryside, and its face is transformed]. *Meishu* [Fine arts] (June 1958): 6.

Wenhuabu pipanzu [Ministry of Culture Criticism Group]. "Ping 'san tuchu'" [Criticism of the "three prominences"]. *Renmin ribao* [People's daily], 18 May 1977.

Wenxue chuangzuo [Creative writing]. Shanghai: Fudan Daxue zhongwenxi, 1976.

Witke, Roxanne. *Comrade Chiang Ch'ing.* Boston: Little, Brown, 1977.

Wittig, Monique. *Straight Mind and Other Essays.* Boston: Beacon Press, 1992.

"*The Wrath of the Serfs:* Old Tibet in Sculpture." *China Reconstructs,* March 1976.

Wu Guanzhong. "Shi Lu de 'qiang' ji qita" [Shi Lu's "operatic tune" and other matters]. *Meishu* [Fine arts] 9 (September 1983): 41-43.

Wu Hung, ed. *Chinese Art at the Crossroads: Between Past and Future, Between East and West.* Hong Kong: New Art Media, 2001.

Wu Tongzhang. "Jinshan nongmin hua de yishu daolu" [The artistic road of Jin Shan peasant painting]. *Meishu* [Fine arts] (August 1982): 40-46.

Wuxian fengguang zai xianfeng: Jiang Qing tongzhi guanyu wenyi geming de jianghua [On perilous peaks dwells beauty in her infinite variety: Speeches on the Cultural and Artistic Revolution by Comrade Jiang Qing]. N.p., 1969.

"Xuexi 'san tuchu' chuangzuo yuanze – buduan tigao chuangzuo ziliang" [Study the creative principle of the "three prominences" – Ceaselessly raise creative standards]. *Meishu ziliao* [Art materials], October 1973.

Yan Jiaqi, and Gao Gao. *Turbulent Decade: A History of the Cultural Revolution.* Translated and edited by D.W.Y. Kwok. Honolulu: University of Hawai'i Press, 1996.

Yang Haizhou. *Zhongguo dianying wuzi chanye xitong lishi bian nianji* [Chronological history of the Chinese film product manufacturing system]. Beijing: Zhongguo dianying chubanshe, 1998.

Yang Jian. *Wenhua da geming zhong de dixia wenxue* [Underground literature during the Cultural Revolution]. Beijing: Chaohua chubanshe, 1993.

Yang Mu. *'Wenge' chuangjiang feng shen bang* [Pathbreakers of the Cultural Revolution]. Beijing: United Publishing House, 1993.

Yao Wenyuan. "Ping xin bian lishiju *Hai Rui ba guan*" [Criticism of the recent historical drama *Hai Rui Dismissed from Office*]. *Wenhuibao* [Cultural gazette], 10 November 1965.

Ye Jian. "Yongxin xian'e de yichang naoju" [An intentionally evil drama]. *Meishu* [Fine arts] 5 (May 1978): 14-16, 35-36.

Ye Jian, and Shi Dan, eds. *Shi Lu yishu wenji* [Shi Lu's art-related literary works]. Xi'an: Shaanxi People's Art Press, 2003.

Yin Chengzong. "Yi Jiang Qing tongzhi wei guanghui bangyang, zuo yongyuan zhongyu Mao zhuxi de geming wenyi zhanshi" [Taking Jiang Qing as a glorious example, be a revolutionary cultural soldier always loyal to Chairman Mao]. *Guangming ribao,* 6 July 1968.

Yizhi changdao gongchanzhuyi [Singing all the way to communism]. Shanghai: Renmin chubanshe, 1975.

Yu Hong, and Deng Zhengqiang. *Zhongguo dangdai guanggao shi* [History of contemporary Chinese advertising]. Changsha: Hunan kexue jishu chubanshe, 2000.

Yu Huiyong. "Yu Huiyong tongzhi de jianghua" [Speech by Comrade Yu Huiyong]. *Hongqi* [Red flag], May 1967.

Zhai Jiannong. *Hongse wangshi: 1966-1976 nian de Zhongguo dianying* [Red past: Chinese film 1966-1976]. Beijing: Taihai chubanshe, 2001.

Zhang Nan. "Lai zi gongnong hua gongnong" [Paintings of workers and peasants by workers and peasants]. *Renmin ribao* [People's daily], 5 December 1972.

Zhang Shaoxia, and Li Xiaoshan. *Zhongguo xiandai huihuashi* [A history of painting in modern China]. Nanjing: Jiangsu Art Press, 1986.

Zheng Qian, and Han Gang. *Wannian suiyue – 1956 nian hou de Mao Zedong* [The later years – Mao Zedong after 1956]. Beijing: Chinese Youth Publishing House, 1993.

Zheng Shengtian. *Fang Gangmin.* Vancouver: Asia Pacific Art Promotion, 1996.

Zhongguo dianying juben xuanji [Selected scripts of Chinese films]. Beijing: Zhongguo dianying chubanshe, 1963.

Zhongguo dianying ziliaoguan, Zhongguo yishu yanjiuyuan dianying yanjiusuo, eds. *Zhongguo yishu yingpian bianmu, 1949-1979* [Catalogue of Chinese art films, 1949-1979]. Beijing: Wenhua yishu chubanshe, 1982.

Zhongguo dianyingjia xiehui dianyingshi yanjiubu, ed. *Zhonghua renmin gongheguo dianying shiye sanshiwu nian, 1949-1984* [Thirty-five years of the film industry in the People's Republic of China, 1949-1984]. Beijing: Zhongguo dianying chubanshe, 1985.

Zhongguo Hu Xian Nongmin Hua [Chinese Hu County farmer paintings]. Xi'an(?), 1984.

Zhongguo nongmin hua [Chinese peasant paintings]. Beijing: Renmin meishu chubanshe, 1984.

Zou Yuejin. *Xin Zhongguo meishu shi* [History of the art of New China]. Changsha: Hunan meishu chubanshe, 2002.

Acknowledgments

The inspiration for this book came from an exhibition titled Art of the Great Proletarian Cultural Revolution, which took place in 2002 in Vancouver. It was organized by the Morris and Helen Belkin Art Gallery at the University of British Columbia, generously sponsored by the Audain Foundation, Stephanie Holmquist, and Annie Wong, and funded by the Canada Council for the Arts and by the Hampton Fund Research Grant in the Humanities and Social Sciences, University of British Columbia. Accompanying the exhibition was a conference called "Cultural Production and the Cultural Revolution," which brought together scholars, artists, and students from Canada, China, the United States, Europe, and Australasia, some of whom made contributions to this book. It was organized by the Morris and Helen Belkin Art Gallery in collaboration with the Department of Asian Studies, University of British Columbia; the Departments of History and Pacific and Asian Studies, University of Victoria; and Charles H. Scott Gallery, Emily Carr University. Funding for the conference was provided by the Social Sciences and Humanities Research Council of Canada.

Publication of this volume was made possible by grants from the Chiang Ching-kuo Foundation and the Millard Meiss Publication Fund of the College Art Association.

The editors and authors gratefully acknowledge the scholarly contributions of Alison Bailey, Yomi Braester, Sulan Dai, Francesca dal Lago, Feng Bin, Donghui He, Shuyu Kong, Wendy Larson, Michael Schoenhals, Kuiyi Shen, Catherine Swatek, Muli Tang, Wang Mingxian, Xia Wei, Yan Shanchen, and Lan Yang; the support and assistance of Cindy Richmond, Naomi Sawada, Mary Williams, and Annette Wooff at the Belkin Gallery, Emily Andrew at UBC Press, and Stella Chan at the Centre for Asia-Pacific Initiatives, University of Victoria; and the advice of the three unnamed readers who reviewed the manuscript for UBC Press.

Contributors

Julia F. Andrews is professor of East Asian Art History at The Ohio State University. She is the author of *Painters and Politics in the People's Republic of China, 1949-1979,* which won the Joseph Levenson book prize of the Association for Asian Studies, and co-author of *A Century in Crisis: Modernity and Tradition in the Art of Twentieth Century China,* which she curated for the Guggenheim Museum. She has published many articles and catalogue essays on modern and contemporary Chinese art, art institutions, and visual culture. She is currently writing *Art in Modern China* in collaboration with Kuiyi Shen.

Bai Di is Associate Professor and Chair of the Department of German/Russian/Chinese/Arabic at Drew University. She teaches Chinese literature, film, and gender studies, and has published on Western feminisms and modern Chinese literature.

Paul Clark is Professor of Chinese at the University of Auckland, New Zealand, and a specialist on Chinese film and popular culture. He is the author, most recently, of *The Chinese Cultural Revolution: A History* and is completing a book on Chinese youth cultures in 1968, 1988, and 2008.

Ralph Croizier is Professor Emeritus of History at the University of Victoria. His writing on modern Chinese art history includes *Art and Revolution in Modern China: The Lingnan (Cantonese) School of Painting, 1906-1951.*

Britta Erickson is an independent scholar and curator living in Palo Alto. Dr. Erickson is author of *The Art of Xu Bing: Words without Meaning, Meaning without Words* and *On the Edge: Contemporary Chinese Artists Encounter the West.* Her current research interests focus on contemporary Chinese art.

Gu Xiong is a multi-media artist and an Associate Professor in the Department of Art History, Visual Art, and Theory at the University of British Columbia. Widely exhibited and represented in many collections, his work has received significant critical recognition. He is the author of *The Yellow Pear* and the illustrator of *The Boy in the Attic.* His practice centres on hybrid identity arising from the integration of various cultural origins.

Shelley Drake Hawks is Assistant Professor in the Division of Social Sciences at the College of General Studies, Boston University. Her primary research field is China's twentieth-century political and cultural history, with a particular focus on the lives of artists during the Cultural Revolution.

Richard King is Associate Professor of Chinese at the University of Victoria. He is co-editor of *Global Goes Local: Popular Culture in Asia*, editor and translator of several volumes of contemporary Chinese fiction, and author of a number of articles on contemporary Chinese literature and culture.

Jan Walls is Professor Emeritus in the Humanities Department at Simon Fraser University, where he was founding director of the David Lam Centre for International Communication and of the Asia-Canada Program in the Faculty of Arts. He has taught Chinese language, literature, culture, and communication courses and contributed to Asia-focused program development at the University of British Columbia, University of Victoria, and Simon Fraser University. His publications include translations and studies of traditional and modern Chinese literature.

Scott Watson is Director/Curator of the Morris and Helen Belkin Art Gallery and Professor in the Department of Art History, Visual Art and Theory at the University of British Columbia. He has published extensively in the areas of contemporary Canadian and international art, and curated exhibitions in Europe and North America. His research focus is contemporary art and issues, art theory and criticism, twentieth-century art history, and curatorial and exhibition studies.

Shengtian Zheng was Professor and Chair of the Oil Painting Department of the China Academy of Art in Hangzhou, his alma mater, for more than thirty years. He was Secretary of the Annie Wong Art Foundation and Director of Art Beatus Gallery in Vancouver. In 2002, he founded *Yishu: Journal of Contemporary Chinese Art* and is also a founding member and Board Director of the Vancouver International Centre for Contemporary Asian Art. An independent curator, he has organized numerous exhibitions and writes frequently on contemporary Chinese and Asian art.

Index

Page numbers in italics indicate illustrations.

"800 million people watching 8 shows" *(bayi ren kan bage xi),* 163

1966 Beijing Jeep (painting), 19, *fig. 0.5 (before page 9)*

Acrobatic Art Reflecting Real Life (Fanying xianshi shenghuo zaji yishu), 177

Acupuncture Anaesthesia (painting), 52

Ad Hoc Study Group of Ancient Literary Scholars and Marxist Theorists, 224n36

administrators, academic: demonstrations against, 33; persecution under Cultural Revolution, 96-99; removed from positions during Anti-rightist campaign, 95

allegorical criticism of present, by retelling historical events, 14-15. *See also* Criticizing Lin Biao and Confucius campaign; *Hai Rui Dismissed from Office* (opera)

Anti-revisionism group (Fanxiuzu), 101

Anti-rightist Campaign (1957), 31-32, 95, 137

Anyuan mining workers' movement, 228n30

art. *See* art, of the Cultural Revolution; artists; ballet; music; opera; painting; poetry; sculpture; theatre

art, of the Cultural Revolution: centralized control over, 30; designed to improve viewer's revolutionary consciousness, 123, 130; dismissed in early years after Mao's death, 93-94; emphasis on Mao's revolutionary role, 43; limitations of content, 177; Mao depicted as "red, smooth, and luminescent" *(hong, guang, liang),* vii, 47; Mao, iconic images of, 30; military images and battle-readiness, 12-14, 35, 48, 145, 203-15; phase one (1966-71), 30, 32-45; phase two (1971-76), 30, 45-56; post-Cultural Revolution, as commodities in commercial popular culture, 17-19, 20-21, 56-57, 106; purpose of model revolutionary art, 7, 30, 130; Red Guards, destruction of traditional art by, 8, 35; replacement of traditional art by uniform socialist images, 30, 31; socialist realist style, 44, 55-56, 129; "three prominences" *(san tuchu),* 54, 144, 185, 206-207, 211, 214; and unlocking of human potential through socialism, 137; utopian vision of, 3-4, 11, 31. *See also* ballet; caricatures; drawings; Hu Xian peasant art; Jin Shan peasant art;

Mao Zedong images; model theatrical works *(geming yangbanxi)*; music; novels; opera; painting; posters; sculpture; theatre; woodcuts

Art of the Great Proletarian Cultural Revolution, 1966-1976 (exhibition), vii

Art Society of the Eighteenth at West Lake (Xihu yi-ba yi she), 95

Art Storm (Meishu fenglei) (journal), 36, 37

Art War Gazette (Meishu zhanbao), 38

articles: "Carrying Out Chairman Mao's Line on Literature and Art: Brilliant Models" *(People's Daily)*, 188; "Chinese Peasant Painting, 1958-1976: Amateur and Professional" (Laing), 146-47; "The Death Toll of the Cultural Revolution Amounts to Two Million" (Ding Shu), 104; "On the Revolution in Beijing Opera" (Jiang Qing), 174; "Peasants' Revolutionary Paintings" *(People's Daily)*, 141; "Rent Collection Courtyard: A Revolution in Sculpture" *(China Reconstructs)*, 128; "Study the Revolutionary Model Performances, Defend the Revolutionary Model Performances" *(Red Flag)* (Zhe Ping), 182; "Sweep Away All Ox-Demons and Snake-Spirits" (*People's Daily* editorial), 8; "*The White-Haired Girl* and the Historical Complexity of Yan'an Literature" (Meng Yue), 193; "Writers and Performers, Their Works and Their Audiences, in the First Three Decades" (McDougall), 189. *See also* journals and newspapers; publications, of the Cultural Revolution

Artistic Family (painting), *158*

artists: attacks on, by Red Guards, 8, 33-34; collective collaboration on paintings, 35, 45, 101-3; collective, collaboration on versions of *Rent Collection Courtyard* (1965), 124-26, 128; collective, issues of artistic ownership, 22-23; commercially successful, based on Cultural Revolution images, 20; contemporary, background of "re-education" by peasantry, 10; emigré, 19, 20, 56; mistreatment during Cultural Revolution, 9, 36, 96-99; peasants, workers and soldiers mandated as source of inspiration during Cultural Revolution, 126, 128; professional, invited to submit for national exhibitions, 46; proletarian, 11; revolutionary consciousness of, 102; rusticated youths, 11; "sent-down" professional artists, 45, 137; "Stars" (Xingxing pai), 17, 19. *See also* art, of the Cultural Revolution; "cultural workers"; Hu Xian peasant painters; Jin Shan peasant painters; *names of individual artists*

Attending Party Class (painting), 148, *fig. 6.2 (before page 149)*

authors, Red Guard attacks on, 8-9

Azalea Mountain (Dujuanshan) (opera), 186, 189, 239n14

Ba Jin, 21, 28, 57

Bai Tianxue, 149, *150*

ballet: previous popularity of stories, 170; sinicization of dance form in model works, 170. *See also The Red Detachment of Women* (ballet); *The White-Haired Girl* (ballet)

Banff Centre for the Arts, 118

baoshoupai (conservatives), 99

"beat back the right deviationist wind": campaign, 152; slogan, 16

Beijing Architectural Artistic Sculpture Factory, 125-26

Beijing Chinese Painting Institute, 38
Beijing Jeep. See 1966 Beijing Jeep (painting)
Beijing Normal University, 9
Beijing Painting Institute Mao Zedong Thought Armed Struggle Group Revolutionary Committee, 36
Beijing Planetarium, 9
Beijing University, 33
Belden, Jack, 192
"black paintings," 36, 38, 78-79, *80. See also* "erroneous art"; paintings
books, illegal, 115-16
Boulder Day (Panshi wan) (opera), 187
"brushes are weapons" (slogan), 105-6
"burning books and burying scholars alive" (slogans), 60, 87, 221n5

Cai Guo-Qiang: accused of violating copyright, 133-34; unconventional approach to art, 121; Venice Biennale *Rent Collection Courtyard* (1999), 22-23, 121, *123*, 131, *132*
Cai Ruohong, 62
Cai Yuanpei, 94
Cao Jinying, 153-54
Cao Quntang, 160-61
Cao Yu, 176
"capitalist-roaders," 16, 33, 130, 203, 204, 213
caricatures: created by Red Guards, 9-10; *A Parade of Clowns* (Weng Rulan), 4, 39, *40*, 41, 42
Caricatures: Smashing the Reactionary Line Advocated by Liu Shaoqi and Deng Xiaoping (exhibition), 9-10
"Carrying Out Chairman Mao's Line on Literature and Art: Brilliant Models" (article), 188
C-C Clique, 97, 227n16
Central Academy Middle School, 53
Central Academy of Arts and Crafts, 34, 126
Central Academy of Fine Arts, 9, 35, 36, 47, 49, 125, 126, 143
Central Academy of Fine Arts Middle School, 47
Central Propaganda Department, 45
Central Symphony Orchestra, 178
Chairman Mao. *See* Mao Zedong
Chairman Mao Goes to Anyuan (painting), 7, 43, 45, 103, 106, 108, *fig. 1.6 (after page 44)*
Chairman Mao Inspects Areas South and North of Yangtze River Near Wuhan (painting). *See Man's World Is Mutable, Seas Become Mulberry Fields: Chairman Mao Inspects the Situation of the Great Proletarian Cultural Revolution in Northern, South-central, and Eastern China* (painting)
"Chairman Mao is the red sun in our hearts" (slogan), 48
Chairman Mao's Heart Beats as One with the Hearts of the Revolutionary Masses (painting), 34-35, 43, *fig. 1.2 (before page 35)*
Chairman Mao's Red Guards (musical performance), 176
Chairman Mao's thought entertainment group, 114-15
Chen Boda: arrest as collaborator of Gang of Four, 227n13; in *Chairman Mao's Heart Beats as One with the Hearts of the Revolutionary Masses* (painting), 35, *fig. 1.2 (before page 35)*; meeting with Zhang Yongsheng, 97
Chen Juo-fu, 227n16
Chen Li-fu, 97, 227n16
Chen Rutang, 178
Chen Sihe, 190
Chen Yan'ning, 47
Chen Yifei, 45, 47
Cheng, Arthur Shuren, vii

Cheng Li, 50, *51*
Childhood (poster), 129
Children's Palaces, 45, 51-52, 220n40
China Academy of Arts, 94
China Cultural Development Committee, 126
China Dance-Drama Troupe (Zhongguo wuju tuan), 170
Chinese Artists' Association, 34, 36, 45, 65
The Chinese Cultural Revolution: A History (book) (Clark), 3
"Chinese Peasant Painting, 1958-1976: Amateur and Professional" (article) (Laing), 146-47
City Opera School (Xixiao), 177
clappertalk *(kuaishu)*, 179
Clark, Paul, 3
class origins: and access to employment and education, 34, 39; consequences of being "red" or "black," 116-17; as hereditary, 34, 116; "If the father's a hero, the son's a brave; if the father's a counter-revolutionary, the son's a bastard" (slogan), 34, 42
class struggle: and feminist themes in model ballets, 201; as struggle between moral and immoral, 193-94
Cloth Tiger (painting), 156
The Columbia Anthology of Modern Chinese Literature (Lau and Goldblatt), 189
Communal Fish Pond (painting), 150, 151, *fig. 6.5 (before page 151)*
Confucianist-Legalist Struggle *(Ru-Fa douzheng)*, 15
Confucius: comparison of virtuous ruler to pole star, 223n23; Criticizing Lin Biao and Confucius campaign, 14-15, 78, 81, 142; in work of Shi Lu, 83-87
Confucius (ink painting), 84-85
conservatives *(baoshoupai)*, 99
Consolidate Our Forces: Enter Deeply into Condemnation of Deng Xiaoping's Counter-Revolutionary Revisionist Line (poster), 12, *13*
Criticize Reactionary Painter Shi Lu Task Force *(Pipan fandong huajia Shi Lu)*, 224n36
Criticizing Lin Biao and Confucius campaign, 14-15, 78, 81, 142
Cultural Revolution: allegorical criticism of present, by retelling historical events, 14-15; beginnings in "May Sixteenth Directive," 11, 95, 169, 181; categorization of people by devotion to, 99; codification of class distinctions as hereditary, 34; denunciation as revolt against culture, 16; destructive actions of, 4, 29-30; effect on three generations, 28; expatriate writings on, 3; "four olds" *(sijiu)*, 30, 48; ignored by subsequent political leaders, 27-28; launched by Mao's denunciation of president of Beijing University, 33; as Mao's attempt to resolve Marxism and Leninism, 217n1; Mao's failure to control, 28; phase one (1966-71), 30, 32-45; phase two (1971-76), 30, 45-56; power struggles, reflected in strident campaigns, 14; purpose as removal of Mao's political rivals, 5, 14, 28; referred to as "ten lost years," 27, 31; resurgence of interest in, vii, 56. *See also* art, of the Cultural Revolution; Cultural Revolution Group; Gang of Four; Jiang Qing; Mao Zedong; model theatrical works *(geming yangbanxi)*; Red Guards
Cultural Revolution Group: and Criticizing Lin Biao and Confucius movement, 78, 81; encouragement to students to join in mass criticism and repudiation activities, 95; as

highest authority on cultural matters, 45; Literature and Arts Group (Wenyizu), 38
Cultural Revolution museum, 21, 28, 57
"cultural workers," 5-6. *See also* artists
"Cut Off Liu Shaoqi's Black Hand in the Art World – Thoroughly Eliminate the Poisonous Weeds Glorifying Liu Shaoqi" (conference), 37

Dalai Lama, 130
danwei (work units), 99
Daoji, 62
Daozi, 133
David, Jean-Louis, 148
"The Death Toll of the Cultural Revolution Amounts to Two Million" (article) (Ding Shu), 104
democracy movement, 19
Deng Shu, 39, 50, *fig. 1.3 (before page 35)*
Deng Tuo, 41
Deng Xiaoping: allegorical portrayal in "Sun Wukong beats the White Bone Demoness" (Sun Wukong san-da Baigujing), 16; blamed for "erroneous" art, 38; as complicit in Anti-rightist Campaign, 32; condemnation in painting *Steady as a Rock,* 203-4, 205; condemnation in posters, 12-13; criticized for running Beijing Chinese Painting Institute, 38; criticized in "May Sixteenth Directive" (1966), 32; in *A Parade of Clowns* (poster), 41-42; in power struggle with Gang of Four, 14, 213; rise to power, following Cultural Revolution, 27; second purging of, 16, 152; tolerant towards artistic stylistic innovation, 19
Digging a Well (painting), *151*, 151-52
Ding Shu, 104
Dong Xiwen, 43, *fig. 1.7 (before page 45)*
Dong Zhengyi, 150, 151, *fig. 6.5 (before page 151)*
Double Uniting (Shuangjiehe) campaign, 143
drawings: *From Brother Laowan* (Gu Xiong), *fig. 4.9 (before page 117); Grinding Grain* (Gu Xiong), *113*; *The Moon Is Up* (Gu Xiong), *114*; *Our Kitchen* (Gu Xiong), *111*; *A Parade of Clowns* (Weng Rulan) (caricature), 4, 39, *40*, 41, 42; *Qingping Village Scene in the Daba Mountains* (Gu Xiong), *111*; *Shattering Illusions* (Gu Xiong), *fig. 4.8 (after page 116)*
Du Yinxin, 97, 227n12
Duan Ruixia, 203, 211-13

The East Is Red (painting), 10
The East Is Red (Red Guard faction), 34
Eastern Venus de Milo/Goddess of Beauty (painting), 74, *fig. 2.3 (before page 75)*
"[economic] reform and opening [to the West]" (slogan), 17
Eighth Route Army, 30, 192
emigré artists, 19, 20, 56
"Encountering Sorrow" (poetry) (Qu Yuan), 68, 70
Engels, Friedrich, 231n3
"erroneous" art, 38. *See also* "black paintings"
essays: "On the Power of Mara Poetry" (Lu Xun), 86; "Theory of Class Origins" (Yu Luoke), 116; *Xue Hua Lu* [Notes on the study of painting] (Shi Lu), 221n8
Eulogy for Liu Yingjun (Lin Yingjun zan) (musical performance), 176

Family Histories of the Air Force Fighters (sculpture), 230n28
Fan Zhihua, 151-52
Fang Gangmin, 22, 96, 227n9

Fang Haizhen, *183*, 185
Fang Zengxian, 49
Fanxiuzu (anti-revisionism group), 101
Fei, Ms., 97
Feng Agui, 200
Fighting in Northern Shaanxi (painting), 58, 62-67, *63*
Fighting North and South (Nan zheng bei zhan) (film), 185
Fighting Opera Troupe (Zhandou), 175
film industry: after Cultural Revolution, 17; colour remakes of pre-Cultural Revolution black and white films, 185; rewriting of history of Chinese revolution, 11
films: *On the Docks*, 182, 184; *Fighting North and South (Nan zheng bei zhan)*, 185; *Green Pine Ridge (Qing song ling)*, 185; *Guerrillas on the Plains (Pingyuan youjidui)*, 185; *Heroic Little Sisters of the Grasslands (Caoyuan yingxiong xiao jiemei)* (animated film), 186; *Lenin*, 114; of model theatrical works, 11, 182, 184; *Others Will Follow Us (Zi you houlairen)*, 171, 175; *The Red Detachment of Women*, 170, 195-97; *Sparkling Red Star (Shanshan de hongxing)*, 185; *Taking Tiger Mountain by Strategy (Zhiqu Weihushan)*, 171, 184; and "three prominences," 185; *The White-Haired Girl*, 170, 184, 192, 193, 194-95
A Fine Son of the People (Renmin de hao erzi) (musical performance), 176
Fish Pond (painting), *154*
folk art. *See* Hu Xian peasant painters; Jin Shan peasant painters
Follow Chairman Mao Closely, Grow Up Tempered by Wind and Waves (poster), *51*
Founding of the Nation (painting), 43, *fig. 1.7 (before page 45)*
Four Modernizations, 152
"four olds" *(sijiu)*, 30, 33, 48
From Brother Laowan (drawing), *fig. 4.9 (before page 117)*

Galston, William, 194
Gan Yu reservoir project, 139
Gang of Four: accused of instigating "ten-year disaster" of Cultural Revolution, 16; arrest after death of Mao, 11, 104; and Criticizing Lin Biao and Confucius movement, 15; model theatrical works limited by association with, 187; power struggle with political rivals, 204, 205-6, 213; Smash the Gang of Four campaign, 152. *See also* Jiang Qing; Wang Hongwen; Yao Wenyuan; Zhang Chunqiao
Gao Gao, 3, 239n8
Gao Jingde, 46-47, 50
Gao Xingjian, 17
gender construction, disrupted by model theatrical works, 190-91
General Headquarters of the United Rebel Factions (Shen Lian Zong), 96
"the globe is entirely red!" (slogan), 102
Goddess of Beauty (painting). *See Eastern Venus de Milo/Goddess of Beauty* (painting)
Goldblatt, Howard, 189
The Golden Road (novel), 11
Great Hall of the People, 67
A Great Happy Occasion for the Whole People (musical performance), 176
Great Job! Investigating the Peasant Movement in Hunan (painting), 44, 56, *fig. 1.8 (after page 46)*
A Great Joyous Occasion for the Whole People (Quanguo renmin de da xishi) (musical performance), 176
Great Leap Forward campaign, 5, 71, 110, 136-40

Great Proletarian Cultural Revolution. *See* Cultural Revolution

Great United Congress of Central Academy of Fine Arts Classes and Departments, 36

Great Yak (sculpture), 105

Green Dragon Pond (Qinglong tan) (opera), 184

Green Pine Ridge (Qing song ling) (film), 185

Grinding Grain (drawing), 113

Gu Xiong: "black" class origins, 116-17; career after Cultural Revolution, 22, 118; in countryside, as rusticated urban youth, 10, 108-16, *110;* on growing up during the Cultural Revolution, 107-8; on importance of art, 117-18; photographs of, *109, 110;* sketchbooks of life in countryside, 22, *111, 113, 114, 115, fig. 4.8 (after page 116), fig. 4.9 (before page 117)*

Gu Yuan, 143

Guan Shanyue, 46

Guang Tingbo, 47

Guangzhou Academy of Arts, 47, 49

Guerrillas on the Plains (Pingyuan youjidui) (film), 185

Guomindang (Nationalist Party), 227n16

Gutian Meeting (painting), 48, *49,* 50

Hai Rui Dismissed from Office (opera): as allegory, 14; critiqued by Yao Wenyuan, 6; interpreted as critique of Mao's dismissal of Peng Dehuai, 6

Hao Boyi, 53

Hao Ran, 11

He Jingzhi, 192

He Kongde, 48, *49,* 50

He Long, 41

He Yan, 97

Headquarters of Revolutionary Rebel and Red Guards of Hangzhou (Hong San Si), 96

"Heavenly Questions" (poetry) (Qu Yuan), 222n18

Hebei clapper opera *(bangzi),* 179, 184

Heilongjiang Production and Construction Corps, 53

Helping the Army (painting), 148

Henan Opera Troupe (Yuju tuan), 176

Herds of Cows and Horses (painting), 149

Herds of Livestock (painting), 148

heroic figures: militant battle-readiness, 203-15. *See also* model theatrical works; "three prominences"

Heroic Little Sisters of the Grasslands (Caoyuan yingxiong xiao jiemei) (animated film), 185-86

Hershatter, Gail, 191

A History of Contemporary Chinese Literature (book) (Chen Sihe), 190

Hong Bo, 41

Hong Changqing, 198, 199

hong, guang, liang ("red, smooth, and luminescent"), vii, 47

Hong Lian, 199, 200-1

Hong San Si (Headquarters of Revolutionary Rebel and Red Guards of Hangzhou), 96

Hong Zicheng

Hongweibing zhandoudui (Red Guard Fighting Force), 95

Honig, Emily, 191

Hotel School, of ink paintings, 142, 144

Hou Yimin, 35, *37,* 39, 43, 50, *fig. 1.3 (before page 35)*

Hu Feng, 42

Hu Xian, Jin Shan, Dong Feng United Peasant Painting Exhibition, 155

Hu Xian Peasant Art School, 139

Hu Xian peasant painters: art instruction provided to, 137, 138-40, 143; dissociation from leftist political line, after fall of Gang of Four, 145-46, 153; family (private) studio-galleries, 160-61; and the Four Modernizations, 152; Hu Xian Peasant Art School, 139; national prominence of, 12, 141; as professional artists and entrepreneurs, 157, 159-62; as proof of power of "Mao Zedong thought" and Cultural Revolution, 145; publications, 143; reinvention to fit new era of "reform and opening," 23, 145-46, 152, 153. *See also* Hu Xian peasant painting; Hu Xian peasant paintings

Hu Xian Peasant Painters Association, 139

Hu Xian peasant painting: as alternative to elitist traditional-style paintings, 142, 145; analysis of, 146-47; and Chinese cultural diplomacy, 143, 144-45, 152; exhibitions, 143, 144-45, 152, 155, 233n11, 234n32; folk art traditions of Hu Xian, 140; and globalization, 162-63; international tourist market for, 156, 161-62; as microcosm of history of Chinese revolution, 136, 162; painting as revolutionary act, in breaking monopoly of cultural production by elites, 137; as popular "gifts," 161; revival of folk art under Deng Xiaoping, 153; shift away from political content to folk themes, 156, 157; and Socialist Education Movement, 140, 141-42; stylistic influences on, 12, 146-47, 148, 155-56; and "three prominences," 144. *See also* Hu Xian peasant painters; Hu Xian peasant paintings; Jin Shan peasant painters

Hu Xian Peasant Painting Exhibition Hall, 139, 142

Hu Xian peasant paintings: *Artistic Family* (Liu Fengtao), *158*; *Attending Party Class* (Liu Zhigui), 148, *fig. 6.2 (before page 149)*; *Cloth Tiger* (Li Fenglan), 156; *Communal Fish Pond* (Dong Zhengyi), 150, 151, *fig. 6.5 (before page 151)*; *Digging a Well* (Fan Xiaohua/Zhihua), *151*, 151-52; *Helping the Army* (Zhang Lin), 148; *Herds of Cows and Horses* (Zhang Lin), 149; *Herds of Livestock* (Zhang Lin), 148; *Never Stop Being Industrious and Thrifty* (Zhang Lin), 149; *Night Melody* (Liu Zhide), *155*, 156; *Old Party Secretary* (Liu Zhide), 147, 156, *fig. 6.1 (after page 148)*; *Raising Goats* (Bai Tianxue), 149, *150*; *Spring Hoeing* (Li Fenglan), 149, *fig. 6.4 (after page 150)*; *Treading on a Big Drum* (Liu Zhide), 156

Hua Junwu, 62, 153

Hua Yu Lu (Notes on painting) (Shitao), 221n8

Huang Shiren, 192, 193

Huang Yongyu, 36

Hubei Art Academy, 47

"hundred days' war," of Red Guard factions, 10

Hundred Flowers movement, 117, 229n7. *See also* Anti-rightist Campaign (1957)

Idol (sculpture), 17

"If the father's a hero, the son's a brave; if the father's a counter-revolutionary, the son's a bastard" (slogan), 34, 42

In Praise of Mao Zedong Thought (Gesong Mao Zedong sixiang) (musical performance), 177

In Praise of the Red Guards (sculpture), 230n28

Indian Fort/Tower to Recognize the Heart of Lu Ban (painting), 81-86, *82*
Indian Sage-King/Indian Spirit King (painting), 73, *fig. 2.2 (after page 74)*
ink painting *(guohua):* among influences on Hu Xian peasant painting, 147; attacks on, during Cultural Revolution, 38; Hotel School, 142, 144; landscape, 65; Painting Correction Group, 48-50; Shi Lu's approach, 65-67; socialist realism, 44, 54-55; traditional, 38
ink paintings *(guohua): Confucius* (Shi Lu), *85*; *Eastern Venus de Milo/ Goddess of Beauty* (Shi Lu), 74, *fig. 2.3 (before page 75)*; *Fighting in Northern Shaanxi* (Shi Lu), 58, 62-67, *63*; *Indian Fort/Tower to Recognize the Heart of Lu Ban* (Shi Lu), 81-86, *82*; *Letting the Horses Drink at the Yan River* (Shi Lu), 67; *Qin Shihuang* (Shi Lu), 88-90, *89*; *Winter Plum* (Shi Lu), 79-81, *80*
intellectuals: attacks on, by Red Guards, 8; denunciation of, during Cultural Revolution, 6, 28; imprisonment in "ox-sheds" *(niu peng)*, 9, 36
Invincible Mao Zedong Thought Illuminates the Revolutionary Arts Stage (poster), *fig. 0.1 (after page 8)*

"January Storm," 96
Ji Changchun, 203, 212
Jia Xingdong, 129
Jiang Baoxing, 206, 241n7
Jiang Hua, 96
Jiang Qing: in *1966 Beijing Jeep* (painting), *fig. 0.5 (before page 9)*; allegorical portrayal in "Sun Wukong Beats the White Bone Demoness" (Sun Wukong san-da Baigujing), 16; antipathy to traditional Chinese art, 7, 46; arrest after death of Mao, 8, 11, 28, 104, 174; biographical information, 6-7; blamed for interference in artistic process, 174; in *Chairman Mao's Heart Beats as One with the Hearts of the Revolutionary Masses* (painting), 35, *fig. 1.2 (before page 35)*; condemnation in public demonstrations, 16; at conference on military arts and literature (1966), 32; and Criticizing Lin Biao and Confucius campaign, 15, 78; as cultural standard-bearer for revolution, 15-16; denunciation of Western artistic traditions, 7; as director of Culture Group, 45; in *The East Is Red* (painting), 10; in *Invincible Mao Zedong Thought Illuminates the Revolutionary Arts Stage* (poster), *fig. 0.1 (after page 8)*; and Literature and Arts Group (Wenyizu), 38; meeting with Zhang Yongsheng, 97, 220n42; methods of control, 174; and model theatrical works *(geming yangbanxi)*, 7, 23, 168, 173-74, 174, 179, 181, 239n8; and modernization of Beijing opera, 6, 7, 207; praised by artists, 178; and promotion of "three prominences," 206-7; replacement of traditional art by uniform socialist images, 30; on role of drama in shaping consciousness, 16; self-image as embattled but noble fighter, 174; speech on modernization of opera, 173; use of cultural activities for personal political ambitions, 15, 190, 239n8. *See also* Gang of Four; model theatrical works *(geming yangbanxi)*; opera
Jiang Qisheng, 146
Jiang Shuiying, 211

Jiao Yulu (opera), 175
Jin Lang, 95
Jin Shan peasant painters: *Fish Pond* (Cao Jinying), *154*; folk art style, 153-55; *Welcome Guests* (Zhang Xinying), 154. *See also* Hu Xian peasant painters
Jin Shangyi, 35, 44, 47, 50, *fig. 1.3 (before page 35)*
Jin Shunhua, 45
journals and newspapers, 11, 36, 37, 38, 39, 175, 177, 178, 181, 186. *See also* articles; publications, of the Cultural Revolution
Journey to the West (Xiyouji) (epic), 16
Judd, Ellen, 211
July Twentieth Incident, 100

Kang Sheng, 35, 126, *fig. 1.2 (before page 35)*
Ke Qingshi, 206

Labour-Reform Farm Inmate (painting), *fig. 3.3 (before page 95)*
Laing, Ellen Johnston, 146-47
Lao She, 8-9
Last Supper (painting), 18-19
Lau, Joseph S.M., 189
Legalism, compared with Confucianism, 15
Lei Feng, 107
Lenin (film), 114
"let a hundred flowers bloom" *(baihua qifang)* (slogan), 179, 188
*Let's Go and Watch the Model Theatrical Works (*poster), 12
Letting the Horses Drink at the Yan River (painting), 67
Li Fenglan, 140, 143, 149-50, 156, 159, *fig. 6.4 (after page 150)*
Li Keran, 38
Li Kuchan, 36, 38
Li Na, 227n13
Li Qi, 37-38
Li Shan, 56, *fig. 1.14 (before page 55)*
Li Songtao, 143
Li Xiaoshan, 27
Liao Mosha, 41
Lin Biao: in *1966 Beijing Jeep* (painting), 19, *fig. 0.5 (before page 9);* in *Chairman Mao's Heart Beats as One with the Hearts of the Revolutionary Masses* (painting), 35, *fig. 1.2 (before page 35);* and Criticizing Lin Biao and Confucius campaign, 14-15, 142; and cult of Mao's personality, 5; death in plane crash after abortive coup by (1971), 14, 30, 77-78; in *The East Is Red* (painting), 10; "elitism" of, refuted by Hu Xian peasant paintings, 145; and purging of Liu Shaoqi, 130
Lin Fengmian, 94, 95
Lin Yong, 44, 56, *fig. 1.8 (after page 46)*
Literature and Arts Group (Wenyizu), of the Cultural Revolution Small Group, 38
"Little Red Book" (Mao Zedong), 5, 8, 20, 100
Liu Chunhua, 7, 43-44, 45, 103, 106, 108, *fig. 1.6 (after page 44)*
Liu Fengtao, *157, 158*
Liu Lixun, 105
Liu Qunhan, 157
Liu Shaoqi: in *1966 Beijing Jeep* (painting), *fig. 0.5 (before page 9);* and Anyuan mining workers' movement, 103, 228n30; campaign to discredit, 32, 37, 38, 43; criticized in "May Sixteenth Directive" (1966), 32; death, 42; in *Founding of the Nation* (painting), 43; in *Liu Shaoqi and the Anyuan Coal Miners* (painting), 37; in *A Parade of Clowns (poster),* 41; purging of, 28, 130

Liu Shaoqi and the Anyuan Coal Miners (painting), 37, 39, 43
Liu Wencai, 124
Liu Wenxi, 49, 55
Liu Zhide, 143, 147, 155, 156, 157, *fig. 6.1 (after page 148)*
Liu Zhigui, 148, *fig. 6.2 (before page 149)*
Long Live the Victory of Chairman Mao's Revolutionary Line (exhibition), 10, 43, 101
Long Live the Victory of Mao Zedong Thought Revolutionary Painting Exhibition, 38
Long March, 64
Long Yuli, 131
Lu Ban, 83
Lu Dingyi, 32, 38, 39, 41
Lu Xin, 227n11
Lu Xun, 62, 86, 95, 225n47, 226n6
Lu Xun Academy of Art, 47, 49
Lu Xun Academy of Arts and Literature, 30, 46
Luo Gongliu, 36, 50, *fig. 1.3 (before page 35)*
Luo Ruiqing, 32, 39, 41

Ma Gaihu, 66
MacFarquhar, Roderick, 3
Macherey, Pierre, 200-1
"making foreign things serve China" *(yang wei Zhong yong)* (slogan), 103, 179, 188
Making Revolution Following Chairman Mao Forever (Yongyuan genzhe Mao Zhuxi nao geming) (musical performance), 176
"making the past serve the present" *(gu wei jin yong)* (slogan), 14, 16, 179, 188
Maksimov, Constantine, 47
Man's World Is Mutable, Seas Become Mulberry Fields: Chairman Mao Inspects the Situation of the Great Proletarian Cultural Revolution in Northern, South-central, and Eastern China (painting), 93, *fig. 3.1 (after page 94)*
Mao Zedong: and Anyuan mining workers' movement, 103, 228n30; character, contrast with popular image, 4; contributions of art to cult of personality, 44-45, 56; on history and "making the past serve the present," 14; on limited number of Cultural Revolution products, 185; "Little Red Book," 5, 20; "May Sixteenth Directive" (1966), 11, 32, 95, 169, 181; poetry, 79-80, 93, 226n2; political motivation for Cultural Revolution, 4-6, 28; and purging of Liu Shaoqi, 130; sanction and mandate of Red Guards, 8, 33; self-identification with emperor Qin Shihuang, 87-88; in "Sun Wukong Beats the White Bone Demoness" (Sun Wukong san-da Baigujing), 16; swim in Yangtze River, 50. *See also* Mao Zedong images; Yan'an Talks
Mao Zedong images: *1966 Beijing Jeep* (painting), 19, 54, *fig. 0.5 (before page 9)*; *Chairman Mao Goes to Anyuan* (Liu Chunhua), 7, 43, 45, 103, 106, 108, *fig. 1.6 (after page 44)*; *Chairman Mao's Heart Beats as One with the Hearts of the Revolutionary Masses* (poster), 34-35, 43, *fig. 1.2 (before page 35)*; contemporary popular art, 19, 20; *The East Is Red* (painting), 10; *Fighting in Northern Shaanxi* (Shi Lu) (painting), 58, 63; *Follow Chairman Mao Closely, Grow Up Tempered by Wind and Waves* (Tang Xiaohe and Cheng Li), 51; *Founding of the Nation* (Dong Xiwen) (painting), 43,

fig. 1.7 (before page 45); Great Job! Investigating the Peasant Movement in Hunan (Lin Yong) (painting), 44, *fig. 1.8 (after page 46); Gutian Meeting* (He Kongde) (painting), 48, 49, 50; *Idol* (sculpture), 17; *Invincible Mao Zedong Thought Illuminates the Revolutionary Arts Stage* (Wang Zhaoda) (poster), *fig. 0.1 (after page 8); Man's World Is Mutable, Seas Become Mulberry Fields: Chairman Mao Inspects the Situation of the Great Proletarian Cultural Revolution in Northern, South-central, and Eastern China* (Shengtian Zheng) (painting), 93, *fig. 3.1 (after page 94); New Spring in Yan'an* (poster), 55, *fig. 1.13 (after page 54);* required to be "red, smooth, and luminescent" *(hong, guang, liang),* vii, 47; *The Rouge Series/Rouge Mao* (Li Shan) (painting), *fig. 1.14 (before page 55); We Must Implement the Proletarian Cultural Revolution to the Finish* (painting), 50, *fig. 1.3 (before page 35)*
Mao Zedong's Thought Illuminates the Anyuan Workers' Movement (exhibition), 43
Marx, Karl, 137, 163, 231n3
"matched couplet" debate, 34
May 4 New Culture Movement, 226n6
May anniversary of Yan'an Talks. *See* Yan'an Talks
May Seventh Cadre-schools, 45
May Seventh College of the Arts, 129-30
"May Sixteenth Directive" (1966): as beginning of Cultural Revolution, 11, 95, 169, 181; critique and purging of political rivals, 32-33; theory, guidelines and policies for the Cultural Revolution, 95
McDougall, Bonnie S., 189
Mencius, 78-79, 224n36
Meng Yue, 193
Meserve, Walter, 189
military: as guardian of Mao's prestige, 64; metaphors, and peasant art, 145; military images and battle-readiness in art, 12-14, 35, 48, 145, 203-15. *See also* Red Guards
Milk Maid (painting), 51
Min Lisheng, 72-73
Ministry of Culture, 45
minority culture, songs and dances, 185-86
Mo Pu, 95
Mo Yan, 17
model theatrical works *(geming yangbanxi):* "800 million people watching 8 shows" *(bayi ren kan bage xi),* 23, 167, 180; associated with Gang of Four, 187; attacked by Chinese critics as propaganda, satisfying Jiang Qing's personal ambition, 190; celebration performances, 167, 174-75, 177, 178, 181, 201-2; continuous refinement of, 179; cynicism regarding, 185, 186, 190; definition, 188, 189; excitement of wartime settings, 23, 173, 211; feminist themes, 188-202, 239n14; glorification of revolutionary heroism, 7, 23; heralded as first truly proletarian works of art, 7, 23, 168; iconic status of, 168; as means of overcoming resistance to change in arts and attitudes, 7, 169, 171, 189; as models for other artistic and literary endeavours, 179-80, 211; as models for other performing arts, 179-80; portrayal of comrades-in-arms and Communist Party as family substitutes, 171-72; post-Cultural Revolution renewed interest in, 21, 201-2; reasons for popular success, 172; by

rusticated youth in countryside, 114-15; slogans attached to, 179; stylistic innovations, 172-73; supported by state cultural apparatus, 178, 179, 188; varying popularity, 168, 180-82, 187; in western scholarship, 189, 190. *See also On the Docks (Haigang)* (opera)*; Raid on the White Tiger Regiment (Qixi Baihutuan)* (opera)*; The Red Detachment of Women (Hongse niangzi jun)* (ballet)*; The Red Lantern (Hongdeng ji)* (opera)*; Shajiabang* (opera)*; Shajiabang* (symphony); *Taking Tiger Mountain by Strategy (Zhiqu Weihushan)* (opera)*; The White-Haired Girl (Baimao nü)* (ballet)

The Moon Is Up (drawing), 114

Morris and Helen Belkin Art Gallery (Vancouver), vii

Mount Jinggang (Red Guard faction), 34

Museum of Revolutionary History, 37, 43, 67

Museum of Revolutionary History Revolutionary Rebel United Committee, 36

music: new folk songs *(xin minge)* movement, 238n3; *Red Sun*, 20; revolutionary songs, 20, 116; rice-sprout song *(yangge)*, 170, 171, 238n3; Shajiabang (symphony), 188; songs by rusticated youth, 116. *See also* musical performances; opera

musical performances: *Chairman Mao's Red Guards*, 176; *Eulogy for Liu Yingjun (Liu Yingjun zan)*, 176; *A Fine Son of the People (Renmin de hao erzi)*, 176; *A Great Happy Occasion for the Whole People*, 176; *A Great Joyous Occasion for the Whole People (Quanguo renmin de da xishi)*, 176; *Making Revolution Following Chairman Mao Forever (Yongyuan genzhe Mao Zhuxi nao geming)*, 176; *In Praise of Mao Zedong Thought (Gesong Mao Zedong sixiang)*, 177; *Sending Precious Books (Song baoshu)*, 176; "Songs, dances and Other Artistic Performances," 176; "Songs of Praise *(gesong)* for the Great Leader Chairman Mao," 176; "Songs of Praise for the Great Proletarian Cultural Revolution," 176; *Songs of the Red Guards (Hongweibing zhi ge)*, 176; *Sons and Daughters of the Grasslands (Caoyuan ernü)* (dance-drama), 185-86

Nanbatian, 197

National Academy of Fine Arts, 20

National Art Gallery, 53, 101, 124, 143

National Art Gallery Red Rebel Group, 36

National Artists Association, 153

National Assembly of Red Art Rebels, 36

National Day celebrations (October 1): performance of *Shajiabang* symphony, 171; performances of model theatrical works, 23, 167-68, 175, 181, 184, 186, 187, 201

National Peasant Painting Exhibition, 155

Nationalist Party (Guomindang), 227n16. *See also* C-C clique

Never Stop Being Industrious and Thrifty (painting), 149

new folk songs *(xin minge)*, 238n3

New Spring in Yan'an (poster), 55, *fig. 1.13 (after page 54)*

New Wave art movement, 19, 20

Nietzsche, Friedrich, 225n47

Night Melody (painting), *155*, 156

Nixon, Richard, 144

"Not Just One of the Audience" *(Tebie guanzhong)* (short story):

battle-readiness of hero, 203, 213-14; storyline, 211-14; "three prominences" in, 214
novels: *The Golden Road* (Hao Ran), 11; *The Second Handshake (Di'er ci wo shou)* (Zhang Yang), 116; *Three Kingdoms (Sanguo zhi yanyi)*, 172; *Tracks in the Snowy Forest (Linhai xueyuan)* (Qu Bo), 171, 207, 208, 211; underground, 116; *Water Margin (Shuihu zhuan)*, 172
Nu Wa, 223n21

October National Day. *See* National Day celebrations (October 1)
Old Party Secretary (painting), 147, 156, *fig. 6.1 (after page 148)*
On the Docks (film), 182, 184
On the Docks (opera): celebration performances, 186; and composer Yu Huiyong, 177; feminist themes, 239n14; as model theatrical work, 185, 188; near present-day setting as unusual, 173; performer photograph, *183*
"On the Power of Mara Poetry" (essay) (Lu Xun), 86
"On the Revolution in Beijing Opera" (article) (Jiang Qing), 174
One Hundred Crimes (sculpture), 124
opera: Beijing, transplanted into other opera forms, 184; expansion of Beijing opera repertoire, 186-87; modernizing of, 169-70, 174-77; role of Jiang Qing in promoting, 173-74, 177-78. *See also* operas
operas: *Azalea Mountain (Dujuanshan)* (opera), 186, 189, 239n14; *Boulder Day (Panshi wan)*, 187; *On the Docks*, *183*, 185, 186, 188, 239n14; *Green Dragon Pond (Qinglong tan)*, 184; *Hai Rui Dismissed from Office* (Wu Han), 6, 14; *Jiao Yulu*, 175; *Raid on the White Tiger Regiment (Xixi Baihutuan)* (opera), 167, 188; *Red Cloud Ridge (Hongyun gang)* (opera), 187; *The Red Lantern*, 20, 171, 175, 176, 180, 188, 201, 239n14; *Reed Catkin Stockage (Luhua zhai)*, 184; *Shajiabang*, 20, 171, 172, 175, 176, 180, 188, 201, 239n14; *Song of the Dragon River*, 189, 211, 239n14; *Taking Tiger Mountain by Strategy*, 20, 168, 171, 172, 185, 188, 203, 207-11, 212, 239n14
Others Will Follow Us (Zi you houlairen) (film), 171, 175
Our Kitchen (drawing), *111*
Outlaws of the Marsh (Shuihuzhuan), 207
"ox-demons and snake-spirits," 8, 36, 96, 97
"ox-sheds" *(niu peng)*, 9, 36, 97

painting. *See* Hu Xian peasant painters; ink paintings *(guohua)*; Jin Shan peasant painters; Painting Correction Groups; painting, during Cultural Revolution; painting, traditional; paintings
Painting Correction Groups, 47, 48-50, 54
painting, during Cultural Revolution: approved three-in-one method for cultural production, 206; "black paintings," 36, 38, 78-79, *80*; collective collaboration, 35, 45, 101-3; emphasis shift from wall painting to mass production, 138; military postures and focus on struggle, 12-14; "model" paintings, 43-45; new Jiangsu style of traditional Chinese painting, 46; Painting Correction Groups, 47, 48-50, 54; portrayal of Mao, 47-48; as revolutionary task, 102; socialist realism,

44, 46, 54-55; style of Cultural Revolution, 47-48; "three prominences," 54, 144, 206
painting, traditional: landscape, 65; revival after Cultural Revolution, 17
paintings: *1966 Beijing Jeep* (Shen Jiawei), 19, 54, *fig. 0.5 (before page 9); Acupuncture Anaesthesia* (Tang Muli), *52*; *Artistic Family* (Liu Fengtao), *158*; *Attending Party Class* (Liu Zhigui), 148, *fig. 6.2 (before page 149); Chairman Mao Goes to Anyuan* (Liu Chunhua), 7, 43, 45, 103, 106, 108, *fig. 1.6 (after page 44); Cloth Tiger* (Li Fenglan), 156; *Communal Fish Pond* (Dong Zhengyi), 150, 151, *fig. 6.5 (before page 151); Confucius* (Shi Lu), 84-85, *85*; *Digging a Well* (Fan Xiaohua/Zhihua), *151*, 151-52; *Eastern Venus de Milo/Goddess of Beauty* (Shi Lu), 74, *fig. 2.3 (before page 75); Fighting in Northern Shaanxi* (Shi Lu), 58, 62-67, *63*; *Fish Pond* (Cao Jinying), *154*; *Follow Chairman Mao Closely, Grow Up Tempered by Wind and Waves* (Tang Xiaohe and Cheng Li), *51*; *Founding of the Nation* (Dong Xiwen), 43, *fig. 1.7* (before page 45); *Great Job! Investigating the Peasant Movement in Hunan* (Lin Yong), 44, 56, *fig. 1.8 (after page 46); Gutian Meeting* (He Kongde), 48, *49*, 50; *Helping the Army* (Zhang Lin), 148; *Herds of Cows and Horses* (Zhang Lin), 149; *Herds of Livestock* (Zhang Lin), 148; *Indian Fort/Tower to Recognize the Heart of Lu Ban* (Shi Lu), 81-86, *82*; *Indian Sage-King/Indian Spirit King* (Shi Lu), 73, *fig. 2.2 (after page 74); Labour-Reform Farm Inmate* (Wang Liuqiu), *fig. 3.3 (before page 95); Last Supper* (Zhang Hongtu), 18-19; *Letting the Horses Drink at the Yan River* (Shi Lu), 67; *Liu Shaoqi and the Anyuan Coal Miners* (Hou Yimin), *37*, 39, 43; *Man's World Is Mutable, Seas Become Mulberry Fields: Chairman Mao Inspects the Situation of the Great Proletarian Cultural Revolution in Northern, South-central, and Eastern China* (Shengtian Zheng), 93, *fig. 3.1 (after page 94); Milk Maid* (Tang Muli), 51; *Never Stop Being Industrious and Thrifty* (Zhang Lin), 149; *Night Melody* (Liu Zhide), *155*, 156; *Old Party Secretary* (Liu Zhide), 147, 156, *fig. 6.1 (after page 148); Pingpong Mao* (Zhang Hongtu), 56; *Qin Shihuang* (Shi Lu), 88-90, *89*; *Raising Goats* (Bai Tianxue), 149, *150*; *The Rouge Series/Rouge Mao* (Li Shan), *fig. 1.14 (before page 55); Spring Hoeing* (Li Fenglan), 149, *fig. 6.4 (after page 150); Standing Guard for Our Great Motherland* (Shen Jiawei), 53, *fig. 1.12 (before page 47); Steady as a Rock (Dizhu)* (collective painting), 203-6, *204*; *Treading on a Big Drum* (Liu Zhide), 156; *Vultures* (Pan Tianshou), 97; *We Must Implement the Proletarian Cultural Revolution to the Finish* (collective of senior artists), *fig. 1.3 (before page 35)*, 50; *Welcome Guests* (Zhang Xinying), 154; *Winter Plum* (Shi Lu), 79-81, *80*. *See also* ink paintings *(guohua)*; posters
Pan Tianshou, 97-98, 220n42, 227n10
Pan Xiaoling, 161
A Parade of Clowns (caricature), 4, 39, *40*, 41, 42
peasant painters. *See* Hu Xian peasant painters; Jin Shan peasant painters
Peasant Painting Centre, 160

Peasant Painting Hall, 159-60
"Peasants' Revolutionary Paintings" (article), 141
Peng Dehuai, 5, 6
Peng Zhen, 32, 39
People's Art Publicity House, 143
"The People's Liberation Army Captures Nanjing" (poetry) (Mao Zedong), 93, 226n2
Pingpong Mao (painting), 56
poetry: "Don't complain the cage is cramped and narrow" (Pan Tianshou), 97-98; "Encountering Sorrow" (Qu Yuan), 68, 70; "Heavenly Questions" (Qu Yuan), 222n18; "The People's Liberation Army Captures Nanjing" (Mao Zedong), 93, 226n2; "Verses for chanting by lakes, repairing the sky" (Shi Lu), 68-70
posters: after the Cultural Revolution, 17; big-character *(dazibao)*, as transitory art form, 33; *Chairman Mao's Heart Beats as One with the Hearts of the Revolutionary Masses,* 34-35, 43, *fig. 1.2 (before page 35); Childhood* (Jia Xingdong), 129; *Consolidate Our Forces: Enter Deeply into Condemnation of Deng Xiaoping's Counter-Revolutionary Revisionist Line,* 12, *13*; created by Red Guards, 9; *Follow Chairman Mao Closely, Grow Up Tempered by Wind and Waves* (Tang Xiaohe and Cheng Li), *51*; *Invincible Mao Zedong Thought Illuminates the Revolutionary Arts Stage* (Wang Zhaoda), *fig. 0.1 (after page 8); Let's Go and Watch the Model Theatrical Works, 12; New Spring in Yan'an,* 55, *fig. 1.13 (after page 54); A Parade of Clowns* (Weng Rulan), 39, *40*, 41, 42; *Revolution Is No Crime, Rebellion Is Justified, fig. 1.1 (after page 34); We Must Implement the Proletarian Cultural Revolution to the Finish,* 50, *fig. 1.3 (before page 35). See also* caricatures; paintings
Preparatory Office for the Struggle against Peng, Lu, Luo, and Yang Counter-Revolutionary Revisionist Group, 39
professors. *See* teachers
Proletarian Cultural Revolution Red Painting Guard (exhibition), 38
propaganda: demonizing victims as strategy, 31-32; newspapers as responsive to Mao's wishes, 33. *See also* model theatrical works; posters; slogans
publications, of the Cultural Revolution: *Art Storm (Meishu fenglei),* 36, 37; *Art War Gazette* (journal), 38

Qi Baishi, 38
Qi Benyu, 38
Qian Songyan, 46
Qin Shihuang, 60, 87, 221n5
Qin Shihuang (painting), 88-90, *89*
Qingdao Workers' Fine Arts Creation Collective, *204*, 206
Qinghua University, 10
Qingping Village Scene in the Daba Mountains (drawing), *111*
Qu Bo, 171, 207, 210
Qu Yuan, 21, 60, 68, 70, 222n18
Quan Shanshi, 102

Raid on the White Tiger Regiment (Xixi Baihutuan) (opera): earlier versions, 171; as model theatrical work, 188; as often overlooked, 167; as wartime story in 1950s Korea, 173
Raising Goats (painting), 149, *150*
"rebel artists," 39

"rebellion is justified" (slogan), 8, 33, 135
rebels *(zaofanpai),* 99
Red Art Soldier Beijing Opera Troupe (Hongyibing jingju tuan), 175
Red Cloud Ridge (Hongyun gang) (opera), 187
The Red Detachment of Women (ballet): change of heroine's name in ballet version, 199, 240n31; contrasted with Western ballets of the past, 178; deletion of character of Hong Lian by Jiang Qing, 200; disruption of Chinese gender construction, 190; feminist themes, 239n14; first performance, 170; heroic role of women, 23; Mao's attendance as crucial encouragement for modernizing ballet, 178; as model theatrical work, 188; origins as film, 195-97; performers' photographs, 184, *fig. 8.2 (after page 198), fig. 8.3 (before page 199);* renewed interest in, 20-21, 201, 202; as revealing of Communist Party's limited platform for women's liberation, 201; storyline, 197, 198-99; themes of class struggle and women's liberation, 197, 198-99, 200
The Red Detachment of Women (film): change of heroine's name in ballet version, 240n31; released 1961, 170; storyline, 199-200
Red [Guard] Congress Central Academy of Arts and Crafts East Is Red Commune, 36
Red [Guard] Congress Central Academy of Fine Arts Prairie Fire Armed Struggle Team, 36
Red Guard Fighting Force (Hongweibing zhandoudui), 95
Red Guards: art produced by, 9-10, 39-45, 218n8; and atrocities of Cultural Revolution, 8, 35-36; class distinctions viewed as hereditary, 34; conflict among contending factions, 10, 34, 38-39, 100, 108; construction of new pictorial history of China emphasizing Mao's revolutionary role, 42-43; destruction of older art works by, 8, 35; end of era of, 10, 45; formation of, 8; mandate given by Mao, 33, 107; "matched couplet" debate, 34; movement, as exhilarating experience for youth, 9; "national liaison stations" for art students, 36; publications, 36, 37, 38; as "rebel artists" *(zaofanpai),* 36, 39; and *Rent Collection Courtyard* (1965), 126; sent for "re-education" by peasants in countryside, 10, 29, 45, 104, 108; used by Mao to destroy party apparatus, 28. *See also* Zhang Yongsheng
The Red Lantern (opera): based on film *Others Will Follow Us (Zi you houlairen),* 171, 175; feminist themes, 239n14; in languages of other regions of China, 180; as model theatrical work, 188; popularity of, 175, 176; renewed post-Cultural Revolution interest in, 20, 201
"red, smooth, and luminescent" *(hong, guang, liang),* vii, 47
Red Sun (music), 20
Reed Catkin Stockade (Luhua zhai) (opera), 184
"re-education" of youth, by peasantry. *See* rusticated urban youth
Rent Collection Courtyard (sculpture) (1965): contributing artist, speech by, 38; difference in meaning from 1999 version, 131; documentary on, 175; as epitome of socialist realism,

129; images, *122, 125, 127*; importance of collaborative process of creation, 129; installed at Landlord's Courtyard of Oppression Exhibition Hall, 124; as "model" art of Cultural Revolution, 7, 32, 121, 123; as most prominent sculpture, after Mao's statues, 126; "original" version, contested by institutions and individual artists, 134; originally made of clay, 129; precursors and copies, 124-28, 134; refusal by China to exhibit in Europe, 131; as socialist educational tool, 129, 131; as visual education in class struggle, 175

Rent Collection Courtyard (sculpture) (1999): accused of violating copyright, 22, 106, 133-34; as commentary on China's socialism, 131; critiqued by Chinese, 131-33; difference in meaning from 1965 version, 131; at Venice Biennale (1999), 121, *123*

"Rent Collection Courtyard: A Revolution in Sculpture" (article), 128

Repin Academy of Fine Arts (Leningrad), 102

Revolution Is No Crime, Rebellion Is Justified (poster), *fig. 1.1 (after page 34)*

"revolution is no crime, rebellion is justified" (slogan), 107

Revolutionary Committee of Zhejiang, 96

rice-sprout song *(yangge)*, 170, 171, 238n3

"roll in the mud and gain a red [revolutionary] heart" (slogan), 112

The Rouge Series/Rouge Mao (painting), *fig. 1.14 (before page 55)*

Rubin, Gayle, 194

rusticated urban youth: art produced by, *111, 113, 114, 115, fig. 4.8 (after page 116), fig. 4.9 (before page 117)*; experience of, 108, 110-16; hope of returning to city, 112; painters, 50-54; questioning of Cultural Revolution, 112; removal to countryside, as end of Red Guard era, 10; return to the cities, 116-17. *See also* Red Guards

The Sayings of Chairman Liu (book title in poster), 41

"Sayings of Chairman Mao." *See* "Little Red Book" (Mao Zedong)

Schoenhals, Michael, 3

schools: closure in early Cultural Revolution, 9, 33; re-opening, after end of Red Guard era, 11; rusticated youth as substitute teachers in countryside, 116

sculpture: *Family Histories of the Air Force Fighters,* 230n28; *Great Yak,* 105; *Idol* (Wang Keping), 17, *18*; *In Praise of the Red Guards,* 230n28; *One Hundred Crimes,* 124; *Rent Collection Courtyard* (1965), 7, 32, 38, 106, 121-35, *122, 125,* 175; *Rent Collection Courtyard* (1974-78), *127*; Venice's *Rent Collection Courtyard* (1999), 22-23, 121, *123*, 131, *132*; *The Wrath of the Serfs,* 129-30

The Second Handshake (Di'er ci wo shou) (novel), 116

Sending Precious Books (Song baoshu) (musical performance), 176

"sent-down" urban youth. *See* rusticated urban youth

Shaanxi Provincial Cultural Bureau, 139

Shaanxi Revolutionary Art Association, 71

Shajiabang (opera): based on *Sparks among the Reeds (Lu dang huozhong)* (opera), 171; feminist themes, 239n14; heroine Sister Aqing, 172; in languages of other

regions of China, 180; as model theatrical work, 188; popularity of, 175, 176; post-Cultural Revolution renewed interest in, 20, 201
Shajiabang (symphony): first performance, 171; lack of popularity of, 189; as model theatrical work, 188; praised as "worker-peasant-soldier symphonic music," 178; as sinicization of Western orchestral music, 170-71
Shanghai Art College, 47
Shanghai Beijing Opera Company, 208
Shanghai City Dance School (Shanghai shi wudao xuexiao), 170
Shanhai jing (Classic of mountains and seas) (geomantic text), 178
Shao Jianbo, 207, 208
Shattering Illusions (drawing), *fig. 4.8 (after page 116)*
Shen Jiawei, 18, 19, 53-54, *fig. 0.5 (before page 9); fig. 1.12* (before page 47)
Shen Lian Zong (General Headquarters of the United Rebel Factions), 96
Shengtian Zheng. *See* Zheng Shengtian
Shi Dan, 220n1
Shi Gu Lumanden (Shi Lu), 73
Shi Guo, 66, 74
Shi Lu: accused of being counter-revolutionary, 59, 71; biographies, 220n1; as "black painter," 78-79, 80; Confucian values, 61, 83-90; *Confucius* (painting), 84-85, *85*; on creativity and cultural inheritance, 61; critique of Great Leap Forward campaign, 64-65; critique of Jian Qing, 59; as devout communist, 58, 61, 90; diary, 81, 83, 84225n41; and dispute over *Fighting in Northern Shaanxi* (painting), 62-67, *63*, 90; *Eastern Venus de Milo/Goddess of Beauty* (painting), 74, *fig. 2.3 (before page 75)*; erosion of faith in Cultural Revolution, 58; *Fighting in Northern Shaanxi* (painting), 58, 62-67, *63*; *Indian Fort/Tower to Recognize the Heart of Lu Ban* (painting), 81-86, *82*; *Indian Sage-King/Indian Spirit King* (painting), 73, *fig. 2.2 (after page 74)*; invoking of Confucian legacies as strategy for protest, 60-61, 87-90; *Letting the Horses Drink at the Yan River* (ink painting), 67; mental illness, aspects of, 59, 60, 62, 71, 75-77; mistreatment during Cultural Revolution, 9, 21; on need for imagination in painting, 222n17; objection to Cultural Revolution's assault on traditional arts, 58, 59, 81; personal demarcation between pre- and post-Cultural Revolution, 73, 75; poetry, 60, 68-71, 79, 87; *Qin Shihuang* (painting), 88-90, *89*; revision of old paintings, 72-75; use of art as weapon of cultural resistance, 60, 76, 77-90; wandering in Sichuan, 71; *Winter Plum* (painting), 79-81, *80*, 224n38, 226n55; *Xue Hua Lu* [Notes on the study of painting], 65, 221n8
Shitao, 62, 65, 221n8
short story: "Not Just One of the Audience" *(Tebie guanzhong)* (Duan Ruixia), 203, 211-14
Shu Goa, 220n42
Sichuan Arts Academy, 124, 133
Sichuan Arts Institute, 118
Singing Model Operas, Becoming a Revolutionary (Chang yangbanxi, zuo geming ren) campaign, 189
Sister Aqing, 172
slogans: "beat back the right deviationist wind," 16; "brushes are weapons," 105-6; "burning books and burying scholars alive," 221n5; "Chairman Mao is the red sun in our hearts,"

48; "[economic] reform and opening [to the West]," 17; "the globe is entirely red!," 102; "if the father's a hero, the son's a brave; if the father's a counter-revolutionary, the son's a bastard," 34, 42; "let a hundred flowers bloom" *(baihua qifang),* 179, 188; "making foreign things serve China" *(yang wei Zhong yong),* 103, 179, 188; "making the past serve the present" *(gu wei jin yong),* 14, 16, 179, 188; "rebellion is justified," 8, 33, 135; "revolution is no crime, rebellion is justified," 107; "roll in the mud and gain a red [revolutionary] heart," 112; "throwing out the old and bringing in the new" *(tui chen chu xin),* 179, 188; "up to the mountains, down to the villages," 108; "we have friends all over the world," 162

Smash the Gang of Four campaign, 152

Socialist Education Movement, 140

Song Dong, 131

"The Song of Chongqing" (song), 116

"The Song of Nanjing" (song), 116

Song of the Dragon River (opera), 189, 211, 239n14

"Songs, Dances and Other Artistic Performances" (musical performance), 176

"Songs of Praise *(gesong)* for the Great Leader Chairman Mao" (musical performance), 176

Songs of the Red Guards (Hongweibing zhi ge) (musical performance), 176

Sons and Daughters of the Grasslands (Caoyuan ernü) (dance-drama), 185-86

Sparkling Red Star (Shanshan de hongxing) (film), 185

Sparks among the Reeds (Lu dang huozhong) (opera). *See Shajiabang* (opera)

Spring Hoeing (painting), 149, *fig. 6.4 (after page 150)*

Standing Guard for Our Great Motherland (painting), 53, *fig. 1.12 (before page 47)*

"Stars" (Xingxing pai), 17, 19

Steady as a Rock (Dizhu) (painting): battle-readiness of hero, 203, 204-5; illustration of struggle against capitalist-roaders *(zouzipai),* 203, 205; "three prominences" *(san tuchu)* portrayed in, 206

students: interruption of formal learning, during Cultural Revolution, 29; sent to countryside for re-education by peasants, 10, 29, 45, 104, 108; "worker-peasant-soldier" origins, preferential access to education, 11. *See also* Red Guards; rusticated urban youth

"Study the Revolutionary Model Performances, Defend the Revolutionary Model Performances" (article) (Zhe Ping), 182

Su Qi, 212

Sun Jingbo, 47

Sun Wukong, 209

"Sun Wukong Beats the White Bone Demoness" (Sun Wukong san-da Baigujing), 16

"Sweep Away All Ox-Demons and Snake-Spirits" (editorial), 8

Szeemann, Harald, 131, 133

Taking Tiger Mountain by Strategy (Zhiqu Weihushan) (film): dissemination of (1970), 184; earlier version (1958), 171

Taking Tiger Mountain by Strategy (Zhiqu Weihushan) (opera): battle-readiness of hero, 203, 209-10; feminist themes, 239n14; as model theatrical work, 168, 188; in "Not

Just One of the Audience" *(Tebie guanzhong)* (short story), 212; origins as chapter in *Tracks in the Snowy Forest* (Linhai xueyuan), 171; post-Cultural Revolution revivals, 20; storyline, 207-10; transformation of hero Yang Zirong, 172, 207-11
"Talks at the Yan'an Forum on Literature and Art" (Mao Zedong). *See* Yan'an Talks
Tang Muli, 51-52
Tang Xiaohe, 47, 50, *51*
teachers: attacks on, by Red Guards, 8, 35-36; persecution under Cultural Revolution, 96-99; removal from positions during anti-rightist campaign, 95
"ten lost years," 27, 31, 152. *See also* Cultural Revolution
theatre: local productions by rusticated youth, 114-15; traditional, Cultural Revolution offensive against, 6. *See also* model theatrical works *(geming yangbanxi);* opera
"Theory of Class Origins" (essay) (Yu Luoke), 116
Three Kingdoms (Sanguo zhi yanyi) (novel), 172
"three prominences" *(san tuchu),* 54, 144, 185, 206, 211, 214
Three Stones Museum (Tianjin), 129, 130
"throwing out the old and bringing in the new" *(tui chen chu xin)* (slogan), 179, 188
Tian Han, 41
Tian'anmen Square: Mao's review of Red Guard rallies, 8, 34; massacre (1989), 20
Tianjin Acrobatic Troupe, 177
Tianjin City Beijing Opera Troupe, 175
Tianjin City Northern Opera Troupe (Pingu tuan), 176
Tianjin City People's Art Spoken Drama Theatre (Renyi), 176
Tianjin City People's Recitation Troupe (Shuochang tuan), 177
Tianjin City Shaoxing Opera Troupe (Yueju tuan), 176
Tianjin City Worker-Peasant-Soldier Art School, 177
Tianjin City Worker-Peasant-Soldier Song and Dance Ensemble, 176
Tianjin Special Region Northern Opera Troupe (Tianjin zhuanqu Pingju tuan), 175
Tibet Museum of Revolution (Lhasa), 129
Tong Xiangling, 210
Tracks in the Snowy Forest (Linhai xueyuan) (novel), 171, 207, 208, 211
Treading on a Big Drum (painting), 156
Turbulent Decade: A History of the Cultural Revolution (book) (Yan Jiaqi and Gao Gao), 3

United States, 78
universities: closure during early Cultural Revolution, 9, 33, 95, 96; re-opening, after end of Red Guard era, 11. *See also names of specific institutions;* students; teachers
University of British Columbia, 22, 118
"up to the mountains, down to the villages" (slogan), 108

Venice's Rent Collection Courtyard (1999). *See Rent Collection Courtyard* (sculpture) (1999)
"Verses for chanting by lakes, repairing the sky" (Shi Lu), 68-70
Vultures (painting), 97

Wang Dachun, 193, 195
Wang Dewei, 37
Wang Guangmei, 41

Wang Guanyi, 134
Wang Hongwen, 15
Wang Keping, 17, *18*
Wang Liuqiu: biography, 227n19; *Jade Collection* (paintings), 99; *Labour-Reform Farm Inmate* (painting), *fig. 3.3 (before page 95)*; mistreatment during Cultural Revolution, 98-99
Wang Mantian, 46, 48, 220n42
Wang Nanming, 133
Wang Shikuo, 39
Wang Zhaowen, 62
Wang Zizhi, 85
War of Resistance Song and Dance Ensemble (Kangzhan wengongtuan), 176
Water Margin (Shuihu zhuan) (novel), 172
Watson, Scott, 216n1
"we have friends all over the world" (slogan), 162
We Must Implement the Proletarian Cultural Revolution to the Finish (painting), 50, *fig. 1.3 (before page 35)*
Welcome Guests (painting), 154
Weng Rulan, 39, 40-41
The White-Haired Girl (ballet): class discourse replaces gender/sexual theme in film, 195-97; contrasted with Western ballets of the past, 178; derived from folktale and rice-sprout song *(yangge)* folk-dance form, 170, 171; feminist themes, 190, 239n14; first performance, 170; heroic role of women, 23; as model theatrical work, 188; performers' photographs, *196*; post-Cultural Revolution revivals, 20; renewed interest in, 201; storyline, 192-93
The White-Haired Girl (film): class struggle enacted as fight over ownership of Xi'er, 194-95; musical film version (1951), 170, 192; performers' photographs, 184; post-Cultural Revolution critique of, 193
"'*The White-Haired Girl*' and the Historical Complexity of Yan'an Literature" (article) (Meng Yue), 193
Winter Plum (painting), 79-81, *80*
Witke, Roxanne, 206, 207
women: backlash against degendered image of, in post-Mao China, 191; feminist themes, of model theatrical works, 188-202, 239n14; gender construction, disrupted by model theatrical works, 190-91; gender disparity, increased post-Cultural Revolution, 239n15; as heroic figures in revolutionary model theatrical works, 7-8, 23; peasant painters, 149-50, 153-54; performers' photographs, 184, *196*, *fig. 8.2 (after page 198)*, *fig. 8.3 (before page 199)*; rusticated female youths, 112. *See also* Jiang Qing
woodcuts, 95
work units *(danwei)*, 99
Workers' Propaganda Team, 104
The Wrath of the Serfs (sculpture), 129
"Writers and Performers, Their Works and Their Audiences, in the First Three Decades" (McDougall), 189
writings. *See* articles; essays; journals and newspapers; novels; poetry; publications, of the Cultural Revolution; short stories
Wu Guanzhong, 73
Wu Han, 6, 14, 41
Wu Qinghua, 184, 197-99, 201. *See also* Wu Qionghua
Wu Qionghua, 199-200
Wu Song, 207
Wu Zizhong, 49

Xia Yan, 41

Xi'an Art Academy, 71
Xi'an Art Association, 58, 59
Xi'an Cultural Centre, 139
Xi'an Provincial Art Academy, 160-61
Xiao Chuanjiu, 97
Xiao Li, 97, 104, 227n13
Xie Jin, 170, 187, 197
Xi'er, 191-97
xin minge (new folk songs) movement, 238n3
Xinan Law University, 133
Xu Chunzhong, 45
Xu Junxuan, 102
Xu Yong, 49

Yan Jiaqi, 3, 239n8
Yan Shanchun, 216n1
Yan'an Forum. *See* Yan'an Talks
Yan'an Talks (May 1942): annual anniversary celebrations, 23, 38, 46, 51, 152, 168, 174, 177, 181, 187, 203; Mao's view on role of arts in revolution, 5, 121, 126, 168, 189; on new proletarian culture, 6; in "Not Just One of the Audience" *(Tebie guanzhong)* (short story), 212; as policy statement for the arts, 6, 168. *See also* model theatrical works *(geming yangbanxi)*
Yang Bailao, 192, 193, 195
Yang Lin'gui, 50, *fig. 1.3 (before page 35)*
Yang Shangkun, 33, 39
Yang Zirong, 172, 185, 203, 214
yangge (rice-sprout song), 170, 171, 238n3
Yao Fu (Xia Peng), 95
Yao Wenyuan: arrest as member of Gang of Four, 227n13; and Criticizing Lin Biao and Confucius movement, 15; critique of opera *Hai Rui Dismissed from Office*, 6, 15; at meeting with Zhang Yongsheng, 97, 220n42; as member of Literature and Arts Group (Wenyizu), 38
Ye Jian, 220n1
Ye Qianyu, 36, 38, 40, 41
Yi the Archer, 223n19
Yi Zhong, 45
youth. *See* Red Guards; rusticated urban youth; students
Yu Hua, 17
Yu Huiyong, 177, 206
Yu Luoke, 116
Yuan Hao, 50, *fig. 1.3 (before page 35)*

zaofanpai (rebels), 99
Zhan Jianjun, 50, *fig. 1.3 (after page 34)*
Zhanag Qiuyuan, 143
Zhang Chunqiao: and Criticizing Lin Biao and Confucius movement, 15; as member of Literature and Arts Group (Wenyizu), 38; and Red Guard organizations, 96
Zhang Daofan, 97
Zhang Hongtu, 18-19, 56
Zhang Lin, 148, 149
Zhang Shaoxia, 27
Zhang Xinying, 154
Zhang Yang, 116
Zhang Yongsheng: as art instructor at labour camp, 105, 106; downfall, after arrest of Jiang Qing, 22, 104; leadership position in Red Guards, 46, 96; meeting with Jiang Qing, 97, 103, 220n42; as printmaking student, 95; sent to countryside, 104
Zhao Wangyun, 78
Zhaoxia (Morning clouds) (journal), 203
Zhe Ping, 182
Zhejiang Academy of Fine Arts, 20, 22, 46, 49, 94, 95, 104
Zheng Shengtian: and Art of the Great Proletarian Cultural Revolution, 1966-76 (exhibition), 216n1; confinement by Red Guards, 99-100; *Man's World Is Mutable, Seas Become Mulberry Fields: Chairman*

Mao Inspects the Situation of the Great Proletarian Cultural Revolution in Northern, South-central, and Eastern China (painting), 44, 93, *fig. 3.1 (after page 94)*; as painter during Cultural Revolution, 101-4; on persecution of teachers and administrators, 96-99; post-Cultural Revolution career, 22, 105-6; on the Red Guards, 96, 97, 100-1; as student, 94-95; on Zhang Yongsheng, 95-96, 103, 104, 105-6

Zhong Runliang, 178

Zhou Enlai: in *1966 Beijing Jeep* (painting), *fig. 0.5 (before page 9)*; ascendancy of, 78; attacks on, during power struggles, 14; in *Chairman Mao's Heart Beats as One with the Hearts of the Revolutionary Masses* (painting), 35, *fig. 1.2 (after page 34)*; critiqued in Criticizing Lin Biao and Confucius movement, 15, 78, 142; in *The East Is Red* (painting), 10; on limited number of cultural products during Cultural Revolution, 185; memorial wreaths by populace, 16; in power struggle with Gang of Four, 213; request for removal of image from *We Must Implement the Proletarian Cultural Revolution to the Finish* (painting), 50; stress on formal education, 145

Zhou Ruiwen, 102

Zhou Sicong, 49-50

Zhou Yang, 38, 41, 130

Zhu Naizheng, 47

Printed and bound in Canada by Friesens

Set in Hypatia Sans and Warnock by Artegraphica Design Co. Ltd.

Text design: Irma Rodriguez

Copy editor: Deborah Kerr

Proofreader: Danielle Arbuckle

Indexer: Annette Lorek